ELDER LAW

AND LATER-LIFE

LEGAL PLANNING

SECTION OF REAL | TRUST &
PROPERTY | ESTATE LAW

ABA
Defending Liberty
Pursuing Justice

LAWRENCE A. FROLIK

Cover by Cory Ottenwess/ABA Publishing.

Printed in the United States of America

21 20 19 18 17   5 4 3 2 1

Library of Congress Cataloging-in-Publication Data

Names: Frolik, Lawrence A., author.
Title: Elder law and later-life legal planning / Lawrence A. Frolik.
Description: Chicago : American Bar Association, 2018.
Identifiers: LCCN 2017042046 | ISBN 9781634259668
Subjects: LCSH: Older people—Legal status, laws, etc.—United States. |
   Legal assistance to older people—United States.
Classification: LCC KF390.A4 F76 2018 | DDC 346.7301/30843—dc23
LC record available at https://lccn.loc.gov/2017042046

Contents

CHAPTER 11
Health Care Decision Making   151

CHAPTER 12
Long-Term Care Insurance   165

Preface

This book is for attorneys who have an interest in dealing with the legal problems of their older clients and for attorneys who are interested in practicing elder law or at least having an appreciation and understanding of that practice. It is also designed to be of interest to attorneys who are aging and want to be better informed about the programs and legal choices that they face.

This book focuses on the legal issues that can arise in old age and the various laws and governmental programs that address those issues. An attorney can read through the book or dip into the individual chapters. Each chapter stands alone; every chapter both illuminates an issue and describes how the law has responded.

The book is divided into three parts that reflect the different stages of aging. Part I, Retirement Considerations, discusses the issues that arise with retirement, including income and paying for medical care. Part II, Post-retirement Issues, addresses the issues that most, older individuals face in their 70s, such as housing concerns and identifying alternate decision makers for their property and person. Part III, Later-Life Concerns, focuses on the problems associated with the end of life, such as the need for long-term care and planning for the possible loss of mental capacity.

This book is not intended as a treatise, therefore the lack of extensive footnotes. I have provided footnotes for cases and statutes, but not for the more general statements. Every statement in the book can be verified on the Internet. Those looking for an expanded discussion on any topic are encouraged to search the Internet or consult an appropriate legal treatise or single-volume text that explores the topic in detail.

Note: Like many authors, I do not feel comfortable using the singular pronouns "he," "him," and "his" as a gender neutral term. Even if meant to be gender neutral, they cannot help but be read as referring to men. The gender reference is not avoided by using "she," "her," and "hers." To avoid the gender connotation, many authors now use "he and she." That is awkward, however, and leads to having to use "his and hers" and "him and her." An alternative is to use a plural noun. For example, rather than "The client may prefer to keep his or her finances secret from his or her children, because he or she is a private person," the sentence can read, "Some clients prefer to keep their finances secret from their children, because they are private persons."

Although the plural is preferable, it is not always workable. The better solution, and the one adopted in this book, is to use "they," "them," and "their" to refer to a single individual. For example, "A client may prefer to keep their finances secret from their children, because they are a private person." Some object to that use, claiming it to be ungrammatical. Perhaps, but plural pronouns have long been used to refer to a single person, and the practice is becoming increasingly common. Given the desire of modern writers and readers for gender neutral pronouns, the use of "they," "them," and "their" is going to become evermore common. And so that is how I use those terms in this book.

Retirement Considerations

The book has three parts. Part I, Retirement Considerations, is directed at the legal issues that often arise
around the time of retirement. It begins with a discussion of what elder law is and how it relates and reacts
to the legal issues of aging clients who have retired
or are contemplating retirement. Some retire because
of a loss of physical vigor. Therefore, the physical
reality of aging is described. Next come overviews of
the chief sources of income for older clients—Social
Security, employer-provided retirement benefits, and
individual retirement accounts. Retirement frequently
results in a loss of employer-provided health care
insurance. Part I provides a description of Medicare,
the federal subsidized health care insurance for those
age 65 and older, and also examines veterans' benefits. Part I ends with an overview of other federal
statutes that protect the elderly, including the Age
Discrimination in Employment Act, the Americans
with Disabilities Act, and the Federal Housing Act.

The Practice of Elder Law **1**

I. Why Elder Law?

The driving force behind the need for elder law and legal planning for later life is the growth of those age 65 and older—at present over 12,000 individuals turn 65 every day. Today about 13 percent of the population is age 65 and older, but that percentage will grow to 20 percent by 2040.[1] The ever-increasing number of older Americans creates challenges for society and the law.

Even more significant are the elderly who have suffered a decline in their physical or mental well-being. As individuals age past age 75, they inevitably suffer a loss of physical well-being. Of course, the rate, nature, and extent of that loss varies greatly; for some it is evident at age 70, others remain quite healthy well into their 80s. Nevertheless, whenever the decline in physical capacity occurs, it gives rise to increasing dependence on others. For example, the ability to drive a car is lost, the physical stamina required to maintain a house ebbs away, the ability to manage complex financial arrangements becomes problematic, vision is sometimes lost, and the energy is lacking to sit through long meetings with an investment advisor. Fortunately, there are reasonable responses to physical declines; some are obvious but others require an attorney's advice, planning, and creation of documents.

---

1. https://www.census.gov/content/dam/Census/library/publications/2014/demo/p23-212.pdf.

Although physical decline creates problems, mental decline is even more serious because it may mark the beginning of the end of an individual's autonomy. If the mental decline is severe enough, individuals lose the ability to make decisions on their own behalf and therefore cease to be independent legal actors. The consequences of mental decline can be so devastating that the mere possibility of mental decline and its devastating impact on an individual's life should be enough to cause an older individual to seek out legal assistance and to plan for its possible occurrence.

Physical and mental decline necessitates a legal response for almost all elderly, but that need rises in proportion to the assets owned by the affected individual. The rise in those age 65 and older contributes to the growth in elder law, but it is the rise in the number of those age 65 or older who have more than a minimum of assets that is the real cause for the demand of lawyers with specialized knowledge about the legal issues associated with old age. For an individual, the loss of mental capacity due to progressive dementia is a personal and family tragedy, but if they have assets, the loss of capacity becomes a financial problem that requires the assistance of an attorney. An individual with diminished mental capacity who owns significant assets needs a tailored response, not just the standard practice of resorting to a power of attorney or, even worse, the imposition of a guardianship or conservatorship.

Not surprising, as the need and demand for legal assistance for older clients has grown, attorneys have responded. Beginning in the 1980s, attorneys who are knowledgeable about the special needs of older clients have been referring to themselves as elder law attorneys. Although their practices vary, they share a focus on helping older clients resolve their legal problems. Also referred to as later-life legal planning, elder law usually involves addressing the issues that arise due to a lack of mental capacity, including inter alia, guardianship or conservatorship, planning and paying for long-term care, housing choices, pension and retirement benefit planning, veterans' benefits, qualifying for various public benefits, and estate planning including powers of attorney and surrogate health care decision documents.

The focus of elder law is to provide older clients with customized legal assistance to address the legal issues associated with aging. Of course, the practices of elder law attorneys vary greatly, with some focusing on planning, some on litigation, and others on providing holistic assistance to aging clients. Some elder law attorneys are solo practitioners; others practice in small partnerships; a few are partners in large, full-service law firms; and others head up law firms that employ not only attorneys but nurses, social workers, and elder law trained paralegals. Whatever the case, elder law attorneys typically are called upon to be knowledgeable in a number of legal fields, or at least be aware of the legal issues that can arise. For example, an elder law attorney typically engages in estate planning and so must understand the federal income tax consequences of an inherited IRA. Though most elder law attorneys do not accept elder abuse cases, all must be aware of the possibility of elder abuse and financial fraud and exploitation. Those who write wills must be very alert to possible undue influence that so often occurs with an ageing client who has diminished mental capacity.

As with so many aspects of the practice of law, merely being an attorney with a generalized knowledge of the law is not enough. Specialized knowledge about the legal needs of the elderly is necessary. An attorney interested in practicing elder law or developing a practice with older clients must be familiar with the major government programs that impact the lives of the elderly, including Social Security, Medicare, and Medicaid. Elder law attorneys also need to understand the legal issues and the relevant law concerning health care of the elderly, both acute and chronic care, including the law of end-of-life medical treatment and an individual's right-to-die. Also, elder law attorneys usually draft wills and trusts, and because they are often dealing with clients with diminished capacity they must understand and be alert for undue influence and fraud, and they must appreciate how trusts can be a valuable aid to their clients. An elder law attorney should be familiar with federal estate and gift tax, federal income taxation of trusts, and relevant state inheritance and income taxes. Finally, they must know the signs of elderly abuse, neglect, and financial exploitation and how to respond if they suspect a client is being victimized.

In short, elder law is a practice that demands a great deal of substantive knowledge about the law. It also, however, requires the attorney to have strong "people skills"; an ability to effectively market a practice that rests on a large number of clients; and the judgment and wisdom to guide a client, and often the client's family, through emotionally difficult circumstances.

II. The Role of the Elder Law Attorney

The essence of elder law is planning for the contingencies that arise with advancing age and advising clients on how best to respond to those contingencies. Elder law attorneys deal with clients upon a continuum: those who are concerned with a possible future legal need associated with aging, those at the beginning stages of a life event that has or is about to give rise to a need for legal assistance, and those at a stage of life when remedial or "emergency" legal assistance is required. Whereas some elder law attorneys avoid litigation other than at the administrative level, for others litigation is a focus of their practices. Most elder law attorneys engage in some litigation but spend the majority of their time on advising, planning, and document preparation.

The practice of elder law can be roughly divided into the following three kinds of client needs:

1. Their concern about their finances in light of future care needs.
2. Their need for identifying those who can act on their behalf if they should lose mental capacity.
3. Their fear of dependency caused by physical or mental declines.

Financial concerns are not the same as financial planning. Elder law attorneys are not financial planners; they provide legal advice, not investment advice. The financial concerns addressed by elder law attorneys arise from client concerns about how to manage their financial affairs in the face of declining physical or mental abilities, how to pay for costly long-term care, and how to allocate resources to obtain the necessary care and assistance while providing adequately for a spouse and possibly leaving a legacy to children and grandchildren.

Older clients need legal advice as to how to protect their assets in the event that they should lose the physical or mental ability to do so. The elder law attorney has several responses, including creating a power of attorney, establishing a living trust, and placing accounts or property into joint ownership. Selecting the best response and selecting appropriate substitute decision makers are critical decisions for which the elder law attorney can provide valuable assistance.

Dependency in later life is unfortunately very common. It is sometimes the result of physical decline, but it is more frequently caused by mental decline, and more specifically, dementia. It is estimated that over 40 percent of those age 80 and older have some form of dementia, usually Alzheimer's disease, which is progressive, irreversible, and incurable. Chronic physical illness, such as rheumatoid arthritis, can also lead to dependency, and acute illness, such as multiple organ failure, can require daily assistance from others.

Clients who encounter personal dependency in their later life face two legal issues: how to best prepare for possible dependency and how to pay for the care they need because of the dependency. Addressing these problems is often the key component of an elder law practice, both because the client is concerned about their quality of life in the event that they become dependent, and because they are concerned with how to pay the high cost of personal and medical care that they may require in the future because of a debilitating mental or physical condition.

Some elder law attorneys focus their practices on planning for their clients' need for personal care necessitated by serious physical or mental decline. Their client base is often composed of individuals who have already experienced decline and need to make appropriate plans in the event that they decline even further. Some of these attorneys call this life care planning, and many belong to the Life Care Planning Law Firms Association (LCPLFA)—composed of law firms that offer proactive legal services, care coordination, and advocacy support to elderly clients and their families. The goal is to help clients understand their needs, assess possible solutions, recommend providers of care services, and monitor the care being received. Such firms often employ nurses, social workers, and other professionals as well as paralegals that work as a team to ensure that the client's needs are properly met.

Other elder law attorneys focus more on providing advice as to how to find appropriate care for their clients and how to arrange a client's affairs to pay for needed care, including assisting the client to become eligible for governmental benefit programs. In particular, elder law attorneys help clients become eligible for and enroll in Medicaid, the joint federal-state program that pays for long-term nursing home care and increasingly for home- and community-based care. Merely gaining eligibility, however, is not the goal. Medicaid is a need-based program that requires applicants to spend down almost all of their savings and to spend effectively all of their income toward their care in order to become Medicaid eligible. Elder law attorneys assist their clients to achieve eligibility and still retain or pass on to family members as many assets as possible.

Medicaid planning is complicated and ever changing; it must respond to new state and federal laws, cases, regulations, and procedures. Elder law attorneys spend a good deal of time mastering the subject, keeping current with the law, understanding which alternative is best for each client, and translating all of that into effective planning as well as seeing that the plan works as designed. This is not a field that a lawyer can just dip into; as with so many other legal practices it demands dedication and commitment.

Elder law attorneys also advise clients on how to arrange for private payment of long-term care, including the purchase of long-term care insurance, moving into a continuing care retirement community, using an assisted living facility, and purchasing care in the home. Each of these solutions raises issues and problems to which a lawyer can offer assistance and solutions to enable the client to live a better, more satisfactory life.

The possibility of mental incapacity is so great for the older client that it is imperative for a client to create a plan that will lessen the personal and financial cost should they suffer a serious decline in their cognitive abilities. Elder law attorneys help the client to imagine the possibility of a loss of capacity, and to carefully consider the alternatives. After the client selects a course of action, the attorney will draft the appropriate documents.

The client must appreciate that the longer they live, the more likely they will experience a loss of mental capacity. Proper planning is essential. The cost of not planning may result in the client being placed under an involuntary conservatorship or guardianship. Fortunately, in almost all cases, with the help of an elder law attorney, the client can take steps to avoid the need for conservatorship or guardianship. The attorney will lay out the alternatives available to the client and advise them about who they should consider to make their financial and medical decisions for them, and the attorney will draft an appropriate legal document that enables the surrogate health care decision maker to be able to act in the best interest of the client.

Elder law attorneys must also protect their clients from those who would neglect, abuse, or exploit them. Fortunately, neglect and abuse of the elderly usually does not happen to elderly who have lawyers with whom they are in contact. Either the client will reveal the neglect and abuse to the attorney or the attorney will perceive it. Unfortunately, most neglected and abused elderly are not in contact with an elder law attorney and so must depend on family, friends, or other professionals to report the abuse and neglect to the appropriate authorities.

Financial exploitation, on the other hand, can happen even to an older person who has contact with an attorney. Some exploiters even attempt to enlist the attorney to unknowingly assist in the financial exploitation. The exploiter attempts to manipulate the attorney to assist in making lifetime gifts, creating joint property interests, or leaving a legacy in a will. Elder law attorneys must be alert to such attempts by being watchful for undue influence and fraud by third parties who present themselves as friends of the older person. Sometimes the elder law attorney must protect clients from themselves as they can be prone to covering up for the wrongdoings of those close to them, such as children and grandchildren. The elder law attorney may even have to resort to seeking involuntary conservatorship or guardianship for a client of diminished capacity whose property or person is at risk of exploitation or abuse.

Finally, although elder law can be a "one and done" deal—the client engages the attorney, the problem is solved, and the legal representation is over—that is not usually the case. More typically a client engages the attorney to meet a perceived need or problem, and while dealing with that need the attorney recognizes that the client's needs, opportunities, and risks are much greater than the client imagined. Many elder law attorneys see themselves as engaging in a holistic practice that deals with the entirety of the client's life rather than merely addressing a specific problem.

Whatever the exact nature of their practice, an elder law attorney must have a great deal of substantive knowledge about the law. They must also have strong "people skills" because a successful elder law practice rests on a large number of clients. Finally, an elder law attorney needs the judgment and wisdom to guide a client, and often the client's family, through emotionally difficult circumstances.

Later-life legal problems are not discrete issues but are part of a larger, ever changing mosaic as an individual ages and changes. Because old age is not static, the client is best served by a continuous relationship that permits the attorney to adapt solutions to the changing needs and desires of the client and to the changing legal landscape.

III. Ethical Issues for Elder Law Attorneys

Like all attorneys, elder law attorneys must be careful to practice in an ethical manner. Elder law attorneys, however, face additional ethical issues that may arise when dealing with older clients. First, the attorney must be careful to properly identify who the client is. Second, elder law attorneys must be attentive to their clients' degree of mental capacity.

A. Who Is the Client

For most lawyers, identification of the client is not a problem, but the issue often arises for elder law attorneys who are frequently initially contacted by the children of an older person. The children are worried that their parent is declining physically or mentally and believe that the parent should consult with an attorney. The children often arrange the meeting with the attorney, bring their parent to the attorney's office, and expect to sit in and participate in the interview and initial planning. None of this poses a problem unless the children fail to realize that the parent, not they, is the client. The elder law attorney must make it clear at the beginning of the interview who the client is. Usually that means the older person. The children must be led to understand that regardless of their concern and involvement, and even if they expect to pay the attorney, the parent is the client.

The importance of identification of the client, and making the children aware that it is the older person, is critical. The Rules of Professional Responsibility repeatedly refer to an attorney's duties to the client. For example, Rule 1.4(a) states that the attorney must "reasonably consult with the client about the means by which the client's objectives are to be accomplished." Obviously, accomplishing a client's objectives requires identification of the client and making it clear to the children that it is the client's wishes that dictate what the attorney does, not the desires of the children. It is important for the children to understand that their parent's instructions to the attorney govern the relationship. That is not to say that the children's wishes are of no concern; only that the attorney must only take instruction from the older person. If the client, the older person, wants to give preference to the wishes or needs of their children or other family members, that is the client's right.

Identification of the older person as the client means that it is the older person to whom the lawyer owes duties of diligence (Rule 1.3), keeping them reasonably informed (Rule 1.4(a)(3)), and also keeping client communications confidential unless the client consents to information being shared with named persons (Rule 1.6(a)). When representing an older client, the attorney must take great care not to reveal confidential information of the client to the family absent having been given permission in writing to do so by the client. The attorney should inform the client about the confidentially rule and ask whether the client gives consent to revealing information to their children or other individuals. The attorney should also point out that the client can share some information and hold back other information, and the attorney should advise the client on which information might be shared and which might best be kept confidential.

B. Dealing with the Client's Family

Many older clients are close to one or more family members, such as a child or grandchild, and want to share information as they seek out legal advice and try to make decisions that they hope will benefit both themselves and family members. The attorney must respect the client's concern for their family but still attempt to arrange discussions so that the older client is able to make autonomous decisions and not merely act as some, or all, of the family might want. To do so, the attorney needs to understand the family dynamics of those present and how the older client relates to them. The older client may rely on a family member for transportation but otherwise have little to do with them. Or, in contrast, the client may be very dependent on a particular family member for caregiving and companionship and as a result have a deep emotional connection with that person. Even if the client is normally not dependent on others, if the client has a hearing or vision problem, they may rely on a particular family member to help them communicate with the attorney. They may want a family member present, and waive confidentiality, because they do not trust their hearing or memory. After the meeting with the attorney, they expect to review what happened at the meeting with the family member who was in attendance.

Some elderly clients receive financial support from a child; others benefit from free daily caregiving provided by a child. Whatever the nature of the assistance, the attorney should try to determine if it exists. If so the choices made by the older client may reflect the influence or sense of obligation created by such assistance. The client has the right to treat caregivers and benefactors differently from the other children, including sharing confidential information with them, but the attorney should make it clear to the client that they are not obligated to do so. And at some point, the involvement of a third party can rise to the level of undue influence. Given the nature of their clients, elder law attorneys must be alert to that possibility.

To lessen the chance of undue influence by family members, and to ensure that the client has the opportunity to make autonomous decisions, the attorney must attempt to meet alone with the client as much as possible. Even if the client objects and wants a family member present, the attorney must at least meet once alone with the client. During that meeting, the attorney must determine whether the client has sufficient mental capacity to engage the attorney, consent to a waiver of confidentiality, make decisions as to their person and property, and resist excessive importuning or undue influence by family members.

Once the attorney is satisfied that the client understands what is happening and is making independent choices, additional meetings that include family members should not be a problem. Nevertheless, as the planning continues, the attorney should consider carefully whether a particular topic under consideration requires at least a brief meeting alone with the client. If, for example, the client is planning a new will, the client should meet alone with the attorney to discuss the plan of distribution. The client's decision as to who to name as agent under a power of attorney also should be made by a meeting with only the client and the attorney present. Of course, a client cannot be forced to meet alone with the attorney, but a reluctance to do so should raise a red flag for the attorney. Absent a need for another party to assist the client to communicate with the attorney, there is almost no acceptable reason for a client to refuse to meet alone with an attorney. Whatever the purported reason, it is all too likely that the family member that the client ostensibly wants present is the true instigator and may be guilty of undue influence. Client resistance to meeting alone with the attorney may be the best reason for insisting on meeting alone with the client.

To maintain cordial relations with the client's family often requires the attorney to diplomatically explain why a private meeting with the client is required. If the attorney explains the reason for a private meeting, and what they hope to accomplish, the family is likely to understand and accept the need for the meeting. The attorney may also need to meet with some or all of the family without the client being present. If so, the attorney must make clear to the family that the older person is the client, the attorney does not represent the family members, and that whatever is revealed at the meeting may be passed on to the client. During such a meeting, the attorney can attempt to understand how the family perceives the older client in light of the client's mental and physical capacity. The attorney needs to know if the family believes the client has declined so much that they may lack sufficient mental capacity to engage in sophisticated planning or may no longer have the ability to make rational financial plans. If so, the attorney should take steps to determine the extent of the client's capacity and ability to engage in planning, such as using trusts or making gifts. If the attorney believes that the client has greater mental capacity than do family members, the attorney should document that belief in the event that the client's capacity is later challenged. Family suspicions about the client's mental capacity may indicate possible future challenges to gifts, transfers to a trust, and distributions under a will.

Although the attorney must be cautious when dealing with the family, the attorney must keep in mind that in most cases the family has the best of intentions (or at least some family members do) and is legitimately concerned with the well-being of the older client. It is possible, moreover, for the attorney to represent members of the family as well as the older person. Model Rule 1.7(b)(1) permits representation of multiple persons as long as there is no "concurrent" conflict of interests and, if there are, only if the attorney believes that "the lawyer will be able to provide competent and diligent representation to each affected client." In addition, each client must give informed consent in writing to the existence of the conflict and also be willing to share otherwise confidential information.

IV. Client Competency and Mental Capacity

Elder law attorneys are frequently faced with issues of client competency. The attorney must appreciate that under the law an individual either does or does not have the legal capacity needed to perform a particular act. Mental capacity is best thought of being measured in degrees of capacity. A decline in mental capacity usually takes place in increments, but at some point the decline incapacity is severe enough to cause the law to label the individual as incapacitated. Note, however, that legal capacity varies according to the transaction or the nature of the decision. For the elder law attorney these varying measures of capacity mean that a client may have capacity to perform some acts but not others.

The attorney must first decide whether the older individual has sufficient capacity to enter into an attorney-client relationship. To do so requires that the client have sufficient capacity to enter into a contract; that is, the client understands the nature and consequences of the proposed relationship with the attorney. Assuming that standard is met, the attorney should act in accordance with Model Rule 1.14, Client with Diminished Capacity, which requires the attorney to "maintain a normal client-lawyer relationship." Presumably that means assisting the client to execute documents to the extent possible in light of the client's capacity.

Testamentary capacity, the capacity to execute a valid will, is at the lower end of the legal capacity spectrum. At common law the testator has to:

- Understand the nature of the act of signing a will.
- Understand the nature and extent of their property.
- Know the identity of their heirs—the "natural objects of their bounty."
- Understand how the will disposes of their property.[2]

The application of these tests is not easy. The more complex the estate, the higher degree of capacity required to meet the legal standard. The attorney must weigh the totality of circumstances when deciding whether to permit a client with lessened capacity to sign a will, with the likelihood of a possible will contest a factor to consider. The attorney must also keep in mind that capacity is measured at the moment of the signing of the will. A client can be mentally incapacitated prior to the execution of the will and incapacitated afterward, but can have a moment of lucidity when signing the will and so meet the test for testamentary capacity. The testimony of the subscribing witness, though not determinative, can go a long way to support a later finding, perhaps at a will contest, that the testator, at the moment of the signing, appeared to have testamentary capacity.

The common law standard for the capacity to execute a trust apparently was somewhat higher than testamentary capacity. However, the Uniform Trust Code states that the same capacity is required to execute a revocable trust as is required to execute a will.[3] In practice, because trusts are often will substitutes or a will may pour-over into a contemporaneously executed trust, it makes sense for the two documents to require the same degree of capacity. Still, because of the greater complexity of a trust, the careful attorney may insist upon a marginally greater client capacity to execute a trust as opposed to a will.

Older clients sometimes wish to make substantial gifts, perhaps as part of Medicaid planning. To make a gift requires the same level of capacity needed to enter into a contract, which is a higher state of capacity than testamentary capacity. To enter into a valid contract, an individual must possess sufficient mental capacity to understand the nature and consequences of the act. An older person who wants

---

2. For a detailed discussion as to the levels of capacity required for various acts, see Lawrence A. Frolik & Mary F. Radford, *"Sufficient" Capacity: The Contrasting Capacity Requirements for Different Documents*, 2 NAELA J. 303, 307 (2006).

3. Unif. Trust Code § 601 (2004).

to make a gift, therefore, must understand that if they make the gift they no longer own the property or asset and can no longer enjoy its use or the income in the future that it might produce. They must also understand that a gift is final. They cannot demand the return of the gift regardless of how much they need it or how much they regret having made it.

Similarly, if the client wants to appoint an agent under a power of attorney, state law will require that the client must have the capacity needed to make a contract. That same level of capacity is required if the client wishes to revoke or amend the power of attorney.[4] The capacity needed to execute a valid, advance health care directive or to appoint a surrogate health care decision maker, however, depends upon the applicable state statute. To encourage the use of such documents, states typically only require a level of capacity similar to testamentary capacity or even lower. State statutes often permit the revocation of such documents even if the individual lacks legal capacity. In short, even clients with diminished capacity should be encouraged to sign a health care directive so long as they understand what they are doing. If they later lose capacity to the point that they can no longer give informed consent to decisions regarding their health care, the document that they are signing will mean that a person that they selected will make health care decisions for them rather than someone imposed on them by a court or an individual selected by default under a state statute.

When dealing with a client with diminished capacity, the attorney should proceed cautiously, making sure to not to assume the client comprehends what is happening, take time to explain the basics of what the attorney is trying to achieve, and use non-leading questions to assess the client's understanding. In particular, the attorney must be reasonably certain that it is the client's desires, as opposed to those of the family or a third party, that are being carried out. Yet the attorney must also keep in mind that many older persons welcome input from others. Still, the attorney must be alert for undue influence that results in the older individual undertaking acts that represent not their will, but that of a third party influencer.

Over the course of time, an attorney may conclude that the client's capacity has diminished to the degree that the client is at risk. Model Rule 1.14(b) states that the attorney who reasonably believes that a client is at risk of "substantial physical, financial or other harm," "may take" action to protect the client, including seeking the appointment of a guardian or conservator. Doing so, of course, means resorting to the court to make the determination that the client is legally incapacitated; the attorney does not make that determination. The commentary to Model Rule 1.14, however, suggests that protective action does not necessarily mean resorting to guardianship or conservatorship. The attorney can first attempt less drastic alternatives. The commentary suggests resort to a power of attorney, but that assumes the client has sufficient capacity to execute the power. The commentary also recommends bringing the client to the attention of adult protective

---

4. E.g., *Persinger v. Hols*, 639 N.W.2d 594 (Mich. Ct. App. 2001).

services and other supportive agencies. Here too, the assumption is that the client retains capacity, albeit diminished, and so the client retains the ability and the autonomy to make decisions. If not, guardianship or conservatorship may be unavoidable if the client had not yet appointed a surrogate health care decision maker, executed a power of attorney, or placed assets in a trust. Note that if the attorney takes action to protect a client with diminished capacity, Model Rule 1.6 implicitly permits the attorney to reveal otherwise confidential information about the client, but only to the extent reasonably necessary to protect the client's interests.

Most elder law attorneys are familiar with clients with reduced mental capacity. They usually suffer from dementia, typically Alzheimer's, which is progressive and at present untreatable. In light of the likely possibility that a client may have dementia, the attorney needs a checklist to adequately respond. That list of skills and knowledge should include the following:

- Understanding the signs of dementia.
- Understanding how best to communicate with a client who exhibits signs of dementia.
- Having a list of referral health care professionals who know how to deal with individuals with dementia.
- Being alert to possible ethical issues when dealing with a client with dementia, particularly how to avoid excessive or undue influence.
- Understanding the range of life-planning issues that arise for an individual with dementia.
- Knowing how to arrange the client's finances to avoid financial abuse and exploitation.
- Making sure the client has health care surrogate decision making documents in place, and, if possible, has left instructions either orally or in writing as to their preferred end-of-life care.
- Having an understanding with the spouse and the family about who the attorney will communicate with if the client's capacity continues to decline.

The attorney should also be familiar with screening tests that are used in the health care field to screen for dementia and diminished capacity. Although an attorney in theory could employ such a test, the wiser course is to have a psychiatrist or psychologist test the individual and interpret the results.

The simplest test is the "clock drawing" test. The individual is given a blank sheet of paper and asked to draw a clock with all of the numbers. Next the individual is asked to draw hands on the clock that indicate a specific time, such as a quarter to four. An individual who cannot successfully complete the task may have capacity issues although they may also merely have vision problems, hearing deficits, difficulty holding a pencil, or be unable to draw a picture for mental reasons other than dementia.

Perhaps the most commonly used test is the Mini-Mental State Exam (MMSE). In use since 1975, it asks 11 questions in an attempt to measure the individual's ability to recall, comprehend, and solve visual problems. Some professionals question its accuracy, but at a minimum it is useful in at least flagging a possible loss of capacity if properly interpreted by a trained professional. Other tests include the Montreal Cognitive Assessment and the Saint Louis University Mental Status test. Some professionals believe such tests are too inaccurate or too imprecise to be of much use, and prefer to rely on a half-day or even a full-day examination of the individual in order to properly assess the degree of decline in mental capacity and to identify the mental abilities and life activity skills that have suffered the most decline.

VI. Initial Meeting with the Client

The initial meeting with a potential elder law client, and possibly with members of their family, sets the tone for the relationship. Some elder law attorneys meet for a limited period, such as an hour, without charge, in order for both the potential client and the attorney to determine if the individual has legal needs that the attorney can address. More commonly, the initial meeting is not free but the charge for the meeting is incorporated into the total fee charged to the client if the attorney is engaged. If not, the individual is charged a set fee for the attorney's time.

Whether to charge for the initial meeting depends in part on whether the attorney wants to discourage individuals who are in effect looking for free legal advice as well as those who want to "shop around" among attorneys. If the attorney charges for the initial meeting, the individual is likely to be more serious about intending to hire an attorney and, in particular, has good reason to believe that they expect to hire this attorney. In contrast, an initial free consultation may be effective for an attorney trying to establish a client base. If so, the initial consultation should be "scripted" so that the attorney can uncover the individual's legal issues. The attorney should avoid giving answers or advice and even be somewhat vague about just what documents or actions the attorney expects to undertake. The goal is to impress the potential client that the attorney understands the individual's legal needs and is prepared to provide solutions, but not provide a detailed roadmap that the individual can take to another attorney in an attempt to bargain for a lower fee.

Elder law attorneys almost always use a set fee rather than hourly billing with the proviso that if the work requires increases because of changing circumstances the fee may be increased. Using a set fee requires the attorney to be able to determine both what work is required and how much time that work will require. A third consideration is what the market will bear. Some clients may have an idea of what other attorneys charge or at least have an idea of what they are willing to pay. It is therefore wise to either set a fee that is typical in the region or have an explanation why the fee is higher than might be expected. Except in unusual circumstances the attorney should adhere to a set fee schedule. Lowering the fee for one client is the first step on a slippery slope. If other clients learn of the discounted fee, they too will demand it. It is far better to create a realistic fee schedule and explain to clients that the business of running a law office as well as the talents of the attorney require charging the scheduled fee.

If the client hires the attorney, a written engagement letter must be sent that includes the fee and the scope of representation including documents to be prepared. The engagement letter language that describes the fee should be worded in a manner that will permit an increase in the fee under appropriate circumstances. The letter should also state when the fee is to be paid and how much. For example, is it all due within 30 days or is only a portion due now with additional payments in the future? The letter should state whether the attorney accepts credit cards. The letter should also state whether the fee covers expenses such as mailing or copying or whether those will be billed for as incurred. If the latter, the attorney may want a deposit against which future expenses can be applied. An alternative is to charge an initial retainer against which the fee and expenses are charged, and to bill additionally if the retainer is exhausted. The engagement letter should require that the client sign a consent statement and return that signed copy to the attorney.

If the prospective client declines to hire the attorney, a non-engagement letter should be sent. If the individual left documents with the attorney, but the attorney has decided not to represent them, the attorney should return the original documents and explain that the attorney will not represent the individual, has retained copies of the documents, and is not charging the client for the consultation unless the charge for the consultation was disclosed to the individual at the beginning of the meeting and agreed to by the individual. If the individual engaged the attorney, but failed to pay the fee or retainer, the attorney should notify the individual that the attorney does not represent them because they have not paid the fee or retainer.

A. Client Information

After the client has engaged the attorney, the gathering of information begins. The attorney should have a checklist of questions, many of which can be answered by the client prior to the initial meeting. Based on that response, the attorney should be alerted to what additional information is needed. Sample questionnaires abound. Whatever questionnaire is used, it must be broad enough in scope and detailed enough in questions to elicit needed information and also reveal areas that the attorney should make additional inquiry about. The following topics should guide the client interview and questionnaire.

- **Personal data.** Including the client, their spouse, descendants, parents (if living), previous spouses, siblings, and significant others. Beyond names and addresses, the questionnaire should ask the client to flag individuals with health problems, disabilities, mental health issues both past and current, and any other relevant conditions or circumstances.

- **Parental and sibling health history.** Because many chronic conditions appear to have a genetic component, family medical histories may be a guide to what may happen to the client. Even shared environmental or cultural backgrounds may be predictive.

- **Marriage history.** Both present and prior. If the client has been divorced, focus on the property settlement and any agreements as to pension or retirement fund rights.

- **Occupation or work record.** Many clients will strongly identify with their current or past employment. Knowing what the client did before retirement can be helpful in understanding how to approach them when explaining planning options. For example, explaining end-of-life choices to a retired nurse is different than explaining the topic to a former office administrator.

- **Retirement benefits.** Including pensions, 401(k) plans, other retirement income benefits, IRAs, and retiree health care benefits. If the client is married, be sure to inquire about the retirement benefits of both spouses.

- **Social Security benefits.** Ascertain the dollar amounts of both spouses and explain about the effect on the survivor's benefits when one spouse dies. If they are not yet taking benefits, determine when they expect to begin them.

- **Health of client.** Information should be sought about the current physical and mental health, prognosis of any developing or latent condition, relevant past medical history and client estimation of future health care needs, including personal care or need for assistance.

- **Religious beliefs.** To the extent that such beliefs might play a role in planning for end-of-life health care and funerals. Housing choices can also be affected by religious beliefs. The attorney needs to know enough about the client's beliefs so that the attorney can see that the beliefs are respected even if family members do not agree or are even hostile about them.

- **Secular values.** Many clients do not have religious beliefs but nevertheless have strong opinions as to what is moral, ethical, or proper behavior, particularly when it comes to health care, end-of-life care, funerals, and even housing choices.

- **Professional, community, and social affiliations.** Having the client give a brief summation of affiliations can assist in understanding who the client "is" and to whom they might turn should they need assistance and social support.

- **Relationship with children and their spouses.** The client will need to appoint agents under powers of attorney, surrogate health care decision makers, possibly executors and trustees, and identify possible caregivers. Essentially the questions are who does the client trust, who is available, and who has the knowledge and appropriate temperament to successfully function in the position. Although the children's spouses are not often named, in some cases their hostile attitude about the obligations taken on by the child can interfere with the child performing well. The other demands on the child—personal, family, and financial—should also be understood.

- **Significant others and close friends.** Not every older client has a spouse. Some cohabit and others merely have close friends that they consider as "family." Uncovering these relations requires careful questioning. Essentially, the attorney needs to know if someone other than or in addition to a spouse or family member has a special place of trust in the client's life.
- **Financial obligations.** Both legal and voluntary to children, grandchildren, parents, siblings, and even charitable pledges or moral obligations. The amount of support provided, and whether the client wants it to continue and, if so, under what conditions and subject to what limitations?
- **Legal documents and agreements.** Knowledge of and, if possible, copies of any current will, power of attorney, surrogate health care decision maker, revocable and irrevocable trusts, joint property, powers of appointment, long-term care insurance, Medigap insurance, life insurance, annuities, beneficial interests in a trust, rental leases as tenant or landlord, royalty rights, and mineral leases.
- **Client assets.** A complete list of all intangible assets including all bank accounts, bonds and securities in paper form, brokerage accounts, real estate, deferred annuities, and insurance products. Also all real estate and tangible assets including art, precious metals and collectibles, and any household effects that have significant market value.
- **Passwords.** For the home computer, bank accounts, and all other password protected sites. Insist that the client create either a handwritten version or use a computer password site and keep whichever up-to-date and be sure that the password site is accessible by a trusted third party or the attorney.

B. Dealing with the Client's Spouse

Often the older client is married. If so, the couple is likely to consider that both are clients. The attorney can represent both spouses, but only if the spouses agree in writing to the potential conflict of interest and to the disclosure of confidential information. Obtaining consent to the conflict of interest is usually not a problem because the personal and financial interests of the couple typically overlap. They both want to retain their autonomy, they both are usually willing to assist the other, and they both usually agree about their finances such as whether they are willing to expend their savings on their care or whether they want to pass their savings on to their children. Even if the couple is not in complete agreement, they are likely willing to work with the attorney to resolve their disagreements.

The sharing of otherwise confidential information may be more problematical. The attorney must emphasize that representation of both spouses means that the attorney must share all relevant information. The clients cannot selectively agree which information to share. If either spouse has secrets from the other that they do not want to reveal, they must not reveal that information to the attorney. Many attorneys will not represent a couple if one or both are not willing to waive confidentially as to the other spouse.

The attorney who represents a couple must help them decide how they will react to the care needs of the first spouse to suffer a physical or mental decline. It is important to learn this early in the representation because the answers will directly impact future planning. The couple must estimate how much personal assistance the well spouse will provide and what proportion of the couple's income and financial resource will be used to support the non-well spouse. If the well spouse is willing to provide care and maintain the non-well spouse at home, the need for paid care and institutionalization of the non-well spouse can be delayed with a corresponding savings of income and resources. The "cost" to the well spouse, however, can be considerable in terms of their health and psychological well-being. Even if the well spouse is willing to make that sacrifice, the attorney must lay out the probable scenario of the likely future of the non-well spouse. At some point the condition of the non-well spouse will have declined so much that they will require additional paid assistance and perhaps even institutionalization. The attorney should initiate a discussion as to how the projected cost of care of the non-well spouse will be met and how doing so will affect the quality of life of the well spouse. Often during that discussion it will become clear that the couple's assets and income will be unable to support the cost of care and so the couple should plan on eventually applying for Medicaid to pay for nursing home care or for state-provided home and community assistance to help pay for care in the home. If either of the couple is a veteran, the attorney should review the possible veterans' benefits available to them.

The couple may want to defer institutionalization by using paid in-home care, but the attorney should caution them that such care is expensive and may not best meet the needs of the non-well spouse. The attorney should also warn the couple about the difficulties of finding, supervising, and monitoring appropriate in-home care. If the couple insists on using in-home care, the attorney should note that they will need help in meeting the obligations that come with being an employer, such as payment of wage taxes including withholding for income taxes and the Social Security wage tax. If the couple plans to hire an agency to provide the care, the attorney should suggest that the couple either hire the attorney or a qualified employment attorney to review the contract of care to see that it meets the client's needs.

During the initial interview and throughout the planning process, the attorney must be careful to balance the needs of the two spouses. When discussing plans for long-term care for one spouse, the attorney must emphasize the couple's need to have a contingent plan for the possible future care needs of the other spouse, keeping in mind that every dollar spent on the first spouse is one less dollar available for the other spouse. Of course, the decision on how to allocate their finances is up to the couple, but the attorney has the ethical obligation to make sure that both spouses fully appreciate the consequences of their decisions. The attorney should also emphasize that any plan may not prove to be the best plan in light of future developments. Later-life legal planning is a process. Unanticipated care needs, changes in finances and income, and changes in state and federal law may necessitate amending the original plan. The initial interview is only the beginning of a relationship with the attorney. The clients should plan on a regular review with the elder law attorney about their needs and whether their current plan remains the best approach.

C. Articulating Client Goals

A client typically seeks out an elder law attorney for a particular problem or concern. In all likelihood, however, the client's needs are much broader than those articulated. In most cases, those needs can be grouped into four areas of concern.

1. Long-term care in light of current or projected physical and mental decline.
2. Financial security including financial security for a surviving spouse.
3. Property management during life and distribution of property at death.
4. Housing that is affordable and appropriate in light of the client's current and projected physical and mental condition.

Clients often are focused on only one of these areas and usually fail to appreciate their interdependence. The attorney, therefore, must ask questions that force the client to consider how to plan for the variety of contingencies that go well beyond the immediate concerns that brought the client to the elder law attorney's office.

As the client begins to appreciate that later-life legal planning must be ongoing and respond to changing circumstances, the client may come to appreciate that they need a continuing relationship with the attorney. Or the attorney may convince the client that they have needs that will be best served by continuing to engage the attorney. If the client remains as an active client, the attorney's role is to help the client understand how declines in physical and mental capacity require the client to choose among the continuum of available options. The choices depend upon on the client's values, finances, and social and family support systems.

D. Understanding Available Solutions and the Need for Other Professional Involvement

As the client explains what is important to them, such as aging in place or not being a burden on their children, the attorney can begin to outline choices and solutions that translate vague values and wishes into specific solutions. That may require calling for assistance from other professionals such as geriatric social workers, insurance professionals, and financial advisors.

Many elder law attorneys employ such professionals on their staff. Some employ nurses, social workers, or paralegals with extensive experience in dealing with the issues confronting older clients. Other attorneys employ or consult with other professionals as needed, or merely refer clients with the hope that the other professionals will reciprocate by referring their clients to the attorney. A few elder law attorneys have become licensed to sell insurance so that they can sell clients long-term care insurance when it is appropriate. Some attorneys have become licensed to sell financial products such as annuities or mutual funds in the belief that such products are often essential parts of effective planning in light of their clients' needs. The potential conflict of interest in an attorney selling a product that the same attorney recommends as part of proffered legal advice is obvious. Great care is required to avoid transgressing professional ethical rules.

Elder law attorneys should also be well informed as to the available community support services and housing options. Most states, counties, and even some cities offer services and support to the elderly, often without regard to financial need. The attorney should know what those services are and how to access them. For example, the attorney should know if there is a local senior center and what kinds of programs are available there. Adult day care centers may also exist that the attorney might want to recommend. Many religious entities offer support and outreach to the elderly. The attorney should have contact information for these groups in the event that the client wishes to seek their assistance. The attorney should also have a list of the nonprofit community entities that are a potential source of programming and assistance.

Elder law attorneys need to be familiar with the supportive housing available in their community. Many clients want to age in place, but to do so requires assistance with personal care. The attorney should have a list of agencies that provide in-home care. Giving the client the names of potential care providers is usually unwise. If the client hires the individual and that arrangement does not work out, the client may have doubts about the attorney's advice in other matters. Worse, if the client is harmed, abused, or victimized by an individual recommended by the attorney, it is possible that the attorney might be liable for having made the recommendation. The client can claim that the attorney failed to do due diligence prior to making the recommendation. It is far better to merely provide a list of agencies while noting that the attorney is not recommending them and has no personal knowledge about them; and add that there are other agencies that are not on the list.

It is also important to be familiar with the housing designed for the elderly that is available in their community including continuing care retirement communities, supported housing, assisted living, and nursing homes. The attorney might want to visit some of these facilities, both to be able to describe or recommend them and also to establish relationships with the managers of those facilities. Being able to provide a client with a contact person at a facility can be very useful in assuring the client that they selected the right elder law attorney.

VI. Basic Estate Planning Documents

The initial interview with a client should disclose whether the client has the basic estate planning documents, including a will, a power of attorney, and a document that appoints a surrogate health care decision maker. The elder law attorney should ask to be provided copies of these documents and should review them. Doing so will frequently reveal that the documents are out of date or fail to comport with the client's current wishes. If the client agrees, the attorney should draft new documents.

A. Will

Older clients who have a will have often not reviewed it for several years. Consequently, the document may not express how the client now wants to leave their estate. Alternatively, the client may not have considered how changing circumstances may necessitate a new will. The attorney should discuss with the client the most likely events that may require a new will.

First, the previous wills of many older clients leave everything to the surviving spouse. If there is no longer a spouse or if the spouse named in the will has died, a new will is clearly in order. Even if the spouse is alive, they may have suffered a significant loss of mental capacity that makes leaving the entire estate to them unwise. A reduction of the gift to them or leaving the gift to them in a trust may be more sensible. If the spouse is in a nursing home or is receiving at home care and is receiving Medicaid or is likely to soon receive Medicaid, the client should only leave the minimum required by the state law to that spouse in order to minimize or avoid their becoming ineligible for Medicaid or other state assistance programs. In short, both the present and future physical and mental dependencies and needs of each spouse should be considered when drafting a new will.

The clients should also consider how much of their wealth is part of their probate estate and therefore subject to provisions in the will. Increasingly, wealth is held in IRAs, insurance proceeds, trusts, and jointly held property, none of which are governed by a will. The client needs to carefully review beneficiary designations including successor beneficiaries and review whether it is wise to continue to own jointly held property other than the family home.

Next, the client must review the appropriateness of gifts in the will to their children. When the previous will was executed, the children might have been minors or only young adults. An older client, however, one who is past age 70, will likely have children age 40 or 50. Those children may not be suitable for an outright gift. Problems in their marriage, their business, or with their finances might suggest that a gift in trust is more advisable. If the client has grandchildren, they should be asked whether they wish to leave gifts to those grandchildren and, if so, should the gifts be left in trust.

B. Power of Attorney

The client should have a new power of attorney if only to avoid problems with third parties being reluctant to accept a power signed years ago. Because many states have amended their power of attorney statutes, even though a preexisting power might still be valid, it is advisable to sign a power that comports with the current state requirements. If the client has changed state residency since signing the previous power of attorney, the attorney should insist on the client executing a power that meets the requirements of the current state of residence. If the client has a winter or summer home, they should sign a second power of attorney that meets the requirements of the state where the property is located and that grants agent authority only to deal with that property. The client should also review who they have named as agent and successor agents, as the passage of time may dictate the need for new agents and possibly even new powers tailored to the client's current financial realities.

Finally, the attorney should ensure that the client has a document that appoints a surrogate health care decision maker in the event that the client lacks the capacity to make health care decisions. The document should appoint the agent and a successor, and also detail the kind and extent of end-of-life treatment desired by the client. If the client typically spends time in two or more states, the client should sign separate documents that meet the statutory requirements of each state. Some clients will have or will want a living will, which is a document that attempts to dictate their medical care in the event that they lose the capacity to do so. In most cases, it is preferable to have a single document that appoints the agent for health care decision making and also includes instructions as to the kind of care desired. Attempting to dictate care in the abstract is less effective than providing a surrogate health care decision making agent with appropriate powers and instructing them as to the desires of the client who signs the documents.

For a more detailed discussion of estate planning for an older client, see Chapter 11, Health Care Decision Making; Chapter 16, Trusts; and Chapter 17, Estate Planning with the Very Old Client.

Medical Realities of Aging 2

I. Introduction

Aging is an inevitable progressive process that proceeds at
varying rates among individuals. The consequences of aging are
profound, but they have very different meanings for different
aspects of an individual's life. From the legal perspective the
decline in physical and mental well-being can result in a radical
reordering of the many facets of an individual's life that impact
the individual's role in society and even their legal standing.
Understanding how individuals age and how aging effects behavior and therefore ultimately legal rights is critical for anyone who
advises older clients or who themselves may be aging.

II. The Aging Body

We are all mortal. As we grow older, the likelihood of death
increases and our life expectancy grows shorter. At age 65, ignoring racial differences, the average life expectancy of a female is
about 20½ years; for a male it is about 18 years. More than half
of the women alive at age 65 will be alive at age 85, and for men,
more than half will still be alive at age 83. Even for an 80-year-old,
the average life expectancy is nine years. Today, out of a 100,000
women born 80 years earlier, about 63,400 women are alive and
out of a 100,000 men, about 50,000 are alive.

Absent disease or accidental injury, aging is the steady decline of organs and body functions. The decline in the efficient operation of the heart and blood vessels means less control over blood pressure; it generally becomes higher, but may also drop sharply lower. Other systems, such as regulation of body temperature, become less effective, putting an individual at risk of heat stroke. The body may be less capable of mounting a fever to fight inflection, and less efficient kidneys may not adequately regulate water retention. Skin, which acts as a barrier against bacteria, becomes thinner and more porous and so more susceptible to bruises, wounds, and trauma. Swallowing begins to fail at times, leading to aspiration as liquids or solids enter the lungs instead of the esophagus. Coughing that clears the airways is less effective. A reduction in stomach acids means that bacteria have a better chance of survival. The bladder functions less well. Because the immune system becomes less responsive, cancer is more likely to develop. Noticeable to most is the progressive decline in the delivery of oxygen, which results in a steady decline in physical work capacity; someone age 70 has about half the physical work capacity of a 20-year-old.

Individuals lose height as they age, with most losing two inches by age 80, thanks to compression of the spine and changes in joints. Weight gain is common during one's 60s and 70s; then it declines, although more slowly for women. Most older persons experience the loss of lean muscle mass and an increase in body fat. Bone loss is common, but it is highly variable among individuals. Short-term memory declines, as does hearing. The aging eye is prone to presbyopia making it harder to focus on nearby objects; hence the need for bifocals. The eye also takes more time to adapt to an abrupt change from light to dark and is more sensitive to glare. Taste, smell, and touch all become less sensitive.

A. Skin Diseases and Conditions

1. Pressure Sores

Older persons are more susceptible to ailments that affect the skin. The most serious of these ailments are pressure sores (also known as pressure ulcers), which are the result of soft tissues being compressed for an extended period of time between a bony prominence and another surface, typically a bed or a wheelchair. Pressure sores are classed in four stages with stage 4 being the most severe. At stage 1 the individual suffers soft tissue inflammation with some loss of the epidermal (surface) skin. As the sore worsens and descends through the skin into the underlying subcutaneous fat, it becomes a stage 2, and if not treated, progresses to stage 3. A stage 4 pressure sore features the extension of the sore into muscle and possibly bone. Pressure sores can appear across the body wherever there is extended pressure. Common sites of pressure sores are hips, lower back, heels, and lower buttocks.

Pressure sores frequently fail to heal and significantly increase the risk of death for many elderly. It is often not clear whether a pressure sore is the cause of death or if it hastens death by other causes. Blood poisoning is one complication of pressure sores along with other infections that may lead to death or weaken the individual's ability to ward off other diseases. What is clear is that pressure sores, particularly stage 4 pressure sores, are not only the cause of pain and discomfort, but they also lead to death.

Pressure sores occur most frequently in the elderly with limited mobility. Bed and wheel chair bound individuals are at high risk of pressure sores. Other factors are poor nutrition that may be caused by the individual's refusal to eat and cigarette smoking. The sore is a result of the pressure blocking adequate oxygen to the area. The medical response is to reposition the person at regular intervals—every two hours is recommended—to relieve the pressure. Devices can be used to provide relief, including sheepskins, air pillows, foam pads, and water-filled mattresses.

Pressure sores are not normal, certainly not stage 3 or 4 pressure sores. If a sore advances beyond stage 1, it is almost always due to substandard care. Proper inspection of an individual's body and in particular the sites that pressure sores often develop should reveal a pressure sore in its early stages and permit the appropriate medical or caregiving response. Proper periodical repositioning of the individual should minimize or eliminate pressure sores. Any individual who suffers prolonged pressure sores or severe pressure sores has almost certainly been the victim of substandard care and may have a potential lawsuit against the medical provider or caregiver. Depending on the applicable state law, the lawsuit may be for the tort of personal injury or may be a medical malpractice claim.

2. Shingles

Shingles is a painful skin rash featuring small skin blisters that itch and may cause a burning pain. It is caused by the chickenpox virus. It is more common among older persons or those with impaired functioning immune systems because of stress, injury, or reaction to certain medicines. Shingles occurs when the chicken-pox virus that has been dormant in the nerve roots starts up again in old age. Only someone who had chickenpox can develop shingles. If the virus becomes active, it can only cause shingles, not chickenpox.

There is no cure for shingles, but treatment may shorten the length of the illness and reduce the itching or pain. Treatment includes antiviral medicines to reduce the pain and duration, and pain medicines, antidepressants, and topical creams to relieve the long-term pain that may occur years after the rash has disappeared.

A shingles vaccine roughly cuts in half the chances of getting shingles; or, if the individual has already had singles, the vaccine may help prevent a reoccurrence. The vaccine contains a weakened chickenpox virus, which primes the immune system to defend against the disease.

3. Skin Cancer

Hundreds of thousands of Americans annually report having a skin cancer. It is believed that nearly all skin cancer is caused by exposure of the skin to sun without adequate clothing or suntan lotion. Because skin cancer, particularly melanoma, results from repeated exposure to the sun, the incidence of skin cancer rises with age. Skin cancer appears in three forms. Basal cell carcinoma, the most common, is a small skin tumor that is treatable by removal and has a very high cure rate, estimated to be over 95 percent. Squamous cell carcinoma is usually related to excessive exposure to sunlight and features a scaly red bump, plaque, or non-healing skin ulcer. Like basal cell skin cancer, it is highly treatable unless the tumor has metastasized. Melanoma is a life-threatening skin cancer if not detected early. It is evidenced by moles, usually black or brown. If treated at this stage, the death rate is very low. However, if it has spread beyond the surface skin to the body fat, the survival rate over the next five years is only about 50 percent. If it has metastasized, the death rate is quite high; about 10,000 Americans die from melanoma every year.

B. Diseases and Conditions Affecting Joints, Muscles, and Bones

1. Joints

Aging individuals often experience joint problems; over half of those age 65 and older experience some degree of a joint problem. Joint problems can result from mechanical problems with the joint, inflammatory arthritis, or wear and tear on the joint, known as osteoarthritis. Problems with tendons around a joint, tendinitis or bursitis, can also bring on pain and reduced joint mobility that is often worse at night or in the morning upon wakening.

Mechanical problems with a joint are caused by tears in the joint cartilage or ligament or changes in the bones of the joint. Such problems give rise to intermittent pain. The joints may suddenly "give way" or "lock." This can be painful if the joint is moved in a certain way and often causes swelling around the joint.

Inflammatory arthritis can be sudden. It abruptly causes pain and swelling for 10 to 48 hours and is often accompanied by fever and chills. Chronic inflammatory arthritis, such as rheumatoid arthritis, is characterized by extended periods of morning stiffness in the hands, wrists, ankles, and feet, and may be characterized by thickening around the joints to the extent of deforming the fingers.

Osteoarthritis is a progressive response to the wear and tear on joints. It features the gradual progression of pain and morning stiffness of the joints, particularly the end joints of the fingers, the thumb, the hips, knees and even the base of the big toe. As it progresses, the individual may suffer a decline in their ability to get in or out of a chair.

Certain parts of the body are particularly susceptible to joint pain. Neck pain due to compression of the spinal cord or of a nerve root is common. A compressed cervical disk can result from a ruptured disk in the neck that manifests itself as pain in the neck and shoulders.

2. Shoulders

Many older individuals experience shoulder problems. The three interrelated joints of the shoulder, the tendons, bursae, and the muscles of the rotator cuff are all vulnerable to wear and tear. The rotator cuff muscles and tendons are often the source of pain for aging individuals. Inflammation and small tears of the tendons lead to rotator cuff bursitis and tendonitis that cause pain in the shoulder and upper arm that spikes when the individual undertakes movements such as reaching over the head or putting on a coat. Unfortunately, small tendon tears that for a 20-year-old might heal in two weeks might not heal in two months for an 80-year-old. Usually rest, ice, and physical therapy are enough to enable an individual to recover from a rotator cuff injury, but if the injury is a complete tear of the muscle or tendon, surgical repair may be needed.

Frozen shoulder is the gradual progressive, painful restriction of the shoulder movement. The cause is unknown, but with treatment over several months, the individual usually regains full motion. Steroid injections can help, but often active stretching is enough. For many, time alone seems to be enough, though it may take two years or more to regain full movement of the shoulder.

If shoulder pain and the loss of function are severe, surgery and the insertion of an artificial shoulder may be required because the shoulder in essence has worn out. Surgery, however, is not a complete panacea. It does not fully restore the same level of function that the person had before the damage to the shoulder joint began. But after shoulder surgery, most have much less pain and are able to perform most normal activities, including golfing, riding a bike, swimming and walking for exercise. Those who have the surgery after age 60 can expect the artificial joint to last the rest of their life.

3. Hips and Knees

Many elderly suffer from osteoarthritis of the hip, which is characterized by gradual increase of pain in the buttock, groin, thigh, or even in the front of the knee. The pain intensifies with use, including climbing stairs, but even just standing can bring on pain. Treatment includes use of pain relievers, weight loss, exercise, and use of a cane. Because of increasing pain, many eventually need hip replacement surgery.

Knee problems effect nearly 5 percent of those age 65 and older. As with hips, osteoarthritis is the most common reason for knee pain and loss of movement. For many, knee replacement may be the only solution.

4. Osteoporosis

Osteoporosis is the age-related decrease in bone mass that causes an increase in the susceptibility in bone fractures. Although some bone mass loss is part of normal aging, excessive loss is not. As a result of osteoporosis, for women the incidence of hip fracture increases by 15 percent after age 65. Vertebrae fractures increase even more, but they usually pass unnoticed. Nevertheless, such fractures contribute to stooped posture and the loss of height.

Hip fractures do not always manifest themselves, as victims often do not feel pain. Once discovered, however, hip fractures are usually treated by the surgical insertion of pins into the hip bone. The longer the delay in the surgery, the lesser the chance of recovery. Delay beyond 24 hours of the fracture can lead to the loss of the ability to walk, or even death. Even with surgery, about 10 percent of those who have a hip fracture die within 30 days of the fracture. Patients with heart failure have about a 65 percent likelihood of dying within 30 days. Post-fracture pneumonia is common and leads to a 40 percent mortality rate. Some fractures are of a type that does not heal well and may lead to the need for a hip replacement.

C. Hearing and Vision

Declines in hearing and vision are very common for older individuals. Over 30 percent of those over age 65 have problems with their hearing and it rises with age; 50 percent of those over age 85 having hearing loss. It is possible that a decline in speech recognition may be a reflection of overall slowing of mental processing as well as problems with hearing.

Most hearing loss is a result of presbycusis, which is the progressive, high-frequency hearing loss that effects both ears. Deterioration of the ear and nerve damage also contribute to hearing loss, as does the buildup of ear wax that is common among older individuals. Some medications, particularly antibiotics and diuretics can cause a loss of hearing.

The solution to hearing loss is a hearing aid, although about 20 percent of those who use hearing aids report that they still have trouble hearing. A better fitting device, more regular use of the device, and the use of a more appropriate device, such as one observable by others, may result in a more effective hearing aid that provides improved hearing.

Communication with a hearing impaired person is greatly facilitated if the speaker takes care to:

- Eliminate or reduce background noise.
- Face the listener, maintain eye contact and allow the listener clear view of the speaker's face.
- Speak in a normal tone; shouting usually does not help.
- Repeat and rephrase the content of the conversation.

Loss of vision accompanies aging. Over 90 percent of older individuals require glasses. Even glasses, however, cannot reduce the loss of the ability to adapt from bright light to darkness and the increasing sensitivity to glare, both of which impair driving at night.

Serious loss of vision that cannot be countered with glasses affects about 20 percent of those over age 85. Many are afflicted with one of the four major eye diseases: cataracts, glaucoma, macular degeneration, and diabetic eye disease. Over 40 percent of those over age 75 have cataracts, a progressive clouding of the eye lens. For many, better lighting and stronger glasses are an adequate response. If not, surgery to remove the cataract is a safe and successful procedure that replaces the damaged lens with an artificial lens.

Glaucoma, one of the leading causes of blindness, is a condition that causes optic nerve damage leading to the loss of vision; abnormally high pressure in the eye is the most common cause. Unfortunately, often the only symptom is the gradual loss of vision. Early diagnosis and treatment can minimize the loss of vision. Regular eye exams are key to detecting glaucoma early enough to successfully treat it. After age 60, eye exams every one to two years are recommended, though for African Americans, who often experience an earlier onset of the condition, periodic eye exams starting as young as age 30 are recommended. Because glaucoma appears to have a genetic component, those with a family history of the disease should take particular care to screen for it. Surgery and eye drops are used to lower the pressure in the eye, but may not reverse previous loss of vision.

Macular degeneration causes the loss of central vision. It has two forms: dry and wet. Dry macular degeneration accounts for over 80 percent those with the condition. About 10 percent of those with dry macular degeneration eventually become legally blind, meaning their vision in the better eye is not correctable to 20/200, that is, they can see at 20 feet what a normal person can see at 200 feet. The risk of macular degeneration increases with age and is most common in people older than 65. Risk factors include the following:

- A family history of macular degeneration
- Race—it is more common in whites
- Smoking
- Being severely overweight
- A diet low in fruits and vegetables
- Having cardiovascular disease
- High cholesterol

There is no treatment that reverses dry macular degeneration, but it usually progresses slowly and does not usually lead to blindness. Often only one eye is affected. Those with the condition can usually lead normal lives, albeit with reduced vision. Treatment includes high doses of antioxidant vitamins and zinc, though whether and how effective they are is not clear. A healthier diet featuring fruits, vegetables, healthy fats such olive oil, and omega-3 rich fish, such as salmon, is also recommended.

Wet macular degeneration is the other form of macular degeneration. Its cause is unknown, but it almost always begins as dry macular degeneration. Wet macular degeneration causes vision loss in the center of the field of vision due to abnormal blood vessels that leak fluid or blood onto the macula, which is the oval-shaped pigmented area near the center of the retina. Medications injected directly into the eye may help stop growth of abnormal blood vessels. The injections are repeated every four weeks and may lead to some improvement in vision.

Those with macular generation that has significantly impaired their vision must eventually resort to magnifiers, including devices that use a video camera to magnify the image and project it on a screen.

D. Heart Conditions

The elderly often have heart and circulatory conditions. Although age alone may contribute to cardiovascular decline, for most elderly the decline is due to a disease or condition.

1. High Blood Pressure

Over half of those over the age of 65 have some degree of high blood pressure. If high enough, it can contribute to a heart attack or stroke. Blood pressure is measured as systolic pressure (when the heart is contracting and pushing out blood) and diastolic pressure (when the heart is relaxing and letting blood flow in). Systolic blood pressure is more predictive of heart problems and strokes, the latter being closely associated with high blood pressure. The two readings are combined into a single number such as 120/70. A reading of below 120 and below 80 is considered normal blood pressure. A reading of 120–139 or 80–89 indicates prehypertension, but no medical response is needed. A reading of 140–159 or 90–99 indicates stage 1 hypertension and may require medicine to counteract the rise in blood pressure. A reading of above 160 or above 100 indicates stage 2 hypertension (high blood pressure) and will likely result in the prescribing of one or more medicines. Changes in lifestyle including exercise and a better diet will also be recommended. If blood pressure is reduced below 150/90, the likelihood of a stroke or heart attack is significantly lowered.

2. Coronary Artery Disease

The progressive narrowing of the arteries that supply blood to the heart is coronary heart disease (CAD), which is the leading cause of death for those over the age of 65, although the rate of deaths has decreased dramatically over the last 35 years. CAD is a process that begins during adolescence and slowly progresses throughout life. The risk factors for coronary artery disease are smoking, high blood pressure, obesity, and a sedentary life style. High levels of cholesterol, particularly LDL cholesterol, also appear to be associated with the disease.

LDL cholesterol contributes to plaque, a thick, hard deposit that can clog arteries and make them less flexible. Known as atherosclerosis, if a clot develops it can narrow an artery and cause a heart attack or a stroke. Elevated triglycerides are also associated with atherosclerosis and can result from obesity, smoking, lack of physical exercise, and a diet with excessive carbohydrates. Those with high triglycerides often have a high total cholesterol level.

III. The Aging Brain

Just as the body ages, so does the brain. Normal aging that results in some decline in brain function should not be confused with diseases such as Alzheimer's that erode and degrade brain functioning. The most common aspect of the aging brain is a decline in short-term memory. It is likely due to the brain being less efficient at storing new experiences and input and also the result of declines in sensory perception—vision and hearing—so that less information reaches the brain. Long-term memory may also decline, but it is not clear whether it is a reflection of normal aging or due to a disease or condition. Recall, such as stating a name, appears to decline past age 60. Conversely, judgment may improve with age or it may be that greater experience leads to better choices. Some contend that many older persons grow in wisdom. That may be true if wisdom is defined as an ability to perceive the truth and rise above personal circumstances. Or if may be that the elderly, who often have less personal involvement and who can monitor and control their emotions, are better able to objectively assess a situation.

Whatever the truth about wisdom and aging, unfortunately the aging brain is susceptible to diseases that degrade it and leave it progressively unable to properly function.

A. Dementia

Dementia in the elderly is not a function of normal aging. It is defined as the development of significant deficits in memory and at least one other area of cognition such as abstract thinking, judgment, language, or spatial recognition. More than 60 percent of dementia is caused by Alzheimer's disease, which is progressive, untreatable, and eventually leads to death.

Alzheimer's disease begins gradually and manifests itself by the individual experiencing the loss of memory and having difficulty in learning new tasks. As the disease progresses, long-term memory declines and the individual increasingly suffers from impaired orientation, judgment, word finding, motor skills, and spatial recognition. As the disease becomes more severe, individuals lose the ability to care for themselves. They can no longer feed themselves, bath, or dress themselves and lose toileting skills and become incontinent. Some become depressed and passive; others agitated and aggressive. At some point, they have gait problems and eventually become bedridden.

Alzheimer's is often described by its stages that arise during the years (an average of seven) that an individual will live with the disease. The early stage of mild dementia is characterized by the individual forgetting what they have just read. As a result, they may stop reading books, magazines, and even the newspaper. They begin to repeat the same question and cannot make plans. The disease progresses to the moderate stage, at which point the individual begins to forget the month or the season, has trouble using a menu, and seems to forget details about themselves. They begin to lose track of where they are, cannot remember their address or phone number, and have trouble selecting clothes to wear that are appropriate for the season. In the severe stage, the individual forgets the names of loved ones (and later cannot even recognize their faces); begins to confuse one person for another, such as thinking a daughter is their mother; and believes that they must report to work or have some other need to leave the house because they are convinced that there is someplace that they must get to. In the end stage, the individual will cease being able to eat, walk, or even sit up. They also cease to realize that they need to drink fluids.

Once dementia has progressed to a severe or late stage, death usually occurs within six months to one year. An infection, such as pneumonia, is often the cause of death. Multiple organ failure is another common cause of death because as Alzheimer's disease progresses, the nerves that signal the body organs to perform their function begin to die and that in turn leads to death. Other causes of death are general wasting, malnutrition, and dehydration that arise because the individual no longer can drink or eat without assistance.

Vascular dementia is the second leading cause of dementia, accounting for about 20 percent of all dementia cases. It occurs in individuals who have mini-strokes in their brains, that is, cerebrovascular disease. Each mini-stroke blocks the passage of blood to a part of the brain, which in turn causes some observable degree of dementia such as an inability to read or a lack of recognition of family members. The progression of vascular dementia is more abrupt than is Alzheimer's but it may plateau for a period of time. Some who have vascular dementia also develop Alzheimer's disease.

Lewy body dementia is responsible for about 10 percent of dementia. Not only does the individual exhibit the usual dementia symptoms of loss of memory, loss of judgment, and the like, but the individual will also have visual hallucinations and often exhibits rigidity and posture changes. The individual may have slowed movement, tremors, and a shuffling walk. Dizziness and falls are common. Some physically act out dreams while they are asleep. Long periods of staring into space, long naps, and depression are also typical characteristics.

Early onset dementia describes dementia that affects memory and cognition in those under the age of 65. Dementia has been diagnosed in people in their 50s and even in their 40s. Some early onset dementia is caused by Alzheimer's disease, but more often the individual is experiencing frontotemporal dementia, which is a term for a group of disorders that affect the frontal and temporal lobes of the brain causing them to shrink. The result is a dramatic change in personality and socially inappropriate or impulsive behavior. It leads to a lack of judgment and inhibition, and often the individual loses interest in personal hygiene. Like other dementias, frontotemporal dementia is progressive and incurable.

B. Parkinson's Disease

Parkinson's disease is characterized by tremors, slowness of movement, and postural instability. It is a progressive neurodegenerative disease that becomes more prevalent with advancing age. Many with Parkinson's have a festinating gait, meaning they shuffle with short steps and exhibit stiffness of the leg and hip. The tremor in the hand has the appearance of the individual rolling a pill or marble between the thumb and fingertips. Postural instability often leads to falls. Drug therapies and brain surgery may bring some degree of relief.

C. Depression

Depression is the most common psychiatric disorder in older adults. Geriatric depression can have serious consequences, as the individual experiences functional decline and a diminished quality of life. It can even lead to suicide. Unfortunately it is often undetected, as family, and even physicians, often attribute the symptoms as a normal reaction to aging or to underlying medical conditions.

It is also often misperceived as normal grief or bereavement over the loss of a spouse or loved one. Clinically depressed elderly, however, focus more on themselves than on the deceased and are likely to feel guilt and reduced self-esteem. Normal bereavement typically extends for up to a year before the individual comes to accept the loss. After a year, the individual should begin to redefine who they are and come to accept the death of the loved one. Depressed individuals, on the other hand, continue to exhibit grief and excessive feelings of loss even after a year has passed. They often complain of excessive loneliness and yearn for the deceased. They exhibit feelings of futility about the future, remain in disbelief about the death of the loved one, feel that life is meaningless or empty, and feel that a part of themselves has died.

Depression often accompanies major health problems; congestive heart failure is highly associated with depression as are strokes. Parkinson's disease is also strongly associated with depression although dementia is not. Some individuals with depression, however, also exhibit cognitive deficits and may forget names, repeat the same question, or have poor grooming. They are not, however, demented, and treatment of the depression may reduce the symptoms of the cognitive impairment. Unfortunately older individuals with depression often mask the depression by complaining about physical health problems, with the result that the treating physician focuses on the physical issues and fails to diagnose the depression. Some medications, either alone or in combination, may contribute to depression. Conversely, antidepressive medication along with psychotherapy can often be effective in treating depression.

Social Security 3

I. Introduction

Social Security, or as it is officially called, Old-Age, Survivors and Disability Insurance (OASDI),[1] pays benefits to almost 60 million Americans. Social Security pays benefits to three groups: retired workers; disabled workers; and spousal, survivor, and family benefits. Eligibility for Social Security benefits also entitles the recipients to Medicare at age 65 (see Chapter 5, Medicare). Social Security benefits function much like a private lifetime annuity, as the recipients receive benefits for life, with a few exceptions such as children's benefits. Unlike most private annuities, however, Social Security benefits are adjusted annually for inflation by cost of living adjustments, which were 3.6 percent in 2011 but 0 percent in 2015. Much like private retirement pensions, Social Security benefits are tied to the worker's wages with those workers who had higher wages receiving greater benefits. But unlike private pensions that may or may not be paid based upon the financial solvency of the pension plan, Social Security benefits are backed by the federal government. Although in theory Congress might decide to cut benefits, in reality it is highly unlikely to do so for those who are currently receiving benefits.

---

1. 42 U.S.C. §§ 401–434.

II. Eligibility

Eligibility for Social Security benefits arises from a worker (the term used by the Social Security statute) having worked in "covered employment" and having paid the Social Security wage tax. Covered employment refers to employment that is subject to the Social Security wage tax, which includes almost all employment in the private sector.[2] The biggest exceptions are some public employees, such as teachers, fire and police employees, state correctional officers, and other state or local employees. Federal employees hired before January 1, 1984, did not pay the Social Security wage tax and so that employment did not qualify them as covered employees. State public employees can vote to not subject themselves to the Social Security tax. In some states where state public employees have opted out of the Social Security tax, they are covered if they do not participate in the state or local government retirement system. Members of certain religious groups may avoid being taxed if the group has existed since at least 1950 and is opposed to receiving benefits; the Amish are an example of a qualifying religion. Work by students for a school or college that they are enrolled in is not covered employment. Children under age 18 who are employed by a parent are not covered and neither are those who perform domestic services, for example, babysitting, in a private home.

To receive retirement benefits, anyone born after 1928 must have at least 40 "quarters of coverage."[3] Absent the 40 quarters of coverage, no retirement benefits are paid. A quarter of coverage refers to calendar year quarters, although the quarter could be three months that do not correspond with a calendar quarter. For example, although Nina works only in March and April, if she earned enough, she will be credited with one quarter of coverage. In 2017, a worker must have earned at least $1,300, the required minimum amount, to be credited with a quarter of coverage. (The amount is adjusted annually for inflation.) The amount earned is calculated by cash wages before any deductions for state or federal taxes, but excludes fringe benefits such as employer-provided health insurance. Over a calendar year, a worker can receive credit for only four quarters of coverage, but the earnings need not occur in each quarter. The worker's total wages for the year are divided by four with the result determining how many quarters of coverage will be credited. For example, in 2017, Nicolas earned $16,000 in January but nothing the rest of the year. He will be credited with four quarters of coverage—$16,000 ÷ 4 = $4,000, which exceeds the required $1,300 per quarter.

The rules are somewhat different for self-employed individuals. In 2017, they were credited with four quarters of coverage if they had $5,200 of annual net earnings. For Social Security purposes net earnings are gross income earnings from a trade or business, minus allowable business deductions and depreciation. Dividends are not income unless the individual is a dealer in stocks and securities;

---

2. Information on this and other aspects of Social Security can be found at www.ssa.gov.
3. 42 U.S.C. § 414(a)(2).

interest from loans is not income unless the business is lending money; rents are not income unless the individual is a real estate dealer or regularly provides services for the occupants of the rentals; and income from a limited partnership is not counted as Social Security qualifying income. Self-employed individuals with at least $400 of such earnings may combine them with non-self-employed earnings to obtain quarters of coverage. Household workers, such as babysitters, elder companions, and housecleaners are covered by Social Security if they received at least $2,000 in 2017 from any one employer.

Individuals with questions about their quarters of coverage can request a "Personal Earning and Benefit Estimate Statement" from the Social Security Administration. The statement can be requested online at www.ssa.gov. The report will also show the earnings reported each year. Mistakes in the report can be corrected by a showing of tax returns and Form W-2 earnings statements.

III. Retirement Benefits

A worker who has 40 quarters of coverage is entitled to monthly retirement benefits. To receive benefits, the individual must apply for them with the Social Security Administration either online or in person at a local Social Security office. Individuals have the choice of several ages at which to request the start of retirement benefits.

A. Full Retirement Age

Individuals are eligible for their "primary insurance account" (PIA) at "full retirement age," which is based upon the year of birth.[4] Those born before 1938 have a full retirement age of 65. Those born in 1938 or later have a full retirement age that began at age 65 and two months and gradually rose to age 66. Those born in 1943 to 1954, have a full retirement age of 66. Those born in 1955 or later have a full retirement age as follows:

1955	66 and 2 months
1956	66 and 4 months
1957	66 and 6 months
1958	66 and 8 months
1959	66 and 10 months
After 1959	67 years

B. Early Retirement Options and the Earnings Test

A worker may claim benefits as early as age 62, but doing so permanently reduces benefits compared to taking them at their full retirement age. The amount of

---

4. *Id.* § 416(l)(1).

the reduction is 5/9 of 1% per month for the first 36 months before the age of full retirement and 5/12 of 1 percent for each additional month thereafter. An individual with a full retirement age of 66 who takes benefits at age 62 suffers a permanent reduction of 25 percent compared to what would have been paid had the worker waited until age 66. If benefits are began at age 63, for a worker whose full retirement age is 66, the reduction is 20 percent; if benefits are began at age 65, the reduction is 7.67 percent.

The effect of claiming benefits at different ages is demonstrated by the maximum benefit that can be paid to a worker eligible for the maximum annual benefit. For example, in 2017, for a worker age 62, the maximum benefit was $2,153 per month or $25,836 per year; for a worker age 66 it was $2,687 or $32,244; and for a worker age 70 it was $3,538 or $42,456.

A worker who claims benefits before full retirement age is also subject to the Social Security earnings test that lowers benefits based on the worker's earned income.[5] If the worker waits until full retirement age to claim benefits, the earnings test does not apply. For those under full retirement age, the earnings test does not apply to the first $16,920 of earnings in 2017 (adjusted annually for inflation). Any reduction in benefits due to excess earnings only effects the benefits paid in the year of the excess earnings. Benefits paid in later years are not affected.

Earnings above the exempt amount reduce the recipient's benefits by $1 for every $2 of earning. An example illustrates the effect of the earnings test. Assume Tess turns 62 on December 13. Two years later, at age 64, she claims benefits of $20,000 per year. She, however, continues to work and earns $26,920. Because her earnings exceed the exempt amount of $16,920 by $10,000, she will lose $5,000 of benefits and so will receive only $15,000.

In the year that the recipient reaches full retirement age the earnings threshold is $44,880 (in 2017); earning above this amount reduces the recipient's benefits by $1 for every $3 of earnings but only for the months prior to the recipient reaching full retirement age. Once the worker has reached full retirement age—age 66 until 2021—their earnings after that date have no effect on benefits. In the first year after claiming benefits before the full retirement age, and only for the first year, the earnings test is calculated on a monthly, not an annual, basis. The total earnings for the year are divided by 12 and that number establishes the monthly excess earning limit but only for the months in which income was earned. For example, if the individual began collecting benefits in May, earnings from January through April would not affect benefits paid in May or thereafter.

Note that "earnings" refers only to income from the performance of personal services whether performed as an employee or an independent contractor. Distributions from an "S" corporation are treated as earnings if the shareholder performed services for the corporation. Earnings do not include income such as interest, dividends, rents, annuities, pensions, distributions from retirement plans or

---

5. *Id.* § 403.

IRAs, and capital gains. Deferred compensation is excluded when received if it was earned prior to the worker claiming Social Security benefits. Royalties are also excluded if the patent or copyright was obtained before the claim for benefits, but if the patent or copyright was issued after the commencement of benefits, the royalties are counted as earnings.

The benefit reduction for excess earnings triggers a recalculation in the monthly benefit. When the worker reaches full retirement age, the reduction in the monthly benefit that occurred due to claiming benefits and earning more than the exempt amount is recalculated to account for the benefit reduction caused by the excess earnings. For example, if the worker claimed benefits at age 62 and had excess earnings over the next four years that in total caused a reduction in benefits equal to six months of benefits, when reaching full retirement age, the permanent reduction in benefits thereafter will be recalculated as if the worker had claimed benefits at age 62½. The result is that the monthly benefit will be modestly increased, and, if the worker lives out their actuarial life expectancy, the benefits lost to excess earnings will be recovered.

C. Deferred Retirement Options

A worker does not have to claim benefits at full retirement age even if retired. In recognition that those who delay claiming benefits will actuarially receive benefits for fewer years, the amount of benefits is permanently increased. For every month of deferral past full retirement age (age 66 until 2021) up to age 70, a worker's benefits increase by 0.666 percent or 8 percent per year. A worker with a full retirement age of 66 who delays claiming benefits until age 70 will receive 32 percent more in monthly benefits than if they had retired at age 66. After age 70, delay in claiming benefits does not cause a further increase in benefits.

IV. Calculation of Benefit Amount

Social Security benefits are based upon a worker's "primary insurance amount," or PIA. To the worker the most important aspect of the PIA calculation is that it is based on the worker's "Average Indexed Monthly Earnings," or AIME, which has several noteworthy aspects. First, the AIME is determined only by the worker's earnings that were subject to the Social Security wage tax. Wages in excess of the cap on the wage tax are ignored. For example, in 2008 the wage tax applied to only the first $102,000 of wages. If the worker earned $122,000 in 2008, they would only have paid the Social Security wage tax on the first $102,000 of earnings. Consequently, when calculating the worker's AIME for 2008 only $102,000 would have be included. In 2017, the maximum taxable wages were $127,200.

Second, the AIME is calculated using the highest 35 years of earnings (indexed for inflation). The other years are ignored. If, for example, the worker had 45 years of taxed earnings, only the 35 years of highest earnings are used to calculate the

AIME. If the worker had fewer than 35 years of taxed earnings, the missing years are essentially included as "zero." (The sum of the years of indexed earnings is divided by 35.) Even after a worker commences benefits, the AIME is recalculated by replacing lower earning years (or years of zero income) with higher years, with the result that the worker's benefits increase accordingly. For example, Pat claims benefits at age 66 but continues to work for three more years. If her earnings during those years exceed the inflation-adjusted earnings of previous years, perhaps during her 20s when she was employed in low-paying entry level jobs, Social Security will automatically replace the lower earning years with the higher years, with the result that Pat's benefits will increase modestly.

Finally, the AIME calculation results in a higher percentage replacement of wages by benefits for lower-income workers. For workers who claim benefits at age 66, the percentage of wage replacement runs from about 40 percent for those with a low AIME to about 25 percent of workers who have 35 years of taxed earnings at the maximum amount. For example, in 2015 a worker with 35 years of earnings that equaled or exceeded the cap on the wage tax who at age 66 applied for benefits received $29,464, or about 25 percent of the 2015 wage cap of $118,500.

V. Derivative Benefits: Spousal, Survivor, and Children

In addition to retirement and disability benefits for workers, Social Security pays derivative benefits to their spouses and children.[6] The logic for doing so is that Social Security is designed to replace the loss of income due to a worker retiring, becoming disabled, or dying. Derivative benefits also reflect the idea that a worker with a spouse or minor children has greater financial need than a single worker without children. Note that the payment of derivative benefits does not reduce or otherwise affect the worker's benefits.

A. Spousal Benefits

The spouse of a worker who has filed for benefits is eligible for a benefit equal to 50 percent of the worker's PIA as adjusted for any cost-of-living increases.[7] The spouse will receive the greater of percent of the worker's benefit or, if the spouse files for benefits based upon their earnings record, what the spouse receives based on their PIA. For example, Katy, age 66, files for retirement benefits. Based on her PIA, she is eligible for $2,000 a month. Her husband, Karl, also age 66, files for spousal benefits of $1,000 per month. (Karl cannot receive spousal benefits unless Katy is receiving benefits.[8]) Based upon his own earnings record, Karl

---

6. For information as to spousal and other derivative benefits see www.ssa.gov.

7. 42 U.S.C. § 402(b)(2).

8. Prior to 2016, Katy could file for benefits and then suspend them. Her filing would enable her spouse, Karl, to claim spousal benefits. After April 29, 2016, using the "file and suspend" method no longer creates a spousal benefit.

would be eligible for $800 per month but as a spouse Karl will receive $1,000 per month. Conversely, if Karl's earnings record entitled him to $1,150 per month, he would receive $1,150 per month. Social Security automatically pays the higher benefit amount unless the spouse files a restricted application that requests only spousal benefits. Only spouses born on or before January 1, 1954, can file a restricted application, however.

To be eligible for the spousal benefits the applicant must be at least age 62 or have in their care a child below the age of 16, and must have been married to the worker for at least one year.[9] Also, the other spouse must have begun their own benefits. If the applicant for spousal benefits applies before their full retirement age (66 until 2021), they permanently reduce their monthly benefit by 25/36 of 1 percent for the first 36 months and 5/12 of 1 percent for each of the potential additional 12 months, with the result that the spousal benefit may be reduced from 50 percent to only 32.5 percent of the worker's primary insurance amount. For a spouse who is not entitled to benefits on his or her own earnings record, this reduction factor is applied to the base spousal benefit, which is 50 percent of the worker's primary insurance amount. For example, if the worker's primary insurance amount is $1,600 and the worker's spouse chooses to begin receiving benefits at age 63, which is 36 months before their full retirement age, the calculation of their spousal benefit is as follows. First take 50 percent of $1,600 to get an $800 base spousal benefit. Then compute the reduction factor, which is 36 times 25/36 of one percent, or 25 percent. Applying a 25 percent reduction to the $800 amount gives a spousal benefit of $600. Thus, in this case, the final spousal benefit is 37.5 percent of the primary insurance amount of the other spouse.

The spousal derivative benefit is based on the PIA of the other spouse, not the actual benefit amount that is being paid to the other spouse. For example, Erik, age 66 is married to Eliza, age 62. Erik files for benefits at age 66, his full retirement age. His benefit is $3,200 per month. At age 66, Eliza files for benefits. Based on her earnings record, her monthly benefit is $1,000. If Erik had not filed for benefits until he was age 70, and so received $4,224 a month, Eliza would still only receive 50 percent of what Erik would have received had he filed for benefits at age 66, or 50 percent of $3,200. The only exception is that Eliza will receive 50 percent of the inflation adjusted benefit amount. For example, if the benefit that Erik would have received at age 66 when adjusted for annual inflation increases had grown to $3,450, Eliza would receive 50 percent of $3,450. Also, if Erik's PIA is increased because his post-age 66 work years replace lower income years in the calculation of his benefit, Eliza's 50 percent benefit will be based upon that higher PIA. Note that Eliza is not eligible for spousal benefits unless Erik has filed for benefits. If Eliza filed for benefits before Erik filed, she would not be eligible for spousal benefits until Erik filed. Once he filed, she would be eligible for a spousal benefit equal to 50 percent of Erik's PIA, that is, the benefit he would have received at age 66, not

---

9. 42 U.S.C. § 416(b)(2).

50 percent of the larger amount he received because he deferred claiming benefits until a later age.

B. Surviving Spousal Benefits

A surviving spouse of a deceased worker has rights to benefits based upon the earnings record of the deceased spouse.[10] To be eligible, the surviving spouse must have been married to the deceased spouse for at least nine months, though this requirement is waived if the worker's death was accidental or incurred in the line of duty as an active member of the armed services. The surviving spouse cannot remarry before age 60, but if the surviving spouse remarries, after one year, they are eligible for spousal benefits based on the earnings record of the new spouse. However, remarriage by the surviving spouse after reaching age 60 will not disqualify them from surviving spouse benefits. After they have been married one year, Social Security will pay only whichever benefits are greater—as a surviving spouse or as the current spouse in the new marriage.

The surviving spouse who has reached their full retirement age (currently age 66) has a right to receive an amount equal to 100 percent of what the deceased spouse actually received. If the deceased spouse had taken benefits early, such at age 62, or delayed benefits until age 70, the surviving spouse receives 100 percent of the reduced or increased benefits, as the case might be. Of course, a surviving spouse can file for benefits on their own work record if that would pay more than the 100 percent of the deceased spouse benefit.

A surviving spouse may claim "mother's" or "father's" benefits if they have in their care a child of the deceased spouse who is either under age 16 or disabled. If a surviving spouse is disabled and the disability began before or within seven years of the death of the other spouse, they can claim benefits at age 50. Remarriage after age 50 will not terminate the benefit. After reaching age 60, a surviving disabled spouse may be entitled to greater benefits based on their own earnings record or that of a current spouse. Social Security will pay whichever is the greater benefit.

If the surviving spouse has not yet reached full retirement age their benefits are reduced based upon the number of months remaining until they reach full retirement age. The surviving spouse must be at least age 60. At that age the surviving spouse receives 71.5 percent of what the deceased spouse was receiving. The 28.5 percent reduction is spread equally over the 72 months (this assumes the full retirement age is 66).

For many couples, the effect of the surviving spouse benefit means that the death of one spouse results in a reduction in the household Social Security benefits by one-third. For example, Ruby, age 75, is married to Ray, age 78. Ray receives benefits of $2,000 a month. Ruby receives $1,000 a month as a spousal derivative benefit. Together the couple receives $3,000 a month. Ray dies. Thereafter, Ruby will receive $2,000 a month in benefits so that the household receives one-third

---

10. *Id.* § 402(e),(f).

less than when Ray was alive. If Ruby had predeceased Ray, he would continue to receive $2,000 a month or one-third less than what they had received as a couple. Suppose while Ray was alive, Ruby received $1,800 a month based on her earnings record. When Ray died, she would receive $2,000 a month as derivative surviving spouse benefits.

A surviving spouse of any age is entitled to a one-time payment of $255 (in 2017).[11]

C. Divorced Spouse Benefits

A divorced spouse who was married for at least ten years to a worker and has been divorced for at least two years can claim spousal benefits on the former spouse's earning record.[12] Similar to a married spouse, the divorced spouse must be at least age 62 and unmarried. They will receive a reduced benefit if they claim benefits before reaching their full retirement age. Moreover, the earnings limit applies if they have not reached their full retirement age. The divorced spousal benefits are available when the former spouse reaches their full retirement age, age 66 in 2017. The benefits are available without regard to whether the former spouse has applied for benefits.

Remarriage by the former spouse does not affect the right of the divorced spouse to benefits. Remarriage by the divorced spouse, however, terminates their benefits unless that marriage ends because of death, divorce or annulment.

A divorced spouse born on or before January 1, 1954, can file for benefits at full retirement age and elect to receive benefits based on the former spouses work record while delaying the payment of their own benefits until age 70, thereby increasing the benefit amount paid based on their work record. When they apply for benefits based on their own work record, they will receive the greater of benefits based on their work record or on the work record of their former spouse.

The benefits paid to a divorced spouse have no effect on the benefits paid to the former spouse or the current spouse or any other spouse of the former spouse.

D. Children's Benefits

Children of a worker who has claimed retirement benefits or of a deceased worker are eligible for benefits if they are under age 18, under age 19 and still attending high school, or over age 18 but became mentally or physically disabled before age 22.[13] They must be unmarried and dependent upon the worker for support. A child includes adopted children, stepchildren and children born out of wedlock. Grandchildren also qualify if they are dependent upon the worker for support. The children's benefit is generally one-half of the retired worker's primary insurance amount (PIA) and 75 percent of a deceased worker's PIA. However, the children's benefit is subject to a family maximum that, though not limiting the amount of the

---

11. *Id.* § 402(i).
12. *Id.* § 402(b),(c).
13. *Id.* § 402(d); 20 C.F.R. § 404.1500 et al.

worker's benefit, can restrict the total, combined derivative benefits of a spouse and children.

VI. Disability Benefits

Social Security pays benefits to disabled workers as well as derivative benefits to their spouses and children. Disabled workers who are at least age 21 but who have not reached their full retirement age can qualify for disability benefits. Disabled is defined as being unable to perform "any substantial gainful activity by reason of any medically determinable physical or mental impairment."[14] However, the disabled individual can still receive benefits during a trial work period that is allowed so that the individual can test their ability to work for at least nine months. There is no limit on how much they can earn each month as long as they report their work and continue to have a disability. In 2017, a trial work month was any month in which the individual had total earnings over $840. The trial work period continues until they have worked nine months within a 60-month period. After the trial work period ends, the individual can work for the next 36 months and still receive benefits in 2017 for any month in which their earnings did not exceed $1,170 ($1,950 if blind).

If the individual is disabled and if the disability is expected to last at least one year, the individual is eligible for benefits equal to their full primary insurance amount regardless of their age. The full primary insurance amount is based on their earnings record prior to their becoming disabled. To qualify for disability benefits, the individual must be "fully insured" by having sufficient quarters of coverage. Before age 24, the individual must have earned six credits earned in the 3-year period ending when the disability started. From age 24 to 31, an individual can qualify if they have credit for working half the time between age 21 and the time they became disabled. For example, if they become disabled at age 27, they would need credit for three years of work or a total of 12 credits out of the past six years. After age 31, the number of credits rises with age until it reaches 40 credits at age 62.

Benefits are payable after five months of the onset of the disability. Note that disability benefits can be the basis for derivative benefits payable to a spouse or child or other qualifying individual.

VII. Federal Income Taxation of Benefits

Social Security benefits are subject to the federal income tax based on the calculation of two "tiers" of income and based on their other income that "triggers"

---

14. 42 U.S.C. § 416(i).

taxation.[15] The other income is determined by a formula that is the sum of the taxpayer's adjusted gross income, plus interest-free income, and one-half of the taxpayer's Social Security benefits. The "first tier" arises if the total of this income exceeds $25,000 for a single taxpayer or $32,000 for a married couple filing a joint return. If the Social Security beneficiary has income in excess of the triggering dollar amount, one-half of the excess income is treated as taxable income. There is a "second tier" that includes a higher percentage of the taxpayer's benefits. If the formula calculation results in income that exceeds $34,000 for a single taxpayer or $44,000 for a married couple filing a joint return, the taxpayer must include 85 percent of the excess income in taxable income.

To illustrate. Assume Betty and Bart, both age 71, are married and file a joint return. Betty receives $30,000 per year in Social Security benefits while Bart receives $20,000, for a total of $50,000. They have adjusted gross income other than their Social Security benefits of $30,000 and they receive $5,000 in tax-free interest (interest on municipal bonds) for a total of $35,000. To determine the taxability of their Social Security, they add to that $35,000, one-half of their Social Security benefits—$25,000. For purposes of calculating whether their benefits are taxable they have "income" of $60,000. For the first tier, income above $32,000 up to $44,000 ($12,000), they must include 50 percent of the excess or $6,000 of Social Security benefits in their taxable income. For the second tier, they must include 85 percent the benefits in excess of $44,000, or 85% × $16,000 ($60,000 – $44,000), or $13,600 of Social Security benefits in taxable income. When added together— the first tier inclusion of $6,000 and the second tier inclusion of $13,600—the total Social Security benefits added to their taxable income is $19,600 out of their total benefits of $50,000.

VIII. Administration and Appeals

The Social Security Administration, a part of the Department of Health and Human Services, administers the program through the Field Office, the Office of Disability Adjudication and Review (ODAR), and the Appeals Council. The Field Office, operating through district offices, handles applications for benefits, initial appeals, and process requests for administrative hearings.

The Office of Disability Adjudication and Review (ODAR) handles appeals from initial disability determinations and reviews. It employs administrative law judges (ALJs) who hear the appeals. It also employs staff attorneys who are empowered to issue decisions favorable to claimants in disability cases.

The Appeals Council is the appellate division that can accept or deny a claimant's request for review and may also reverse, uphold, or remand decisions by the ALJs.

---

15. 26 U.S.C. § 86.

Whereas denied claims for disability frequently result in appeals and even litigation, claims for Social Security retirement benefits rarely do. The disputes that do arise are usually over whether the worker's earnings were properly credited. Actual benefit amounts are not subject to any discretion; if the earnings record is correct and the worker's age is properly entered into the record, the benefit amount is not subject to dispute.

IX. Benefit Claiming Strategies

As individuals enter their 60s they increasingly ask at what age they should claim their Social Security retirement benefits. Unfortunately, there is no certain answer because of two unknowns. First, almost no one knows how much longer they will live. Second, no one knows their future financial situation, neither their future income nor their future expenses. Despite the uncertainty as to how long they will live and how much income they will need, individuals should nevertheless consider what might be the best time for them to claim benefits.

Individuals can claim benefits "early," that is, before their full retirement age of 66 (the age will begin to rise in 2022), at age 66, their full retirement age, or they can "delay" taking them until after reaching age 66. Disregarding the special rules for some spouses, surviving spouses, and children, the earliest that an individual can claim Social Security benefits is age 62, while delaying past age 70 does not result in an increase in benefits. The three most relevant ages are thus 62, 66, and 70. Note that individuals qualify for Medicare at age 65, which makes that age very significant to them but not relevant to a discussion about when to claim Social Security benefits. Of course, an individual can claim benefits beginning at age 62 and every month thereafter, but typically the discussion is framed as whether to claim at age 62, 66, or 70. There may be reasons, however, to claim at other ages between 62 and 70, which are discussed when relevant.

In 1983, when the current age 66 was established as the age to determine full Social Security benefits, the average male life expectancy at age 66 was about 14 years and for females it was about 18 years. For males at that time if the individual began their benefits at age 62, if they lived closed to their actuarially life expectancy, they would have been paid about the same amount of total benefits as if they had delayed beginning benefits to age 70. (Because of their longer life expectancy, women would have been better off in the amount of total benefits by delaying to age 70.) But in 2017, a male at age 66 has a life expectancy of almost 17 years and a woman 19 years. If they live to their life expectancy, both men and women will collect more in total benefits if they defer claiming until age 70 rather than claiming at age 62.

Much of the literature advises, whenever possible, to delay claiming benefits until age 70. That advice reflects the reality that Social Security retirement benefits starting at age 70 are 32 percent higher than if started at age 66, and 76 percent higher than those started at age 62. In some instances, however, starting benefits earlier than age 70 might be wise.

First, if the individual needs the income. Imagine an individual who is fired at age 67 with no pension and limited savings. They might not be able to wait until age 70 to claim benefits, though they should first spend down their savings before claiming Social Security benefits.

Second, the individual's health is another reason that might suggest taking benefits sooner. If at age 62, an individual has a serious medical condition and is no longer employed, taking Social Security benefits may be a reasonable decision. If the individual does not expect to live long after initiating the payment of benefits, taking their benefits early makes sense.

A third reason to start benefits is to enable an otherwise qualifying young or disabled child to begin collecting a child's benefit. This may also trigger spousal benefits if the spouse is caring for the child.

A. Single Individual, Never Married, with No Children

Claiming strategies for a single individual are less complicated than for a married individual because there is no spouse whose benefits can be affected by the individual's choice.

Even for a single individual there is no obviously right age at which to claim benefits. The current conventional wisdom is to delay claiming benefits until age 70. This ensures the largest monthly benefit. Although true, that strategy ignores individual variables and preferences that can point to a different age.

Claiming benefits can be seen as a series of decision points that first arise at age 62. At present, age 62 is the most popular age at which to claim benefits, with about 40 percent of claimants beginning benefits at that age. Doing so, which is in decline, is attributed to many individuals retiring at or before that age, and individuals who were collecting Social Security disability benefits being automatically switched to Social Security retirement benefits. Some others who claim benefits at age 62 are retired but continue to work part time and keep their earnings below the dollar amount that would result in diminished benefits due to the reduction in benefits in the event that they have excess earnings as explained in Section III.B. Early Retirement Options and the Earnings Test.

The decline in the percentage who claim benefits at age 62 can be explained by a decline in the number who retire at that age. That in turn is a reflection of the decline in the percentage of retirees who have a pension. As pensions disappear, more individuals feel the need to continue working. It is also a reflection of the growing understanding that at age 62 an individual's life expectancy is over 20 years and so it may be sensible to delay retirement. Many, however, involuntarily retire at or even before age 62 because they were laid off or fired and have been unable to find a job. Others have jobs but they pay so little or are so difficult to perform, particularly for an aging worker, that retirement at age 62 seems less of an option than a necessity.

It should be apparent that it is unwise to claim benefits at age 62 if the individual expects to continue to work and have earnings high enough to cause a reduction in the benefit amount. All earning above that limit reduces Social Security benefits by $1 for every $2 of such earnings. The effect is a "tax" of 50 percent on earnings above the limit. That "earnings tax" is joined by a possible federal income tax on the Social Security benefits and by the imposition of the Social Security wage tax of 6.2 percent plus the Medicare wage tax of 1.45 percent on the earnings for a total of 7.65 percent. The cumulative effect of the taxes and reduction in Social Security benefits makes claiming benefits while continuing to work full-time an unwise choice. However, claiming benefits and working part-time with earnings below the annual limit is a popular option. Either working part-time by limiting the number of hours worked, or taking on work as a "consultant" with compensation that does not exceed the annual limit is the choice of many early retirees. After reaching age 66, at which time the earnings limit no longer applies, some retirees chose to again work full-time or increase the number of hours they work part time, or consult.

A single individual can retire at age 62 but not claim benefits, but rather delay claiming until age 66 or even age 70. Not claiming benefits until age 66 avoids the 25 percent reduction that is caused by claiming at age 62. Delaying until age 70 adds 32 percent over the benefit amount at age 66. For example, ignoring possible cost of living increases, Janelle at age 66 is eligible for $28,000. If she claims at age 62, she will receive $21,000 but if she delays until age 70, she will receive $36,960. At whatever age she claims benefits, the amount is set for life, except for possible increases in the benefits bases on the cost of living. Assume Janelle retires at age 62. If she has adequate income from other sources such as a pension or investment income, she might decide that she would be better off to claim benefits at a later age. Of course, she can claim benefits at any time after reaching age 62. For example, she could claim at age 63 or 68. If she does not claim at age 62 but later finds she needs additional income, she can always file at that time.

Janelle can calculate the effect on what she can expect to receive for the remainder of her life. If she assumes that at age 62 she has 20 years to live, she can expect to receive the following amounts:

Start benefits at age 62   20 years at $21,000/year = $420,000
Start benefits at age 66   16 years at $28,000/year = $448,000
Start benefits at age 70   12 years at $36,960/year = $443,520

Because the total benefit amounts do not take into account the time value of money, the value of claiming at ages 62 and 66, as compared to claiming at age 70, are somewhat greater than the mere total of benefits collected.

If Janelle assumes she will live 30 years (the average life expectancy of a woman at age 62 is about 23 years), deferring the start date of benefits until age 70 makes sense:

Start benefits at age 62   30 years at \$21,000/year = \$630,000
Start benefits at age 66   26 years at \$28,000/year = \$728,000
Start benefits at age 70   22 years at \$36,960/year = \$813,120

In contrast if Janelle should only live for ten years after starting benefits, delaying them would not have been a wise choice.

Start benefits at age 62   10 years at \$21,000/year = \$210,000
Start benefits at age 66   6 years at \$28,000/year = \$168,000
Start benefits at age 70   2 years at \$36,960/year = \$73,920

Janelle's problem and the problem for most claimants is that they do not know how long they will live. A few claim their benefits early because they have been diagnosed with a fatal illness and so do not expect to live long, others may not have a terminal illness or condition but may have a history of poor health and so do not expect to live long, and a few will believe that because their parents and perhaps siblings died young that they, too, will not live long. Statistically, those with lower earnings during their working years and those with fewer years of education do not live as long as the higher earning, more educated counterparts. African Americans have on average shorter lives and, of course, a man at age 62 has a live expectancy about four years shorter than that of a 62-year-old woman.

Although current health, family history, economic status, race, and gender are predictive for a group they tell individuals very little about how long they can expect to live past age 62. The unknowable nature of life expectancy creates a risk that the individual may live a long time, which might be desirable in many respects, but it means that individuals who began Social Security benefits at age 62 may have to live with reduced benefits for many years with the result that their total lifetime benefits, even considering the time value of money, would have been greater had they not taken benefits until they were older, such as waiting until age 70.

When faced with a risk of financial loss, in this case the risk of living many years after having begun Social Security benefits, the rational response is to "insure" against the risk by deferring the start of the benefits, at least until age 66, and even better until age 70. If Social Security benefits are perceived as insurance that protects against the risk of living a long life without sufficient income, delaying the onset of benefits is the prudent choice for a single individual. Even an individual who retires at age 66 might be wise to wait until age 70 to claim benefits.

Although when to start benefits depends upon a number of factors that vary from individual to individual, for a single individual, a few presumptions prevail:

- Do not claim benefits before age 66 if your projected wages exceed the annual earnings limit.
- Begin benefits if you are diagnosed terminally ill or are very likely to die within ten years.

- Because benefits are based on the 35 years of highest earnings, the more years you work, the more likely you are to replace lower earning years with higher earning years and so modestly increase your benefits.
- After retirement, but before age 70, delay benefits until age 70 if you have adequate income and spend down savings in order to permit you to defer starting benefits.
- Delaying benefits from age 66 to 70 means you must live at least until age 82½ (ignoring the time value of money) to have been paid as many dollars compared to having begun benefits at age 66.
- If you work past age 66, you might start benefits before age 70 if you intend to not spend the benefits but invest the after-tax proceeds. If you invest wisely, the investment returns will further delay the age at which delaying benefits until age 70 will match the total dollars paid (plus investment returns) had you begun them at age 66. Conversely, if you are still working it is more likely that some portion of your Social Security benefits will be subject to the federal income tax.
- You may want to begin benefits at 68 or 69 because you have costly travel plans or another identifiable need for more income, with the idea that income at age 68 is more "valuable" than dollars received at a much older age, such as age 85.

Of course, for many the choice of when to take Social Security benefits is less of a choice than a necessity. For almost half of current retirees, Social Security benefits compose 90 percent or more of their income. Once they have retired, for these individuals delaying benefits is not a viable option. Retirement may also not be much of an option in light of the ability of the aging individual to perform a physically demanding job or to continue working a job that is very stressful, low paying, or distasteful to perform. But most middle and upper middle class individuals have options that deserve their careful consideration.

One option available is to claim benefits, but withdraw the claim within 12 months and pay back all amounts received. An individual who was unemployed at age 66 and in need of income might file for Social Security benefits. Six months later, however, the individual finds a job that pays enough to alleviate the need for Social Security benefits. By withdrawing and paying back the benefits, the individual is treated as if they never applied for benefits, with the result that benefits rise every year until the age they reapply for benefits or reach age 70. Because of the new job, the individual can forego benefits at age 66 for larger benefits after age 70.

Because of the need to pay back benefits, withdrawing is not always an option. Fortunately, the application for Social Security benefits is not immutable. A recipient can suspend benefits. Suspension does not result in any obligation to pay back benefits; it merely suspends benefits until either the individual reaches age 70 when benefits are automatically restarted or until the individual reverses the suspension and reinstates benefits. For the months that the suspension is in effect, the benefit rises by the appropriate percentage. For example, if the individual claims benefits at age 66 and later suspends them at age 69 for 12 months, when the benefits resume, they will be 8 percent higher (plus any cost of living increase).

One additional option is the right to suspend and later reverse the suspension and receive a lump sum equal to the amount of benefits foregone during the period of the suspension. For example, the individual might have begun benefits at age 65, but suspended them on February 1 when they turned age 66. After six months, on July 1, at age 66½, the individual decides to restart benefits retroactive to the date of the suspension. Having done so, the individual will receive a lump sum equal to the amount of benefits that would have been paid during those six months absent the suspension. The retroactive reversal of the suspension means, however, that the amount of the benefit reverts to what it would have been at the time of the suspension except for any subsequent increase due to inflation.

B. Married Couples

When to claim benefits is much more complicated for married couples than single individuals because of the derivative spousal benefits. As discussed, if a couple has been married for at least a year both qualify for spousal benefits. The spouse is entitled to a benefit equal to 50 percent of the primary insurance amount (PIA) of the other living spouse. The surviving spouse benefit is equal to 100 percent of the benefit of a deceased spouse. Both spousal benefits are subject to age restrictions. And the spousal benefit is paid only if it exceeds what the claimant would receive in Social Security benefits on their earnings record. Only one spouse at a time can claim spousal benefits. Excess earnings by either spouse reduce the benefits paid to the couple.

A husband or wife can claim spousal benefits if age 62 or older, or if at the time of applying for benefits they are caring for a child entitled to children's benefits. The amount of the benefit is based on what the other spouse would receive at age 66, their full retirement age even if the other spouse has not yet reached that age. The other spouse must have applied for benefits for there to be a spousal benefit. However, applying for spousal benefits before reaching full retirement age (age 66 for those born before 1955) reduces the benefits paid unless the spouse is caring for a qualifying child. Spousal benefits started at age 66 are 43 percent higher than if started at age 62.

Spouses born on or before January 1, 1954, who have reached their full retirement age can file a "restricted" application for benefits application by which the spouse files *only* for spousal benefits, not for benefits on their own earnings record. By doing so, the spouse's benefits based on their earnings record can rise every year while they collect benefits equal to one-half of their spouse's. For example, Tina, age 66 is married to Tom, age 71. Tom began his benefits at age 70 that are $39,600 a year. However, his full retirement benefits at age 66 would have been $30,000. Tina's work record would pay benefits at age 66 of $32,000 a year. At age 66 Tina files a restricted application, meaning she is only applying for her spousal benefits, not benefits based on her own work record. Tina will be granted benefits equal to 50 percent of Tom's full retirement age benefits, or $15,000 a year. She will collect that $15,000 a year for four years until she is age 70 when she will file for benefits based on her own work record. At age 70, those benefits will have grown to $42,240 a year. By deferring her own benefits to age 70 she will have increased them by 32 percent. She will have given up four years of benefits at $32,000 a year or $128,000 but will have received spousal benefits of $15,000 a year for four years or $60,000. By giving up $68,000 ($128,000 – $60,000 = $68,000) she will have increased her own benefits by $10,240 a year for life. In just over six and a half years, her increased benefits will offset the forgone $68,000 and thereafter she will receive an additional $10,240 a year for the remainder of her life. Note, however, that because of legislation enacted in 2016, use of a restricted application will no longer be available beginning in 2020, because in that year, all spouses who are age 66 will have been born after the cutoff date of January 1, 1954.

Delaying benefits is a "winning" choice only for those whose lives exceed their projected life expectancy or if the delay is chosen as a form of insurance against the possibility of living longer than one's life expectancy. Because of differences as to when spouses want to quit working, their life expectancies, their financial needs and desires, and the other sources and amounts of retirement income, it is impossible to state an optimum claiming strategy. But there are scenarios that suggest what might be the best claiming strategy for a couple.

1. Spouses of Similar Age with Similar Earnings Records

Spouses of similar age with similar earnings records are usually going to collect benefits on their own work record rather than receive the spousal benefit. One strategy, however, as explained earlier, is for the spouse who would receive smaller benefits on their earnings record to file a restricted application to only receive spousal benefits. This strategy assumes that the couple has sufficient other income to accept four years of reduced benefits for the spouse who files the restricted application for restricted benefits, that is, they file to collect benefits equal to 50 percent of the other spouses benefits. As discussed, this technique is available only to those who born on or before January 1, 1954.

2. Spouses of Similar Age with Unequal Earnings Records

If the couple has significantly different earnings records, the lower earning spouse may qualify for spousal benefits. For example, Beth and Bill, both age 66, want to retire. Their financial situation does not permit them to delay taking benefits until age 70. Beth's benefits at her full retirement age of 66 would be $11,000. Bill is entitled to $32,000. Both retire and file for benefits. Beth will automatically receive $16,000 as the spouse benefit equal to one-half of Bill's benefit of $32,000. Although a spouse can file for a spousal benefit at age 62, doing so permanently reduces the amount of the benefit. Unless the couple cannot financially afford to live without the younger spouse claiming at age 62, they should not do so.

3. Spouses of Different Ages

Spouses of different ages must carefully calculate at what years they should claim benefits. If financially feasible, the older spouse should file for benefits at age 70 in order to maximize their benefits. If born before 1954, the younger spouse should file a restricted application for benefits at age 66 in order to claim the spousal benefit while permitting their own benefit to rise until they reach age 70. If both delay claiming benefits on their earnings record until they reach age 70, the couple will maximize their annual benefits. For example, Cally and Cole are married and Cally is three years younger than Cole. Cally expects to work until age 68 while Cole will retire at age 67. Cole delays filing for benefits until he is age 70 when Cally is age 67. At age 67, Cally, though still employed, having been born before December 31, 1953, files a restricted application for benefits so that she receives 50 percent of what Carl is receiving. Note the earnings "tax" does not apply because she is past age 66. Meanwhile Cally's benefit amount grows at 8 percent per year for three years until she reaches age 70. At 70, Cally switches from spousal benefits to benefits based upon her own earning record. Note that this strategy does not depend upon who was entitled to greater benefits, Cally or Carl. However, the strategy does depend upon the couple being able to afford Cally collecting benefits only equal to 50 percent of Carl's full retirement benefits for the three years until she turns age 70 and begins to claim benefits on her own earnings record.

If one spouse starts benefits at age 62 that does not affect the amount of the spousal benefit of the other spouse. So if Ed is age 62 and has started his benefits, and his spouse, Eve is age 66, she can file a restricted application for spousal benefits and receive 50 percent of what Ed would have received at age 66, his full retirement age, not 50 percent of what he is actually receiving. At age 70, Eve will file for benefits on her own earning record, having permitted them to rise to the maximum amount. Note that if Ed has not reached age 66, Eve must have reached her full retirement age, 66, to file for spousal benefits, otherwise she will be deemed to have filed for retirement benefits based on her own earning record. At age 66, her full retirement age, however, assuming she was born before 1954, she can file a restricted application for spousal benefits and permit her own benefits to grow by 8 percent per year until she is 70.

4. Strategy to Benefit a Surviving Spouse

A surviving spouse who claims benefits at their full retirement age is eligible for a benefit equal to 100 percent of the *actual* amount of the benefit paid to the deceased spouse if that amount is greater than the benefit paid to the surviving spouse on their own earning's record. Although a surviving spouse can claim benefits at age 60, doing so reduces the amount of benefits by a percentage amount for each month that the individual is under age 66. Waiting until full retirement age 66 avoids the penalty for claiming early and results in a benefit that is 40 percent higher than if claimed at age 60. The surviving spouse has the option of claiming benefits on their own earnings record at age 62 and later, after reaching their full retirement age of 66, claiming survivor benefits if that amount exceeds the amount of their retirement benefit that they began at age 62.

Because the survivor benefit is based on the actual benefit that had been paid to the deceased spouse, the higher-earning spouse should consider deferring benefits in order to possibly increase the amount of the benefit for the other, surviving spouse. For example, Gale is 66 and Guy is 62. Gale would have received a benefit at full retirement age 66 of $30,000, but she deferred filing until she was age 70 and so increased her benefit to $39,600. At age 71, she died. Her husband, Guy, filed for benefits at age 66. His earnings record paid him benefits of $25,000 per year. But after Gale died, Guy, now age 67, was awarded surviving spouse benefits equal to Gale's benefit of $39,600. This strategy should be considered when the older spouse is considerably older and so can be expected to predecease the other younger spouse whose retirement benefits will be lower than the amount of the older spouse's deferred benefits.

5. Divorced Couples

An individual who was married at least ten consecutive years to an individual qualified to receive Social Security benefits can receive a benefit equal to 50 percent of that individual's benefit amount at their full retirement age, currently age 66. A benefit paid to the former spouse is based on what the former spouse would receive at full retirement age (age 66 in 2017), not the actual benefit paid to the former spouse. The divorced spouse can claim benefits at age 62 but doing so will permanently reduce the amount of the benefit.

An unmarried, divorced spouse of a deceased worker is eligible for survivor benefits and can file for benefits as early as age 60, but that reduces the amount of the benefit as compared to waiting until full retirement age, currently age 66. If the divorced spouse files for survivor benefits at full retirement age, the divorced spouse of the deceased worker will receive a benefit equal to that which was being paid to the worker at the time of death.

The worker has no ability to affect the benefits paid the divorced spouse. Even if the worker does not claim benefits, if the worker is at least age 62 and the divorce has been final for at least two years, the divorced spouse can receive Social Security benefits. If the worker has already reached full retirement age, 66, the two-year waiting period does not apply. Excess earnings of the worker that reduce their benefit will not reduce the derivative benefit of the divorced spouse. A divorced spouse can receive benefits immediately upon the divorce if the other eligibility requirements are met. The divorced spouse loses spousal benefits if they remarry, but they may qualify for greater benefits on the earnings record of the second spouse.

If the divorced spouse had more than one marriage that lasted at least ten years, the Social Security automatically selects the ex-spouse whose earnings record would pay the larger benefit. Multiple ex-spouses can collect benefits based on a single worker's earnings without affecting that individual's benefits.

Retirement Income: Pensions and IRAs 4

I. Introduction

For many, the most important aspect of aging is retirement and the accompanying loss of income. How to replace the income lost due to retirement is a question that almost all older persons must face. For most, income in retirement arises from three sources: savings, employer provided retirement income, and Social Security. During retirement, older persons convert savings into consumable income. Just how to do that, however, is often not clear, and how to do so without spending all the savings can be formidable. In the past, that choice was less often presented because the retired employee might have an employer-provided lifetime pension. Today, increasingly pensions are disappearing and being replaced by defined contribution accounts, typically a 401(k) account that, much like the retiree's savings, must be invested with care and husbanded so that it will last for the rest of the individual's life. Social Security retirement benefits (see Chapter 3, Social Security) provide a lifetime pension that grows with inflation but those benefits typically do not provide sufficient income to support most retirees in the manner in which they desire.

Although almost 85 percent of those age 65 and older receive Social Security retirement benefits, only about one-third have an employment-related pension or retirement account such as a 401(k). However, among those retirees in the highest quintile of income, 55 percent had retirement benefits that provided them with income. Given that such income is less and less likely to be in the form of a pension and increasingly likely to arise from a defined contribution plan, such as a 401(k), for retirees, how to handle their retirement income options and retirement accounts is crucial.

II. Private Pensions

Private employer-provided pensions are almost always governed by the Employee Retirement Income Security Act (ERISA),[1] which is a federal statue that preempts state laws that attempt to regulate employee pensions. The statute applies to private employers including nonprofits but it does not apply to government plans and most plans operated by churches. ERISA governs two kinds of employee benefit plans: (1) pension or other retirement income plans and (2) welfare benefits plans, such as health or disability insurance for employees or retirees.

Employers create pensions and retirement plans to provide employees with a source of retirement income. By doing so, the employer hopes to attract and retain quality employees. If the pension or retirement plan comports with the requirements of ERISA and with the requirements of the Internal Revenue Code, the plan will be considered "qualified"[2] and will receive favorable federal income tax treatment that makes such plans attractive to both employers and employees.

A plan must comply with numerous detailed requirements to be considered qualified. But if it is qualified, the plan is granted significant tax advantages. First, the plan will hold assets that will be used to pay the retirement benefits in a trust that is tax-exempt so that the plan asset investment income is not subject to the federal income tax.[3] The employer contributions to the plan are deductible from the employer's income just as if the contributions were wages.[4] Employees, however, do not have to report the employer contributions to the plan as current income.[5] The employee is not taxed until actual receipt of a distribution from the plan. Even then, the employee may be permitted to take a lump-sum distribution from the plan and roll it over, tax free, into an individual retirement account (IRA), which also does not pay taxes on its investment income.[6] Distributions from the IRA, however, will be subject to income taxation.

---

1. 29 U.S.C. § 1001 *et seq.*
2. I.R.C. § 401(a).
3. I.R.C. §§ 401(a), 501(a).
4. I.R.C. § 404.
5. I.R.C. § 402(a)(1).
6. I.R.C. § 402(c).

A. Defined Benefit Plans

There are two fundamental forms of retirement plans: defined benefit and defined contribution. A defined benefit plan can take many forms, but its essential feature is that the plan promises the employee, having reached a designated normal retirement age, that after "separation from service" (which may be because the employee retired or may have merely switched employers) the plan will pay a lifetime pension. The amount of the pension is usually based on a formula that includes the number of years the employee worked for the employer and participated in the pension plan multiplied by a percentage amount and multiplied by the employee's average wages for a defined period of years, typically the last three. For example, the employee might have been employed for 30 years with average wages in the last three years of $60,000. If the annual percentage multiplier is 2 percent, the employee will have an annual pension of $36,000 (30 × 2% × $60,000).

To protect spouses of employees, unless waived by the employee's spouse, generally plans are required to pay the pension to married employees in the form of a joint and survivor annuity payable to the retiree during their lifetime and to their spouse after the retiree's death.[7] If the employee dies before the pension begins, the plan must provide a "qualified preretirement survivor annuity" to the employee's surviving spouse, unless the employee waived that right with the consent of the spouse.[8]

The joint and survivor annuity must pay benefits for as long as the retiree and their spouse are alive. The amount paid to the surviving spouse must be no less than 50 percent and no more than 100 percent of the amount paid to the retiree. A preretirement survivor annuity pays a lifetime annuity to the surviving spouse with payments beginning no later than the date that the employee would have reached the plan's normal retirement age, which cannot be later than age 65 or five years after the employee joined the plan.[9]

An employee, with the written consent of their spouse, may elect to waive the right to a joint and survivor annuity or a preretirement survivor annuity. Doing so increases the amount of the pension paid to the retiree, but it does so at the risk of leaving the surviving spouse without a pension. Waiving the right to the spousal annuity makes sense, however, if the spouse has a short life expectancy due to an illness or condition and so is not expected to outlive the retiree. If the spouse is considerably older than the retiring employee spouse, the couple might waive the spousal benefits because they do not expect the older spouse to outlive the retiree and so there is little value in having a pension that continues until the death of both spouses. Finally, if both spouses have pensions of about equal value, they may decide to both waive the spousal benefit knowing that whoever survives will have an adequate pension.

---

7. 29 U.S.C. § 1055.
8. *Id.*
9. 29 U.S.C. § 1002(24).

A defined benefit pension plan may also offer retirees the option of taking a lump-sum distribution actuarially equal in value to the pension that they would otherwise receive. The death of a participant before starting the pension may also trigger a lump-sum payout. The recipient of a lump-sum payout has several options. The recipient can report the entire distribution as ordinary income in the year received. This is usually not advisable because it pushes the income into higher marginal rates and accelerates the tax. Another option is to treat the taxable part of the distribution from participation before 1974 as a capital gain and the taxable part of the distribution from participation after 1973 as ordinary income or use a 10-year tax option to calculate the tax on the distribution attributable to participation in the plan after 1973. Typically, the best choice is the third option, which is to rollover the distribution into an individual retirement account (IRA). If done soon enough after the receipt of the lump sum, the distribution is not taxable. Thereafter, only amounts distributed from the IRA are taxed in the year they are distributed. The IRA is tax exempt and its investment earnings are not subject to the federal income tax.

ERISA prevents a retiree or a surviving spouse from assigning or alienating a pension.[10] Known as the anti-alienation provision, it prevents an employee or retiree, or surviving spouse, from bargaining away benefits or having the benefits subject to creditor's claims. The employer must pay the pension to the retiree. Of course, once the retiree or surviving spouse receives the pension distribution, the funds may be subject to a creditor's claim.

The exception to the anti-alienation prohibition is the requirement that a pension plan must recognize and follow a "qualified domestic relations order."[11] A qualified domestic relations order is any judgment, decree, or order including the approval of a property settlement agreement that relates to the provision of child support, alimony, or marital property rights that is made pursuant to the state domestic relations law. A qualified domestic relations order can specify that a former spouse of the employee or retiree shall be treated as the surviving spouse rather than the current spouse of the employee or retiree and so receive the spousal benefits such as a lifetime annuity.[12]

To fund promised retirement pensions, the employer is required to create a pension trust and make contributions to it that, as actuarially calculated, will be sufficient to pay the pensions to the employees. The amount contributed by the employer is a function of how many employees will qualify for a pension, how many years will a pension be paid to each retiree, the expected size of the pensions, and how much investment income is expected to be earned by the pension trust assets.

Pension plans are declining in popularity. The number of pension plans has gone into steep decline because employers do not want to be required to make

---

10. 29 U.S.C. § 1056(d).
11. *Id.*
12. *Id.*

annual contributions that can vary greatly from year to year. There are many reasons for the variation in annual contributions but the main reason is the variation in the amount of investment income. If the investments, typically in stocks and bonds, have poor returns, the employer must make greater contributions to keep the fund actuarially solvent. Rather than being held hostage to the success or failure of plan investments, employers increasingly no longer offer pension plans. Instead they offer defined contribution plans.

B. Defined Contribution Plans

Pension plans are being supplanted by define contribution plans, specifically 401(k) plans, also known as 403(b) plans if established by a school or university, or 457 plans if established by a governmental entity. (The plans are named after the sections in the Internal Revenue Code that govern them.) A 401(k), or similar plan, is a cash or deferred arrangement (CODA) that permits participating employees to choose whether to contribute a portion of their wages or salary to a qualified defined contribution plan account. Normally if an employee has the choice of whether to accept cash or make a contribution to a retirement account, the doctrine of constructive receipt would require the employee to report either the cash or the contribution as current income for purposes of the federal income tax. The Internal Revenue Code, however, permits the employee to make an elective contribution to a retirement account without being taxed on the amount of the contribution.[13] There are limits on the dollar amounts that an employee can contribute with the amount being adjusted annually for inflation. The employer can make contributions to the employee's 401(k) account, and though those contributions are deductible by the employer, they are not income to the employee until distributed.[14] When the account balance is distributed to the employee, the employee must report the distribution as taxable income or roll the amount over tax free to an IRA, which in turn will make taxable distributions to the IRA owner.

Unlike a defined benefit plan, which has a single fund managed by the trustees of the fund, each participant in a 401(k) plan has their own account. Over 90 percent of 401(k) plans permit employees to direct the investment of the funds in their accounts subject to a list of permitted investment choices. Typically a participant can invest in a family of mutual funds, buy certificates of deposit issued by a named bank, and purchase the stock of the employer. Upon "separation from service," that is, upon terminating work with the employer who sponsored the 401(k) plan, the participant has the choice of leaving his account in the plan, taking a lump-sum distribution of the assets in the plan and paying income tax on the value of that distribution, or, as most departing employees do, chose the tax-free rollover of the funds in the 401(k) account into an IRA. To qualify as a tax-free

---

13. Treas. Reg. § 1.401(k)-1(a).
14. I.R.C. § 402(g)(9).

distribution, the rollover must take place within 60 days after the receipt of the lump-sum distribution.[15]

Whether the funds are left in the 401(k) account or rolled over into an IRA, an individual who is age 59½ or older can take distributions from the account. Unless the account contains a Roth IRA or the IRA is a Roth IRA, all distributions are taxed as ordinary income. Distributions are permitted without regard to whether the individual is retired. The individual does not have to take distributions, however, until they turn age 70½. After that, if they have separated from service, they must take a required minimum distribution (RMD) by April 1 of the year following the year in which they turned 70½.[16] In subsequent years, they must take the RMD by December 31. The RMD is determined by dividing the adjusted market value of the IRA (or retirement account) as of December 31 of the prior year by an applicable life expectancy factor taken from the IRS Uniform Lifetime Table that is available online. If the individual has multiple IRAs, the RMD is based upon the total in all of the IRAs although the distribution can be made from a single IRA. If the individual has both an IRA and a 401(k) account, however, the RMD calculated based on the value of the 401(k) account must be distributed from that account. The RMD is usually, but not necessarily, taxable as ordinary income if the IRA was funded by pre-tax dollars, which is the case with a 401(k) that was rolled over into an IRA.

The RMD also applies to IRA's that were funded with after-tax contributions. The IRA itself is non-taxable, meaning that the investment income earned by the IRA is not taxed. But because distributions from such IRA's represent both a return of the after-tax contributions and investment income that was never taxed, only the investment income is subject to income taxation. The nondeductible IRA is added to all other IRAs including those resulting from a rollover from a 401(k) to determine the total annual RMD.

Distributions from a retirement plan or account do not have to begin until after the individual has "separated from service," that is, quit working for the employer who established the plan. Even if the individual is past age 70½ the RMD does not apply if the individual is still employed by the employer who created the account. If however, the individual is employed by a different employer, the RMD will apply to an account or accounts established by or a rollover IRA funded by a retirement plan created by a former employer. The exception is if the individual is self-employed who created and funded a Savings Incentive Match Plan for Employees Individual Retirement Account or SIMPLE IRA. Even if the individual continues to be self-employed and even if the individual continues to make annual pre-tax contributions to the SIMPLE account, the individual will be required to take an annual RMD by April 1 of the year following the calendar year in which they reach age 70½.

---

15. I.R.C. § 402(c)(3)(B).
16. Required minimum distribution rules are contained in I.R.C. § 401(A)(9) and the regulations issued thereunder.

Distributions taken before the individual has reached age 59½ are subject to income taxation and also incur a 10 percent tax penalty. There are exceptions, however. Distributions before age 59½ do not trigger the 10 percent penalty, if

- Unreimbursed medical expenses are more than 7.5 percent of an individual's adjusted gross income for that year.
- The individual lost their job, received unemployment compensation, and paid for medical insurance.
- A physician determines an individual is unable to do any substantial gainful activity due to physical or mental conditions.
- The distribution is used to pay for higher education expenses.
- The distribution is used to purchase, rebuild, or build a first home up to an amount of $10,000.

If an individual dies before reaching age 59½, their IRA can be distributed to their beneficiaries or estate penalty free.

Spouses who inherit an IRA (or similar defined contribution plan such as a SIMPLE or SEP account) are also subject to the RMD, but they have several options as to whose life is used to determine the RMD if they are the sole beneficiary of the IRA.[17] The options depend on whether the account owner died before reaching age 70½. If so, first, the surviving spouse may treat the IRA as their own and wait until they are 70½ to begin the distributions. To avoid the 10 percent penalty tax, they cannot take distributions until after they turn 59½. Second, they can transfer the account into an IRA in their own name. Thereafter they must begin distributions no later than the year that the decedent would have turned age 70½. The amount of the RMD is calculated based on their age in the year after the year of death of the owner of the account. The annual RMD is based upon the age of the surviving spouse. Third, they can withdraw the entire amount in the account no later than the fifth year following the death the account owner's death. Although the entire distribution is taxable, it is not subject to the penalty tax if the distribution occurred before the surviving spouse turned age 59½. Fourth, they can take a single, lump-sum distribution without being subject to the 10 percent penalty tax if they are under age 59½, but the entire amount of the distribution is taxable income in the year received.

If the account owner dies after reaching age 70½, a surviving spouse who is the sole beneficiary has three options. First, they can transfer the account to an IRA in their name and treat it as if it were their account and base the RMD on their age. If they take distributions before they are age 59½, they will be subject to the 10 percent penalty tax. Second, the annual RMD can be based upon the longer life expectancy of the surviving spouse or of the decedent's life expectancy at the year of their death. Such distributions are not subject to the 10 percent penalty tax

---

17. For information about inherited IRAs, see https://www.irs.gov/publications/p590b/ch01.html.

even if the surviving spouse is under the age of 59½. Third, the surviving spouse can take a lump-sum distribution of the entire amount in the account. Although such a distribution is not subject to the 10 percent penalty tax, it is all taxable income in the year of receipt.

A non-spouse beneficiary who inherits an IRA must begin taking an RMD by December 31 of the year after the year of death of the original owner. For example, if the original owner died in 2016, the first RMD must be taken by December 31, 2017. The non-spouse beneficiary must directly roll over the inherited assets to an inherited IRA in their own name and thereafter use their own age for calculating the first year RMD. For each year after, they subtract one year from the initial life expectancy factor to calculate the RMD. The same RMD rules apply to an inherited Roth IRA. Although the original owner was not required to make RMDs, a non-spouse, inherited owner will be forced to take annual RMDs, but all of the distributions are tax-free.[18]

If an IRA is left by the decedent to more than one individual, each beneficiary should set up their own inherited IRA by December 31 of the year following the year of the decedent's death. That will ensure that each IRA will be subject to an RMD based on the life of the individual owner. If those who inherited the IRA do not establish separate inherited IRA assets by December 31 of the year following the year of the decedent's death, the IRA will use an RMD based on the age of the oldest beneficiary whose name was on the account as of December 31.

C. Qualifying Longevity Annuity Contracts (QLAC)

Although the rollover IRA and retirement plan accounts are very popular with many retirees, they lack the income security offered by pensions. A retiree must husband the lump sum to ensure that they do not outlive their retirement nest egg; this requires intelligent investment of the lump sum as well as carefully calculated withdrawals. Poor investment returns or excessive withdrawals may leave the retiree without sufficient retirement income. One way to create a guaranteed stream of income would be to use part or all of the lump sum to purchase an immediate pay, lifetime annuity. A married couple could purchase a two-life, immediate pay annuity. Few retirees do so, however. Many find it difficult to spend a sizeable portion of their IRA or retirement account. The difference in the dollar amount of the cost of the annuity, hundreds of thousands of dollars, and the much smaller annual payout, discourages them from buying an annuity.

Some consider buying a deferred annuity to ensure that they will have income in their later years, such as past age 85. In the past, the federal income tax made that impractical. Today, the use of a deferred annuity is both possible and may be attractive to some retirees.

---

18. For information about inherited Roth IRAs, see https://www.irs.gov/publications/p590b/ch02.html.

In the past, when a plan account or an IRA held a deferred annuity, the account balance used to determine the RMD had to include the actuarial present value (APV) of the annuity, a number that is not reflected in the annuity's cash value, which may be zero. The APV inclusion in the value of the IRA or retirement account effectively precluded deferred annuities from being purchased inside an IRA because in the years before the annuity began to payout, even though the APV was included in the amount of the IRA or retirement account calculation of the RMD, the APV would not provide any cash to help make the RMD payments.

In response, and in an effort to assist retirees to create a stream of income available to them in their later years, in 2014 the Treasury issued new regulations that permit an owner of an IRA, 401(k), 403(b), or 457(b) account to purchase an annuity without triggering taxation upon the distribution of the amount used to purchase it.[19] The regulation permits the distribution of up to the lesser of 25 percent or $125,000 (subject to future inflation increases) of the total amount in a traditional IRA or 401(k) account to purchase a qualified longevity annuity contract (QLAC). The amount distributed and used to purchase the annuity lowers the amount subject to the RMD. For example, if an IRA had $600,000, after purchasing the QLAC at a cost of $125,000, the RMD would then be calculated on $475,000.

The QLAC need not be, and is not expected to be, an immediate pay annuity. Rather the regulations provide that the annuity qualifies so long as the starting date of the annuity is not later than the first day of the month following the annuitant's 85th birthday. The concept is that income provided by the deferred annuity will provide lifetime income. The annuity payments are taxed as ordinary income as they are received. However, the annuity payments do not count as part of the RMD that is required to be paid out from the remaining funds in the IRA or retirement account.

The cost of the annuity is the initial premium or price of the annuity; there are no annual fees. The annuity payments must be fixed; indexed or variable annuities cannot qualify as a QLAC. Depending on what a carrier (seller of the annuity) projects as the probable income return of an annuity premium, for a 65-year-old male who pays $100,000 for an annuity beginning at age 85, the annual benefit would be about $44,000. For a 65-year-old female who pays $100,000 for an annuity beginning at age 85, the annual benefit would be about $35,000. Depending on the carrier that sells the annuity and the annuity's terms, the annuity can include cost-of-living increases in the amount of the annual annuity until the start of the annuity payments.

To qualify as a QLAC, the annuity contract must state that it is a QLAC, and the annuity must not have any commutation benefits (the right to surrender the annuity for a lump-sum payment) or cash surrender value. If the annuitant dies on or after the starting date of the annuity, the permissible benefits are either a life annuity payable to the surviving spouse in an amount not to exceed 100 percent of the periodic payment that was being made to the annuitant or a life annuity payable to a designated beneficiary. The amount of an annuity to a non-spouse beneficiary

---

19. Treas. Reg. § 1.401(a)(9)-5.

must be equal to a percentage of the annuitant's annuity. The percentage is based on the difference is age between the annuitant and the non-spouse beneficiary and begins at 100 percent if the age difference is two years or less and decreases to 20 percent if the age difference is 25 years or more.

If the annuitant dies before the start of the annuity, the surviving spouse can be paid a lifetime annuity but it cannot exceed the amount that would have been paid to the annuitant. The amount of the annuity, however, can exceed the amount that would have been paid to the annuitant if necessary to provide a qualified pre-retirement survivor annuity as defined in 29 U.S.C. § 1055(e)(2). If the beneficiary is a non-spouse, an annuity will be paid, but it will commence at the date of the death of the annuitant and will be subject to the age difference percentage reduction. But because the annuity will have started earlier than the planned date in the annuity contract, the amount of the annuity will be reduced as if it had been projected to commence at the date of the annuitant's death and continue to pay benefits for the annuitant's projected life expectancy. In the alternative, the annuitant can elect a death benefit that will equal the cost of the premium.

The advantages of a QLAC are a guaranteed stream of income in the annuitant's later years and a modest lowering of the amount in the account or IRA that is subject to the RMD. The QLAC can be purchased long before retirement. Some advocate its purchase as young as age 50. The earlier is it purchased, the larger the yearly payout when it finally begins. For example, the distribution from the IRA or retirement account of $125,000 to purchase a QLAC would not be taxed, although the annuity when paid would be fully taxed as ordinary income. But the delay in taxation until age 85 and later provides another reason to purchase a QLAC.

When the purchaser of a deferred annuity retires and reaches age 70½ and is required to take out the RMD, the amount of the RMD will be lower because the IRA or retirement account will have $125,000 less (assuming the maximum allowable amount is used) as well as the investment income that the $125,000 might have earned for the 21 years (age 50 to 71). If the $125,000 earned 6 percent compounded annually (recall the investment income is not taxed until it is distributed), it would be worth about $440,000 at age 71. In addition, because the $125,000 plus investment earnings is not part of the IRA or retirement account, the RMD is significantly lower. The income taxes on the $125,000 and the investment earnings generated by that amount will have been deferred until receipt of the annuity payouts.

D. Roth IRA Withdrawal Rules

Individuals may own a Roth IRA, which is an IRA funded with after-tax dollars that is never thereafter subject to the income tax. Both the after-tax amounts contributed to the Roth IRA and the never-taxed investment income on the IRA assets are distributed tax-free.[20]

---

20. For information on Roth IRA distributions, see https://www.irs.gov/publications/p590b/ch02.html.

Individuals are not required to take an RMD from a Roth account, but they may take a distribution from a Roth IRA if they have reached age 59½ and if five years have passed since the first year they made a contribution to the Roth IRA or converted a traditional IRA to a Roth IRA. Because of the tax advantages of accumulating tax-free investment income in a Roth IRA, however, it is generally unwise to take distributions until needed, usually during the later years of retirement.

As with a traditional IRA, there are exceptions to the early withdrawal rules.

- If the account holder dies before reaching age 59½, their Roth IRA can be distributed to their beneficiaries or estate without the imposition of the 10 percent tax penalty.
- If a physician determines an individual is unable to do any substantial gainful activity due to physical or mental conditions, they can make withdrawals not subject to the 10 percent penalty.
- Account holders can take an early withdrawal from a Roth IRA if they use the money to purchase, rebuild, or build their first home or if the home is the main home and the first home of their spouse, children, grandchildren, a parent, or another ancestor.

Note that after the death of the Roth IRA owner, if the spouse inherits the IRA, there is no RMD. However, a Roth IRA inherited by a non-spouse, such as a child, is subject to the RMD rules and the amount of the RMD is determined by reference to the age of the non-spouse who inherited the Roth IRA.

III. IRA Tax Planning

When they retire, individuals who own an IRA or who expect to rollover a 401(k) or similar plan account into an IRA need to consider the tax ramifications of that IRA, including whether it is possible and advisable to transform part or all of a traditional IRA to a Roth IRA. They also need to plan the amount of distributions they expect to take from the IRA during their retirement years.

A. Converting a Traditional IRA to a Roth IRA

Without regard to their income, since 2010, individuals have been permitted to convert part or all of a traditional IRA into a Roth IRA. Whereas the traditional account contains pre-tax funds and untaxed investment earnings that are taxable upon distribution, a Roth IRA contains after-tax funds which are not taxed upon distribution; the Roth IRA investment earnings that have never been taxed are also not taxed upon distribution. Note that some individuals have after-tax IRAs. The contributions to the IRA were after-tax dollars, but the investment earnings are not taxed until distributed. This type of IRA can also be converted into a Roth IRA.

Conversion of a traditional IRA into a Roth IRA subjects the IRA funds to income taxation (only the investment earnings of a non-tax deductible IRA). The tax does not have to be paid out of funds in the IRA; those who convert an IRA to a Roth IRA typically pay the federal income tax out of non-IRA funds. The reasoning behind a conversion is to avoid taxation on future earnings in the IRA as well as avoiding the RMD and the resulting income tax on the RMD. The advantage of conversion rests upon the expectation of not making any distributions from the Roth IRA for 20 to 30 years. Absent that, a conversion will yield only modest, if any, benefit. Conversely, an owner of an IRA funded with after-tax dollars can convert it into a Roth IRA and only pay income taxes on the accumulated income. After the conversion, the Roth IRA will accumulate tax-free income, which should soon offset the cost of the income tax incurred at the time of the conversion.

Whether the Roth IRA owner can make additional contributions to the IRA, depends on their income. In 2017, an individual could contribute up to $5,500, or $6,500 if age 50 or older, if their modified adjusted gross income (MAGI) was $116,000 or less (amounts are adjusted annually for inflation). If their MAGI was between $118,001 and $133,000, they could contribute a reduced amount. If their MAGI exceeded $133,000 they could not contribute to a Roth IRA. Married taxpayers filing a joint return could contribute the full amount if their combined MAGI was $186,000 or less, a reduced amount if their MAGI was between $186,001 and $196,000. If their MAGI exceeded $196,000 they could not contribute to a Roth IRA.

MAGI is adjusted gross income with a number of additions and deletions. The calculation of MAGI is illustrated on the IRS website, https://www.irs.gov.

B. Withdrawal Strategies

Because of the advantage of the deferral of taxation on the dollars held by the IRA, beyond the RMD distribution, the IRA account should be the last account from which distributions are taken. It is preferable to spend dollars that have already been taxed such as savings, Social Security benefits, and pensions. By doing so, the individual defers taxation and permits the further accumulation of tax-free investment income. Some retirees have sufficient income from these other sources to not need to spend any of their IRA beyond the RMD. Most, however, will need to spend part or all of their IRA to have adequate income. If the individual is spending savings that was previously taxed, and if the savings is in stocks or other assets that have appreciated, the individual should first sell and spend assets that have the least amount of appreciation and thereby defer taxation on that appreciation. An individual with both a traditional IRA and a Roth IRA should first distribute the assets in the traditional IRA and only after it has been exhausted, begin to take distributions from the Roth IRA.

Medicare 5

I. Introduction

Medicare is the federal subsidized health care insurance program for those age 65 and older that is operated by the Centers for Medicare & Medicaid Services (CMS). Medicare is financed in part by the Federal Insurance Contributions Act (FICA), which is a tax on the wages of employees and the self-employed, by premiums paid by Medicare beneficiaries, and by general tax revenues. Medicare provides benefits to over 50 million individuals though four parts: Medicare Part A covers hospital care; Medicare Part B pays for physicians; Medicare Part C, known as Medicare Advantage, provides the option of managed care; and Medicare Part D reimburses prescription drug costs. The law governing Medicare is found in Title XVIII of the Social Security Act in Title 42 of the United States Code.

II. Finance Sources

Medicare Part A is financed by a dedicated, mandatory payroll tax of 1.45 percent on all wage income with the employer paying a matching amount, for a total tax of 2.9 percent.[1] Self-employed individuals pay a tax of 2.9 percent on their employment income. An additional tax of 0.9 percent is paid only by the employee or

---

1. https://www.ssa.gov/news/press/factsheets/colafacts2017.pdf.

Table 5.1   Part B Premiums

Yearly income in 2015 was:			Part B Premium in 2017
File individual tax return	File joint tax return		
$85,000 or less	$170,000 or less		$134.00
above $85,000 up to $107,000	above $170,000 up to $214,000		$187.50
above $107,000 up to $160,000	above $214,000 up to $320,000		$267.50
above $160,000 up to $214,000	above $320,000 up to $428,000		$348.30
above $214,000	above $428,000		$428.50

self-employed individual and applies to wages and self-employment income that exceed the threshold amount of $200,000 for a single taxpayer and $250,000 for a married couple filing jointly. These amounts are not adjusted for inflation.

Medicare Part B, which pays for physicians and some other costs, is financed by a combination of monthly premiums and general revenues. Part B is optional, although almost all Medicare beneficiaries enroll in it. By law, 75 percent of the cost of Part B is paid out of general revenues. Part B premiums are supposed to pay for the remaining 25 percent of its cost with the result that the annual premium for Part B changes annually. The premium rises along with the total adjusted gross income and tax-exempt interest income of the beneficiary as reported on their federal income tax return from two years earlier, that is, the 2017 premium is based on the individual's income tax return for the year 2015. In 2017 the Part B premiums were as shown in Table 5.1.

The higher premiums reflect the percentage subsidy, which is 75 percent for those with adjusted gross income and tax-exempt income of less than $85,000 for a single individual and $170,000 for a married couple filing a joint return, down to 20 percent for those charged the highest premium. Beginning in 2018, the income tax brackets are reduced, for example, the $124,000 to $320,000 is reduced to $214,000 to $267,000 so that more Part B beneficiaries will be subject to the higher premiums.

The standard Part B premium amount for 2017 was $134 for first-time enrollees, but most Part B beneficiaries pay less because the Part B premium is not permitted to rise more than the percentage cost-of-living increase in the monthly Social Security benefit. As a result, in 2017 the average Part B premium was $109.[2]

---

2. https://www.medicare.gov/your-medicare-costs/costs-at-a-glance/costs-at-glance.html#collapse-4809.

The annual Part B increase applies to those:

- Who enroll in Part B for the first time.
- Who do not receive Social Security benefits.
- Who are billed directly for Part B premiums rather than having the premium deducted from Social Security benefits.
- Whose state of residence pays their premiums by way of the state Medicaid program.
- Whose modified adjusted gross income as reported on their federal income tax return from two years prior exceeded $85,000 for a single tax payer or $170,000 for a married couple filing a joint return.

Medicare Part C, Medicare Advantage, is funded by the diversion of the Part B premium to the managed care provider, by premiums that the managed care provider may charge enrollees, and by general revenues.

Medicare Part D is paid for by premiums charged by the provider of the prescription drug plan and by general revenues.[3]

III. Eligibility

A. Part A

Because Medicare is part of the Social Security system, eligibility for it is tied to eligibility for Social Security benefits. Anyone who is 65 years old and is eligible for Social Security benefits (or Federal Railroad Retirement benefits)—whether they are taking such benefits or not—is entitled to Medicare Part A for which there is no charge or premium. Because Part A is "free" at age 65, those eligible for it should enroll in Medicare Part A even if they are still working or have not yet claimed Social Security benefits. There is no advantage in not enrolling.

Conversely, merely receiving Social Security benefits, such as claiming them at age 62, does not create eligibility for Medicare. The individual must be 65 or older. Public employees who were hired after March 31, 1986, who paid the Medicare wage tax, but who are not eligible for Social Security because they did not pay the Social Security wage tax, and who are at least age 65 are eligible for Medicare. Also eligible for Medicare, but who do not need to be age 65 or older, are individuals who have received Social Security disability benefits for at least 24 months and individuals with end stage renal disease.

Those with derivative Social Security benefits based on their status as a spouse or a surviving spouse of someone eligible for Social Security or Railroad Retirement benefits, *and* who are age 65 or older are also eligible for Medicare Part A benefits. A divorced spouse whose marriage lasted at least ten years and who has not remarried can qualify for Medicare based on the participation of a former

---

3. https://q1medicare.com/PartD-The-2017-Medicare-Part-D-Outlook.php.

spouse in the Social Security program. It does not matter if the former spouse remarried or and if their current spouse is eligible for Medicare based on the former spouse's participation in Social Security. Those with derivative benefits can enroll in Medicare even if the spouse or former spouse is not yet eligible because they have not yet reached age 65.

Individuals who are not eligible for Medicare may voluntarily buy Part A, and must also buy Part B, by paying a monthly premium. The monthly premium for Part A varies depending on whether the individual ever paid Social Security wage taxes and, if so, for how many quarters. The premium also rises if the individual does not sign up at the time they turn age 65.

If an individual enrolls in Medicare Part A but is still working and their employer provides group health care insurance, Medicare is a secondary payer; the employer's health care insurance is the primary insurer. However, if the employer has fewer than 20 employees, Medicare is the primary payer. If the individual is self-employed and has employer provided group health care insurance or the individual is covered by group health care insurance provided by the individual's spouse whose employer has 20 or more employees, Medicare is the secondary payer.

B. Part B

Anyone eligible for Medicare Part A is also eligible for Part B. Individuals, age 65 and older, who are not eligible for Part A or who have not bought it, can buy Part B if they are either a U.S. citizen or a resident alien who has lived in this country during the preceding five years.

An enrollee in Part B must pay a monthly premium as described earlier in Section II, Finance Sources. Enrollees in Part A who are still employed and have health care insurance through a group plan offered by their employer often enroll in Part A but not in Part B. Those who do not buy Part B when they enroll in Part A—typically at age 65—can later enroll in Part B but when they do, the premium is permanently increased by 10 percent each year that they could have enrolled. (This is to prevent adverse selection by those who wait until they are in need of physician's services before they enroll.) The premium does not increase, however, if they were covered as an employee or spouse of an employee, but not as a retiree or spouse of a retiree, by an employer provided group health care insurance. The 10 percent increase per year is only suspended during the period of employment. After the individual retires from the employment that provided the health care insurance, the penalty will apply unless the individual enrolls in Part B in a timely fashion. Usually individuals who are about to retire enroll prospectively in Part B to avoid the penalty for late enrollment.

C. Part C—Medicare Advantage Plans

Individuals have the option to enroll in a Medicare Advantage Plan if they are enrolled in both Medicare Part A and Part B.[4] In 2016, about one-third of Medicare

---

4. https://www.medicare.gov/sign-up-change-plans/medicare-health-plans/medicare-advantage-plans/medicare-advantage-plans.html.

enrollees elected to participate in a Medicare Advantage Plan. They can enroll when they turn age 65. If they have Part A and enroll in Part B for the first time at a later age, they can choose instead to enroll in Medicare Advantage. They can also enroll between a date in mid-October and a date in late December when they can also switch or drop Medicare Advantage Plans. In January and up to a date in February, those enrolled in Medicare Advantage Plans can leave the plan and switch to Medicare Part A and B, known as Original or Traditional Medicare. Other than the prescribed enrollment periods, an enrollee in Medicare Advantage must stay enrolled for the calendar year with certain exceptions that include moving out the Plan's service area, being a resident in a nursing home, or having qualified for Medicaid.

D. Part D

Those eligible for Medicare Part A have the option of enrolling in Medicare Part D prescription drug coverage.[5] If they decide to enroll, they have two choices. If they are enrolled in Original Medicare, that is, obtaining coverage through Part A and B, they can add drug coverage enrolling in a stand-alone Medicare Prescription Drug Plan offered by a variety of providers including health care insurance companies. The alternative is to enroll in a Medicare Advantage Plan that provides prescription drug coverage so that they receive Medicare Part A, Part B, and Part D through the Medicare Advantage Plan. Those who enroll in a stand-alone Medicare Prescription Drug Plan on average have a choice of among 30 such plans.

Individuals can enroll during their initial enrollment period when they are eligible to enroll in Part A and Part B. If they defer enrollment in Part B, they can join a drug plan when they enroll in Part B, and can also enroll during the annual open Medicare enrollment period that occurs during mid-October through early December. Enrollment at any time of the year is permitted if the individual moves out of a Medicare Advantage Plan service area, resides in a nursing home or if the individual loses other creditable prescription drug coverage, which means coverage that was actuarially equivalent to Part D coverage. Retirees who have employer-provided retiree health care insurance may have creditable drug coverage, and many enrollees in Medicare Advantage Plans also have creditable coverage.

Failure to elect Part D coverage when eligible, that is, when the individual enrolls in Part A and Part B, triggers an enrollment penalty of 1 percent increase in the premium for each month of delayed enrollment. The increase is permanent and is calculated by being applied to the average base premium paid by Part D enrollees ($34.10 in 2016) and added to the monthly premium paid by the enrollee for Part D coverage. If, however, the enrollee had creditable drug coverage during the period of non-enrollment, no penalty is assessed.

The monthly premium for a Part D plan varies by the plan. Individuals select a drug plan based upon the drugs that they need and those provided by the plan,

---

5. https://www.medicare.gov/part-d/.

known as the formulary, and the monthly premium charged by the plan. Some Medicare Advantage Plans include the cost of the drug coverage in the monthly premium for the Plan, others charge a monthly fee for prescription drug coverage. The charge for independent plans varies along with what drugs are covered. All such plans, however, are subsidized by Medicare. In line with charging higher income Medicare beneficiaries more for their participation, individuals who elect a drug plan rather than a Medicare Advantage Plan and who have incomes above $85,000 for those filing individually or $170,000 for a married couple filing a joint return are subject to a higher Part D plan premium. Individuals who select a drug plan may elect to have the monthly premium deducted from their monthly Social Security benefit check.

IV. Coverage

A. Part A

Part A covers medical care received as an in-patient in a hospital, nursing home, or hospice.[6] The care provided must be "reasonable and necessary" for the diagnosis or treatment of illness or injury or for functional improvement.[7] Medicare pays for semiprivate rooms, usually rooms with two patients. There is an annual deductible: $1,316 in 2017.[8]

Medicare Part A pays for only a limited number of days spent in these institutions for each "spell of illness," defined as beginning with the first day of admission to the facility and ending 60 days after the discharge. After the annual deductible has been paid, Part A pays for up to 90 days of hospitalization. The first 60 are covered in full but for the last 30 days, the enrollee is subject to a daily co-pay, which in 2017 was $329. Each spell of illness resets the counter on the days of coverage, but readmission to the hospital within 60 days of discharge, even for a different illness or condition, is counted as a continuation of the first 90 days of coverage.

After the first 90 days, if the individual is still hospitalized, days 91–150 are covered by the 60 lifetime reserve days, which once used, are no longer available for the rest of the individual's life. The lifetime reserve days have a daily co-pay of $658 in 2017.

Part A pays for up to 100 days of skilled nursing care if provided in a Medicare-approved facility. Most, but not all nursing homes are Medicare approved; some have only certain areas, that is, beds that are Medicare approved. The patient must need skilled nursing care to be eligible for Part A and must have spent at least three continuous days in a hospital within 30 days prior to being admitted to the nursing home. To qualify for the three continuous days in a nursing home, the

---

6. For information about Medicare coverage and costs, see https://www.medicare.gov/.

7. 42 U.S.C. § 1395y(a).

8. https://www.medicare.gov/your-medicare-costs/costs-at-a-glance/costs-at-glance.html.

individual must have had in-patient status in the hospital; outpatient status for the purpose of observation does not count even if the individual was physically residing in the hospital. After a qualifying admission to a nursing home, Medicare pays for all costs for 20 days. For the next 80 days, the individual has a co-pay ($164.50 per day in 2017). After 100 days, Part A ceases to pay for skilled nursing home care. Medicare does not pay for non-skilled care, known as custodial care, even if it is provided in a nursing home.

Medicare pays for hospice care,[9] which is end-of-life care that focuses on pain relief and control of symptoms rather than treatment of the underlying medical condition. Its goal is comfort, rather than seeking a cure. To be eligible for Medicare hospice the individual must have been certified by the hospice physician and their personal physician as having no more than six months life expectancy and sign an agreement to accept hospice care, although they can elect to leave hospice at any time and accept treatment. Hospice is provided under Original Medicare Part A and Part B. Individuals enrolled in Medicare Advantage revert to Original Medicare while they are in hospice. All of those who receive hospice care must continue to pay the Part B premium.

Hospice is most often provided in the home of the individual, but it is also provided in hospitals, nursing homes, and even in stand-alone facilities. A team of professionals, paid caregivers, family caregivers, and volunteers provide holistic care that attempts to meet the individual's physical, emotional, social, and spiritual needs. Medicare hospice provides a variety of services including physical care, counseling, drugs, supplies, and equipment. Medicare hospice is designed to cover all the individual's medical needs that arise from the terminal illness. It even provides up to five days of in-patient hospice for those being treated in their home as respite for family caregivers. The hospice patient may be required to pay a co-payment of no more than $5 for each prescription drug.

Medicare Part A provides hospice care for two 90-day periods followed by an unlimited number of 60-day periods. At the start of each period, the hospice must recertify that the individual has a life expectancy of six months or less. The individual has the right to change providers once during each benefit period and can stop the hospice care at any time for any reason and revert to the form of Medicare that they had prior to electing hospice.

Medicare Part A provides some home health care services for individuals unable to leave their homes except to seek medical assistance with help from others or by using a device such as a walker or wheelchair.[10] To qualify, the individual must contact a Medicare-approved home health agency, which creates a written plan of care established by a physician and reviewed every two months by a physician. Home health services include physical, occupational, and speech therapy; durable medical equipment; medical supplies; and "part time and intermittent"

---

9. 42 U.S.C. § 1395d(d).
10. *Id.* § 1395d(a)(3).

nursing care,[11] which is care of less than eight hours per day and no more than 28 to 35 hours per week.

There are no co-pays or deductibles for home health care except for a co-pay of 20 percent on durable medical equipment. However, Part A home health care is only available if the individual had been hospitalized for at least three consecutive days or had received post-hospital care in a skilled nursing facility and the home health care begin within 14 days after being discharged from the hospital or the skilled nursing facility. And coverage is limited to 100 visits within a home health care spell of illness, which begins on the first day the individual receives services and continues until 60 days after the day they are no longer receiving home care services and have not been an inpatient in a hospital or a skilled nursing facility.

Medicare does not pay for 24-hour-a-day care at home; meals delivered to the individual's home; homemaker services like shopping, cleaning, and laundry if that is the only care needed by the individual; and personal care given by home health aides like bathing, dressing, and using the bathroom if this is the only care needed.

B. Part B

Part B pays for the cost of physicians and certain outpatient services.[12] Physician services are covered no matter where they are provided: in a hospital, a nursing home, the patient's home, or in the physician's office. Outpatient services include diagnostic tests, dialysis, surgery, and therapeutic services. Part B also covers ambulance services. It does not cover routine eye examinations, dental services, and routine podiatry services. Cosmetic surgery is excluded unless done in connection with accidental injury. Part B does not cover routine physical examinations but it does cover an initial physical examination during the enrollee's first year of coverage. Also covered are annual flu shots and other preventive vaccinations, mammograms, and prostate cancer screening. Finally, Part B covers outpatient blood transfusions and medical supplies such as a splint or cast.

Part B generally pays 80 percent of Medicare approved charges; the enrollee pays the other 20 percent. There is also an annual deductible of $183 in 2017. Medicare only pays for approved charges that it considers reasonable. If the physician charges more than the approved charge, Medicare will only pay for 80 percent of what it considers a reasonable charge with the enrollee obligated to pay the excess.[13] In many states, however, state law requires physicians to "participate" in Medicare, meaning that the physician cannot charge more than the Medicare-approved rate. If the physician does not participate, the physician is limited to billing no more than 15 percent of the approved charge. For example, if the Medicare approved charge for a procedure is $100, a physician who participates can only bill the patient $100 of which Medicare pays 80 percent or $80. If the physician does not participate, the physician can bill the patient $115 of which Medicare will

11. *Id.* § 1395x(m).
12. *Id.* § 1395k(a).
13. *Id.* § 1395(a).

pay $80. In both cases the enrollee is responsible for the portion of the bill not paid for by Medicare, in this case $35.

C. Part C—Medicare Advantage Plans

Medicare Advantage Plans is an alternative to Original Medicare, Part A and Part B. Individuals eligible for Medicare have the option of electing a Medicare Advantage Plan, assuming one is available where they live. Medicare Advantage Plans are a form of managed care. The individual pays less for their care but gives up the right to choose any willing provider, as they are limited to providers approved by the Medicare Advantage Plan. By law a Medicare Advantage Plan must provide all the coverage of Medicare Part A and Part B except hospice care; an enrollee who desires hospice must leave the Medicare Advantage Plan and enroll in Original Medicare, Part A and Part B.

In order to attract enrollees, Medicare Advantage Plans not only match the coverage offered by Medicare Part A and Part B, but typically offer additional coverage such vision, hearing, dental, wellness programs, and even free membership in exercise clubs. Most Plans offer prescription drug coverage, sometimes at no additional cost. Those enrolled in Medicare Advantage Plans continue to pay Part B premiums and may be required to pay an additional monthly premium for the Medicare Advantage Plan. The Plan may have an annual deductible and may charge a co-pay or co-insurance.

CMS pays the Medicare Advantage Plans an annual, capitated amount for each enrollee. Because the amount received by the Plan is a fixed amount per enrollee, in order to be able to provide all the required services, and possibly additional benefits, the Plan must carefully monitor its costs. Plans do so by operating as a Health Maintenance Organization, HMO, or another form (such as a Preferred Provider Organization, PPO) that restricts the physicians, hospitals, and other providers that the enrollee can use. The Plan may also restrict access to specialists unless the enrollee is referred to them by a primary care physician.

Anyone considering enrolling in a Medicare Advantage Plan should consult the annually updated publication, "Medicare & You" published by the Centers for Medicare & Medicaid Services available either in print or online.[14]

D. Part D

Part D prescription drug coverage is available either as a free-standing plan or as part of a Medicare Advantage Plan. The amount of the premium is based on the individual's income two years prior; that is, the 2017 premium is based on the individual's income in 2015. Current information as to the income levels and premiums is available at https://www.medicare.gov/your-medicare-costs/costs-at -a-glance/costs-at-glance.html.

---

14. https://www.medicare.gov/Pubs/pdf/10050.pdf.

In addition to charging those who enroll in the plan a monthly premium, plans can impose an annual deductible up to $400, although the amount varies by plan, and some plans do not have a deductible. After the deductible has been reached, the plan can impose either a co-payment, either a set dollar amount per prescription or a percentage of the cost. The amount of a co-payment depends by the plan selected.

Part D free-standing plans feature an annual coverage gap that is commonly known as the donut hole. The coverage gap begins after the enrollee and the plan have spent a designated amount for covered drugs, with the amount changing annually. In 2017, the gap began at $3,700. After reaching the coverage gap, in 2017, the enrollee paid 45 percent of the plan's cost for brand-name prescription drugs and 51 percent of the cost for generic drugs. Medicare pays the remaining cost of these drug purchases. The percentage paid by the enrollee gradually declines until 2020 when the enrollee will pay 25 percent of the cost of both brand-name and generic drugs after the enrollee has met the plan's annual deductible.

The coverage gap ends when the enrollee is credited with having spent $4,950 in 2017 on drugs. Once out of the coverage gap, for the remainder of the year, the individual is automatically eligible for catastrophic coverage that covers the costs of drugs except for a small co-payment or coinsurance amount. In 2017, the enrollee paid the greater of the co-pay of $3.30 for covered generic drugs and $8.25 for covered name-brand drugs or a 5 percent coinsurance amount.

To be eligible for catastrophic coverage, the enrollee must be credited with having spent enough on prescription drugs: $4,950 in 2017. The enrollee cannot count the cost of the monthly drug plan premium, but can count the annual deductible, co-payments and coinsurance, and out-of-pocket cost of drugs paid while in the coverage gap. Also credited to the enrollee are the discounts of 50 percent received on brand-name drugs purchased while they were in the coverage gap, which when added to the 45 percent paid by the enrollee, means that 95 percent of the cost of a name-brand drug is credited toward spending to get out of the coverage gap. For generic drugs, only the actual payment made by the enrollee, plus any dispensing fee, are counted toward the spending that is required to get out of the coverage gap.

V. Appeal of Claim Denials

If Medicare refuses to pay for a provided medical service, usually the provider of the service is not reimbursed because the individual cannot be required to pay for the care. Known as a waiver of liability, it applies if the individual did not know or could not have known that Medicare would not pay for the services. The individual will be financially responsible, however, if the medical service was not "reasonable and necessary" as defined by Medicare, the care was custodial rather than acute, or if the care was home health care but the individual was not home-bound or was not receiving acute care on an intermittent basis.

If the individual is deemed financially liable for medical services, the individual has a right to appeal beginning with a request for a redetermination from the outside contractor hired by Medicare to process the Medicare claims. The contractor must respond to the appeal within 60 days. If denied, the individual can request a reconsideration by a qualified independent contractor (QIC), an outside organization hired by Medicare. The QIC has 60 days to respond. The QIC decision can be appealed to an administrative law judge (ALJ) within the Department of Health and Human Services. The ALJ decision can be appealed to the Medicare Appeals Council of the Department of Health and Human Services that must decide the case within 90 days of receiving the request for its review. Finally, a decision of the council can be appealed in a federal district court.

If the individual is in a Medicare Advantage Plan, an adverse decision by the provider not to provide care or not to provide acceptable care must be appealable under procedures provided by the Plan. These appeal procedures must be similar to appeal rights available under Part A and Part B.

VI. Medigap Policies

Because of the deductibles, co-pays, and limitations on hospital coverage and other potentially uncovered expenses, many Medicare beneficiaries purchase Medigap insurance policies that provide supplemental medical insurance. Medigap policies are offered by private insurance companies who may charge different premiums for identical policies subject to state oversight of policies and premium rates for policies sold in the state. Under federal law, all Medigap policies must be offered as one of ten standardized policies that are identified as policies A through N.

The policies represent a range of coverage, with A policies providing the least amount of coverage of the costs not covered by Medicare and N policies providing the greatest amount of coverage. From policies A to N, the coverage gradually expands, although some policies add coverage while deleting other coverage. Plan A provides the basic, core coverage. Its coverage must be included in all Medigap policies. Plan K and L have higher out-of-pocket costs but usually charge lower premiums. No Medigap policy can cover the Part D co-payments.

Plans A and B, which dominate Medigap sales, have similar coverage except that Plan B covers the first-day deductible for Part A hospitalization. Both Plans cover the following:

- All Part A hospital co-payments
- 100 percent of additional hospital days up to a lifetime maximum of 365 days

- The 20 percent of the Part B co-pay
- First three pints of blood each calendar year
- Hospice cost-sharing requirements

Plan C covers everything that Plan B covers and also the day 21 through 100 co-pay of nursing home stay and the Part B annual deductible. The additional Plans add to and delete some of what is covered by Plans A, B, and C.

After reaching age 65, and if not receiving health care insurance from an employer, an individual has a six-month open enrollment period to buy a Medigap policy. They cannot be denied the right to purchase a policy offered by the issuing insurance company even for a preexisting condition. As long as the insured pays the premiums, a Medigap policy cannot be cancelled.

Veterans Benefits 6

I. Introduction

America has almost 19 million veterans; over 9 million are age 65 and older.[1] Veterans are entitled to a variety of benefits, but this chapter focuses on benefits for older and disabled veterans as well as their spouses who may also be entitled to benefits. The benefits available to older or disabled veterans and their spouses generally require proof of eligibility. Providing that proof can be difficult and frustrating. If eligibility is denied, the individual who wishes to appeal often faces a set of challenging procedures. Older claimants who have physical or mental limitations find it difficult to navigate the bureaucracy to obtain what they are due. If they have lost mental capacity, they may find that the Veterans Administration (VA) has appointed a fiduciary to manage their benefits. Even if the veteran has a valid power of attorney, the VA does not have to recognize it and can appoint a fiduciary of its choosing. Delays in the processing of claims by the VA often mean the veteran has a long wait for benefits. The reality is that for many veterans, the obtainment of benefits can be difficult or even impossible.

To qualify under federal law as "a veteran" an individual must be a "person who served in the active military, naval, or air

---

1. https://www.census.gov/newsroom/facts-for-features/2016/cb16-ff21.html.

service, and who was discharged or released therefrom under conditions other than dishonorable."[2]

II. Veterans Pension Benefits

As a qualified veteran, an individual may be eligible for the VA pension, which is a need-based, monthly cash benefit. It is available to disabled or older veterans and to their surviving dependents who lack sufficient income and assets.

A. Pensions for Disabled or Older Veterans

To qualify for the VA pension, the veteran must have had sufficient length of "active military service,"[3] with at least one day of service having taken place during a "wartime period"[4] (the veteran need not have served in a war zone). The wartime periods are:

- World War II (December 7, 1941–December 31, 1946)
- Korean conflict (June 27, 1950–January 31, 1955)
- Vietnam era (February 28, 1961–May 7, 1975 for veterans who served in the Republic of Vietnam during that period; otherwise August 5, 1964–May 7, 1975)
- Gulf War (August 2, 1990 through a future date to be set by law or Presidential Proclamation)

The veteran must also have "countable income" below the maximum annual pension rate that is set by Congress.[5] The veteran must also not have "excessive"[6] net assets, but there is no set amount that is deemed excessive. Since March of 2015, a veteran's net worth, however, is not a factor when the VA determines eligibility or co-payments for health care benefits. In 2015, the VA issued proposed regulations that would establish an asset limit keyed to the amount of the community spouse resource allowance under Medicaid, but those regulations have not yet been finalized. In addition, the veteran must be permanently and totally disabled[7] or be at least age 65 or older.[8]

A surviving dependent is defined as a surviving spouse or unmarried child of an eligible veteran. To be eligible the individual must have countable income and net worth under the prevailing threshold amount.

---

2. 38 C.F.R. § 3.1(d).

3. 38 U.S.C. § 101(2); 38 C.F.R. § 3.12(a).

4. 38 U.S.C. § 1521(j).

5. For the current pension rate, see http://www.benefits.va.gov/pension/current_rates _veteran_pen.asp.

6. 38 U.S.C. § 1522.

7. *Id.* § 1521.

8. *Id.* § 1513.

To meet the time in service requirement, for service on or before September 7, 1980, the veteran must have served at least 90 days of active military service, with at least one day during a period of wartime. Veterans who enlisted after September 7, 1980, must have served either for a continuous 24-month period or for the full period of duty to which they were ordered to active duty. For example, a veteran discharged because of a hardship or a service-related disability does not have to meet the 24-month requirement.

Countable income includes virtually all the income of the veteran except for public assistance. Note that income includes disability benefits and retirement benefits including pensions. Not included are Supplemental Security Income (SSI) or food stamps. Unreimbursed medical care expenses that have been paid and that exceed 5 percent of the pension's maximum benefit are deducted from countable income.[9] What is considered allowable medical expenses is quite expansive and includes caregiver expenses (even if provided by a family member other than a spouse), assisted living fees, nursing home fees, health care premiums, prescription drugs, long-term care premiums, incontinence products, vitamin supplements, and over-the-counter drugs.[10]

When reporting income, the veteran must provide the gross income amount, including projected income for the next 12 months from any interest-bearing account and distributions from IRAs or other tax-deferred accounts even if the distribution includes the return of principal. All Social Security benefits are included without subtracting any deduction to pay the premium for Medicare Part B (that payment, however, can be deducted as a non-reimbursed medical expense).[11]

Trust property is counted to the extent that it distributes funds to the veteran or if the veteran can direct the funds in the trust to be used for their benefit.[12] Thus, assets held by a trust with the power to make discretionary distributions to the veteran are not counted as assets of the veteran. However, the entire value of a special needs trust are counted as assets because the assets are available for the veteran's support.[13] Because there is no penalty for gifting away assets, a veteran could transfer assets into an irrevocable trust that is solely for the benefit of their children and grandchildren and thereby reduce countable assets to an acceptable level.

No pension will be awarded if the veteran has sufficient assets to provide for their own maintenance.[14] Excessive net worth has no fixed definition,[15] but the VA typically begins to raise the issue if a single veteran has more than $50,000 in assets or a married veteran has more than $80,000. Spousal assets are included in the calculation, but certain assets are specifically excluded from the calculation of net worth, including the primary residence and personal effects.[16] Jointly held assets

---

9. *Id.* § 1503(a).
10. 38 C.F.R. § 3.272(g).
11. Op. Gen. Counsel, Precedent 1-97 (U.S. Dep't of Veterans Affairs, Jan. 8, 1997).
12. Op. Gen. Counsel, Precedent 72-90 (U.S. Dep't of Veterans Affairs, July 18, 1990).
13. Op. Gen. Counsel, Precedent 33-97 (U.S. Dep't of Veterans Affairs, Aug. 29, 1997).
14. 38 C.F.R. § 3.274(a).
15. 38 U.S.C. § 1522.
16. 38 C.F.R. § 3.275(b).

are counted to the extent of the veteran's ownership share.[17] Whether assets are "excessive" depends on whether the veteran's assets are sufficient to their basic needs for a reasonable period of time. Therefore, the individual's life expectancy, countable income, number of dependents, rate of depletion, and unusual medical expenses are all considered.[18]

Assuming the veteran qualifies for a pension, the amount is determined by subtracting the countable income from the Maximum Annual Pension Rate (MAPR) divided by 12 to determine the monthly benefit. In 2017, the MAPR for a veteran with no dependents was $12,907, meaning that the maximum monthly benefit was $1,076. The pension is reduced to less than $100 per month if the veteran is receiving Medicaid and residing in a long-term care facility.[19] A veteran with a spouse may be eligible for a pension up to $16,902 in 2017.

A veteran can apply for a pension by completing VA Form 21-534EZ, "Application for DIC, Death Pension, and/or Accrued Benefits" and mailing it to the Pension Management Center that serves the veteran's state of residence.

B. Aid and Attendance

The aid and attendance[20] benefit is available to veterans who are eligible for a pension and who meet the following five criteria:

1. Ninety days of active service, one day of which must have been during wartime (see Section II.A. for list of wartime periods)
2. Have limited income and assets
3. Were not dishonorably discharged
4. Over the age of 65 or permanently and totally disabled
5. Have need for regular aid and attendance[21]

The need for aid and attendance is not required to be constant, but only regular. That requirement can be met by establishing that the individual resides in a nursing home, is blind or nearly blind, or is significantly disabled so as to require regular aid and attendance.[22] The proof of the latter will usually require the submission of a physician's affidavit indicating the need for assistance as well as evidence of the receipt of such assistance, such as an invoice from a home health agency or from an assisted living facility. Regular need for medical care, including assistance with prosthetic appliances, is also grounds for aid and attendance.[23]

---

17. *Id.*

18. *Id.* § 3.275(b).

19. *Id.* § 3.551(i).

20. http://www.military.com/benefits/veteran-benefits/aid-attendance-and-house-bound -benefits.html.

21. For information about Veteran benefits, see http://www.veteransaidbenefit.org/eligibility _aid_attendance_pension_benefit.htm.

22. 38 U.S.C. § 3.351(c)(1); 38 C.F.R. §§ 3.23(d)(2), 3.351.

23. 38 C.F.R. § 3.352.

If the veteran seeking aid and attendance benefits is over age 65 and lives in a nursing home, it is likely that they receive or soon expect to receive Medicaid reimbursement for the cost of the nursing home. If they live in a nursing home and receive Medicaid, their monthly aid and attendance benefit is reduced to less than $100 a month.[24]

C. Housebound Benefits

Veterans who have a disability that makes them eligible for a pension also qualify for housebound benefits if they are permanently disabled and totally disabled.[25] Housebound benefits are paid in addition to a VA pension, but a veteran cannot receive both aid and attendance and housebound benefits; rather the veteran will be paid the higher benefit of the two.

D. Pension Benefits for Surviving Spouses and Dependents

Surviving spouses[26] and unmarried, dependent children of deceased veterans may be eligible for pension benefits known as "death pensions."[27] The unmarried dependent child must be under the age of 18, in school and under the age of 23, or be incapable of self-support since before the age of 18. To qualify, the deceased veteran must have served at least one day of active military service during a war-time period, at least 90 days of active military service (24 months if the veteran entered active service after September 7, 1980) or the full period of required active duty, and received a discharge that was not dishonorable. Like a veteran, the surviving spouse or dependent child is subject to the annual countable income limit, with the addition that the unreimbursed final medical and burial expenses of the deceased veteran are deductible from countable income. Like veterans, they too cannot have excessive net worth.[28]

In addition to the death pension, a surviving spouse or unmarried, dependent child may also be eligible for aid and attendance or housebound benefits. Marriage by the surviving spouse or dependent child terminates the benefits.

III. Compensation for Disability

A veteran can receive lifetime compensation for injuries suffered while on active duty. The amount of compensation depends on the severity of the injury or disability; the age of the veteran is not relevant. All veterans with a discharge other than dishonorable are eligible if they suffer from a disability that was incurred

---

24. *Id.* § 3.551(i).
25. *Id.* § 3.350.
26. The marriage must have occurred before a specified date that is determined based on the period of wartime service. 38 U.S.C. § 1541(f).
27. *Id.* § 1541.
28. *Id.* § 1543.

during service or was the result of an aggravation of a preexisting injury or disease. No compensation is paid if the disability was a result of the veteran's willful misconduct or abuse of alcohol or drugs.[29]

The veteran must have incurred the disability "in the line of duty," meaning during the period of military service. Any disability incurred or aggravated during that time frame will be grounds for compensation. A veteran whose knee was injured playing recreational softball while in the service is just as eligible for disability compensation as a veteran whose knee was injured in combat.

There are five ways that a disability can be service connected.

First, if the condition was incurred or aggravated during the veteran's service. A disability can be an in-service disability, if the current disability was chronic, or if the symptoms caused by the original disability are consistently recurrent.

Second, a condition that preexisted the veteran's service that was aggravated during service is service connected if the increase in disability exceeded the natural progression of the condition and not just a temporary worsening of symptoms.

Third, there is a presumption of a service connection for certain conditions that were not manifested during service. For example, if the veteran served in Vietnam, certain tropical diseases such as dysentery, malaria, and yellow fever are considered to be service related even if there is a lack of evidence that establishes that they were incurred while the veteran was in service.

Fourth, if the disability is a secondary result of another service-oriented condition, the disability is considered to be service connected.

Finally, a disabling condition that was a consequence of any VA-provided health care is considered to be service related. For claims arising after September 1, 1997, there must be proof of VA fault or negligence in the provision of the care.

There is no "statute of limitations" on applying for compensation for a service-related disability. The claim is never "time barred." Many veteran claims, however, fail because the veteran cannot prove that the disability was service connected. The surest way to prove the disability is by evidence in the veteran's service medical records that substantiates the claim. Even if those records do not help, the VA presumes that certain disabilities are service connected. For example, multiple sclerosis is presumed to be service connected if it is contracted within seven years of the veteran's separation from service.[30] Exposure to radiation during the period of service or having been a prisoner of war also creates a presumption of a service-related cause of disability for many conditions.[31] Even without such a presumption, to establish the service-related cause of a disability, a veteran can introduce medical evidence, lay testimony, and even testimony from those with whom the veteran served.

If the VA agrees that the disability was service related, it must establish the "effective date" for that disability. The benefits begin with the effective date of the disability. The degree or level of disability determines the amount of the

---

29. *Id.* § 1110; 38 C.F.R. § 3.303.
30. 38 U.S.C. § 1112(a)(4).
31. *Id.* § 1112; 38 C.F.R. § 3.309.

compensation benefit. The VA uses a disability percentile schedule to determine the disability level ranging from zero, or no disability, to 100 percent, or total disability. The disability percentages measure the impairment of a veteran's average earning capacity and are divided into increments of 10 percent, with the monthly benefit increasing as the percentage increases. Higher benefits are paid for listed anatomical losses.[32]

Veterans with extreme disabilities, including those who are housebound, or who need regular aid and assistance, are eligible for supplemental benefits. These payments are collectively known as Special Monthly Compensation (SMC).

A veteran who is totally disabled will have a 100 percent disability rating. Alternatively, the veteran may be classified as having individual unemployability (IU) and so be granted a 100 percent disability rating.[33] To qualify for IU status, the individual veteran must have at least a 60 percent disability rating, or if the veteran has two or more disabilities, the combined rating must be 70 percent or more. A veteran may be considered unemployable even though an average person with the same disability would still be able to secure gainful employment because the IU standard takes into account personal circumstances such as the veteran's education and prior employment history. The VA, however, may not consider the veteran's age or non-service-connected conditions when attempting to determine eligibility for IU benefits.

A veteran can receive both VA disability and Social Security disability benefits. The two programs, however, do not have the same definition of complete disability. The VA defines it as the veteran being completely unable to work. However, Social Security defines it on its website as follows:

- You cannot do work that you did before;
- We decide that you cannot adjust to other work because of your medical condition(s); and
- Your disability has lasted or is expected to last for at least one year or to result in death.[34]

Therefore, merely because a veteran is receiving Social Security disability benefits is no guarantee that the veteran will qualify as disabled for purposes of VA individual unemployability benefits. Moreover, to qualify for VA benefits, the veteran must prove that the disability is service related.

Disability compensation is also available to surviving, unmarried spouses and dependent children if the veteran has been found to be totally disabled for at least ten years before death or five years before death if the disability has been determined before the veteran has been found totally disabled before discharge from active duty. The surviving spouse must also have been married to the veteran

32. http://www.benefits.va.gov/COMPENSATION/types-disability.asp.
33. http://www.benefits.va.gov/COMPENSATION/claims-special-individual_unemployability.asp.
34. http://www.ssa.gov/planners/disability/dqualify4.html.

for at least one year, had a child with the veteran, or married the veteran within 15 years after the veteran's discharge from military service.[35]

IV. Other Benefits

If a veteran's death was the result of a service-connected disability or if the veteran died while on active duty, an allowance up to $2,000 for burial expenses is provided, plus limited reimbursement for associated expenses. Veterans receiving compensation or pension benefits who died from a non-service-connected disability are entitled to a burial allowance of up to $300 and up to $700 if at the time of death they were hospitalized in a facility operated by the Veterans Administration. Also, veterans and certain family members are entitled to be buried in a national cemetery.

The VA is required to furnish medical care for veterans with a service-connected disability, for veterans who are entitled to disability compensation, for former prisoners of war, and for veterans exposed to a toxic substance or radiation.

Veterans with non-service-connected disabilities are eligible for VA medical assistance only if they are unable to afford medical care. A veteran is unable to pay for medical care it they are receiving pension benefits or if their income is below the VA income guidelines. Veterans with non-service-connected disabilities and those with incomes higher than the threshold previously described "may" receive care at VA hospitals or nursing homes depending on the availability of resources and facilities. In reality, there is almost no likelihood of there being available resources and facilities.

Under appropriate conditions, the VA will provide disabled veterans with automobiles and adaptive equipment, trained guide dogs for the visually impaired, or prosthetic devices and rehabilitative aids.

V. Applications and Appeals

A veteran seeking a pension or disability compensation must file VA Form 21-526, Veteran's Application for Compensation and/or Pension, at the nearest VA regional office. If the VA approves the request for a pension, the recipient also can seek aid and attendance or household benefits by writing to the same regional office and requesting those benefits. The veteran must supply supporting medical evidence of the need for personal assistance. Typically this will be a physician's report stating that the veteran cannot independently perform one or more activities of daily living.

---

35. 38 C.F.R. § 3.54.

If the veteran has applied for disability compensation, the regional office will have a veterans service representative (VSR) contact the veteran to arrange for the veteran to be examined by a VA physician. After the examination, a rating VSR in the regional office examines the veteran's file. The VSR determines the percentage of disability, if any, and its effective date. A veteran who disagrees with the disability rating or the effective day has a right to appeal.

An appeal is commenced by filing within one year from the date of the decision a Notice of Disagreement with the VA explaining exactly why the veteran believes the regional office decision was in error.[36] Failing to meet the one-year deadline is an absolute bar to the right to appeal. If the veteran appeals, the regional office responds by mailing the veteran a statement of the case explaining why it is disallowing the claim and appeal.[37] It also sends a substantive appeal form to the veteran who can file it to request a non-adversarial personal appearance either with the regional office or with the VA Board of Veterans Appeals. The veteran must return the substantive appeal form within the later of 60 days from when it was mailed or one year from the date the VA mailed its original opinion.[38] Alternatively, the veteran can file a formal appeal to the VA Board of Veterans Appeals to make a de novo determination as to the merit of the veteran's claim. The veteran has the right to introduce new evidence to the board. If denied by the board, the veteran can ask the regional office to reopen the claim because of a showing of new evidence, ask the board to reconsider because it made an error, or file an appeal with the U.S. Court of Appeals for Veterans Claims within 120 days after the board mailed its decision.[39] From there, the veteran can appeal to the U.S. Court of Appeals for the Federal Circuit.[40]

A veteran is permitted to hire an attorney once the veteran has filed the Notice of Disagreement objecting to the decision of the regional office.[41] (Prior to that level of review, a veteran can be represented by a pro bono attorney.) However, only attorneys who have been accredited by the VA are permitted to represent veterans in their claims for benefits.[42] This permits the VA to screen out disbarred or suspended attorneys and to oversee the attorney's fee arrangement.[43] To be accredited, an attorney must have a thorough knowledge of VA disability benefits available to veterans or their survivors and must meet the VA continuing legal education requirements. The accreditation process is started by filing VA Form 21a with the VA Office of General Counsel in Washington, DC, along with three character references.

---

36. *Id.* § 7105.
37. *Id.*
38. *Id.* § 20.302.
39. 38 U.S.C. § 7292.
40. *Id.* § 5904(a)(5).
41. *Id.*
42. *Id.*
43. *Id.* § 5904(a)(5).

VI. Mentally Incapacitated Veterans

Some veterans have lost mental capacity or, as the VA terms it, are mentally incompetent.[44] The rating agency that determines the benefits that a veteran is entitled to has the sole authority to determine whether a veteran is incompetent for purposes of deciding whether the veteran has the competency to accept and manage the distribution of benefits. If the veteran is found to be incompetent, the VA will develop information about the veteran's social and economic circumstances, appoint a federal fiduciary, or appoint the spouse of the veteran to receive the payments to the veteran.[45] Note that the VA does not have to recognize an agent appointed under a power of attorney executed by the veteran.[46]

The fiduciary appointed by the VA has complete control over the payments made by the VA. For their efforts, the fiduciary is eligible to receive a commission of up to 4 percent of the value of the annual benefits.[47] The veteran or the veteran's agent under power of attorney has the right to appeal the VA fiduciary appointment.[48]

VII. Attorney Fees

Fees can be awarded only to accredited attorneys for their services in representing a veteran who has been denied benefits for which they applied.[49] The attorney, however, can only be paid a fee if they have successfully complied with the power of attorney requirements found in the federal regulations.[50] The fee must be reasonable and can be based on a fixed fee, an hourly rate, or a percentage of the benefits recovered.[51] What is a reasonable fee is based on the extent and type of the services, the time spent, the level of skill of the attorney, the results achieved, the level of review of the claim, and what other attorneys charge for similar services.[52]

---

44. *Id.* § 3.353(a).
45. *Id.* §§ 3.12, 3.353(b).
46. Solze v. Shinseki, 2012 WL 4801411 (Oct. 10, 2012).
47. 38 U.S.C. § 13.64(b).
48. Freeman v. Shinseki, 24 Vet. App. 404 (2011).
49. 38 C.F.R. § 14.636(b).
50. *Id.* §§ 14.631, 14.636(c).
51. *Id.* § 14.636(e).
52. 38 C.F.R. § 14.636

Statutes That Protect the Elderly | 7

I. Introduction

Several federal statutes protect the elderly in regard to employment discrimination and housing. This chapter describes those laws. Many states have enacted similar acts that track the federal laws or expand upon them. The federal Age Discrimination in Employment Act, though including many who are too young to be considered elderly, nevertheless was enacted specifically to protect older workers from discrimination because of their age. In contrast, the Americans with Disabilities Act (ADA) was passed to protect all of those with disabilities, not just the elderly. However, because so many elderly are disabled, either because they were disabled when younger or they became disabled when elderly, the ADA has particular importance to them. Finally, the Fair Housing Act, although targeted at eliminating discrimination in housing based on race, religion, sex, or the presence of children, nevertheless offers the elderly the right to live in age-segregated housing.

II. Age Discrimination in Employment Act

The 1960s saw the federal "War on Poverty" that was responsible for the enactment of a number of social programs designed to ameliorate poverty. At the time, poverty among those age 65 and older was much higher than that of the general population. One cause of that poverty was the result of many employers subjecting their employees to mandatory retirement on account of age, which resulted in forcing older workers out of the workforce. As part of the attack on elderly poverty, in 1967 Congress passed the Age Discrimination in Employment Act (ADEA)[1] to help promote employment of older workers by barring any employment decision—hiring, firing or promoting—based on the age of the individual. For example, no longer could individuals be forced to retire from a job merely because they had reached the age of 65. The act also applies to employment agencies and labor unions.[2]

Although an employer cannot fire an employee merely because of age, the employer can terminate an employee who is not adequately performing the job even if the reason for the sub-par performance arises from the individual's age. For example, the employer cannot fire or demote an employee because the employee is age 70 or because the employer would prefer that a younger employee occupy the position. However, if the employee can no longer physically perform the job requirements, even if that is due to the employee growing older, the employer may terminate the employee. Of course, if sued, the employer may have to produce evidence that the termination was due to the employee's job performance and not merely because the employer considered the employee to be "too old."

When originally enacted, the ADEA applied only to workers between the ages of 40 and 65. Today the act applies to workers age 40 and older. In 1974, the act was extended to apply to federal, state, and local government employees, but a Supreme Court opinion, citing the 11th Amendment, prohibited lawsuits by individuals against state and local governments. The act still applies to state and local employees, but only the federal Equal Employment Opportunity Commission (EEOC) can bring a lawsuit alleging a violation of the ADEA by a state or local government.[3]

The ADEA applies to all private sector employers with 20 or more full-time employees. (Employers with 20 or fewer employees may be subject to state laws that bar age discrimination in employment.) The employer must have 20 or more employees for each working day of the week for 20 weeks (not necessarily consecutive). Part-time employees are not counted in the determination of whether the employer is subject to the ADEA, but if the employer is covered by the ADEA, all employees including part-time and temporary employees are protected.[4] The act applies to the domestic operations of foreign employers and to U.S. citizens who work abroad for U.S. corporations.[5]

---

1. 29 U.S.C. §§ 621–634
2. 29 U.S.C. § 629(b), (c).
3. Kimel v. Fla. Bd. of Regents, 528 U.S. 62 (2000).
4. 29 U.C.S. § 630(b).
5. Id. § 630(f).

The ADEA only protects employees. It does not protect independent contractors, partners, directors, or owners of businesses. The determination of who is an independent contractor depends on the particular facts and circumstances and has been the subject of considerable litigation. Who is a partner has proven very troublesome. Smaller entities with a limited number of partners who share the traditional partner arrangement where responsibilities and pay are based upon shares are considered true partnerships. Even larger entities, such as law firms, can be partnerships whose partners are not employees and so the firm can subject the partners to mandatory retirement at a specified age. But other large entities that purport to be partnerships, particularly large accounting and law firms, have been the subject of litigation when some of the alleged partners assert that they are employees despite having the title of partner. For example, a 2002 case held that a law firm of over 500 partners may have violated the ADEA when it demoted 32 of its equity partners to of-counsel status.[6] Although the 32 may have been partners under state law, it did not follow that under the ADEA the 32 were partners and not employees. Even a shareholder-director may be an employee. An individual's employment status is determined by a set of factors developed by the EEOC that can be applied whenever there is doubt as to whether an individual is an employee:

- Whether the organization can fire the individual or set work rules;
- Whether and to what extent the organization supervises the individual's work;
- Whether and to what extent the individual is able to influence the organization;
- Whether the parties expected the individual to be an employee; and
- Whether the individual shares in the profits, losses, and liabilities of the organization.[7]

The ADEA does not prevent compulsory retirement of employees who are age 65 or older and for the two years immediately before retirement who were "employed in a bona fide executive or high policy making position" and were entitled to an immediate non-forfeitable annual retirement benefit of at least $44,000.[8] A "bona fide" executive is a manager who has oversight responsibilities. A "high policymaking" position includes non-managers, such as a chief economist, who have significant influence in creating policy. The ADEA also does not apply to firefighters or law enforcement officers, which includes police officers and prison guards.[9]

---

6. Equal Emp't Opportunity Comm'n v. Sidley Austin Brown & Wood, 315 F.3d 696 (7th Cir. 2002).
7. Clackamas Gastroenterology Assocs., P.C. v. Wells, 538 U.S. 440, 449 (2003).
8. 29 U.S.C. § 631(c)(1).
9. *Id.* § 623(j).

III. Proving Age Discrimination in Employment

The employee who alleges age discrimination has the burden of proof. The discrimination because of age may take the form of refusing to hire, terminating the employee, forcing the employee to retire, failing to promote, paying less, changing the nature of the job requirements, or in the language or manner used to advertise an available position. The majority of complaints of violations of the ADEA arise from claims of termination or being forced to retire on account of age.

A. Plaintiff's Burden

The surest way to win a claim of an ADEA violation is to provide direct evidence of discrimination. Often communications such as e-mails between the employee's immediate supervisor and higher management yield evidence of discrimination like "she's too old" or "he is over the hill." Often the statements do not directly relate to the action taken against the employee, but nevertheless are probative evidence, such as "he is getting older and really slowing down" or "at her age she doesn't appeal to our customers." Some age derogatory statements that were cited in some earlier cases, however, were held not to be evidence of age discrimination; they include when a company official said he liked his salespeople "young, mean and lean"[10] or when a supervisor stated that he "needed younger blood."[11]

Often the employee will not be able to uncover statements that indicate age bias was the reason for termination or other action. In response, courts permit employees to establish a prima facie case if they can prove four elements that were originally established in the Supreme Court case of *McDonnell Douglas Corp. v. Green*,[12] which involved a discrimination claim under Title VII rather than an ADEA claim. The elements necessary to establish a prima facie ADEA claim are as follows:

1. The individual belonged to the protected class—was age 40 or older;
2. The job the individual applied for, or was employed in and was qualified for, was a job for which the employer was looking to hire;
3. Despite the individual's qualifications, they were rejected, demoted, passed over, or otherwise discriminated against; and
4. After the discriminatory act the job or position remained open, and the employer continued to seek applicants with qualifications similar to the plaintiff's or filled the position with another employee with comparable qualifications.

If the plaintiff establishes a prima facie case, the defendant has the burden of going forward.

10. Carpenter v. Am. Excelsior Co., 650 F. Supp. 933, 938 (E.D. 1984).
11. Barnes v. Sw. Forest Indus., Inc., 814 F.2d 607, 612 (11th Cir. 1987).
12. McDonnell Douglas Corp. v. Green, 411 U.S. 792, 802 (1973).

If the plaintiff provides proof of age discrimination, the defendant employer can counter by offering proof that it would have taken the same action in regard to the plaintiff even if it had not taken the plaintiff's age into account.[13] The plaintiff, in turn, can claim that the reason offered by the employer, though legitimate, was not the true reason for the action but was only a pretext. As put by one court, "Pretext exists when an employer does not honestly represent its reasons for the dismissal."[14] But if the plaintiff claims the employer explanation is pretextual, the plaintiff still has to prove discriminatory actions to win an ADEA claim. Proof that the employer's explanation was false does not establish the claim of age discrimination absent evidence of age discrimination.[15] Finally, the plaintiff must prove that age discrimination was not just a motivating factor but the "but-for" cause of the adverse employment action.[16]

B. Summary Judgment

Many ADEA cases turn on whether the plaintiff can survive a defendant's motion for summary judgment. Under Federal Rule of Civil Procedure 56(c), summary judgment must be entered into against a party who fails to make a showing sufficient to establish an element essential to that party's case. Employers often move for summary judgment based on the claim that they have produced evidence of a nondiscriminatory motive for the alleged age discriminatory action. If the motion for summary judgment is denied, employers often settle the case rather than risk the possibility of a more onerous judgment should they lose at trial.

To withstand summary judgment when the employer has articulated a legitimate reason for its actions, the plaintiff is required to produce something more than a prima facie case. The plaintiff must offer some evidence that the employer's explanation was a mere pretext for the discriminatory act. However, it is not a defense for the employer to claim that the plaintiff was replaced or the person hired was age 40 or older. So long as the other employee is younger than the plaintiff, the action may have violated the ADEA.[17] Retaliation against an employee who has made a claim of age discrimination also violates the ADEA.[18]

C. The Bona Fide Occupational Qualification Exception

An employer can legally discriminate on the basis of age "where age is a bona fide occupational qualification reasonably necessary to the normal operation of the particular business."[19] This exemption has been held to apply to airline

---

13. Price Waterhouse v. Hopkins, 490 U.S. 228 (1988).
14. Miller v. Eby Realty Grp. LLC, 396 F.3d 1105, 1111 (5th Cir. 2005).
15. St. Mary's Honor Ctr. v. Hicks, 509 U.S. 502 (1983).
16. Gross v. FBL Fin. Services, Inc., 557 U.S. 167 (2009).
17. O'Connor v. Consol. Coin Caterers Corp., 571 U.S. 308 (1996).
18. Gomez-Perez v. Potter, Postmaster General, 553 U.S. 474 (2008).
19. 29 U.S.C. § 623(f)(3).

pilots[20] and bus drivers.[21] In the main, however, courts have not been sympathetic to employers' claims that they must rely on the arbitrary factor of age because they have no other way of determining or measuring whether an employee is capable of effectively and safely performing their job. Merely because reliance on the employee's age is more convenient, economical, or even reasonable is not enough. The employer must offer compelling proof of the need to rely on age as a proxy for safety or other job requirements.

IV. Waiver and Release

Employers who wish to legally terminate an employee who is age 40 or older and so protected by the ADEA may fear being sued on grounds of age discrimination. The employer, who wants an employee to retire, can encourage them to do so by offering termination pay or additional retirement benefits. In return, the employee will sign a waiver of their right to later sue the employer for age discrimination. In requesting the waiver, the employer is not admitting that it may have violated the ADEA. The employer is just trying to avoid costly litigation and bad publicity.

The ADEA specifically provides for the right of an employee who voluntarily retires to waive their rights under the statute in exchange for consideration.[22] The waiver must be in writing, be understandable to the average employee, must specifically refer to the waiver of ADEA rights and claims, and must advise the employee to consult with an attorney before signing the waiver. The employee must have at least 21 days to consider the agreement (45 days if part of an exit incentive program also offered to other employees). Finally, the employee must have at least seven days in which to revoke the agreement after signing it.

V. Enforcement Procedures, Remedies, and State Law Remedies

Employees or job applicants who believe that they have been the victims of age discrimination cannot file suit until after pursuing all administrative remedies. Federal law requires an individual to first file a complaint with the state agency that enforces that state's anti-age discrimination statute, if one exists.[23] Next, the individual must file a charge with the EEOC within 180 days following the alleged discrimination or 300 days if the claim occurs in a state that has an anti-age discrimination statute or involves employment by the federal government.[24] After

---

20. Rasberg v. Nationwide Life Ins. Co., 671 F. Supp. 494 (S.D. Ohio 1987).
21. Usery v. Tamiami Trail Tours, 531 F.2d 224 (5th Cir. 1976).
22. 29 U.S.C. § 626(f).
23. *Id.* §§ 200–219.
24. *Id.* § 626(d).

filing the charge with the EEOC, the employee must wait 60 days before they can file a private lawsuit. The delay is intended to allow the EEOC time to attempt to resolve the dispute. If the EEOC cannot reach a resolution and decides to sue the employer, the employee may not pursue private litigation.[25] If however, the EEOC terminates action against the employer, the employee, having waited the 60 days without the EEOC suing, but not more than 90 days, may then sue and continue that suit even if the EEOC should later also sue.

If the employee wins, the ADEA provides for a variety of remedies including reinstatement; back pay, including the value of lost employee benefits; front pay, a substitute for lost future earnings; and injunctions against future violations.[26] The employee, however, has the duty to mitigate damages, including accepting a reasonable offer of reemployment with the employer or by taking another job comparable to the former position that was lost. There is no right to punitive damages, but if the discrimination was found to be willful, the award of back pay is doubled. Successful plaintiffs are usually awarded attorney's fees.

Many states have anti-age discrimination laws that parallel the ADEA, but often apply to employers with fewer employees than required by the ADEA. State law may also provide additional remedies including punitive damages and recovery for pain and suffering that may have arisen from the employer committing the tort of the intentional infliction of emotional distress.

VI. Americans with Disabilities Act

Originally enacted in 1990 and significantly amended in 2008, the Americans with Disabilities Act (ADA) was enacted to redress and reduce prejudice against those with physical and mental disabilities and to remove societal, institutional, and legal barriers to their full participation in American life.[27] Congress intended the ADA to eliminate discrimination against those with disabilities, defined as any physical or mental impairment that substantially limits one or more of the individual's major life activities.[28] The ADA applies to employment, public transportation, and public accommodation by private entities.

For older individuals, who have higher rates of disability than the general population, the ADA can be an important source of protection and a path to a better life. Title I of the act prohibits discrimination in employment against individuals with disabilities. Employers with 15 or more employees are required to make "reasonable accommodations" to the work environment to remove barriers to employment for a "qualified individual with a disability" as long as the accommodation

---

25. *Id.* § 626(c)(1).
26. *Id.* § 626(b).
27. 42 U.S.C. §§ 12101–12213.
28. *Id.* § 12102(2)(A).

does not cause the employer "unreasonable hardship."[29] In 2008, in response to Supreme Court rulings that narrowly interpreted who the statute protected, Congress enacted amendments that broadened who is covered and what kind and degree of disability qualify for protection.

The 2008 amendments to the act make clear that the determination of whether an individual is disabled, meaning having an impairment that limits a major life activity, must be conducted without regard to efforts at mitigation of the disability except for the use of eyeglasses or contact lenses intended to fully correct the person's vision. For example, a plaintiff with serious back pain who takes pain medication may still be disabled.[30] The original ADA defined the term "disabled" as a physical or mental impairment that "substantially limits one or more major life activities."[31] Even after the 2008 amendments, however, a hearing problem, for example, was not considered an impairment, even if it resulted in the individual being unable to perform a particular job if it otherwise was not serious enough to severely restrict his ability to work.[32] The 2008 amendments expanded the definition of disabled to include impairments with eating, sleeping, standing, lifting, bending, reading, thinking, concentrating, and communicating, and impairments with the "operation of major life functions" such as brain, respiratory, or bladder functions.[33] A brain tumor, for example, was held to impair a major life activity.[34] Although temporary or transitory impairments are not protected, the disability need not be permanent. For example, a broken leg and tendon injury, which caused the employee to be unable to walk for seven months, were found to be a disability even though only temporary.[35] The act also protects persons who are "regarded as" disabled but who do not have a disability regardless of whether the impairment is perceived to substantially limit the person in a major life activity.[36] For example, an employer violated the ADA when it fired an employee with Parkinson's disease when the employer regarded the employee as being disabled even though the employee was able to perform the essential functions of his job.[37] Finally, retaliation against an employee who alleges a violation of the ADA is a violation of the act.[38]

An employer may not discriminate against a qualified individual with a disability, but the individual must prove his or her qualification for the position. A qualified individual with a disability is someone who with or without reasonable accommodation can perform the essential functions of the job. An example of someone who was not qualified for the job was a plaintiff suffering from cancer

---

29. *Id.* § 12112(b)(5)(A).
30. Molina v. DSI Renal, Inc., 2013 WL 29348 (W.D. Tex. Jan. 4, 2012).
31. 42 U.S.C. § 12102(1).
32. Cocharan v. Holder, 2010 WL 447013 (E.D. Va. Feb. 1, 2010).
33. 42 U.S.C. § 12102(2).
34. Meinelt v. P.F. Chang's China Bistro, Inc., 787 F. Supp. 2d 643 (S.D. Tex. 2011).
35. Summers v. Altarum Inst. Corp., 740 F.3d 325 (4th Cir. 2014).
36. 42 U.S.C. § 12102(3).
37. Williams v. Phoenix Specialty Mfg. Co., 513 F.3d 378 (4th Cir. 2008).
38. *See, e.g.*, Wofsy v. Palmshores Ret. Cmty., 285 F. App'x 631 (11th Cir. 2008).

and coronary bypass surgery who could not walk or breathe comfortably.[39] An employee of a drugstore with osteoarthritis could not perform an essential job function even though she could sit in a chair as a cashier and perform that function because that job also required the employee to stock shelves and mop floors, jobs that she could not perform even with an accommodation.[40]

VII. Federal Fair Housing Act

As discussed in Chapter 8, Housing Choices, age-restricted housing is legally possible because the Federal Fair Housing Act, while outlawing most discrimination in housing, permits the sale and rental of housing specifically designed for and occupied by older persons.[41] The act does bar discrimination in housing on the basis of race, color, religion, sex, familial status, or national origin.[42] Familial status is defined as one or more individuals below the age of 18 who live with a parent or another person having legal custody of the child. It also includes pregnant women and those who are securing legal custody of an individual under the age of 18.

The act, however, creates an exception from the prohibition against discrimination against those under the age of 18 by legalizing "housing for older persons"[43] that in turn can come in either of two forms:

- Housing intended to be occupied only by those age 62 and older, or
- Housing in which at least 80 percent of the units are occupied by at least one person age 55 and older.[44]

Housing exclusively for those age 62 and older means just what it says; no one under the age of 62 can live there. Though this may sound desirable, a potential resident should consider whether circumstances might arise that would force them to move out. For example, a marriage to a spouse under the age of 62 would mean either not living with the spouse or moving out. Living with a partner or relative under the age of 62 would also be barred. If an adult child has a need to temporarily live with a parent, perhaps because of relocating due to divorce or unemployment, that would be prohibited unless the child were age 62 or older.

The less restrictive standard only requires 80 percent occupancy by at least one person age 55 or older. Although it is a more flexible standard, it may not house sufficient "old" residents to meet the desires of an older person who prefers living only with other elderly persons and wants to avoiding living near children, teenagers, and other younger residents. The "80 percent" standard requires that

39. Amsel v. Texas Water Dev. Bd., 464 F. App'x 395 (5th Cir. 2012).
40. EOC v. Eckerd Corp., 2012 WL 2568225 (N.D. Ga. July 2, 2012).
41. 42 U.S.C. § 3607(b)(1).
42. *Id.* § 3604(a).
43. *Id.* § 3607(b)(1).
44. *Id.* § 3607(2)(A) & (C).

the housing facility publish and adhere to policies and procedures that demonstrate the intent to meet the 80 percent requirement. The housing facility also must verify by surveys and affidavits that it is adhering to the 80 percent requirement.

The prospective buyer of age restricted housing should inspect the deed and any rules imposed by a lease, homeowners association or the condominium deed and declaration, as well as the rules of the condominium association to determine the extent of age restrictions in the use of the unit. For example, is an underage, overnight visitor permitted? A renter should demand to see the policies and procedures as well as the advertising for the facility to determine what standard of age discrimination the landlord applies to new residents.

An older resident of housing that claims to be open only to those age 62 and older, who finds that younger persons are residing in a unit (as opposed to merely being a temporary visitor, which may be permitted unless otherwise prohibited) may file a complaint with the local Office of Fair Housing and Equal Opportunity of the Department of Housing and Urban Development.[45] A resident of the 80 percent requirement can ask the landlord for proof that 80 percent of the units have at least one resident age 55 or older. If that proof is not provided, the resident can file a complaint with the local Office of Fair Housing and Equal Opportunity.

If the occupant of age-restricted housing is a renter, the lease will detail whether anyone under the age limit, such as a grandchild, may stay as a visitor and if so, for how long. Some age-restricted housing that is open only to those age 62 or older also bars anyone under age 62 from even being an overnight guest. If the occupants own their living units, the deeds should contain the age restriction, which can be removed only if all the unit owners agree. As for rental property, absent a provision in the lease provision, the landlord has no legal obligation to maintain the property as age restricted housing and has no obligation to continue to provide recreational facilities or services designed to appeal to older residents.

---

45. 24 C.F.R. § 103.10.

Post-Retirement Issues

Part II focuses on legal issues that arise for clients who are typically in their 70s. These clients often confront the need to reconsider their housing in light of their changing physical and mental capabilities. The practical and legal issues that arise when the client considers housing choices is described and alternative arrangements are discussed. Many older clients also own a vacation or weekend home. How to maintain and pass on that home are discussed in detail in Chapter 9. Next Chapter 10 explains how to arrange for the management of property owned by a client with diminished mental capacity. Chapter 11 describes how clients must also make plans for how their health care decisions will be made in the event that they lose the mental capacity to make those decisions. Finally, Part II concludes with Chapter 12, a description and analysis of long-term care insurance.

Housing Choices 8

I. Introduction—Housing Choice Determinates

Housing needs and realities change over time. Aging, with its inevitable physical and mental decline, gives rise to a need for housing that accommodates an individual's "new" realities. Those who fail to respond and adapt their housing to their changing needs not only face a diminished quality of life, but expose themselves to the risk of physical danger and social isolation. Simply put, appropriate housing is a key element of successful aging.

As individuals pass age 70, they must face up to the realities of growing older—loss of physical strength and vigor. Bones lose calcium and so become weaker and more prone to break, joints become stiff and even painful, muscle mass and strength decline, eyesight grows weaker, and hearing is dimmer. Although the degree and speed of physical decline varies greatly, in time, all who survive long enough will experience it to a greater or lesser extent.

Those who are willing to recognize their present and anticipated future physical decline often admit that it is a determinative factor in their choice of housing. For a homeowner, the loss of muscle strength has cascading effects. Climbing stairs becomes more difficult and is compounded by a decline in aerobic capacity and growing joint pain. Home maintenance grows more onerous. Lawn care changes from a way to be outdoors for a few hours to a difficult task that takes more and more time with each passing year. House cleaning changes from a chore to a burden with some aspects, such as moving furniture, becoming impossible. Climbing a ladder to clean out a gutter becomes a risky adventure. Carrying the laundry to the basement becomes a scary exercise in balance. In short, physical decline often means it is time for a home-owner to move to age-appropriate housing.

Age-appropriate housing refers to housing that meets the physical, social, emotional, and financial needs of the occupant. If housing is appropriate for an individual or couple, it adds to the quality of life. If it is inappropriate, it diminishes the quality of life and can even endanger the life of the occupant. Because the elderly vary so much in what they need and want, what is appropriate housing is highly individualistic, but three key factors are: age, the individual's health, and their financial resources.

The older the individual, the more likely that they may need to either move into different housing or pay for ever-increasing assistance for home maintenance and repairs. A decline in physical health translates into a need for housing that is accessible and less demanding. Mental decline may necessitate personal care, which suggests the need for supportive housing that is obtained either by moving to a facility that provides in-unit assistance or by employing personal aides in the current home. Choosing housing that is best for the individual will be constrained by what the individual can afford. For example, a desire to never move may not be possible if the individual cannot afford the ever-increasing costs of personal care and upkeep of the house.

As with so many life challenges, "experts" now advertise their availability to advise aging individuals on when they should move and where they should live. Their advice is based on their knowledge about the physical and mental aspects of aging and how that translates into appropriate housing. These experts also often suggest that the individual's financial planner be called in to discuss how much the individual can afford to spend on their current and probable future housing needs. The advisors may also claim detailed knowledge about what housing for the elderly is available in the community. It is likely, however, that a search of the Internet by the individual or the family could reveal the nearby townhouses, apartments, planned communities, or even towns that specialize in housing the elderly. If the client chooses to call on a senior housing specialist, be aware that some do not charge for their services; rather they are paid by the entity that provides the housing that is selected by the older individual. If, for example, the advisor recommends the individual move into an assisted living facility, the advisor will provide a list of possible facilities. Because the advisor may only get paid if the individual moves into a facility with which the advisor has a contractual arrangement, it is likely that the list of recommended facilities will include only those facilities.

A. Age

When considering what factors determine appropriate housing, age is a good starting point, but considered alone, it is only a crude indicator. Chronological age is deceptive, as individuals vary greatly in their physical and mental health. One person at age 75 can be frail and confused; another 75-year-old may be vigorous and clear minded. One who is age 80 may seem to have more in common with the "average" 70-year-old, whereas another 80-year-old may seem like the "average" 90-year-old. Rather than chronological age, it is "biological age" that is determinative; the person's physical and mental condition that determines what kind of housing is appropriate. But aging is real, and chronological age cannot be ignored. It is the proverbial canary in the coal mine that should alert individuals to the need to consider whether their current housing is appropriate and, if so, will it still be appropriate five or ten years from now.

B. Health

Health is often paramount in determining what is appropriate housing. The effect of physical health is obvious, as it determines, for example, whether stairs are acceptable and home maintenance is possible. The loss of physical strength and vigor are apparent. But often overlooked as creating a need for different housing is the loss of vision associated with glaucoma, cataracts, and, possibly the most destructive, progressive macular degeneration. The latter makes many household tasks impossible, from replacing a light bulb to paying a bill. Loss of hearing is also very common and can effect what is acceptable housing. An individual with a hearing loss may find it difficult to communicate with a spouse in a sprawling home or a person living alone may fear the existence of unheard dangers.

Although the need for a different kind of housing is often apparent, such as the need for housing without stairs for an older person with deteriorating knees, what may not be so obvious is how the individual's physical condition also determines whether the location of the housing is appropriate. Physical limitations or conditions can be a key factor in the decision of where to live. Individuals with progressive macular degeneration either cannot drive or soon will not be able to drive, which suggests they should live where driving a car is not an imperative or, in the alternative, be sure they live with someone who can drive and is willing to drive them about town as needed. Even whether a car service, such as Uber, is available may help determine where they can live. Individuals with chronic health conditions that require regular visits to health care providers should consider living close to those providers. And physical health is not measured only today, but it also includes the projected health over the next few years. The time to seek out appropriate housing is while an individual is still physically well enough to engage in the process of looking for housing that will be appropriate in light of their future physical condition.

Mental well-being is also critical to housing choices. Short-term memory loss is nearly universal among the elderly. It is not a sign of dementia and does not signal a loss of the ability to make rational decisions. But combined with a loss of physical vigor, short-term memory loss can cause many elderly to become stressed and anxious about making decisions or in dealing with the outside world, such as engaging someone to repair an appliance in the home. The combination of declining physical vigor, loss of vision and hearing, and short-term memory decline can result in maintaining a house difficult if not impossible.

The onset of dementia often forces a change in housing. Dementia and related mental diseases such as Parkinson's eventually make independent living, even in an apartment or condominium, impossible. The two most common forms of dementia are Alzheimer's, which is progressive and currently untreatable, and vascular dementia, which is the manifestation of a series of mini-strokes that cut off blood to small portions of the brain. Whatever the cause of the dementia, the result is the loss of brain function, including memory and executive functioning, which includes reasoning and problem solving. The result is that any individual diagnosed with dementia must adapt their housing situation to this unfortunate reality.

But it is not just the appearance of dementia, but also its future likelihood that must be considered in determining what is appropriate housing. With dementia rates climbing to as high as 40 percent after age 85, anyone age 80 or older ought to begin to consider whether their current housing will still be appropriate in the years to come.

C. Financial Resources

Financial resources play a critical role in what is appropriate housing because what is "appropriate" largely depends on what the individual can afford to spend on housing. Aging individuals must undertake a reasonable assessment of how many dollars they have available today—and in the years to come—to devote to their housing. The cost of housing is a function of three factors: first, the fair market value of the home; second, the annual out-of-pocket cost including taxes, repair, and maintenance, with the understanding that as time passes more of the maintenance and repair costs will change from do-it-yourself to purchased services; and third, the need to purchase supportive services ranging from housecleaning and homemaker services to personal care.

The fair market value of the home is best conceived of as capital dedicated to housing that results in foregoing a stream of income that could be obtained if that capital were invested. An older person who has retired and is living off of Social Security, a pension, and income from savings should make an honest assessment of whether the foregone stream of income that results from dedicating a sum of capital to housing makes sense. If the amount spent on housing is excessive in terms of an individual's other needs for income, the individual should consider relocating to less expensive housing in order to free up capital and thereby increase their investment income.

If the individual owns a house, in addition to the foregone income from the capital invested in the house, the individual must also consider the out-of-pocket costs such as property taxes, utilities, repair and maintenance, and the average annual cost of capital improvements. That, plus the lost investment income on the value of the house, represents the total annual income dedicated to housing. The amount is likely to rise over time. If it does not, it is likely due to the individual not adequately maintaining the property with the result that the "savings" in the cost of upkeep are more than offset by a decline in the fair market value of the property.

The upkeep cost of owning housing is often underestimated because homeowners typically invest their own time to maintain their property. Their ability to continue to maintain the property, however, is likely to diminish with age. Older homeowners often find themselves forced to pay for home maintenance and repairs that formerly they had done themselves. As a result, the out-of-pocket cost of the house increases over time and can dramatically increase if the homeowner suffers a physical or mental decline.

Estimation of the future cost of housing should take into account the cost of personal care. Along with age, dependency on others increases over time. Some elderly have spouses who will provide care as needed, but at some point both spouses may need assistance, or only one spouse will be alive. Others have children or grandchildren living nearby who provide assistance that ranges from providing transportation to more personal care such as helping the individual bathe. But in time the need for personal care can become too great for a spouse or family member to provide, thereby necessitating that the older person pay for their personal care. However, the cost of personal care provided in the home, which is usually preferred by an older individual, may not be affordable. If that is the case, a move to a facility, such as assisted living, may be unavoidable.

D. Spouse and Family Aspects

For those who never married and had no life partner, entering old age as a single person holds no surprises. Their greatest concern is that living alone puts them at risk if they should have a serious accident in the house or become too ill to access help. One solution is to create a support network that would respond if they should not be heard from for a period of time. For example, some older women create a morning telephone "tree" whereby A calls B who calls C who calls D who calls A. If C does not hear from B, she will either personally investigate why B did not call her or alert a neighbor of B or the authorities to visit B and see whether she needs assistance.

For those who have been married or have had a life partner, the death of that spouse or life partner (hereafter the term "spouse" will be used to include a life partner) can have serious repercussions, including as to what are appropriate housing choices. The death of a spouse can either encourage the survivor to remain in place because the house holds warm memories or it can cause them to move to avoid the pain of what has been lost. Others may at last be free to move where they have always wanted to live but were prevented from doing so because the deceased spouse refused to move. For some, financial and practical considerations are paramount. The house that was shared by two is too expensive to maintain by one or the loss of the spouse meant a loss of income that must be replaced by devoting less capital to housing and more to income-producing investments.

Family can play a significant role for many when making a choice in housing. It is estimated that two-thirds of older persons live within a 30-minute drive of one of their children, with others living close to siblings or other relatives. If the child moves away, the parent may follow. Others are willing to live far from their children but choose housing with an expectation that the children and grandchildren will frequently visit. To accommodate an extended family, older persons buy or continue to live in a house larger than they need or even purchase a second, vacation home, thereby allocating a significant part of their capital to housing. Whether such a choice is sensible depends upon the extent to which the older person is willing to sacrifice disposable income in favor of having "excess" housing—a large home or a vacation home—that will be used by visiting children for only part of the year.

E. Moving Because of Recreation or Because of Weather, Safety, and Transportation Concerns

A minority of the elderly relocate to a different region, usually soon after retirement. The reasons are typically for better weather, more recreational opportunities, to be nearer to family, or to live in a region with a lower cost of living or lower taxes. Others move into age-restricted housing including retirement communities located where the weather is better, to housing that offers more social activities, or to housing designed for older residents with physical limitations. For some, a move results in purchasing less expensive housing and so freeing up capital. Others become "snowbirds" who split time between two residences; some with the intention of eventually moving full time to the warm weather residence.

Some elderly move but remain in the same region. Often the reasons for moving involve safety and transportation issues. A lack of security or an unsafe housing situation is unacceptable to the elderly with the financial resources to solve the problem. Security refers to the safety of the home or building in which the older person lives. Some find that a single-family house that seemed secure enough when they were younger has begun to feel less safe as they age and are less physically and mentally able to care for themselves. Even a row house with a street entrance may seem less safe, and so the resident might prefer an apartment with a doorman. Others will have lost a spouse and not want to live alone, isolated in a suburban house. Security also refers to how safe a neighborhood is and how safe the individual feels walking about it or frequenting shops and restaurants. What might have seemed "quaint" and "edgy" at age 55 may seem foreboding and unsafe at age 75.

Transportation concerns cause some elderly to relocate. Most Americans assume that they will drive their cars to wherever they need to go. As long as they can drive, they are usually willing to trade off travel time for a more desirable location. However, as individuals age, driving becomes more problematic and, for some, impossible. After age 80, many who are less capable of or willing to drive begin to rethink where they live and to seek out housing that is closer to goods and services, which often means moving to an urban core or living near public transportation.

F. Housing Needs Change over Time

If "old age" begins at age 65, the elderly span over 35 years. Not surprisingly, that group is not homogeneous and so have different housing needs. Gerontologists label the elderly by three groups:

- the "young" old, those age 65 to 75
- the "old," those age 75 to 85
- the "old" old, those age 85 and older

The housing needs of the "young" old usually do not change much. Retirement or a desire for something new may prompt a move. Some, looking to the future, do move. They often downsize by moving from a house to a condominium or apartment. They relocate into housing that they hope will be appropriate for the next 20 to 25 years in light of their health, financial resources, weather, and recreational opportunities.

Those who do not move before age 75, often find that during the "old" years, age 75 to 85, life's circumstances necessitate a change in housing. Decline in physical or mental health is the most common cause of a move. Even some who moved in their 60s find that the two-story townhouse on a golf course that they moved to at age 65 is no longer appropriate for an 80-year-old with arthritis that prevents them from playing golf and who cannot negotiate the stairs to the second floor. Financial concerns may drive a need to access the capital tied up in a large house or cause the sale of a second home. Snowbirds may decide that they no longer have the desire or energy to change households twice a year. For others, an inability to drive may spur a move to a more centralized location where services are either close by or can be delivered to the home.

After age 85, the "old" old period of life, almost everyone has to be concerned with their ability to live independently as spouses die, health deteriorates, and friends move away. Often family members insist that an aging parent relocate nearer to them or move into in a smaller, safer, and more supportive environment. Even a prior move into a condominium by a couple at age 70 may no longer serve the needs of a 90-year-old widow. Every elder person should consider and plan for the need for housing that is appropriate as they enter the "old" old period of life. It is better for aging individuals to make their own plans, than it is to ignore reality and leave it to others to make appropriate housing choices for them.

G. Sale of a House

When aging homeowners decide that it is time to sell their home, the sale often does not result in taxable income because a couple can exclude up to $500,000 of gain on the sale of a house; a single individual can exclude up to $250,000.[1] A surviving spouse who sells a house within two years of the death of the deceased spouse may exclude up to $500,000 of gain. To qualify for the exemption, the

---

1. I.R.C. § 121(b)(1).

house must have been owned and used as the individual's principal residence for at least two of the previous five years.[2] The house does not have to be the principal residence at the time of the sale and the two-year use as the principal residence does not have to be continuous. Temporary absence due to vacations or even seasonal absences are counted as periods of use even if the house is rented during those periods.[3] A principal residence does not have to be a house; condominiums, houseboats, mobile homes, and stock owned by a tenant-shareholder in a cooperative housing corporation all qualify.[4]

Whether a particular property qualifies as the principal residence depends upon the facts and circumstances. If a couple alternates between two properties, the property that the couple uses for a majority of the year is the principal residence. Other factors that help determine what is an individual's principal residence include where the individual is employed; the address used for voting, driver's license, and automobile registration; the mailing address for correspondence; the location of the individual's banks; and the location of religious organizations or recreational clubs that the individual is a member of.[5]

If the individual becomes physically or mentally incapacitated and incapable of self-care and so moves into a licensed care facility, such as a nursing home, the individual is considered to still reside in the home and be using it as a principal residence.[6] It is not clear whether residence in an assisted living facility similarly does not terminate residence in the home. It might qualify because the regulation only requires that the facility, such as a nursing home, be licensed by the state to care "for an individual in the taxpayer's condition."[7]

Other absences from the home also can still be counted for the two-year use requirement. For example, a divorced spouse who owns a residence is considered to be using it as principal residence even if the former spouse has been given the exclusive use of the house under the terms of the divorce or separation.[8] A divorced spouse's basis in a house is the combined basis of the owner and the former spousal owner, which means the basis is the same as it would have been had the couple not divorced. The basis for the owner spouse is not affected if, as part of the divorce settlement, they paid money to the other spouse who no longer owns the house.

The exclusion of gain applies to a house held by a revocable trust because the trust is ignored for application of the income tax.[9] Even if the house is held in an irrevocable trust, the exclusion applies if the trust is a grantor trust, meaning that

2. *Id.* § 121(a).
3. Treas. Reg. § 1.121-1(c)(1).
4. Treas. Reg. § 1.121-1(b)(1).
5. Treas. Reg. § 1.121-1(b)(2).
6. I.R.C. § 121(d)(7).
7. Treas. Reg. § 1.121-1(c)(2)(ii).
8. I.R.C. § 121(d)(3)(B).
9. IRS Private Letter Ruling 1999-12026, issued on March 26, 1999.

the settlor of the trust has retained sufficient powers over the trust to be taxed on the trust income.[10]

If the individual does not meet the two-year use rule, the exclusion is prorated if the sale was due to a change in employment located at least 50 miles away, for reasons of health if recommended by a physician and not just for the individual's well-being, or unforeseen circumstances such as a natural disaster that include becoming eligible for unemployment insurance, the death of the individual, divorce, or separation.[11] Also, the two-year residency rule does not apply if the move occurred to obtain or provide medical care or personal care for the cure or treatment of an illness or injury to the homeowner of a family member, which includes parents, children, in-laws, and siblings.

Despite the amount of the exclusion—$500,000 for a couple—some sellers of highly appreciated property have gain in excess of the excludable amount. Gain is the difference between the basis of the property and the sale price. Basis is the original cost of the property plus the cost of all capital improvements during the ownership of the property. Examples include a new addition, rehabilitation of the kitchen or a bathroom, landscaping, flooring, a furnace, and installation of a security system. A list of what are capital improvements can be found in IRS publication 523, Selling Your Home, available at http://www.irs.gov/pub/irs-prior/p523–2015.pdf.

Homeowners who in the past took a depreciation deduction because they used part or all of the home as a trade or business may have to report gain. That depreciation must be deducted from the cost of the home to establish the basis. If the home sold for more than its basis, a portion of the gain must be allocated to the business use portion of the home. The gain attributed to the business use is not permitted to be excluded and is recaptured as ordinary income.

II. Appropriate Housing Options

A. Aging in Place

Aging in place refers to older individuals staying where they are and not moving even though they may experience mental or physical decline. Those who, while standing in the kitchen of their house, proclaim "They will have to take me out of here feet first" are planning to age in place. Whether that expectation is realistic depends upon the individual's or spouse's health. For most elderly, at some point either their physical abilities or their mental capacity will decline to the degree that a move is unavoidable. But until that occurs it is possible to take steps that will defer the need to move or make a move unnecessary and so successfully age in place.

---

10. *See* I.R.C. §§ 671–679.
11. Treas. Reg. § 1.121-5(e).

Aging in place is foremost a question of finances: can the individual or couple afford to procure the necessary services where they now live? The first step in answering that question is to determine what it costs to live in the current house, which requires an accurate listing of the average monthly cost—not just a rough estimate but the actual cost. Most homeowners underestimate their monthly housing cost. Filling out the list of expenses in the worksheet in the Appendix at the end of this chapter should help them appreciate the true cost.

The worksheet also points to possible cost savings. If there is a mortgage, refinancing at a lower interest rate may be possible. If the individual has savings, it might be sensible to refinance and pay down part of the mortgage if the interest rate on the mortgage (even after refinancing) is higher than the rate of return on the savings. Homeowners should investigate whether they are eligible for property tax relief by the county or city in the form of homestead exemptions, special tax relief for veterans, property tax freezes or deferrals, and circuit breaker programs that limit property taxes or provide a state supplied tax credit based on the income of the homeowner. Low-income elderly may qualify for assistance in paying for heating and cooling by the Low-Income Home Energy Assistance Program (LIHEAP) operated by the state and usually administered by the local Area Agency on Aging.

1. Sale and Leaseback

Some older homeowners may need to reduce the amount of capital devoted to their housing. One way to do so is to sell the house to their children and then pay rent to occupy it. The rental payments can be equal to the children's out-of-pocket costs including property taxes and the cost of maintenance and repair. The parents can use some of the sale price of the home to pay the rent, with the remaining funds used to produce additional income for the parents. If the children take out a mortgage to finance the purchase of the house, the rental payments can be high enough to meet the monthly mortgage payments. Although the rent is income to the children, that can be offset by the costs of maintaining the house, property taxes, and depreciation. When the parents no longer want to live in the house, the children can sell it and recover their investment.

2. Reverse Mortgages

A popular way of accessing the value of a home is to take out a reverse mortgage, a form of a home equity loan. The amount of the reverse mortgage depends on the value of the house that secures the debt, the age of the borrower, and the rate of interest on the mortgage. The younger the borrower, the smaller the mortgage. This is because the longer time until the mortgage is likely to be paid back, the greater the amount of interest accrues on the mortgage. Since the value of the house secures both the mortgage and the accrued interest, the greater the amount of interest, the smaller the mortgage.

The concept of a reverse mortgage is based upon the expectation that the proceeds of the sale of the house, possibly caused by the death of the borrower, will be used to repay the loan. The borrower will have the enjoyment of the mortgage proceeds, while the estate of the borrower will be reduced by the amount of the loan and accrued interest.

A reverse mortgage does not have to be paid back until the borrower dies, ceases to use the house as the principal residence, or sells the home. Upon one of those events occurring, the entire loan plus interest that accumulated over the years becomes due. Although typically the reverse mortgage loan comes due if the borrower moves out of the house, usually the borrower can live in a nursing home or other medical facility for up to 12 consecutive months before the loan must be repaid.

The most popular reverse mortgage is obtained from a private bank or other lender and is an FHA Home Equity Conversion Mortgage (HECM) that is overseen by the U.S. Department of Housing and Urban Development (HUD). It is the only reverse mortgage insured by the federal government and is available only through an FHA-approved lender. In practice, the vast majority of reverse mortgages are FHA insured HECMs.

Because of past losses on failed reverse mortgage transactions, in 2015, HUD issued new requirements for loan applications. Applicants for reverse mortgages must complete a financial assessment, including as assessment worksheet, before they will be granted an insured reverse mortgage.[12] Based on the information in the forms, some applicants are required to create a Life Expectancy Set-Aside of funds sufficient to guarantee their ongoing payment obligations, and some, who cannot demonstrate a willingness and ability to pay property taxes, homeowner's insurance, and flood insurance for the lifetime of the loan, will be required to fund the set-aside by an escrow account. If an applicant is required to partially or fully fund the set-aside, the full amount of the set-aside is taken out of the reverse mortgage.

To be eligible for an HECM, the borrower must be age 62 or older. The amount of the mortgage depends upon the value of the house, if more than one person such as a married couple is taking out the mortgage, the age of the younger borrower, current interest rates, and the type of mortgage. An HECM mortgage cannot exceed $625,500. Before applying for an HECM, the borrower is required to meet with a counselor from an independent government-approved housing counseling agency, who explains the loan's costs and financial implications. With an HECM, there generally is no specific income requirement, but the borrower must have sufficient income to pay for the cost of maintenance, hazard insurance on the house, mortgage insurance, and the property taxes.

The amount of the reverse mortgage—as determined by the value of the home, the age of the borrower, and the interest rate—establishes the initial principal limit. Generally, in the first year of the loan, the borrower can take out up to

---

12. HUD Mortgage Letters 2014-21 and 22.

70 percent of the initial principal limit. This first-year limit applies to the available payout options, which are:

- A line of credit with the amount that can be borrowed increasing over time as the borrower ages, which shortens the probable time the mortgage will have to be repaid. As long as the borrower meets the requirements of the reverse mortgage, the line of credit cannot be suspended or canceled.
- A monthly tenure option that pays the borrower a fixed monthly payout for as long as they live in the house.
- A monthly term payout of a fixed monthly payout for a fixed number of years.
- A lump sum up to 70 percent of the initial principal amount at a fixed interest rate. Thereafter the remaining initial principal amount is available.

The borrower can combine a line of credit with either the monthly tenure or monthly term payouts. The line of credit, monthly payouts, and combination options are only available with an adjustable rate loan.

Some married borrowers list only one of the couple as the borrower on the mortgage. This might occur if the marriage took place after the mortgage was taken out or because the unlisted spouse is under the age of 62 and not eligible for an HECM reverse mortgage. Some might leave off an eligible younger spouse in order to increase the amount of the mortgage. To do so, the couple would quitclaim the deed to the older spouse. For example, if John, age 80, and Ann, age 65, are married, if the house is deeded solely in John's name and Ann is not on the mortgage, the shorter life expectancy of John will permit him to borrow considerably more than if Ann were also on the mortgage. This tactic, however, can lead to a difficult situation. If John dies, with Ann surviving, the reverse mortgage comes due because the lender can demand payment at the death of the borrower. As a result, Ann would likely have to sell the house to repay the reverse mortgage. However, after paying off the debt, Ann likely would not have enough money to purchase or even rent a home of a similar quality.

In 2013, the Federal District Court for the District of Columbia held that the Housing and Urban Development (HUD) regulation, which allowed lenders to demand immediate payment even if the home were occupied by a surviving spouse, violated federal law.[13] In response, HUD issued a new policy that states the non-borrowing spouse may remain in the home after the borrower dies and the repayment of the loan is deferred so long as:

- The non-borrowing spouse was married to the borrower at the time of the loan and remained married for the duration of the borrower's lifetime,
- Their spousal status was disclosed at the time of the closing of the loan,
- The non-borrowing spouse is named in the loan documents,

---

13. Bennett v. Donovan, 4 F. Supp. 3d 5 (D.D.C. 2013).

- The non-borrowing spouse occupied and continued to occupy the home as their principal residence,
- The non-borrowing spouse establishes legal ownership within 90 days of the death of the borrower, and
- The non-borrowing spouse meets all of the obligations described in the loan documents.[14]

If the non-borrowing spouse does not meet all of the requirements, the loan becomes due and payable. The requirements applied to any HECM taken out on or after August 4, 2014. For loans taken out before that date, HUD announced in May of 2015 that the lenders have the option, in certain cases, to delay foreclosure proceedings for up to 60 days after the death the borrower.

B. Age-Restricted Housing

Some elderly chose to relocate to age-restricted housing, which has a variety of attractions. Many prefer to live among others of a similar age who are likely to have shared interests and attitudes arising from their age. A quieter life away from children and teenagers appeals to some. Age-restricted housing also often features special recreational, social, and community activities tailored to the desires of older residents.

Age-restricted housing is legally possible because the federal Fair Housing Act permits two types of housing for older persons: housing that can only be occupied by those age 62 and older and housing in which only 80 percent of the units must be occupied by at least one person age 55 or older.[15] The potential occupant must ask whether they prefer all of their neighbors to be at least age 62 or whether they are willing to live where only 80 percent of the units must have at least one occupant age 55 or older. The latter permits a building or development to mix in some younger residents and permits it to sell or rent to couples, only one of which need be age 55 or older. But it also means that many of the residents may be younger than age 55, and so the building or development might not be as focused on the needs of its older, over age 65, residents. The facility may even contain families with young children or teenagers, or multi-generational families with only one member of the family being at least age 55.

Age-restricted housing is available in many forms: a rental building or condominium, a mobile home park, a subdivision, or a retirement village. There are even self-contained small cities and towns designed exclusively for older residents. For example, Sun City in Arizona has over 45,000 residents. These age-restricted towns feature detached single-family houses, townhouses, and condominiums. The towns typically have extensive recreational facilities, including shuffleboard courts, swimming pools, tennis courts, recreation buildings, and even golf courses.

---

14. HUD Mortgagee Letter 2014-07.
15. 42 U.S.C. § 3607(2)(A) & (C).

Shops, banks, and restaurants are located close enough in the town center that many residents can walk or take a personal scooter or golf cart.

The prospective buyer of age-restricted housing should inspect the deed and any rules imposed by a homeowners association or the condominium deed and declaration as well as the rules of the condominium association to determine the extent of age restrictions in the use of the unit. They also must understand that the recreational facilities and supportive services available today, may not be available in the years to come. Nothing in the Fair Housing Act requires any services or facilities geared to older residents. After age-restricted housing units open, the initial residents grow older, sometimes to the degree that recreational facilities, such as a tennis court, that once appealed to residents no longer do. As a result the complex may vote to replace the tennis court with green space. Beloved social events may cease. For example, an annual New Year's Eve ball may no longer find attendees when the average age of the complex passes age 80. Prospective purchasers should also be careful to choose housing that will be suitable as they age. For example, at age 70 walking up to a second-floor unit may not be a problem for the unit owner, but at age 88 and with arthritis, the stairs to a unit on the second floor may prove insurmountable. Unfortunately, the condominium association is not required to make the second floor units accessible.

A prospective renter should inquire as to whether the lease provides that the housing will remain age restricted for some definite period of time. The lease should state whether anyone until the age limit, such as a grandchild, may occupy the unit and if so, for how long. A prospective resident should inquire as to the facilities policy as to overnight guests staying in the units. Some age-restricted housing bars anyone under the age of 55 or 62 from even being an overnight guest. Others permit it, but limit the number of days or bar any young guests, such as anyone under the age of 18. However, some buildings and developments have guest space that can be rented by the night and for which there are no restrictions on who may rent it so long as they are recommended or signed up by a resident.

If the occupant owns a free-standing unit that is subject to an age-restricted covenant, the deed should contain the age restriction, which can be removed only by unanimous agreement of all the unit owners whose property is also subject to the restriction. Owners of property subject to an age-restricted covenant often also share in the ownership of recreational facilities and other common areas. Before buying property in such a development, the individual should ascertain how those facilities and common areas are maintained and governed. In many cases, a majority or super-majority vote of the unit owners can change the use of the areas and increase the maintenance fees. In some developments, the recreational facilities are not owned by the unit owners, but are owned by the developer who charges a fee for their use and has the final say in the maintenance and even the continuation of the facilities.

C. Condominiums and Cooperatives

Many older homeowners sell their homes and move into condominiums. A condominium owner owns the unit outright, can mortgage it, and pays property taxes on its value. Still, there are important ownership limitations that a potential condominium owner needs to understand. A condominium, whether newly constructed or the conversion of a preexisting building, is a form of property ownership that owes its existence to state law. Typically the statute will require that the condominium is created by the filing of a master deed or declaration of condominium ownership. Depending on state and local requirements, the declaration will describe the land, the form, and boundaries of the individual units; describe and list the common elements such as the entrance, roof, and halls; the percentage ownership of the common areas by each individual unit; unit owner voting rights in the condominium governance; and the rights and responsibilities of the owners association governing board, including the right to make assessments to pay for the upkeep and taxes on the common areas. If the building is newly constructed, the developer will control the owners association until some prescribed number of units have been sold (usually 60 percent) when the developer will turn control of the building to the owners association. The developer, however, can continue to vote for the units that it still owns.

If the condominium has been operating for a period of time, the unit owners association will have adopted rules and regulations that are binding upon unit owners. Before buying a unit, the prospective purchaser should ask to see a copy of those rules and regulations (also known as bylaws). Of particular interest are limits on pets by number, size, and breed; limits on modifications to the outside of a unit such as no window awnings; and prohibitions such as no outdoor grills on balconies, no uncovered wooden floors, and no renting of the unit. Beyond adopting bylaws, the chief function of the unit owners association is to manage the common areas and pay for their maintenance, repair, and taxes. The condominium declaration will empower the board of directors to allocate the costs of the common areas to the unit owners. That allocation is legally enforceable without regard to whether the unit owner agrees with the expenditure or even uses the common area, such as recreational facilities. Decisions by the association or by the board of directors can only be challenged on grounds that proper procedures were not employed or that the rule or bylaw exceeds the authority of the association (some rules must be adopted by the vote of all unit owners) or exceeds the authority of the board of directors. For example, limits on the outside appearance of a townhouse condominium may or may not be permitted. Even minor items, such as whether a unit owner can decorate the outside door with a Christmas wreath, depend upon the declaration and bylaws. The best rule when buying a condominium is not to assume that any action that affects the outside of the unit is permitted. Always inquire of the board of directors what limits exist. Do not assume, for example, that a television satellite dish will be permitted.

Before there were condominiums, there were cooperative ownership associations. A cooperative is a corporate association whose members by virtue of their ownership of shares in the association are permitted to lease an apartment unit. Members of the cooperative do not "own" their units; they have a right of occupancy to a particular unit by virtue of buying shares in the cooperative. They do not pay rent. Instead, the tenant is required to pay the maintenance charges of the cooperative including the cost of common utilities, the real estate taxes, and any share of a mortgage owned by the cooperative. For example, the cooperative might have taken out a mortgage to pay for extensive rehabilitation of the common heating and cooling facility. The tenant is also liable if the cooperative levies an additional assessment to pay for the common costs of the building, such as a significant upgrade to a recreational facility.

Cooperatives have great latitude in determining who may purchase shares and occupy a unit. Those who wish to purchase a unit must have the approval of the association board of directors, who can deny approval for almost any reason other than race, religion, national origin, or familial status. A poor credit rating of a prospective buyer is the most common reason for rejection. Many cooperatives require a buyer to pay cash for their shares and will not approve the sale of shares financed by a mortgage.

Federal income tax law treats cooperative owners the same as condominium owners. An allocable portion of real estate taxes on the cooperative are deductible by the tenants as well as any mortgage interest paid by the cooperative. The sale of the cooperative stock is treated as the sale of a house or condominium and so qualifies for possible tax-free exclusion of any gain.

D. Planned Communities

Planned communities feature a comprehensive development plan supported by zoning, covenants, equitable servitudes, and easements all designed to force unit owners to abide by the plan. Some feature condominiums, but more common are free-standing homes owned in fee simple with common ownership of recreational facilities such as swimming pools and tennis courts. If the streets in the community are commonly owned, the community can restrict access, and the community may be gated with a guard who bars entry by anyone but homeowners, their guests, and approved service providers.

Planned communities are governed by a homeowners association whose power comes from covenants placed on the individual lots. The covenants cannot be removed unless all the lot owners agree. The association, acting through a board of directors, usually has a great deal of control over the appearance of the individual homes and their use and occupancy. Many older persons enjoy the uniformity, calmness, and attractiveness of a planned community. Others do not because they do not like the loss of individual control over their property. Some find planned communities sterile and lacking in commercial services whereas many are attracted to the peace and calmness of narrow streets with little traffic and housing that attracts those of similar economic background.

States, by enacting special zoning, make planned communities possible. The day-to-day regulation of planned communities, however, arises from the easements and covenants that run with the land. A seller cannot remove the easements and covenants, and a buyer is bound by them. As a result, buyers should take care to have the deed examined. For example, they may discover that the lot they are contemplating purchasing may have an easement across it that permits all the other lot owners to cross the property to gain access to a commonly owned facility, such as a lake. The lot will almost surely be subject to a covenant that grants the homeowner association the right of architectural control. Often the association will delegate supervision over architecture to an architectural review committee. The degree of control of the committee depends on the wording of the covenants on the land, but a buyer should assume that the committee must approve any change in the appearance of the unit, and that approval of even "minor" changes may not be forthcoming. A denial of the architectural review committee can be challenged in court, but most challenges fail.

Although the law does not favor law use restrictions and so interprets covenants strictly, courts usually defer to good faith, reasonable decisions made in the best interest of the community.[16] Sometimes the committee may agree that the request from the lot owner makes sense, but have no choice under the covenant but to reject the request because the proposed request would violate the restrictive covenants placed on the land.

---

16. Tierra Rancho's Homeowner Ass'n v. Kitchukov, 165 P.3d 173 (Ariz. 2007).

Appendix 1
Housing Expense Worksheet

Recurring	**Monthly**
Housecleaning	_____
Homemaker and personal care assistance	_____
Mortgage	_____
Rent	_____
Condominium or co-op monthly assessment	_____
Homeowner (HOA) assessment	_____
Recreational fees	_____
Insurance prorated per month	_____
Utilities	
Heating & cooling monthly average	_____
Electrical	_____
Water	_____
Sewage	_____
Garbage	_____
Landline phone	_____
Cell phone(s)	_____
Cable or satellite	_____
Internet	_____
Lawn maintenance	_____
Swimming pool maintenance	_____
Repairs, interior and exterior	_____
Other	_____
Total	_____
Yearly Total	_____

Nonrecurring or Capital Improvements	**Yearly**
Average structural repair based on prior three years	_____
Interior decorating, for example, painting	_____
Major appliance replacement	_____
Lawn maintenance equipment	_____
Other	_____
Total	_____

Anticipated Repair Costs	**Yearly**
Roof and gutters	_____
Sidewalks and driveway	_____
Outside painting	_____
Heating and cooling unit replacement	_____
Swimming pool	_____
Other	_____
Total	_____

Grand Yearly Total	_____

Family Vacation Homes 9

I. Introduction

Many older clients own a second home, variously referred to as a vacation home, a weekend home, a summer home, or a cottage. It is estimated that there are over 5 million vacation homes. For some, the vacation home represents merely a place to vacation. But for many older owners, the home is more than just where they relax; the home is where the extended family gathers. It is filled with memories and provides a sense of permanence as family members move about the country. As the couple ages, the home often takes on greater importance, as it is seen as an essential part of keeping the family together by permitting family members to continue a tradition of vacationing together at a location that otherwise they might not be able to afford.

The aging owners of a vacation home are often concerned as to how to pass on the home in a way that will encourage and enable the heirs to continue to use and enjoy it. Unfortunately, without an adequate plan, a vacation home can become a burden rather than a benefit, and rather than promoting family harmony, it can be the source of significant friction and hostility. An effective succession plan, however, can go a long way in ensuring that a vacation home is enjoyed by the heirs for years to come. Still, in some instances the older client will come to realize that the heirs are better served if the vacation home is sold, either to an outsider or to one of the heirs.

II. Client Objectives

Clients have different attitudes about their vacation homes. Some see a vacation home as "their" home and have little concern about passing it on. A few will sell theirs before they die because the vacation home no longer fits their needs or becomes too great a burden to maintain. Others will want to ensure the house is passed on to their spouse to enjoy, and let the surviving spouse make the ultimate decision about whether the home should be sold, retained and treated as a special legacy gift, or retained as merely another asset of the estate.

In contrast, many vacation homeowners, whether individuals or couples, see the home as something special, as having value beyond its market value and thus worthy of special planning. Their objective is to keep the home in the family as long as possible, hopefully for multiple generations. Some are driven by the sentimental memory of the good times shared by the family and the hope that those will continue. Others consider the home to be a way of passing on a valuable asset that will grow in value more rapidly than alternative investments. They want to tie up the property so that the heirs cannot sell it and so fail to realize the future gain. Some see the house as a way for the heirs to stay in touch and have a place to gather. A few have such strong emotional attachment to the home that they cannot bear to think of it being owned by strangers.

Older clients are often aware of the possible threats to passing on the vacation home and its being enjoyed by the heirs, which include the following:

- The surviving spouse selling the home, either because of financial need or feeling it no longer serves the family purposes;
- The surviving spouse remarrying and leaving the home to the new spouse;
- Heirs facing a lack of liquidity to pay inheritance or estate taxes arising from owning the home;
- Heirs, over time, coming to need money more than a vacation home;
- Heirs facing financial crisis or extreme need, such as bankruptcy or having a child with special needs;
- Heirs who misuse the home or refuse to cooperate with the other owners;
- A creditor of an heir putting a levy on the heir's ownership interest;
- The share of the home owned by an heir passing by divorce or death to their spouse, who in turn either does not want the home or wishes to occupy it with others who have no blood relation to the rest of the family;
- Conflicts among the heirs as to maintenance, repairs, and remodeling that lead to serious family quarrels;
- Conflicts among the heirs over who occupies the home;
- Personality conflicts among the heirs that make it very difficult to share usage of the home; and
- The inability of the heirs to afford the upkeep and property taxes on the home.

Although all of these client concerns are valid, too many elderly clients do not want to consider the most fundamental problem about passing on a vacation home—some or all of the potential heirs do not want it. They want the value of the home, but they do not want to own it and would prefer to have its monetary value to consume or invest. Some heirs may like the home but do not think that its value as a vacation home is commensurate with its market value. Faced with selling the home and taking a percentage share worth $X or having the right to occupy the home for Y number of days per year, some heirs would rather have the money. Surprisingly, the desire for money may not necessarily reflect their economic circumstances. Heirs who are financially secure nevertheless may not believe it makes sense to tie up a considerable amount of assets in a vacation home. Others in greater financial need, such as those faced with paying for college for their children, despite having a great fondness for the home, may feel that they have little choice but to prefer having liquid assets rather than the right of occupancy of a vacation home along with the costs of taxes and upkeep.

Before engaging in planning on how to keep the home available to the family, the client should inquire among the potential heirs whether they wish to retain a right to use the home after the client's death. The client needs a clear understanding of which heirs want to continue to have access to the home. The client should also inquire whether the heirs will need financial assistance to maintain the home and pay the taxes. And, of course, clients need to decide as to how many generations they want to preserve the home for. Certainly the children, possibly grandchildren, but does the client expect the home to be passed on to great-grandchildren and beyond? If so, the client must arrange the ownership of the house in a way that permits more distant heirs to opt out of ownership and be financially recompensed. Otherwise the potential number of homeowners or occupants (including their families) will be overwhelming. Multi-generational ownership is also likely to include heirs who have no interest in occupying the home.

III. Common Tenancies and the Right of Partition

The simplest way to leave a vacation home, but probably the worst, is to leave it to the heirs, whether named—"Jane Doe and Doris Doe"—or identified as a class—"my children"—as tenants in common who each own an undivided interest in the home. Tenants in common need not each have the same percentage of ownership. The client could leave the property to three or more children or other heirs in unequal percentage ownership. That is unusual. The more likely scenario of unequal ownership interests arises when tenants in common who owned an equal share die and bequeath their interest to two or more children (the client's grandchildren) with the result that the grandchildren own a smaller fractional share than the original common tenants (their aunts and uncles). Common tenants also have the right to give or sell their interest to any person at any time.

For example, a child who is a tenant in common could sell their interest to their children or they could transfer their interest to an ex-spouse as part of a divorce settlement.

The cost of maintaining the property is divided according to the ownership interest of the common tenant. A common tenant with a 33⅓ percent ownership interest is responsible for 33⅓ percent of the expenses of the property. No matter what the ownership interests, however, no tenant in common has the right to exclusive occupancy. Each has the right to occupy the property when and for as long as they like, although they can reverse that common law right by agreeing by contract to individual times of occupancy. A tenant who occupies the property does not owe rent to the other owners. Although all are liable for the cost of maintaining the property, none is entitled to be reimbursed for the cost of making improvements to the property. Absent an agreement to the contrary, tenants are also not required to reimburse a fellow tenant who expends money or time on managing the property, such as arranging for the property to be rented. A tenant in common is also not entitled to reimbursement for repairs or improvements to the property unless the repairs were capital repairs necessary for the preservation of the property.

Though the rights associated with a tenancy in common can often be disruptive, the greatest threat to continued family ownership of the vacation home, however, is the right of partition. If a tenant wishes to sell their interest, and the other tenants are not willing to buy that tenant's share or not willing to pay fair market value, a tenant can sue for partition by where a court orders the property sold at fair market value and the proceeds distributed to the tenants in proportion to their ownership interest. A tenant who wishes to retain ownership of the property will be permitted to purchase it at fair market value or to buyout the other tenants at fair market value. If more than one tenant wishes to buy the property, the tenant willing to pay the highest price will be awarded the property. The right of partition means that leaving a vacation home to the heirs as tenants in common is unlikely to preserve it as a family-owned and family-enjoyed property.

A vacation home can be left as a joint tenancy with a right of survivorship, but that is almost never a good choice. As the name implies, a joint tenancy with a right of survivorship means that at the death of a joint owner, neither the will of the deceased owner nor the state intestacy law govern who takes the property; the ownership of the home passes by law to the other joint owners. In most states, joint tenants must own an equal share. If there are two joint tenants each owns half; if three, each owns a third. If there are three joint owners and one dies, the remaining two owners each own half.

Fortunately those left property in joint tenancy can easily defeat the survivorship interest. If a joint tenant sells or gives away their interest, the new owner is a tenant in common. Moreover, the joint tenants can agree to convert the tenancy into a tenancy in common without survivorship interests. Even without the agreement of the other owners, a joint owner can convey their interest to a third party in a straw transaction, thereby creating a tenancy in common where the third party immediately conveys the tenancy in common back to the original owner. Some states now permit a joint owner to convert their ownership to a tenancy in common without going through a straw transaction.

In light of the ease of terminating the joint survivorship interest, it is difficult to imagine why it would ever be employed by the owner of a vacation home. In the few states that permit an indestructible joint tenancy that cannot be destroyed by a sale or gift, the survivorship feature means that the original owner has no idea who will eventually take the property. The longest living tenant will eventually own it outright and have the right to sell, bequeath, or give it to whomever they desire.

IV. Limited Liability Company (LLC)

A. Introduction

In lieu of a tenancy in common tenancy or joint ownership with survivorship, the home can be put in a trust or it can be owned by a partnership. The use of a trust creates the problem that the trustees control the property, which can mean that if some of the trust beneficiaries, those who have a right to occupy the home, are not trustees, they may have no input into the management of the home. The division between the legal interest and control of the trustees and the beneficial interests of the users of the home is very likely to lead to disputes and family disharmony. An alternative is to have the home owned by a partnership, but doing so exposes the assets of the partner-owners to creditors. A limited partnership can provide creditor protection for the limited partners but requires at least one general partner whose assets are not protected. Also over time, as more heirs, who have a right of occupancy, become partners, the increase in the number of the partners will make it increasingly difficult to agree on how to manage the home.

In most cases, to avoid personal liability, ownership by a corporation would be preferable to a partnership. Ownership of the home could be held by a close corporation that does not require annual shareholder or director meetings and that obtained S status for federal income tax purposes, that is, it is treated as if it were a partnership. However, because maintaining S status requires a degree of vigilance as to who owns shares, most recommend using a limited liability company.

B. State Law Requirements for LLCs

Every state authorizes limited liability companies (LLCs). The details of incorporation and the organization of the LLC are determined by state law but the vacation home need not be located in the state in which the LLC is created. An LLC is formed by filing articles of incorporation with the appropriate state agency. The incorporation records of the LLC must identify an individual to receive notice of a lawsuit against the LLC as well as a mailing address of the office of the LLC. Often an attorney or accountant serves as the agent for the LLC for service of process and other official notifications.

C. Federal Income Tax Treatment

An LLC with at least two members is classified as a partnership for federal income tax purposes unless it files Form 8832 and elects to be treated as a corporation.[1] An LLC with only one member is treated as an entity that is disregarded as separate from its owner for income tax purposes. If the LLC elects to be treated as a partnership, all income and deductions of the LLC pass on to the shareholders in proportion to their ownership interests. As a practical matter, because the LLC will not have income (unless it charges rent to those who use the vacation home), the shareholders will not report income but will be able to deduct the allowable expenses such as property taxes.

D. Creation of the LLC

Most vacation homeowners are focused on how the home will be owned and used after their death. They should also plan, however, for how the home will be managed during their life in the event they should lose mental capacity. A couple who owns the home jointly with right of survivorship must plan for the death of one of them with the survivor possibly living on to a very old age and so having a high possibility of becoming demented.

If the surviving spouse cannot manage the home, perhaps due to dementia or merely because of advanced aged, someone else must take on the task. Although the surviving spouse can appoint a child as an agent under a power of attorney to handle the home, doing so might be the cause of family disharmony if the child who is acting as the agent appears to be managing the occupancy of the home in a way that disadvantages other family members. For example, the child as agent might claim the right to occupy the home during prime dates, such as the July 4th holiday, or might insist on sole use of the house for several weeks in summer when other children would also like to use the home.

Rather than naming a child as agent, it would be preferable to transfer the vacation home to an LLC. The partners of the LLC would be the surviving spouse and all the children. That would ensure that the maintenance and use of the home would be jointly controlled by all the children or they could appoint or elect a manager who might be one of the children to operate it. Such an arrangement would merely accelerate the timing of the transfer of the home to an LLC so that it took place during the life of the surviving spouse rather than at their death. Note, however, that re-deeding the home may result in state or local transfer taxes or fees, or the transfer might trigger a reassessment of the home for property tax purposes.

---

1. I.R.C. § 280A.

If the aging owner desires to transfer the home to an LLC, the owner must make a number of decisions. First is the state of incorporation; the owner's state of residence is one choice, as is the state where the home is located. The owner must choose a name for the LLC; the family name is often used but it may already be the name of a corporation and not be available. After the LLC has filed the necessary papers with the appropriate state agency, and come into being, the vacation home must be transferred by deed to the LLC. The owner also must decide whether to transfer the contents of the home, the furniture and the like, or to retain possession. That decision depends on whether the owner intends to transfer the personal property as part of the home or devise it as part of their will. Transfer of the personal property by will may be appropriate if there are possessions of high value, such as a sail boat, or have special value to an heir. A painting or photograph, for example, may be desired by a child but have little importance to the other heirs. Other personal property associated with the vacation home might be transferred to the LLC, including smaller boats, recreational gear, and vehicles that are used only in conjunction with the vacation home. If other family members regularly use the home and leave personal property at the home, such as golf clubs or furniture that they do not have room for in their own homes, the older homeowner should inquire whether the younger heir has donated the personal property or do they still consider themselves to own it. The older owner must also be sure to ensure that the property and the contents are properly insured. The property insurance may be affected by the transfer of the property. After the LLC comes into existence, the owner must abide by state law requirements that require annual meetings, make the necessary state filings, and also report the income and deductions arising from the LLC to the partners so that they can report those items on their federal income tax returns. If the property has a mortgage, it will be necessary to obtain the consent of the lender to the transfer of the property to the LLC. If not, the mortgage may become due upon the transfer.

The older owner must decide whether to add other family members as shareholders in the LLC. By retaining sole ownership, the older owner retains complete control over the property. The older owner, however, could transfer the home to an LLC and give shares in the LLC to their children, but retain majority ownership and thereby have control over the property. If the older owner, or couple, is the only shareholder, they need not share the management with others. But as discussed earlier, there may come a time when neither of the couple is capable of managing the property. If so, the other LLC members could manage the property. If the older owner loses capacity and has appointed an agent under a power of attorney, the power should be worded to deny the agent the right to sell or gift the older owner's shares in the LLC. This will ensure that at the death of the older owner the shares are passed according to the will.

The LLC operating agreement must be in writing and state law may require it to be signed by the members of the LLC. The LLC can, but is not required to, issue certificates of ownership to its members that identify the owner and the number units in the LLC owned by the member. The number of units in total is up to the creator of the LLC, but having many units makes it easier to pass on units to succeeding generations that may result in an increasing number of owners. For example, if a couple is leaving a vacation home in an LLC in equal shares to three children, there might be 90 units so that each child would receive 30. Those children in turn might each divide their 30 units among their children.

The alternative to transferring the home to the LLC during the owners' lives is to transfer it at the death of the last to survive (assuming a married couple owns the home). The LLC will be established while the couple is alive. The LLC can be transferred to a revocable trust. The home will then be left to the LLC by will or, if the home is owned in trust, by deed from the trust. Alternatively, the LLC would not receive ownership of the home until after the death of the second of the couple to die. If the LLC is owned by a trust, the trustee will accept ownership of the home into the LLC and then distribute the ownership of the LLC as provided by the trust instrument. If the LLC is owned by a trust, the trustee should be empowered to amend the LLC as needed to comport with changes in state law.

E. Management of the LLC

1. Voting Rights

The members of the LLC can directly manage the vacation home. The operating agreement can state that a majority of unit owners can make the decisions about the property, such as when to make repairs. If a majority can rule, the voting rights of unit owners must be spelled out; for example, do the owners of each generation have one vote and succeeding generations split that vote. If so, must they unanimously agree in order to cast their vote?

The alternative is to require unanimity. Unfortunately, unanimous agreement places a great deal of power in the hands of unit owners who can refuse to accede unless they are "rewarded" in some manner, such as being granted use of the home during a particular time. The agreement could call for majority control but also require unanimous agreement for some decision, such as placing a mortgage on the property or renting it to non-owners.

Direct member management becomes difficult as the number of unit owners increases and as individuals of different generations own units. The alternative is for the operating agreement to permit members to designate a manager, likely a family member, who has whatever power the members feel comfortable in granting. At a minimum, the manager (or managers) should have the power to authorize repairs and maintenance and pay ordinary expenses including property taxes. Because occupancy of the home is the point of being a member, how the occupancy is determined is critical. The power can be delegated to a manager but the manager's discretion should be limited by an agreed occupancy agreement among the members. The manager might only have the power to maintain the schedule of occupancy, the details of which have been agreed upon by the members.

2. Occupancy Agreements

At the beginning of each year, the members can agree to how to allocate the occupancy rights. Usually each member has a right of occupancy whose duration is determined by the number of unit shares that the member owns. For example, if there are 30 unit shares that were originally divided equally among three children, ten unit shares create the right to occupy the home for one-third of the occupancy time. If one child dies and leaves their ten shares in equal shares to two children, each of those children would have only one-half as much occupancy time as would one of the original three heirs.

The members have to agree on how many weeks a year that the home can be occupied and allocate those accordingly. If the home has two seasons of use, such as a home in a ski area that is in most demand in the winter but is used some in July and August, the members might agree to have separate occupancy rights for each season.

An annual agreement requires that some method exist to deal with disagreements. The parties could draw lots and choose a date in order of the number they drew or they could establish an order of choice that rotates each year so that in year 1, member A chooses first, but in year 2, member B chooses first, member C second and member A chooses last. The agreement could also require a minimum number of unit votes to participate. An LLC with 30 units of ownership might require ownership of at least ten units to have the right to participate in the allocation occupancy times. If two members each own five units, they would have to join together to use their combined ten units to be eligible to participate in the process that determines allocation of the times of occupancy of the home. They, in turn, would have to agree how to divide their joint right of occupancy.

The parties must agree as to the period of occupancy such as a week or a month, but unit owners should be permitted to trade dates and periods of occupancy with each other. If the home can house many, the agreement might permit multiple occupancy, particularly at dates of peak demand such as around Labor Day. Though any unit owner is free to permit another unit owner to share occupancy or to invite other guests, whether the right of occupancy can be given away to a friend or other nonmember depends upon the occupancy agreement. The agreement should also address the right of a unit owner to permit college age children to occupy the home without the unit owner being present. Whether the right to rent the home rather than occupying it is permitted should be spelled out in the agreement, as should the right to bring pets onto the property. If pets are permitted, the unit owner might be required to have the home thoroughly cleaned after having occupied it with a pet. Rights of occupancy should be lost or suspended for members who fail to pay their share of the expenses of the home.

3. Successor Ownership Rights

The agreement should define who can be a unit owner—typically descendants of the couple that originally owned the home. If so, the language should address the issue of adopted children. The right of occupancy of a surviving spouse should also be considered. The agreement, for example, could permit a surviving spouse to own and vote on the deceased spouse's units but only bequeath the shares to the issue of their marriage, thereby preventing the units passing to the spouse or children from another marriage.

Some who inherit units may not wish to occupy the home nor be responsible for the costs of its upkeep. One solution is to permit that person to return the units to the LLC, which in turn would cancel the units. Another solution is to permit the unit owner to sell their shares back to the LLC with the remaining unit owners contributing their proportionate share of the cost of the shares.

The right to sell the shares must be accompanied by a method of determining the per unit sale price. Any one of a number of methods can be used. The simplest is to state a fixed value, such as $X per unit and add a yearly compound percentage increase to account for inflation and growth in market value. Another method is to set a price subject to the right to reopen the price every X years if a majority of unit owners elect to do so. The new unit sale price would then be set by a vote of the majority of owners but in no case be lower than the original sale price.

A more accurate valuation method is to have the property valued each year (or only when a unit owner wishes to sell) by a qualified appraiser. That valuation would then set the value of each unit share. A unit owner could attempt to force the LLC to purchase the owner's units at the current valuation less some percentage discount in recognition of the below market value of owning a right of shared occupancy. The deeper the discount, the less likely a unit owner will want to sell their unit. But a sale of units to the LLC increases the occupancy time of the remaining owners so they may prefer imposing only a modest discount to encourage some unit owners to sell back their ownership interest. If either the LLC or the selling unit owner disagrees with the appraiser's value, the parties should have agreed to submit to mandatory arbitration.

The agreement should also state the terms of the buyout—such as cash within 90 days, half on the date of the sale and half one year later, or a down payment of 20 percent with installment payments stretching out over five to ten years. If an installment sale is allowed, it should permit the purchasing unit owners to accelerate the payments at their option. The rate of interest on the debt should be stated in the agreement but it should be subject to modification based on a prevailing interest rate such as the National Mortgage Contract Interest Rate.

4. Renting the Vacation Home

Assuming that the local zoning laws permit the home to be rented, and there are no property restrictions as to renting the property, such as covenants, the question is whether the LLC unit owners will agree to rent it. There are two options. One is to permit individual unit owners to rent out the home for the period that they have a right of occupancy. By doing so, the individual unit owner takes on the responsibility for having adequate insurance, monitoring the behavior of the renters, and restoring the property by cleaning and repairs after the renters have departed. Because of the likelihood that an individual unit owner may not properly perform these duties and because the LLC will very likely be liable to the renter and to third parties whatever the unit owner agreed to, this option is usually not desirable.

Instead of permitting renting by individual LLC unit owners, any renting of the home should be done by the LLC. The rental income can either accrue to the benefit of all the unit owners or the LLC can rent out the home for the benefit of a unit owner who does not want to occupy the home and would prefer to rent it out. If the LLC rents out the home for the benefit of an individual unit owner, the LLC should charge a fee commensurate with the cost in time and money for doing so. Any remaining funds from the rental would be passed on to the unit owner who agreed to rent the property rather than occupy it.

Whether the home is rented by the LLC for the benefit of all the owners or rented in lieu of occupancy by a single unit owner, the best way to proceed is to engage a rental management company to handle renting the home. A rental management company should know how to solicit tenants, screen possible tenants, draw up a rental agreement that protects the LLC, prepare the unit for rental occupancy, monitor the renter's use of the unit, address any problems that arise during the rental period, inspect the unit after the renters have left, handle the security deposit and deduct proper amounts for any damages or excessive wear, and prepare the property for the next rental or occupancy by a unit owner. As indicated by this lengthy list, renting out a vacation home is usually best left to a professional.

Management of Property of a Person Who Is Mentally Incapacitated

10

I. Introduction

One of the most feared aspects of aging is the possible loss of mental capacity. Not just the normal decline in short-term memory or the inability to remember names, but a serious loss of mental capacity due to dementia, stroke, or another irreversible brain disease or condition. The loss of mental capacity means the loss of self; that is a terrible thing to happen, but the psychological aspect of the loss of mental capacity is a separate topic. For the law, what is relevant is that the loss of mental capacity, if severe enough, can mean the loss of the individual's ability to make legally binding decisions. A severely mentally incapacitated person ceases to be a legal actor. Although that person is still recognized by the law as an individual with legal rights and protections, the loss of capacity means that the individual can no longer make legally binding decisions on their own behalf.

If the incapacitated person cannot make decisions, someone else must make decisions concerning the individual's person and property. The legal framework for decision making for the person is discussed in Chapter 11, Health Care Decision Making. This chapter focuses on decision making for the property of a mentally incapacitated person who is mentally incapacitated as that term is defined by the law.

A note on nomenclature. Those who deal with younger persons who have a disability often employ the language of "putting the person first," which attempts to avoid labeling someone by a disability or condition. Thus, rather than "disabled person," it is preferable to say, a "person with a disability." For older persons who have lost mental capacity the term often found in statutes is "incapacitated person." Some, however, advocate for the term, a "person with reduced capacity." While acknowledging the reasoning and values behind "putting the person first," this chapter will, in the main, use "incapacitated person" because that is the term most commonly used in statutes and case law.

II. Mental Incapacity and Property Management

The law assumes that every adult has the requisite mental capacity to make legally valid decisions about their property. Mental capacity is defined as the "mental ability to understand the nature and effects of one's acts"[1] and is measured or assessed by the decisions made by the individual, by medical tests, and by cognitive and psychological assessments. Mental capacity is not binary; one is either or not mentally capacitated, but rather mental capacity is a continuum from very good to very bad. On that continuum, the law sets standards for whether an individual has sufficient mental capacity to engage in the activity in question. "Different activities or actions require different levels of mental capacity."[2] Individuals can have legal capacity[3] for some actions but not for others. The law has established the levels of capacity necessary for a variety of acts concerning property.

The law of almost every state distinguishes between testamentary capacity and the capacity to execute a trust, versus the capacity to enter into a valid contract or make a gift. Testamentary acts require the lowest level of capacity. In the past, the law appeared to require a higher level of capacity to execute a trust, but the modern approach is to require the same level of capacity for either a will or trust. The law, however, still requires a higher level of capacity to legally enter into a contract or to make a gift. And though the law permits an individual to name an agent who can enter into a contract or make a gift on behalf of an individual who lacks the capacity to do so, the law will not permit an agent to execute a will on behalf of an individual who lacks the legal capacity to do so.

---

1. Black's Law Dictionary 220 (8th ed. 2004).
2. Lawrence A. Frolik & Mary F. Radford, *Sufficient Capacity: The Contrasting Capacity Requirements for Different Documents*, 2 NAELA J. 303, 304 (2006).
3. Capacity refers hereafter only to mental capacity, not physical capacity.

A. Capacity to Execute a Will or a Trust

Under most state laws, the lowest level of capacity is that needed to execute a valid will. Known as testamentary capacity, it is set very low because the law does not favor intestacy. A low level of capacity means that more individuals, particularly those in old age, are able to execute a valid will even if they have experienced some loss of capacity. The legal preference of the right of an individual to execute a valid will not only honors the right of individuals to distribute their property at death as they prefer, but it also encourages loyalty and devotion by family members, including caring for the physical needs of the aging individual. By being attentive to an aging relative, and particularly one who because of diminished capacity requires support and assistance, family members can hope that they will be favored in a will written near death when the testator may have suffered from diminished capacity but still retains testamentary capacity.

Testamentary capacity is a creature of state law; in some cases it is defined in a state statute but in most states case law defines it. The case law of virtually all states holds that four elements are required for a showing of testamentary capacity.

1. Did the testator understand the nature of the act they were performing?
2. Did the testator know the nature and extent of their property?
3. Did the testator know the identity of those who were the "natural objects of their bounty?"
4. Did the testator understand how the will disposed of their property?

While the tests are not complicated, their application has raised many questions and much litigation. For example, what is adequate knowledge of one's property? Is it enough that the individual understand the value of their estate and have some concept of the nature of the assets, for example, real estate or stocks, or must the individual have a fairly detailed understanding of the assets whose distribution will be governed by the will? Does the individual's educational attainment change the standard, with greater capacity being expected of someone with an MBA as opposed to a high school dropout? Understanding the distribution of property directly to individuals, such as equal shares to all my children, does not require much capacity. But what of an elaborate estate plan drawn up by a knowledgeable estate planner. Does the law require an aging client to understand why the gift to the spouse is a gift in trust rather than outright gift? (See Chapter 17, Estate Planning with the Very Old Client.)

In the past, case law sometimes appeared to require a higher level of capacity to execute a revocable trust. But despite language that seemed to require a higher standard of capacity, in reality the capacity to execute a valid trust was the same as for a will.[4] Today, the Uniform Trust Code (UTC) states that the capacity to

---

4. Frolik & Radford, *supra* note 2, at 303, 211.

execute a revocable trust is the same as that needed for a will.[5] Having the same standard is sensible because so often a will pours over into a testamentary or inter vivos trust or a trust is used as a will substitute. The standard for funding an irrevocable trust by a non-testamentary transfer, however, requires proof of the higher standard of capacity that is required to make a valid gift or enter into a contract.

B. Capacity to Make a Gift or a Contract

The capacity needed to make a gift or a contract (or to execute a deed) is the same: did the individual have the ability to understand the nature and effect of the act.[6] A donor of a gift must also have sufficient mental capacity to form the intent to make the gift, that is, give up ownership of the item being given, and those entering into a contract must have the intent to be legally bound by the terms of the contract.

Contractual and gift capacity require a higher degree of capacity than does testamentary capacity. An individual entering into a contract must "understand, in a reasonable manner, the nature and effect of the act."[7] It is the "reasonable manner" requirement that sets contract and gift capacity above testamentary capacity, or at least permits courts to invalidate contracts or gifts because of a lack of capacity if the court believes that doing so is in the best interest of the person with reduced capacity.

Contractual capacity also has a twist that is missing from testamentary capacity or the capacity to make gifts. The lack of necessary capacity for making a will, a trust, or a gift voids the transaction. The will or trust is invalid or the gift is voided and the property returned to the donor. In many states, however, a contract entered into by a party who lacks sufficient capacity is only voidable. The contract is valid unless the person who had reduced capacity or their legal representative chooses to void it. This permits, for example, an individual whose capacity varies over time and who lacked capacity at the time the contract was entered into, but who later recovered sufficiently to be able to enter into a contract, to enforce the contract previously entered into. It also permits the legal representative, such as a conservator, to enforce a contract that is in the best interest of the incapacitated person who entered into the contract.

Other states hold that contracts entered into by a person with insufficient capacity to be void from the inception, not merely voidable, because the transaction was missing the basic element of a contract, the assent by two persons with the requisite capacity to appreciate the consequences of entering into the contract and the mutual promises that they made. Although voiding all contracts entered into by incapacitated individuals offers a great deal of protection to individuals

---

5. UNIFORM TRUST CODE § 601 & comments (2004).
6. *In re* Estate of Clements, 505 N.E.2d 7 (Ill. Ct. App. 1987).
7. 17A C.J.S. CONTRACTS § 143 (2005).

who lack capacity, doing so also eliminates the possibility of enforcing a favorable contract.

Because the law presumes every adult to have legal capacity, the burden is on those who claim the contract is void due to one of the parties lacking capacity. Sometimes the incapacitated person or his or her representative will attempt to void the contract because of the alleged lack of capacity. Other times the other contracting party will attempt to void the contract, which is now seen as disadvantageous, on grounds that the other individual lacked contractual capacity. If the contract is only voidable, the individual who lacked capacity at the time the contract was entered into can unilaterally enforce the contract.

Whether an individual lacked contractual capacity at the time the contract was entered into is not always clear because of possible fluctuating capacity, the difficulty in ascertaining capacity at some past point in time, and applying the legal standard of whether the individual had a reasonable understanding of the terms and conditions of the contract. The need to establish the lack of capacity is unnecessary if the individual is under a conservatorship or plenary guardianship.[8] By law the individual cannot enter into a valid contract.[9] Note that guardianship does not necessarily mean that an individual lacks testamentary capacity; individuals under a conservatorship or plenary guardianship may have sufficient capacity to execute a valid will. However, because the burden of establishing the validity of the will is on its proponents, the existence of a guardianship or conservatorship must be overcome in the attempt to prove that the testator had testamentary capacity. (See Chapter 17, Estate Planning with the Very Old Client.)

III. Powers of Attorney

In anticipation of the possible loss of mental capacity, many aging clients execute a power of attorney for property management. (Powers of attorney for health care decision making are discussed in Chapter 11, Health Care Decision Making.) Powers of attorney are creatures of state law. Before creating one, the applicable state statute must be examined as to what powers can be delegated to the agent and the procedures to be followed in executing the power. Also, some states require the power to contain designated language that is meant to alert the principal and the agent of the powers and the responsibilities that the power grants to the agent.

At one time, by state statute, powers of attorney terminated upon the mental incapacity of the principal. To avoid that, state statutes were amended to permit the principal to designate the power of attorney as being "durable," meaning that it was still valid even if the principal lost capacity. Today, in most states, powers of

---

8. RESTATEMENT (SECOND) OF CONTRACTS, § 13 (1981).

9. *But see* Thames v. Daniels, 544 S.E.2d 854 (S.C. Ct. App. 2001) (An 80-year-old woman under a guardianship was found to have contractual capacity and so could execute a power of attorney.).

attorney are presumed durable, although the principal can reverse that presumption and have the power terminate upon his or her incapacity. Few do, however, because it is the fear of incapacity that gives rise to the desire for a power of attorney. As a result, powers of attorney are no longer referred to as "durable" since that is presumed to be the case. Also, the agent acting under a power of attorney in the past was referred to as the "attorney-in-fact." That term was confusing to the public and has given way to the term "agent." Today, a power of attorney is often referred to by the initials POA.

A. Legal Requirements to Execute a Valid POA

State law determines the requirements for a valid POA, but some generalities are possible. The principal who executes the POA must be an adult who has the requisite mental capacity, which in most states is the capacity necessary to execute a contract. Because that standard is higher than testamentary capacity, some individuals may have the capacity to sign a valid will but not a POA. Assuming that the principal has sufficient capacity to execute a valid POA, the state execution requirements must be observed. At a minimum, the state will require the POA to be in writing, dated and signed by the principal. Some states permit another to sign for a physically incapacitated but mentally competent principal. Other state requirements include the need for witness and notarization. Some states also require the agent to sign the POA, often after a statement that alerts the agent to the responsibilities of the position and the possible sanctions that can be brought to bear if the agent violates their obligations. The principal may even have to sign a statement that they understand the authority and control over the principal's property that the POA grants to the agent.

Because POAs are frequently signed only after the principal has suffered a loss of capacity, many lawsuits have been brought challenging whether the principal had sufficient capacity to execute a valid POA. Note that it is the mental capacity of the principal at the time of the execution of the POA, not physical capacity, which determines whether the POA is valid. An Arizona court found a principal to have capacity despite his being in a wheelchair, on oxygen, on a catheter, on several prescription drugs, partially deaf, and showing signs of dementia. The court found him to have sufficient capacity, relying in part on testimony by his physician and several lay witnesses that the principal was alert and understood that he was signing a power of attorney.[10] But if the principal has advanced dementia, it is very likely that the POA will be held to be invalid if anyone challenges it. Often whether the principal has sufficient capacity is not clear. The family, who very much wants the individual to sign the POA, may strongly urge the attorney to prepare and submit the POA despite the possibility that the principal lacks sufficient capacity. At least one court has held that an attorney did not commit malpractice when he permitted his client to sign a POA

---

10. *In re* Estate of Pouser, 975 P.2d 704 (Ariz. 1999).

even though later that person was found to have lacked capacity at the time of the execution of the POA.[11]

Signing two or three copies of the POA may be desirable. The agent may need to provide a signed original, as opposed to a photocopy, to a third party before the third party will acknowledge the agent's authority. Professionals, such as an accountant who represents the principal, may need a signed copy of the POA to show to those with whom they have business transaction that the professional is correct in taking direction from the agent. In some states, an agent who wishes to deal with real property owned by the principal is required to file a signed original POA with the appropriate Register of Deeds. And an additional signed copy can be very helpful if the original POA is lost or inadvertently destroyed even though state law may authorize a photocopy or electronic version of the POA to be treated as if it were an original, signed copy.

B. Springing and Standby Powers of Attorney

A POA goes into effect at the time designated by the principal, which can either be at the date of the execution of the POA, known as a "standby" POA, or when the principal loses mental capacity, known as a "springing" POA. Although springing POAs were once popular, experience with them has led to their being used much less often. Their major disadvantage is identifying when the agent's power under the POA takes effect. Typical mechanisms that trigger the POA include testimonials from one or more physicians or another professional that the principal has lost capacity. Unfortunately, obtaining the necessary testimonials can be expensive, time consuming, and, in some cases, very difficult, particularly if the principal does not believe that they have lost capacity and so will not cooperate with being examined. Moreover, the POA must define the level of incapacity that triggers the POA. It is difficult to describe the degree of the loss of capacity that will cause it to "spring" into action and even more difficult to apply. The physicians who examine the principal may not be familiar with the language used in the POA and so may be uncertain as to whether the principal is "incapacitated," as that term is used in the POA. Even if the physicians declare the principal to be incapacitated and so the POA is triggered, third parties may be reluctant to deal with the agent, because they may fear that the conditions that would trigger the POA may not have occurred.

In light of the problems associated with springing POAs, most POAs are now standby; the agent has full authority to act the minute the POA is properly executed. The principal does not expect or want the agent to act, however, unless the principal loses capacity and is unable to properly handle their financial affairs. Just how incapacitated the principal must be depends on the principal. If the agent should invoke the POA too soon, the principal can revoke it. If, however, the principal wants to revoke the POA, but has lost contractual capacity, the principal's

---

11. Persinger v. Holst, 639 N.W.2d 594 (Mich. Ct. App. 2001).

attempt to revoke the POA will be ineffective. Of course, a principal who still retains the capacity to revoke a POA, but whose loss of capacity has made it difficult to manage their finances may not choose to revoke the POA, but rather permit the agent to act as needed, or the principal and the agent may work together to make decisions about the assets and property of the principal.

There are ways to minimize the possibility of an agent using the POA before the principal would want him or her to do so. In order to deal with third parties, the agent must have a signed copy of the power, but the agent does not need to be given the POA until such time as the agent is needed. Many principals retain the POA, place it in a file, tell the agent where the POA is, and instruct the agent to retrieve it if the principal should lose capacity. This assumes the agent will always have access to where the POA is stored, and that may be the case if the agent is the spouse or child of the principal. Agents who are not so closely related to the principal may find it difficult to gain possession of the POA.

Often the attorney who drafted the POA will retain possession of it until such time as they determine that the mental condition of the principal necessitates action by the agent and then deliver the POA to the agent. This, too, has pitfalls because the attorney may not have enough contact with the principal to know when the principal is incapacitated enough to warrant releasing the POA to the agent. The expectation, however, is that the agent will approach the attorney and present proof enough to satisfy the attorney that the time has come for the agent to act.

The final protection from the agent prematurely acting under the POA is the right of the principal to revoke it. A principal with capacity can revoke the POA, name a new agent, or appoint a co-agent to act as a check on the other agent. Although the revocation of the POA is immediate, third parties who have been honoring the authority of the agent may not be aware of the revocation of the POA. Thus, if the principal revokes or alters the POA, the principal should notify third parties, such as their brokerage firm, and inform them that the POA has been revoked and the agent no longer has authority to act.

C. Selection of the Agent

The decision as to who to appoint as agent and successor agent deserves careful consideration. Most married principals name their spouse as agent unless the spouse has mental or physical limitations that would prevent them from performing as an agent. Those without a spouse (or a partner) usually name a child or grandchild. Those with no children sometimes name a sibling, a niece or nephew, or a friend. Some name an attorney or other professional. The principal must select not just the initial agent, but at least one successor agent. Co-agents can be named, but it is not preferred. If two agents are named, they must both agree to any action. Even if the two agents usually agree, they may find it difficult to find time to meet and carry out what needs to be done. Third parties, seeing that the POA appointed co-agents, may be reluctant to accept instructions from only one agent, even if the POA permits that, and demand that the other agent affirm the requested action.

It is best if the agent resides near the principal, though modern communication devices such as Skype lower the need for an agent to live in close proximity. Although not required, the agent ought to have enough interaction and communication with the principal to understand what the principal needs and how the agent can use the assets of the principal to meet those needs. The principal should select an agent who has the time, skills, and judgment to carry out their responsibilities. Perhaps the most underrated attribute of a good agent is that they be trustworthy. Not just in the sense that the agent will not steal from the principal, but trustworthy in the sense that the agent will act in good faith to loyally and diligently promote the best interests of the principal. Legally, an agent has a fiduciary obligation to the principal, but more importantly, the agent must be trusted to act in the best interest of the principal, not just because of the law, but because the agent wants to make the principal's life as good as possible.

D. Specialized Powers of Attorney

Although by law, a properly drafted POA that meets the state's formalities of execution and content should be accepted by all, some third parties are reluctant to accept a standard POA. Despite state law that often mandates that third parties accept a POA that appears valid on its face, they prefer or insist on the principal using a form of POA that they created. Financial institutions are the most likely to prefer the client use a form that they have created. An agent may find it much easier to deal with those institutions if the agent is appointed both by a standard POA and also by the form supplied by the institution.

Agents may find it difficult to deal with banks in which the principal has only modest-sized accounts because the agent will be confronted by a branch bank manager or employee who may be reluctant to honor a non-bank form POA. To avoid such problems, the principal should contact his or her bank, brokerage account, and investment entity and ask if they have a POA form that they prefer be used. If they do not, the principal should ask whether he should provide them with a signed original or photocopy of the POA and ask them to review the document to see if it properly empowers the agent to access and manage the principal's assets. If not, the principal should redraft the POA so that it contains the necessary language.

If the principal has unique assets, the drafter of the POA might include specific reference to those assets and detail the right of the agent in regard to those assets. In some cases, the principal may not want to grant the agent full authority of those assets. For example, the principal may not grant the agent the power to sell those assets or may insist that the agent obtain agreement from a third party before selling those assets. Assets with a foreign situs may also require a separate POA. For example, real estate located in another state likely requires an agent appointed under a POA that comports with the law of the state in which the property is located.

E. Powers Granted to the Agent

Principals usually want to grant their agent full authority to control and manage their assets. To that end, the POA should include all of the powers that the applicable state statute permits to be granted to the agent in order to ensure that the power confers sufficient authority on the agent to be able to handle whatever situation arises. Over the years, the tendency has been for state statutes to define more specifically what powers can be granted to an agent and the definition of or what is included within such powers. Most statutes contain a list of powers that the principal can grant to the agent. Typically, principals will want to grant all those powers absent a compelling reason not to. In doing so, the best practice is to track the exact language of the statute. As a general rule, a drafter should have an identifiable reason for substituting their own language for that of the state, because language that may seem "better or more correct" to the drafter, may seem opaque and confusing to a third party. If the language is different, a third party may assume that the principal intended to limit the power of the agent—otherwise why not use the language of the statute?

State law may bar certain powers to the agent unless specifically included in the POA. For example, the POA may have to specifically grant the agent the power to create, amend, or revoke an inter vivos trust; elect against a will; make gifts; change rights of survivorship on accounts; change beneficiary designations in life insurance policies, IRAs, or annuities; waive the principal's right to be a beneficiary under a pension or annuity; or disclaim property under a will. Even if state law does not require powers such as these to be specifically included in the POA, a careful drafter will ask the principal whether they want such powers to be granted to the agent, and draft the POA accordingly with specific language that clearly expresses what powers the principal wished to grant to the agent.

Care should be taken in granting the agent broad general powers because such language may be interpreted as granting expansive powers to the agent beyond those that the principal intended to grant. This may result in the agent taking actions never contemplated by the settlor, such as electing against the will.[12] A careful principal will grant broad powers because an agent must be able to deal with unexpected circumstances, but the principal will also specifically withhold from the agent powers that would permit the agent to take acts not desired by the principal.

Case law is replete with courts granting an agent authority to take actions that may not have been contemplated by the principal. For example, courts have held that an agent has the right to file a personal injury suit on behalf of the principal because of the general grant of authority under the POA.[13] A Texas court found that the daughter of the principal, acting as his agent under a POA, could execute

---

12. Matter of Lando, 809 N.Y.S.2d 901 (2006).
13. Miller v. Jackson Hosp. & Clinic, 776 So. 2d 122 (Ala. 2000); *In re* Guardianship of Savell, 876 So. 2d 308 (Miss. 2004).

a contract for prearranged funeral services and direct the disposition of the principal's body over the objections of the principal's widow.[14] Courts have split as to whether an agent can agree to arbitration when entering a contract for the principal. The issue has arisen when an agent admits the principal to a nursing home and signs an admission contract in which the agent agrees on behalf of the principal to submit any dispute to compulsory arbitration. Later, when the agent wants to sue the nursing home for injuring or causing the death of the principal, the nursing home invokes the arbitration agreement. The agent claims it does not apply because the agent lacked the authority to commit the principal to arbitration. The issue has been considered in several Florida cases with the outcome depending on the wording of the POA. One court upheld the arbitration agreement because of the POA's catchall language.[15] In another Florida case, however, the court found the agent's power to handle the principal's finances did not extend to agreeing to compulsory arbitration.[16]

Even very specific grants of authority in the POA may grant more authority to the agent than the settlor intended. A Colorado court interpreting a POA that specifically granted the agent the power to enter into a trust agreement held that the agent also had the power to revoke a trust even though the POA did not specifically grant that power.[17] A South Carolina court held that a POA that granted the agent the power to create trusts meant that the agent could create an irrevocable trust, fund it with the assets of the principal, and successfully resist a later attempt by the principal to revoke the trust. The principal was unsuccessful in convincing the court that the creation of the irrevocable trust by the agent was tantamount to creating a will, a power that is not permitted to be granted to an agent.[18]

The POA should also address whether the agent has authority to access the principal's online accounts and other digital assets. If so, the principal must arrange to make available to the agent the name of such accounts, passwords, and account numbers. The principal should maintain a file, preferably in hardcopy held in a secure file that holds the passwords to financial accounts as well as more personal information, such as photos that are stored in the cloud.

If the principal owns a pet, the POA should empower the agent with the authority to pay for and provide the care necessary to keep the pet comfortable and in good health. The POA could direct the agent to personally care for the animal or in the alternative to arrange for and pay for its care by another. To keep the cost of the pet care in bounds, the POA could authorize expenditures as necessary to maintain the pet in the manner that the principal did. In the alternative, the POA could direct the agent the power to give the pet to another person or entity that will provide appropriate care and permit the animal to live out its natural life. The

---

14. Carruth v. SCI Texas Funeral Servs. Inc., 221 S.W.3d 134 (Tex. Ct. App. 2006).
15. Sovereign Healthcare of Tampa, LLC v. Estate of Huerta, 14 So. 3d 1033 (Fla. Ct. App. 2009).
16. Carrington Place of St. Pete, LLC v. Estate of Milo, 19 So. 3d 340 (Fla. Ct. App. 2009).
17. *In re* Schlagel Trusts, 51 P.3d 1094 (Colo. Ct. App. 2002).
18. Watson v. Underwood, 756 S.E.2d 155 (S.C. Ct. App. 2014).

agent might also be authorized to make a one-time grant of money to the person or entity that agrees to take on the care of the pet.

An agent is a fiduciary with obligations of loyalty who must avoid self-dealing and must act in good faith. Even if state law does not recognize an agent as a fiduciary, the agent still must act in good faith and in the principal's best interest. It is likely that these fundamental duties are not waivable by the principal, though it is unclear why a principal would not want the agent to be required to act in good faith and in the best interest of the principal. Other state rules that govern an agent may seem to the principal to be unnecessary, particularly if the agent is the spouse or a trusted child. For example, the principal may not object to the agent, such as a spouse, comingling their funds with those of the principal. If so, the POA should so state. A principal may also want to modify the kind of records kept by the agent; requiring them to be either more or less detailed than required by state law. What the principal expects of the agent will depend on the relationship of the principal and the agent; the value, nature, and location of the principal's assets; and the likelihood of others objecting to the agent's acts.

The principal should also consider whether the POA should be worded in a way that will prevent the agent from doing anything that would disturb the principal's estate plan. In particular, the principal should either permit or bar the agent from actions that effect the value and nature of the principal's assets, including investing in assets or property that would burden the principal's net worth with high taxes or maintenance expenses or that would increase the principal's estate to greater exposure of income, estate, inheritance, or gift taxes.

The principal should carefully consider whether it is wise to grant the agent the power to make gifts. Many agents have misused that power to enrich themselves or made inappropriate gifts to others, such as their spouse or children. In response to incidents of agents abusing the power to make gifts, many states have modified their power of attorney statutes. In the past, many state statutes automatically gave the agent the power to make gifts. Over time many of these statutes were changed to reverse the presumption so that today in many states an agent has the power to make gifts only if the POA specifically grants that power. More recently, states now require that a POA that permits the agent to make gifts must contain language warning the principal of the risk associated with letting the agent make gifts.[19] Regardless of the applicable state law, the POA should specifically address whether the agent has the power to make gifts and the limitations, if any, on that gifting power.

A principal who wants the agent to have the power to make gifts should consider placing limits on the amount of such gifts and for some gifts require the agent to seek approval from a third party. One commonly used method is to limit an amount of gift to an amount not to exceed the annual dollar limit of the federal gift tax exclusion ($14,000 in 2017). The POA could bar the agent from making gifts

---

19. E.g., 20 Pa. C.S.A. § 5601(c).

to himself, his spouse, or his immediate family. The POA could also limit the manner in which the agent could make gifts. The agent could be denied the power to make gifts by changing the title on joint accounts, the named beneficiary on a Pay on Death account, the beneficiary on annuity payments, or by placing the assets of the principal in a joint survivorship account with the agent. Some principals require the agent to have any gift above a certain dollar amount approved by a named third party. The POA should include an exception to the limits on gifts if the agent believes it wise to give away assets as part of a plan to create Medicaid eligibility. (See Chapter 14, Medicaid.) Even this exception might require the approval of a named third party to ensure that the gifts not only address the need for Medicaid eligibility for the principal, but that the gifts are made in a manner consistent with the principal's estate plan.

F. Medallion Signature Guarantee

Agents who need to transfer securities in their physical form, as opposed to directing a brokerage firm to do so, will likely need to have their signature validated by a medallion signature guarantee stamp. The guarantee is required to prevent fraud because securities are bearer instruments; mere possession establishes a presumption of ownership. The agent can obtain a medallion signature guarantee from a financial institution, such as a commercial bank or a broker dealer that participates in one of the following programs:

- Securities Transfer Agents Medallion Program (STAMP) whose participants include more than 7,000 U.S. and Canadian financial institutions,
- Stock Exchanges Medallion Program (SEMP) whose participants include the regional stock exchange member firms, and clearing and trust companies, or
- New York Stock Exchange Medallion Signature Program (MSP) whose participants include NYSE member firms.

Notarization by a notary public is not a substitute for a medallion signature guarantee.

IV. Representative Payee

Many who receive Social Security benefits (or Supplemental Security Income) because of mental or physical deficits need assistance managing those benefits. In response, the Social Security Administration (SSA) provides that benefit payments may be made to a representative payee rather than the beneficiary.[20] Representative payees may be used for any SSA benefit including spousal and disability payments. A representative payee (commonly referred to as a "rep payee") only

---

20. 20 C.F.R. § 404.2010.

has the authority to handle funds provided by the SSA; they have no power to handle any other income or assets of the individual.

The SSA appoints the representative payee if the individual, the beneficiary of SSA funds, is unable to handle his or her payments. The beneficiary must be

- legally incompetent or mentally incapable of managing the benefits, or
- physically incapable of managing or directing the management of the benefits.[21]

Note that a representative payee will be appointed even if the beneficiary has a conservator or guardian or has a valid power of attorney. If so, usually the conservator, guardian, or agent will be appointed the representative payee.

The request for a representative payee can originate from the beneficiary or a third party, such as a family member or guardian, or the SSA can appoint one on its own initiative if it believes that doing so would best serve the beneficiary even if the beneficiary is legally competent. The SSA only appoints a representative payee upon a showing that one is needed based on the beneficiary's physical or mental condition. Proof may be in the form of a judicial declaration of guardianship, a physician's statement of the beneficiary's condition, a statement from the medical officer of a nursing home where the beneficiary resides, or similar evidence that the beneficiary's interest would be best served by the appointment of a representative payee. The appointment of the representative payee can be terminated if the beneficiary recovers enough, physically or mentally, to be able to manage the benefit payments.

Most representative payees are individuals, such as spouses or adult children, but agencies, organizations, or other institutions may also be appointed.[22] Although no one can be forced to act as a representative payee, the SSA has an order of preference.

- The beneficiary's guardian, spouse, or other relative with custody who has a "strong concern" for the beneficiary;
- A custodial friend or friend with a "strong concern" for the beneficiary;
- A custodial institution; or
- Another person who volunteers.

After investigating the probable representative payee, the SSA will select the person or entity with the ability to look after the needs of the beneficiary and who will best serve the interest of the beneficiary.[23] Although most representative payees are volunteers, a community-based nonprofit organization that serves as a representative payee may be paid a modest fee.[24]

21. *Id.*
22. *Id.* § 404.2020.
23. *Id.*
24. 42 U.S.C. § 405(j)(4)(A).

The representative payee must report annually to the SSA as to how the payments were used, except that spouses who live with the beneficiary need not do so unless requested by the SSA.[25] The representative payee must use the funds for the beneficiary's "maintenance," which includes food, shelter, clothes, the cost of institutionalization, medical care, and personal care needs. Any remaining funds may be used to support the beneficiary's support obligations to a spouse, parents, or children.[26] The representative payee cannot be forced to use the benefit funds to pay creditors of the beneficiary for any debts incurred before the payee began receiving the benefits, although the payee can pay off prior debts after having met all current and reasonably foreseeable needs of the beneficiary.[27] Amounts not spent are encouraged to be invested, preferably in an insured savings account or U.S. Savings Bonds. The representative payee, not the SSA, is liable to the beneficiary for any misuse of the funds.[28]

For detailed information about representative payees, see https://www.ssa.gov/payee/NewGuide/toc.htm#Needs_payee.

V. Joint Property

Many older persons own assets jointly, most often with a spouse. Joint ownership has three forms: tenancy by the entirety, joint tenancy, and tenancy in common. Tenancy by the entirety, which does not exist in some states, is a form of joint ownership available only to married couples (except in Hawaii and Vermont where designated civil union couples qualify) that permits them to own real property as a single legal entity. In some states, the couple must state in the deed that ownership is by the entirety, while in other states the conveyance of property to a married couple is presumed to be a tenancy by the entirety unless otherwise stated. At the death of one spouse, the surviving spouse becomes the sole owner of the property by force of law; the property is not subject to the provisions of the will. The tenancy by the entirety provides protection from creditors because the creditor of an individual spouse may not attach and sell the interest of the debtor spouse. However, if the debtor spouse survives and takes the property, the debt attaches to the entire property, not just the portion contributed by the debtor spouse. Neither spouse can sever the tenancy (give away or sell their share) without the consent of the other.

Joint tenancy most commonly is found in regard to real property and creates a right of survivorship in the other joint tenants. The death of one of the tenants means the other tenant shares equally in the interest owned by the deceased tenant. If the joint tenancy is between two tenants, the surviving tenant becomes the

---

25. 20 C.F.R. § 404.2065.
26. *Id.* § 404.2040.
27. *Id.* § 404.2040(d).
28. *Id.* § 404.2041.

sole owner upon the death of the other tenant. The ownership passes by law and is not subject to the deceased tenant's will. However, during life a joint tenant can sever the tenancy by selling their share or, in most states, by filing a document that changes the tenancy to a tenancy in common that does not have a right of survivorship.

Joint bank accounts and other joint financial accounts are creatures of the institution that created them. As a result the ownership interests vary. The account may state that it does not create survivorship interests, but usually the account is merely titled as a joint account and is silent as to whether it is a survivorship account. Typically a joint account that is silent as to the matter is presumed to have a created a right of survivorship, but that presumption is rebuttable if it can be shown that the deceased party never intended to create a survivorship interest in the other account holder. The heirs of the deceased joint account owner, who want to inherit under the will or by intestacy, will attempt to defeat the presumption that the deceased intended to create a survivorship account. They will claim that the account was a "convenience" account created so that the now surviving joint owner could access the account to manage the funds of the deceased account owner, such as paying their bills. Despite the title of the account, the deceased account owner never intended to create a survivorship interest. Although some courts have held that the deceased owner opened a "convenience" account and so rejected the presumption of survivorship, other courts have held that those who claimed the account was a convenience account failed to meet their burden of proof, and thus found that the account was a survivorship account and awarded ownership to the surviving account owner.[29]

Tenancy in common is joint ownership of property without a right of survivorship; the parties may sell or give away their interest in the property without the consent of the other tenant. At death, the ownership passes by will or intestacy. Many who open joint bank or other financial accounts with someone other than a spouse, such as an adult child, intend to create tenants in common. Unfortunately, the language used in the document that creates the account may create a joint account with right of survivorship or the language may be ambiguous or confusing. Anyone opening a joint financial account must take care that the account correctly reflects their intent as to the ownership interest and survivorship rights.

Joint financial accounts with right of survivorship between spouses are very common. These joint accounts serve two functions: they are will substitutes and they permit access to the asset by both spouses. Even couples who have wills that leave all their assets to the other spouse often use joint accounts to permit the survivor to have access to and control the asset or funds immediately upon the death of the other spouse without having to wait for the will to be probated. Spouses also want access by both spouses to assets because it is their understanding that the

---

29. E.g., Konfirst v. Stehlik, 13 N.E.3d 278 (Ill. App. Ct. 2014); *In re* Byrne Estate, 2014 WL 1233708 (Mich. App. Ct. Mar. 25, 2014).

assets are truly jointly owned and should therefore be accessible to both spouses without regard to which spouse was the source of the asset.

Older couples often find that joint ownership is very helpful if one spouse loses mental capacity. Thanks to the joint ownership of their assets, the well spouse can access the funds, pay the bills, and manage the investments without the need to rely on a power of attorney or to seek guardianship for the incapacitated spouse.

Creating a joint account with someone other than a spouse is problematical. Older individuals without a spouse sometimes open a joint account with an adult child so that the child can assist them with paying bills. Unfortunately, too often the child uses the account for their benefit by withdrawing sums to pay bills of their own or to invest in accounts solely in their name. Some attempt to justify their behavior by claiming that they "earned" the money because of their efforts on behalf of the parent. Because of the risk of misuse of the account by the child and the confusion as to the ownership interests of the parties, joint accounts with anyone other than a spouse are best avoided.

The better solutions to paying bills and managing an account are representative payees for Social Security benefits and a power of attorney for other finances. It is also possible to add another signature, such as that of a child, to a checking account without granting that person any ownership rights. This permits the child to write checks on the account without having any right to the funds. The safest solution to possible misuse of funds is the use of a power of attorney that requires the agent to disclose the use of the funds in the account to a third party. One child, for example, could be the agent who pays the bills, but would have to show the bank statements or permit online access to the account by another child.

VI. Trusts

The use of trusts as a means of providing property management is discussed fully in Chapter 16, Trusts.

Health Care Decision Making

11

I. Introduction

Every adult has the right to control their health care as long as they have sufficient mental capacity. Because mental capacity is presumed, the burden is on those who allege the adult lacks sufficient mental capacity to prove that assertion. Absent such evidence, an adult can make health care decisions even if they suffer from diminished capacity.

Patients must affirmatively consent to medical treatment. Such consent must be "informed consent," meaning that the patient understands the costs, benefits, and burdens of the proposed medical treatment and the alternatives, including the costs, benefits, and burdens of such alternative treatments. A patient has full autonomy; no one, not doctor, the family, or the state, has the right to make medical treatment decisions for a competent patient.[1]

For the medical community, the goal of informed consent is not merely to uphold the patient's self-determination, but to result in a patient who is well informed and who asks questions that enable the patient to make a decision that reflects medical realities and expresses the patient's values and hopes. Medical treatment is a process; a sharing and evaluation of information. A

---

1. Cruzan v. Director, 497 U.S. 261 (1990).

patient's medical care is not a single decision but a series of ongoing decisions as the doctor and the patient respond to the patient's changing condition. Some decisions are easy, some difficult. For older clients, their age and physical condition often mean that medical treatment decisions that they are asked to make literally have life and death consequences.

A competent patient has the right to refuse or terminate life-sustaining medical treatment even if that should lead to the patient's death. The refusal to accept life-sustaining treatment is not suicide (though suicide is not a crime); it is merely the expression of the right of an individual to accept or reject medical treatment as they see fit.

The exception to the need for a patient to grant consent arises in emergency care situations. If the patient is rendered incompetent because of a medical emergency, such as an accident or a medical event like a stroke, medical personnel have the right to provide medical care without consent until they have stabilized the patient and insured that the patient is not going to deteriorate or die. Once the patient has been stabilized, the treating personnel can continue to treat to maintain that stabilized condition, but cannot undertake treatment designed to improve the patient's condition. The emergency exception to the informed consent rule has important application to older patients who may experience an incident that requires medical treatment. If so, necessary treatment can be provided even if the patient would not have agreed to it. For example, the patient may be very old and may have been willing to die from the medical incident rather than endure the pain and discomfort associated with the treatment. If, however, the patient is treated under the emergency exception, after being stabilized and regaining competency, the patient can either agree to the continuation of the treatment or order that it be discontinued even if doing so might lead to their death.

II. Mental Capacity to Make Health Care Decisions

Competency to make medical decisions, or "mental capacity" as is the current preferred term, means the patient has sufficient capacity to understand the choices presented; to understand the nature of the medical condition and the probable consequences of the proposed treatment. The degree of capacity required is very fact specific—the more complicated the decision, the more variables involved, the less certain the outcomes—the more capacity that is required. The arbitrator of whether the patient has sufficient capacity is the treating physician who is required to obtain informed consent. If the treating physician doubts the patient can give informed consent, the physician should not proceed. Instead, the physician must turn to another decision maker who has the authority to make medical decisions for the patient. For older patients the most common causes of lack of capacity are the underlying illness or condition, reaction to prescription drugs or invasive treatment, and perhaps most commonly, dementia.

In theory, a physician who doubts that the patient has capacity or a patient who has been told that they lack capacity could petition a court to make a determination as to whether the patient has sufficient capacity to make medical treatment decisions. In practice, resorting to a court is rare. Sometimes the patient and physician come to agreement that the patient has diminished capacity but still is capable of making their medical decisions or at least the decision that must be made at that time. In other situations, if the physician decides that the patient lacks the capacity to give informed consent, the physician must turn to another, legally designated health care decision maker to make the medical treatment decision.

III. Advance Directives and Surrogate Health Care Decision Makers

A. Guardians

If the patient lacks the capacity to make health care decisions, the physician or other medical provider is not permitted to make them. Rather a lawful surrogate decision maker must be identified. The appointment of a guardian to make medical treatment decisions for the incapacitated person is one alternative. A guardian of the person or a plenary guardian will normally be empowered to make health care decisions. In some instances, the patient has a guardian of the estate or a conservator who had authority to manage the patient's assets but not their personal life or their medical care. If that is the case, the guardian or conservator should petition the court and ask it to enlarge the scope of the guardian or conservator's power to include making health care decisions or to appoint another guardian with the authority to make health care and other personal decisions.

A possible issue for a guardian who has the authority to make health care decisions is whether the guardian has the right to terminate or refuse life-sustaining treatment for the incapacitated person. State law differs on this point. Increasingly guardians are given the power to make health care decisions that may hasten the death of an incapacitated person. However, in some states, the court may require the guardian to petition for the court's approval before terminating or refusing life-sustaining treatment.

B. Spouses and Family Members

If the patient is incapacitated and cannot give informed consent and has not appointed a surrogate health care decision maker, guardianship will usually not be sought. Rather a spouse or family members, such as adult children, will make the necessary decisions. Many physicians are comfortable meeting with the spouse and the children and working out a plan of care. Even Justice Brennan of the Supreme Court noted that informal arrangements are often resorted to.[2] The

---

2. *Id.* at 314 n.15.

courts are rarely resorted to because of the cost, the delay in making the decisions, and the possible publicity.

Informal arrangements, however, may break down if the family disagrees about what is appropriate care or if they reject the physician's advice and, in the opinion of the physician, the family's decisions are not in the best interest of the patient. Even then, rather than going to court, the physician may wait and keep talking to the family, who, after the passage of hours or days, may finally agree to a course of treatment that is acceptable to the physician. Frequently, for example, the family may initially refuse to terminate life-sustaining treatment that the physician has determined to be futile. But after a few days and appropriate counseling by hospital professionals, the family will finally agree to terminate treatment and permit the patient to die.

C. Statutorily Appointed, Surrogate Health Care Decision Makers

Informal family decision making for an incapacitated patient has become less prevalent because many states have enacted laws that designate a surrogate health care decision maker if the patient has not previously done so. These laws are designed to avoid the need to seek a guardianship and to clearly identify those who have the authority to act for the incapacitated patient. Most of these state statutes are modeled after the Uniform Health-Care Decisions Act.[3]

State surrogate health care decision maker acts typically permit the attending physician to determine whether the patient lacks capacity. The physician does not have to go to a court, but merely declares that the patient is incapacitated and unable to make a health care decision. If the patient has not appointed an agent for health care decisions or does not have a guardian authorized to make health care decisions, the statute provides a list of surrogates in descending order empowered to made health care decisions on behalf of the patient. The state law may also permit the statutory designated person to act even if the patient has appointed an agent if that agent is not available or cannot be made available in time to make a necessary health care decision. Assuming the statute is invoked, the usual priority of surrogates is the spouse (absent a legal separation), an adult child, a parent, an adult sibling, or a person with a special relationship or concern for the patient. No one on the list can be compelled to act as a surrogate. If, for example, the spouse declines, the option to act as surrogate devolves to the next in line, typically an adult child.

If there is more than one member of the designated class, such as more than one adult child, in most states all of the class who agree to serve as surrogate are designated as surrogates. But the state may permit the health care provider to select a single surrogate out of a class of eligible individuals. If there is more than one surrogate and they do not agree, the decision by the majority of the surrogates controls in some states. In others, there must be unanimity. If the surrogates are

---

3. Uniform Health-Care Decisions Act, 9 U.L.A. § 5 (West 2005).

evenly divided, the law may disqualify them as surrogates and may provide for the power to decide to devolve to the next class of surrogates on the list. If disputes as to how to care for the patient results in the disqualification of all the statutory listed surrogates, a resort to a guardian may be necessary.

The state statute will likely require the surrogate to make decisions in a manner that the patient, but for the incapacity, would have made. This is known as the substituted judgment standard; the surrogate substitutes the judgment of the patient in lieu of doing what the surrogate might think best. To determine how the patient might have reacted to the medical decision faced by the surrogate, the surrogate can rely upon the patient's written statements, oral pronouncements, expressed moral or religious beliefs, or even the patient's lifestyle.[4] If the surrogate lacks knowledge of how the patient would have decided, the surrogate will probably be required to make decisions in the best interest of the patient. The state might require the surrogate to act in good faith, which presumably means in the patient's best interest. What is the patient's best interest depends on the facts at hand; in most instances what the patient would want if they were a reasonable person is the best way to define what is in their best interest.

States differ on the authority of the surrogate to terminate or refuse life-sustaining treatment, although if no one objects to what the surrogate decides, the decision will prevail without regard to what the statute says. The right of a surrogate to terminate the artificial provision of nutrition and hydration may also be limited or denied by the statute, although again, unless an objection is raised, and if the provider and family members are willing to go along, the decision of the surrogate may prevail over the language of the statute.

Neither the authority of the surrogate or the decisions made by the surrogate requires judicial approval. The purpose of these state statutory surrogate statutes is to greatly reduce judicial involvement in health care decisions for incapacitated persons. The statutes are intended to identify a surrogate who has a relationship with the patient that is significant enough to permit the surrogate to make informed decisions for the patient.

D. Living Wills

Every state permits an individual to execute a living will to control or direct their medical care in the event that they lose the mental capacity to do so. The instructions in the living will are the attempt by the individual to prospectively determine their course of medical care near the end of life. The state statute defines what kinds of medical decisions can be controlled in a living will and also defines the conditions under which the living will is operative. By definition, a living will becomes effective only upon the individual becoming incapacitated. In addition, in many states the individual must also either be permanently unconscious or terminally ill. Permanent unconsciousness or as it is also known, a persistent

---

4. *In re* Fiori, 673 A.2d 905 (Pa. 1996).

vegetative state, is usually caused by brain trauma resulting from an accident. It is a nonreversible state from which the individual is not expected to ever awake. The individual is not responsive or aware of their surroundings and is kept alive only by artificial nutrition and hydration and sometimes by a respirator. Although not brain dead, the individual will never regain consciousness. Most individuals do not want to be kept "alive" if they are permanently unconscious and so state in the living will. Death is brought on by removing the respirator, if there is one, or by terminating artificial nutrition and hydration.

The requirement in most living will statutes that the individual be terminally ill is more problematic. The term usually means that the individual's condition is incurable and that death is certain. Some state statutes refer to death being not only certain but imminent, soon or in a short time. What those terms mean is unclear. The "certainty" of death is defined in some statutes as being to a reasonable degree of medical certainty, which is not a precise definition. Some statutes define terminal as when medical treatment will only serve to prolong the process of dying. Advances in medicine, however, have increased the chance of a successful recovery, or at least extension of life, to the point that most physicians will not declare a patient to be terminal until death is very close, only hours or days away. The result is that fewer patients are terminal, so fewer living wills take effect and so many dying patients who lack capacity are aggressively treated far longer than they might have imagined or desired.

State statutes enumerate the procedural requirements to create a valid living will. The exact state requirements should be examined and carefully followed. Many state living will statutes provide a model form. When available the model form should be used. Otherwise, third parties in that state may not believe that a customized form is valid even if it is. To execute a valid living will the individual must have sufficient mental capacity; the exact degree is often not defined, but the individual should understand the concept of a living will and the consequences of signing such a document. The individual must sign the living will; oral living wills are not valid. Most states require the living will to have two witnesses and many require it to be notarized. Some states restrict who may act as a witness and so prohibit anyone with a conflict of interest, such as a potential heir, from being a witness. Some states bar an employee of a nursing home or other facility where the individual lives from being a witness.

A careful drafter of a living will would always have it witnessed by at least two witnesses and also have it notarized. If an individual signs more than one living will, the most recent document prevails. States generally do not recognize living wills as valid unless the document meets the state's procedural requirements even if the document was valid in the state where it was executed.

Most state statutes permit an individual to declare in a living will that they do not want artificial nutrition or hydration, although state law may require the provision of artificial nutrition and hydration as necessary for the patient's comfort.

Some states require language in the living will that specifically refers to the termination of artificial nutrition and hydration, but even if not required by statute, the living will should specifically state the patient's preference.

A living will takes effect only if the individual is mentally incapacitated and meets the state requirements, such as being terminally ill. The health care provider must also be aware of the existence of the document with the duty on the individual to provide it to the provider. Federal law requires that a hospital must ask newly admitted patients whether they have a living will or other advance health care directive.[5] Physicians and other health care providers also typically inquire whether the patient has a living will or advance health care directive. If the patient is incapacitated, they will often ask the spouse or family if they know of a living will. Once the physician is aware of the living will, state law requires that the directions in the document be followed. Failure to do so may make the physician liable for civil or even criminal penalties depending on state law. Conversely, physicians and other health care providers have immunity if they follow the dictates of a valid living will. If the physician or hospital refuses to follow the dictates in the living will, perhaps because of religious beliefs, they must arrange to transfer the patient to a facility or a different physician who will honor the document.

An individual can revoke a living will at any time by physical destruction, by executing a later dated living will, by a written declaration, and even by an oral revocation. Of course, the revocation takes effect only after the physician has been notified. Many states even permit an incapacitated patient to revoke a living will. In practice, this means that a physician should respect a patient's statement that they want to revoke their living will and continue treatment even if it is unclear whether the patient lacks the capacity to make a rational decision.

Although very popular, in practice living wills are not thought to have much influence on a patient's end of life care. Because the patient must be terminal, the living will often does not apply to very sick patients or those with very serious conditions because there is still hope, albeit not much, that the continued medical treatments and procedures might either cure the patient, or more realistically, keep the patient alive for at least a few more days or weeks. Spouses and families also often object to the termination of medical care in the belief that care should be provided as long as there is a chance of recovery or continued life even if that chance is very slim. As long as the patient is in a hospital setting, the odds are high that termination of life-sustaining treatment will not cease until the patient is very close to death regardless of the language in a living will or the patient's intent. Rather than relying on a living will, a patient while still having capacity should consider electing hospice care where the goal is to provide palliative care and cease attempting to cure the patient or prolong their life. (See Chapter 13 for a discussion of hospice care.)

---

5. 42 U.S.C. § 1395c(f).

E. Appointment of a Surrogate Health Care Decision Maker

The failure of living wills as a means of controlling end-of-life care has resulted in individuals appointing surrogate health care decision makers. Often referred to as health care powers of attorney, these documents are similar to traditional powers of attorney in that they identify a person, the agent, who will make health care decisions for the declarant. Unlike traditional powers of attorney that typically appoint the agent with standby powers that take effect immediately upon the execution of the power, individuals appoint a surrogate health care decision maker (surrogate) whose authority only arises if the declarant loses the mental capacity necessary to give informed consent to health care decisions. Every state has a statute that permits the appointment of a surrogate, sometimes referred to as a proxy decision maker. The statutes vary, but all recognize that while a living will is an attempt by the individual to control or dictate when life-sustaining treatment should be terminated, the appointment of a surrogate is the delegation of health care decision making to another person. It is based on the concept that because an individual has a constitutional right to control their health care, in the event that they lose the capacity to exercise that right, they have the corresponding right to delegate the authority to make their health care decisions to another person.

The degree of authority that an individual can delegate to a surrogate varies by state statute; some attempt to limit the surrogate's authority in regard to end-of-life decisions. Whether those statutes could pass constitutional muster is unclear. If an individual has the right to refuse life-sustaining treatment even if the individual is not terminally ill, it is not clear why the individual cannot delegate that power to a surrogate. Fortunately, the issue is largely moot. If the physician is willing to respect the decisions of the surrogate and no one objects, the statutory limitations are usually irrelevant.

The procedural requirements of appointing a surrogate depend upon state law. The declarant must have sufficient mental capacity to execute the document. As with a living will, the drafter should always have at least two witnesses and have the document notarized even if not required by the state statute. The drafter should pay close attention to the state statute, however. The state may have a mandated form, but whether that requirement is constitutionally valid is uncertain. A few state statutes require the document to contain language that warns the declarant of the legal effect of appointing a surrogate.

Some statutes permit a power of attorney to contain language that appoints the agent as the health care decision maker. Other statutes permit the principal to grant limited authority to an agent to make some health care decisions. Consequently, care must be taken not to inadvertently delegate health care decisions to an agent appointed to handle property. In some states, granting an agent all the powers listed in the state statute might inadvertently grant the agent the power to make health care decisions.

Other states combine the creation of a living will with the appointment of a surrogate. If the individual does not want a living will, preferring instead to only appoint a surrogate, it is best not to use the state's model form or the language of the statute, but instead to draft a document that clearly states that the declarant is appointing a surrogate decision maker and is not creating a living will. If the document does contain a living will, it should make clear whether the surrogate has the authority to override the instructions in the living will or whether the living will declarations circumscribe the authority of the surrogate. Like a living will, the document that appointed the surrogate is revocable by the declarant by physical destruction, written revocation, by the creation of a newer document appointing a surrogate, or by an oral pronouncement. State law may permit an incapacitated individual to revoke the document. Of course, because the document will do no good unless the health care provider is aware of its existence, the patient must be sure that the document accompanies them to wherever they may be obtaining treatment.

A drafter in a state that has a model form, even if not mandated by law, should carefully consider whether to use the form or at least make only minor changes in it rather than draft an original, more personalized document. Use of the model form ensures that the document meets the statutory requirements. More importantly, third parties, such as physicians, may be familiar with the statutory form and feel comfortable with it. As a result, they may be more willing to accept the surrogate's authority. If faced with an unfamiliar form, the physician may not be sure whether it is legal. Even if the physician is willing to accept the authority of the surrogate, the physician might be fearful that the power of the surrogate may be limited in some manner by the language of an unfamiliar form, particularly if the form is several pages long.

Some clients, however, may wish for a more personalized form that contains more detail and is more expressive of what the client wants. The client may want to include precatory language that informs the surrogate about the client's attitudes toward end-of-life treatment or how the client would want to be treated if severely demented but not otherwise terminally ill. Unfortunately, such details may confuse the treating physician and the surrogate rather than bringing clarity. The physician merely wants the document to identify the surrogate and state whether the surrogate can refuse or terminate life-sustaining treatment to the extent allowed by the state statute. A complicated, detailed document is likely to cause the physician to refer it to the hospital, which in turn may send it on to an ethics committee or to its legal counsel. All this takes time and may prevent the surrogate from making essential decisions as to the medical treatment of the declarant. Moreover, the surrogate's power only arises when the declarant has lost capacity and requires medical treatment, which can be an emotionally difficult time for the spouse and family of the declarant as well as for the surrogate (who may be the spouse). Even the surrogate may not be sure of the extent of the power granted, either never having been sure or having become confused and distracted by the illness of the incapacitated declarant.

Rather than putting detailed instructions or advisory language in the document, the client should create a separate advisory letter for the surrogate that explains in detail the client's desires and attitudes about medical care and, in particular, end-of-life care. Ideally, the individual would have a conversation with the surrogate and go over the items in the letter with the hope that the surrogate will better understand the wishes of the client and feel more confident in carrying them out. The surrogate can supply the physician with the shorter document that appoints the surrogate and that briefly states the scope and extent of the surrogate's authority. If necessary, the surrogate can show the advisory letter to the physician should there be any question whether the surrogate is acting in a manner consistent with the client's desires and expectations.

If the client has a known illness or condition, the document that appoints the surrogate could refer to that illness or condition and give specific guidance to the surrogate based on expectations as to the kind of medical decisions that are likely to arise at a time after the client loses capacity. It is best not to include binding instructions but rather to include precatory language that indicates the client's treatment preferences with the understanding that the surrogate will ultimately make decisions after consulting with the physician.

Be very careful when naming the surrogate. It is best to name only one surrogate and name one or two successor surrogates. Physicians prefer to deal with a single health care decision maker. Having two or three joint surrogates means that time may be lost in getting all the surrogates together. More surrogates also makes in more difficult for the physician to be sure that all understand the patient's condition, the choice to be made, and why the physician recommend a particular choice. More than one surrogate can also lead to disagreements as to how to proceed. If there are two surrogates, a disagreement can prevent any decision or can permit the more stubborn or least flexible surrogate to dominate the decision making. Three surrogates may mean the majority can decide (if that is what the document states), but that can lead to divisiveness, hard feelings, and escalating disagreement.

The need for successor surrogates is apparent because the surrogate may die, become incapacitated, refuse to serve, or resign as surrogate. The client must be sure to have a conversation with the successor surrogates similar to the conversation with the initial surrogate to ensure that the successors, like the initial surrogate, understand the client's attitude toward end-of life treatment and are willing to make decisions that will implement the client's wishes.

The selection of the surrogate is critical. Whoever is selected must meet the requirements of the applicable state law. Typically the surrogate must be an adult and cannot be a health care provider and certainly not the attending physician. Under many state statutes, if the declarant resides in a facility, such as a nursing home, no employee of that institution can serve as their surrogate. Most declarants name their spouses as the initial surrogate and an adult child as the first successor. If there is more than one child, the child who is selected depends upon which child lives closest, which child is emotionally capable of making end-of-life decisions, which child is best at understanding medical procedures, and, of course, which child is willing to accept the burden of acting as the surrogate.

The state statute will define the powers that can delegated to the surrogate. The declarant should delegate as broad of authority as permitted in order that the surrogate will be able to act and make decisions under any possible scenario. The document should state whether and under what conditions the surrogate can refuse or terminate life-sustaining treatment for the declarant. The document should also state whether the surrogate can withhold or terminate artificial nutrition and hydration, both of which are considered forms of medical care and so can be withheld just as any other form of life-sustaining treatment. A surrogate cannot be authorized to engage in mercy killing or assisted suicide.

The declarant should consider carefully what kind of medical treatment they want in the event that they become severely demented to the extent that they longer recognize their family or friends, do not know where they are and apparently are no longer capable of rational thought. Should that come to pass, the question arises whether the declarant would want routine medical care or prefer that it be discontinued. For example, if the declarant is severely demented would they want an annual flu shot or a pneumonia vaccination? Or would the declarant be willing to become infected and possibly die; an outcome that they might believe acceptable if they are so severely demented that they no longer recognize family members.

One approach to instructing the surrogate is for declarants to declare in general terms how they want to be treated based on the conditions of their life. The declarant states that they either do or do not want to continue living if

- Due to dementia, they cannot understand what they read or cannot carry on a conversation;
- They need to stay in a nursing home for the rest of their life; or
- They need someone to take care of them for the rest of their life, that is, bathe, feed, or dress them or assist them because they are incontinent.

If the declarant does not want to continue living under any of the these conditions, they should instruct the surrogate to approve only palliative care—pain relief and comfort care—but not treat infections, diseases, or conditions even it not treating them may lead to death.

IV. Advance Directives That Require Physician Authorization

A. DNR Orders

Many older clients fear that a "natural" or "inevitable" death may be blocked or delayed by the administration of cardiopulmonary resuscitation, known as CPR, administered to restore cardiac function, that is, restart a heartbeat, if the individual has suffered cardiac or respiratory arrest. An individual whose heart has stopped beating suffers a loss of blood to the brain that leads to brain damage and eventually death if the heart function is not quickly restored. CPR is administered by chest compression, use of a defibrillator, electric shock to the chest, provision of cardiologic medications, and aids to breathing, such as the insertion of a breathing tube.

If the Emergency Medical Service (EMS) is called because of cardiac heart failure, an advance health care directive, either a living will or one that appoints a surrogate decision maker will usually not help. By law, EMS must attempt to resuscitate the patient and transport them to a hospital. The administration of medical care, even without the patient's consent, is appropriate under the emergency care exception to the requirement of informed consent, which permits third parties to engage in emergency medical care to stabilize the victim and maintain them in that condition until the patient or a surrogate can engage in making medical treatment decisions. Some states by law declare that a patient is presumed to have consented to care by the EMS including CPR.

In order to prevent the use of CPR by EMS, an individual can execute a Do Not Resuscitate Order, or DNR, if authorized by a state statute. Although the statutes vary, most permit any adult to execute a DNR; some limit the use of a DNR to those in a terminal condition, if CPR would be futile, or by other terms that limit the circumstances under which third parties must honor the document. Statutes also define what CPR is and what kind of procedures can be barred by a valid DNR.

A DNR is essentially a medical treatment order. An individual who wants a DNR must request that their physician issue it and make it part of the treatment plan contained in their medical records. To be valid is must be signed by the patient's attending physician, signed by the patient, and be witnessed. The DNR becomes part of the patient's medical record. It is a physician's treatment order, consented to by the patient about how the patient is to be treated, in this case, no provision of CPR. Many statutes contain model DNR forms; in some states a state agency is delegated the task of creating a model form.

A patient, working with their physician, can create a DNR designed to prevent third parties, including the EMS, from employing CPR if the EMS personnel are aware of the DNR. To make sure that the existence of the DNR is known, some states permit patients to wear a bracelet or a necklace stating that they have a physician authorized DNR with which the medical personnel must comply. In almost all states, physicians must either comply with a DNR or transfer the patient to another physician or facility that is willing to abide by it. However, if the physician believes that the patient's condition has improved enough to make the DNR order inappropriate, the physician can try to persuade the patient to rescind it. If the patient is incapacitated, a surrogate decision maker, depending on state law, may have the authority to withdraw the DNR. Whether a surrogate should do so depends on how the surrogate believes the patient would respond to the physician's request to rescind the DNR if the patient had capacity.

B. POLST—Physician Order for Life-Sustaining Treatment

A physician order for life-sustaining treatment, or POLST, is a physician order that reflects the patient's end-of-life treatment preferences. (In some states, a POLST is known as MOLST, COLST, MOST, or POST.) Unlike living wills and the appointment of a surrogate health care decision maker that are executed by the patient, a POLST is created by the physician. It is a medical order that is made part of the patient's medical records and takes effect immediately. The course of care detailed in the POLST, like any medical order, must have been approved by the patient under the doctrine of informed consent. The POLST, therefore, can only be issued after the physician has consulted with the patient and obtained the patient's consent.

POLSTs are creatures of state laws or state regulations and so differ from state to state. However, they all are designed to encourage the physician and the patient to engage in a conversation about the available medical treatment choices, the patient's preferences, and what medical treatments or procedures that the patient consents to. Depending on the state law or regulation, the POLST may be available only if the patient has a year or less to live.

A typical POLST will first address whether the patient desires CPR. If not, the POLST can serve as a DNR order. Next, the POLST will address whether the patient consents to a list of potential medical interventions including incubation, intensive care, the use of antibiotics, chemotherapy, and the like. If the patient desires hospice care, the POLST may contain consent only for palliative care or comfort care. Finally the POLST should address whether the patient desires artificial nutrition or hydration. Specifically, does the patient consent to the use of a feeding tube?

Because a patient can give informed consent only if they have sufficient mental capacity, a patient who lacks mental capacity cannot consent to a POLST. Because of a possible loss of capacity, all potential patients should appoint a surrogate decision maker. Whether a surrogate designated by the patient can consent to a POLST depends on state law. Some states grant surrogates, whether appointed by the patient or designated as surrogate by a state statute, the authority to agree to a POLST. A few states limit the authority of a statute-designated surrogate to do so. Some states permit the surrogate to agree to a POLST but not to the termination of life-sustaining treatment. Of course, a patient who appoints a surrogate can limit the authority of the surrogate and prohibit them from agreeing to a POLST or limit the kinds of medical treatment that can be included in the POLST. A patient who has already agreed to a POLST, for example, might bar the surrogate from revoking or replacing that POLST. Or the patient might include language that makes clear that the surrogate can only agree to a new POLST if it is consistent with the intent and wishes of the patient and is in the patient's best interest.

A POLST is often printed on a pink page or otherwise printed in a manner designed to ensure that it is not overlooked. As a medical directive it is part of the patient's medical records and should accompany the patient wherever the patient may be, such as in a nursing home or a hospital. As the patient's condition varies, and particularly if it worsens, the POLST should be reviewed and modified as needed in light of the patient's changing condition.

The role of a lawyer advising a client about a POLST is limited. The lawyer cannot draw up a POLST and there is no need for the lawyer to review a POLST any more than a lawyer would review any other medical directive. What a lawyer can do is inform a client, the client's spouse, or family about a POLST if the client is very frail or very sick and advise the client to discuss the creation of a POLST with their physician.

Long-Term Care Insurance 12

I. Introduction

Long-term care is expensive. Depending on its location, a nursing home may cost from $70,000 to over $130,000 a year. An assisted living facility may cost $30,000 to $70,000 a year. Home care can be prohibitively expensive. At an average hourly cost of $20, daily care for 24 hours in the home would be $480 or over $175,000 a year. A few elderly individuals do have sufficient income and savings to pay for their cost of long-term care. Most, however, cannot; or, even if they can initially, over time paying for their long-term care will deplete or exhaust their estates and severely compromise the income available to the well spouse. For many, the apparent solution is to purchase long-term care insurance to pay for some of their cost of care. What is long-term care insurance and who should purchase it, is the subject of this chapter.

For many, the purchase of long-term care insurance is problematic. When the cost of the insurance is balanced against the possible benefits, some will conclude that its purchase is not sensible. Others will discover that because of their age or health, they are not insurable. And some elderly decide that they can afford to pay for long-term care and so have no need to purchase insurance.

Long-term care insurance (LTCI) is not a good purchase for everyone. The potential purchaser must be able to afford the annual premiums. Like any insurance, paying the annual premium means that the insured trades off current consumption for future protection against a possible loss, in this case in the form of the cost of long-term care. The question is always whether the cost in terms of a lower standard of living today is worth the reduction of the risk of an uncertain loss tomorrow. For example, if a couple, both age 75, have a combined annual gross income of $60,000, is it worth it to them to pay $3,000 a year in premiums for LTCI? Although the LTCI offers a limited degree of protection against the cost of long-term care (see Section III. Coverage) the cost of the LTCI lowers their consumption for the rest of their lives. Whether the cost of LTCI is worth it depends on the cost to the insured as measured by the loss of income versus the degree of risk of paying for long-term care, which in turn is comprised of the likelihood of the loss (the need to pay for long-term care) and the probable amount of the loss (the cost of such care). Unfortunately for the potential purchaser of insurance, only the loss in income due to the cost of the premiums for LTCI is known; the likelihood of needing long-term care and the cost of that care are both unknown.

II. The Features of Long-Term Care Insurance

Long-term care insurance describes a number of insurance products that pay benefits triggered by the insured paying for long-term care. LTCI can be "pure" long-term care insurance; the policy only pays benefits for the long-term care costs. Increasingly, however, LTCI is offered as part of a larger schedule of benefits, particularly death benefits, or the LTCI benefits are a subpart of benefits paid under an annuity contract. As more LTCI policies are sold as part of larger, more complex insurance products, it has become more difficult to compare policies or to understand the cost of the long-term care benefits as opposed to the cost of the insurance or annuity product.

Even for stand-alone LTCI policies, there is no "standard" policy. Each company offers its own policy and that policy will usually come in several variations. Because LTCI is regulated by the states, there is no federal "law" of LTCI. Each state has its own requirements of what a LTCI policy must contain. Moreover, state insurance regulatory agencies must approve the premiums charged by LTCI so that the same insurance product offered in different states may have a different premium. Despite differences in state requirements and differences among policies offered by different insurance companies, however, all policies do contain some fundamental features that are consistent from state to state. Almost all policies, for example, are written to be "tax qualified" so that they can take advantage of the federal income tax code deduction that permits some or all of the premium to be deducted and the policy benefits to be excluded from the income of the recipient. (See discussion in Section II.D.)

Insurance can be divided in to two kinds: casualty and life. Casualty insurance covers risks that are uncertain to occur and for which the amount of loss is also uncertain, though the policy benefit is limited either by the value of what is being insured or by the benefit limits stated in the policy. Fire insurance on a home is a classic example of casualty insurance. In contrast, life insurance insures death, a risk that is certain to occur—although it is uncertain as to when it will occur—and the amount of the benefit is also certain because it is selected by the insured. What both casualty insurance and life insurance have in common is that the insured loss—the casualty such as a house fire or death of the insured—are losses that can be accurately estimated for a group, but are highly uncertain for any particular policy as to whether they will occur, in the case of the insured casualty loss, or when they will occur, in the case of life insurance.

To some extent, LTCI resembles life insurance in that it is usually taken out for life, whereas casualty insurance is taken out only for the period that the risk presents a possible loss to the insured. For example, homeowner's fire insurance is terminated when the house is sold. Yet, LTCI resembles casualty insurance more than life insurance because it insures a risk of loss that may never occur—the insured may never need or pay for long-term care and so never trigger the payment of benefits by the policy. And whereas the death benefit of a life insurance policy is a set amount, the benefits paid for long-term care depend on the long-term care costs incurred by the insured up to the maximum amount paid for by the policy, which is similar to casualty insurance that only pays for actual losses and then only up to the limit of the policy.

Most purchasers of LTCI never collect any benefits. In 2014, the executive director of the American Association for Long-Term Care Insurance posted the responses of long-term care insurance actuaries to his question, "What percentage of people who purchase long-term care insurance will utilize their policy at some point before they die?"[1] The answer was that about 35 percent ever qualify for benefits. This low percentage exists even though adverse selection drives the purchase of LTCI. The likelihood is that those who have some reason to believe that they will need to pay for long-term care are more likely to purchase it. The reasons that some believe that they are more likely to need long-term care include family history, such as their parents and grandparents having dementia; being overweight or in poor physical condition; or having little likelihood of being the recipient of free care, such as being single or not having children. The latter is a strong determinate of who purchases LTCI. Sixty-five percent of the elderly who need long-term care rely exclusively on family and friends to provide assistance, with the result that only 7 percent who have a family caregiver live in an institution. In contrast, 50 percent of the elderly who need long-term care but have no family available to care for them reside in nursing homes.[2] The profile of those who purchase LTCI therefore undoubtedly reflects both those who fear eventually

---

1. http://www.aaltci.org/long-term-care-insurance/learning-center/probability-long-term
-care.php.
2. http://www.ioaging.org/about/aging-in-america/#sthash.PNJfHax1.dpuf.

needing long-term care and those who anticipate having to pay for long-term care if they ever need it.

If adverse selection is factored in, the fact that only 35 percent of those who buy LTCI collect benefits suggests that the possibility that a relatively healthy, married individual who has children will need to pay for LTCI for an extended period is not as great as some suggest. Although about 1.4 million individuals reside in a nursing home,[3] it is believed that only about 35 percent of those age 65 or older will ever reside in a nursing home. Of those, only a small minority of the elderly stay for an extended period of time in a nursing home. A 2008 survey by the American Association of Long-Term Care Insurance showed the length of nursing home stays:

12%   5 years or more
12%   3 to 5 years
30%   1 to 3 years
25%   3 months to 1 year
20%   less than 3 months

These numbers indicate that almost half of all nursing home stays are for a year or less and only about a quarter last for three years or more. If only about one-third of the elderly will ever spend any time in a nursing home, the probability of an individual residing in a nursing home for three years or more is less than 10 percent. The odds of residing in a nursing home for a year or more are less than 20 percent. Thus, while the possibility of paying for nursing home care exists, the cost for the great majority of elderly is likely to be for less than a year. A risk, to be sure, but a risk that many elderly appear willing to accept, if the low sales of LTCI are any indication. Of course, some of those who live in a nursing home may have paid for long-term care provided in their home or in an assisted living facility prior to moving to the nursing home, which means the duration of the need for long-term care is greater than the study might indicate. Nevertheless, it appears that extended stays in a costly nursing home are limited to a small portion of the elderly population.

A. Eligibility Requirements

Most LTCI is purchased by individuals, although some employers provide LTCI as a benefit to their employees, sometimes subsidizing the policies, other times merely making it available as a payroll deduction. LTCI is also sold to members of national associations, though the association typically has nothing to do with the sale and is only providing access to its members to the insurance company, with the association often being recompensed for doing so.

---

3. http://www.cdc.gov/nchs/fastats/nursing-home-care.htm.

1. Age Restrictions

Insurance companies that sell LTCI will not sell a policy if the potential purchaser is too old. For most companies the limit is age 80, although some companies set the limit at age 84 and a few set the age limit below age 80. The insurance companies impose an age limit because the likelihood of a policy owner having to pay for long-term care rises rapidly with age and correspondingly, the number of years that the insured will pay premiums before becoming eligible for benefits is less. In part, the need for long-term care rises appreciably because of the rising incidence of dementia, which often necessitates paying for long-term care.

2. Insurability

Purchasers of LTCI must pass a physical and mental examination and not have a prohibited preexisting condition. These requirements are estimated to eliminate 20 percent or more of those who apply for LTCI. Of course, presumably many others who suspect or know that they will be eliminated due to a physical or mental condition do not bother to apply. Those who attempt to purchase LTCI must fill out an application form that will inquire about their health. If the applicant falsifies the form, the insurance company has the right to cancel the policy or refuse to pay benefits. The possibility of being denied LTCI because of a health condition is often cited as a reason to purchase it while the individual is relatively young and in good health.

Insurance companies typically do not insure applicants whose physical or mental condition already requires them to need long-term care. To determine whether that is the case, applicants are asked whether they need assistance with the activities of daily living, usually defined as the ability to feed oneself, to bath and dress oneself, to use a toilet, and to be able to get out of bed and transfer (walk) to a chair or to get out of a wheelchair without assistance. A need for assistance with any of these activities may be grounds for being classed as uninsurable. Applicants typically will also be denied insurance if they have a progressive neurological condition, such as Parkinson's disease, had a stroke or a heart attack within the last two years, or have metastatic cancer. A diagnosis of dementia, such as Alzheimer's disease, will also result in a denial of insurance. Because each insurance provider sets its own eligibility standard, some applicants may be denied on account of other, seemingly less serious diseases or conditions.

Some companies will sell LTCI to someone with an otherwise disqualifying medical condition but will charge a higher premium or, more commonly, the policy will stipulate that benefits will not be provided for the "preexisting condition," with the term being defined in the policy subject to any applicable state law or regulation. A common definition might exclude any medical condition for which the insured sought treatment or should have sought treatment within "xxx" months of the policy's effective date (first day of coverage). State laws often limit the period of time that an insurance company can refuse to pay benefits for a preexisting condition, with six months being the usual time limit.

B. Coverage Limits

An LTCI policy, similar to casualty insurance, limits the risks that it covers and how much it will pay for the loss incurred by the risk. Note that LTCI does not insure the risk of incurring long-term care; it insures some portion of the cost of paying for long-term care.

1. Daily Benefit Limits

LTCI policies pay benefits only up to a daily benefit rate. For example, the policy may pay up to $150 per day. Some older policies pay a lower daily benefit for care provided in the home. For example, the policy might pay $150 per day for care provided in a nursing home or assisted living facility, but only $75 for home care. Newer policies tend to pay the same daily rate wherever the care is provided. The daily benefit rate is the maximum that can be paid, but it is not necessarily what will be paid. The maximum daily rate is paid only if the cost of care is equal to or exceeds the daily rate. Thus, if the daily rate is $150 and the cost of care is $190 per day, the policy will pay $150 per day. But if the cost of care is less than the daily rate, which is often the case if the insured resides in assisted living, the policy will only pay the actual cost of care. For example, if the policy benefit is $150 per day but the cost of care in assisted living is $110 per day, the policy will pay only $110 per day.

A purchaser of a long-term care policy should insist that it pay for care wherever provided and that the daily amount of the benefit be the same whether the insured receives care at home or in an institution. In the past, long-term care was usually either provided in the home for free by spouses and family members or in costly nursing homes. Today, paid care is more and more often being provided in settings less expensive than a nursing home. Many who have a physical or mental condition severe enough to qualify for benefits under a LTCI policy do not move into a nursing home. Instead they often live in assisted living, which can house even individuals with dementia so long as they are ambulatory. Others in need of care remain at home (or move in with a child or other relative) and supplement voluntary free care with a limited number of hours of paid care. Others live at home but spend much of the day at adult day care facilities, which cost a fraction of the cost of a nursing home, and depend on a spouse or family member for care during the rest of the day. Some combine adult day care with a limited number of hours of paid care at home that is supplemented with free care provided by the family. Whatever the arrangement, it is important that wherever the care is provided, the policy pays benefits.

The daily benefit limit in the LTCI policy essentially creates a co-pay for the insured to the extent that the benefit amount is less than the daily cost of care. The insured could purchase a policy with a higher daily benefit that equals or even exceeds the cost of care, but the result would be higher premiums. A lower daily benefit means lower premiums but is also an impediment to moving into a nursing home because of the "co-pay." Most insureds who move into a nursing home, move there from their own home where they received most if not all of their care for free from a spouse or family member. Because they receive voluntary, free care, their insurance will not pay benefits. To trigger the payment of benefits requires that they pay for care, but to do so will expose them to what can be a fairly expensive co-pay. For example, if the daily cost in a nursing home is $250 and the daily LTCI benefit is $150, the insured must pay $100 a day to generate $150 a day in benefits. The annual out-of-pocket cost to the insured would be $36,500 for nursing home care while collecting $150 a day or $54,750 a year from the insurance company.

For a higher premium, most policies can be purchased that contain an annual "inflation" increase in the daily benefit; 5 percent per year is common. The annual increase is often referred to as protection against inflation in the cost of care, but, of course, a fixed annual increase may bear no relation to the actual annual increase in the cost of care. Annual increases can be based on simple or compound interest.

A simple interest option limits the increase to a percent of the original daily benefit. For example, a 5 percent increase applied to a $150 daily benefit would increase the benefit by $7.50 each year. After 20 years, the daily benefit would be $300. The simple interest option provides a relatively inexpensive protection option, but it is not likely to keep up with the cost of care in the later years. It may be adequate, however, for older purchasers who expect that it is likely that they will trigger the payment of benefits relatively soon after purchasing the policy.

The alternative is a compound interest increase in the daily benefit rate. A 5 percent annual compound interest would increase the benefit amount by the set percentage applied to last year's amount. For example, a $150 daily benefit would increase by 5 percent, to approximately $158 after the first year. The new daily benefit amount would increase by 5 percent the next year to approximately $166, and so on. After 20 years, the daily benefit would be $382. This option provides a more realistic increase in the benefit amount and provides better protection if the claim for benefits does not occur for many years. Unfortunately, it also results in a considerable increase in the premium.

Another option is a guaranteed purchase option that offers the insured the opportunity to periodically increase the daily benefit amount, typically every two or three years. Of course, because the insured is in actuality purchasing a new policy, the premiums will also rise. In essence, this is not a benefit increase plan but a guaranteed right to purchase a new policy with higher benefits without having to pass a physical or provide proof of insurability.

Finally, if the client cannot afford or chooses not to elect an "inflation" increase in benefits, the insured can purchase a policy with a very high daily benefit with the expectation that years hence when the benefits are likely to be paid, the daily benefit amount will still be a reasonable amount in light of the actual daily cost of care.

Most policies are "pure" indemnity; they pay only for the actual cost incurred, not the daily benefit maximum. If the policy pays less than the daily benefit, the policy may permit the insured to "bank" the difference to be used in the future. If, for example, the policy has a $150 daily benefit but the daily cost of care is only $110, the insured would "bank" the $40 difference that could be used if the insured uses up the limit of insured days. The effect of "banking" unused benefits is discussed fully in the following subsection.

2. Time Limit on Daily Benefits

Almost all policies limit the number of insured days, with the fewer insured days the lower the cost of the insurance. Policies typically limit the number of days to three, four, or five years although some may insure up to 10 years and a few may offer benefits that have no time limit. Depending on the terms of the policy, the limit is usually cumulative. The insured might use one year of benefits, recover enough to move home and stop purchasing care, and then later have to again move into a nursing home. If the policy had a three-year limit, the insured would qualify only for another two years of benefits. At the end of the two years, the policy benefits would have been exhausted.

It is estimated that about one-third of all LTCI policies sold limit the benefits to three years. One study found that only about 13 percent of those who owned such policies survived the three-year limit while collecting benefits. Only about 8 percent of those who owned policies with a four-year limit survived the benefit daily limit and of those who owned policies with a five-year limit, fewer than 5 percent survived the policy limit, with men having survival rates about half as great as women.[4]

In addition to a limit on the number of insured days, policies almost always have an elimination period, which is a "waiting" period or a deductible. The insured selects a period of days for which no insurance benefits are paid. After that time has passed, benefits begin to be paid up to the limit of covered days. Typical elimination periods are 60 or 90 days, although the insured may have the option to select a 180-day elimination period. The longer the elimination period, the lower the cost of the premiums.

The elimination period is similar to a deductible that is often part of a casualty insurance policy. The insured must pay for the cost of care—the deductible—before the insurance begins to cover the cost. For example, if the policy has a 90-day elimination period and the cost of care is $200 per day, the insured must pay $18,000 for care before the insurance benefits go into effect. Note that the insured must pay for care, not just have a need for long-term care. The conditions of the policy determine whether the cost of care must be equal to or more than the daily benefit or whether the elimination period can be satisfied if the insured pays for care at a rate less than that of the daily benefit, such as by receiving care in an assisted living facility.

---

4. For statistical information about long-term care insurance go to the website of the American Association for Long-Term Care: http://aspe.hhs.gov/daltcp/reports/2012/ltcinsRB.shtml.

The elimination period is always applied before the initial payment of benefits, but it may be cumulative so that every period of paying for long-term care counts toward the required elimination period. Policies that do not require the elimination period to be consecutive are said to have an "accumulation" period, which is often three times as long as the elimination period. All qualifying payments for care during the accumulation period count toward the single elimination period. Once the accumulation period has passed, however, a new elimination period goes into effect and the insured must again pay for care up to the number of days of the elimination period.

For example, an insured with a 90-day elimination period and a 180-day accumulation period entered a nursing home for 30 days and then returned home where she received free care from her spouse. After 45 days at home, she returned to the nursing home for an indefinite stay. Because the second entry to the nursing home occurred within the 180-accumulation period (which started the first day she entered the nursing home), she will only have to wait another 60 days to be eligible for benefits. If the policy did not have an accumulation period, she would have to wait 90 days after her second admission to the nursing home to be eligible for benefits. The initial 30 days of paying for care would not count against the 90-day elimination period.

The limit on days insured, when combined with the daily benefit limit, creates a cap on the total benefit dollars payable by the policy. For example, consider a policy that pays $150 per day, with a three-year limit and a 90-day elimination period. On January 1 of year 1, the insured enters a nursing home at a cost of $200 per day. The first 90 days in the nursing home are not covered because of the elimination period. The cost of those 90 days to the insured is $18,000. For another three years, until April 1, of year 4, the insured continues to reside in the nursing home at a cost of $200 per day. For those three years, the policy pays $150 per day or $54,750 per year or a total of $164,250 for the three years. During those three years, however, the insured would pay $50 per day ($200/day cost less $150/day insurance) or $18,250 per year or a total of $54,750 for the three years. The total cost for the three years and 90 days of long-term care for the insured would be $54,750 + $18,000 = $72,750. The LTCI policy would have paid $164,250. In percentage terms, the policy would have paid 70 percent of the total cost of $237,000 and the insured would have paid 30 percent.

The relative value of the LTCI changes if the insured does not immediately move into a nursing home but rather moves into a less costly assisted living facility, but nevertheless has a physical or mental condition that triggers the payment of benefits by the policy. For example, on January 1, the insured moves to an assisted living facility at a cost of $100 per day. The insured pays for the first 90 days of care, the elimination period, at a cost of $9,000. For the next year, the insured remains in the assisted living facility. Because the policy limit is $150 per day, the policy covers the entire cost of $100 per day. The policy, like some, but not all policies, provides that if the cost of daily care is less than the policy's daily benefit limit, the insured "banks" the difference and can draw it down after the policy reaches the benefit limit, which in this example is three years. Because the policy only paid $100 for 365 days, the insured "banked" $50 per day for 365 days or a total of $18,250. After 15 months in the assisted living facility, the insured moves into a nursing home at a cost of $200 per day. After two more years, the insured has exhausted the policy benefit limit even though he continues to reside in the nursing home. Thanks to the "banking," however, he still has $18,250 of benefits that will be paid out at $150 per day (the policy daily benefit limit) or four months (122 days). The total cost of care for the insured over the three years and seven months (three months of the elimination period and four months paid for by the "banked" benefit dollars) was $191,500, of which the LTCI paid $164,250 ($36,500 for the assisted living and $127,750 for the nursing home) and the insured paid $27,250, or in percentage terms, the LTCI paid 85 percent and the insured 15 percent.

The dollar amount of the insurance benefits and the cost of the insurance to the insured would vary from the these examples depending on the amount of the daily rate, the actual cost of the nursing home or other provider of long-term care, the length of the elimination period, and the number of years of benefit coverage.

3. Limits on the Provider of the Care

The benefits paid by an LTIC policy depend upon the terms of the policy. Just because the insured pays for long-term care does not necessarily mean that the policy will pay benefits. The care must be provided by a provider approved by the policy. In the past, policies often paid benefits only for care delivered in a nursing home as that term was defined in the policy. Some of these policies are still in effect. Over the years, however, policies began to include benefit payments for long-term care delivered in other facilities, such as assisted living as well as paid care provided in the home. Today, any purchaser of a long-term care policy should insist that it pay for care wherever provided, and that the daily amount of the benefit be the same whether the insured receives care at home or in an institution.

Although policies will usually pay benefits for care delivered in any institutional setting, some policies are still more restrictive about paying benefits for paid care provided in the home. Most policies will not pay if the care is provided by a spouse or family member, even if the insured pays for the care. The policy may require that home care be provided by trained or licensed personnel to ensure that the care is not merely enhanced maid or personal assistant service.

Potential purchasers of LTCI sometimes cite a desire to remain at home as the motivation for purchasing LTCI as a means of lowering their out-of-pocket cost and so make paid home care financially feasible. These potential purchasers should consider carefully whether that goal would be possible if they need extensive, costly home care. Even with LTCI that pays the same for home care as it does for care in an institution, home care may prove to be too costly for the insured to use for an extended period of time. For example, if the policy pays a daily benefit of

$200 a day and the cost of care in the home is $350 a day and the cost in a nursing home is $240 a day, if the insured lives at home the daily out-of-pocket cost would be $150 but residing in a nursing home would only cost $40 a day. Over a year that would translate into $54,750 to live at home but only $14,600 to live in a nursing home.

4. Limits on Covered Physical or Mental Conditions

The LTCI policy defines the degree of care needed by the insured that is required to trigger the payment of benefits. Some older policies require that the care needed be "skilled nursing care," a very high standard of care. Today, policies still cover skilled nursing care but they also pay benefits for custodial care. Skilled nursing care, as the name implies, refers to care that has medical aspects or requires the attendance of a licensed medical provider, such as a registered nurse (RN). Custodial care refers to non-medical personal care that provides assistance for aspects of daily living. Most policies will pay for custodial care that the insured needs because the insured requires assistance with two (some policies require three) of the Activities of Daily Living, typically defined in the policy as

- Eating (needing help with or being fed by another);
- Bathing (needing assistance from another to accomplish or safely engage in);
- Dressing (needing assistance to accomplish);
- Toileting (lack of continence or needing assistance to perform); and
- Transferring (needing assistance to get out of bed to a chair or to get out of a chair such as a wheelchair).

The reason that the insured needs assistance or cannot perform an Activity of Daily Living could be a physical condition, a mental condition such as dementia, or merely due to extreme physical weakness and frailty. Policies also pay benefits without regard to specific activities of daily living if a physician certifies that the individual is in need of long-term care due to a medical condition.

Alternatively, a significant decline in mental functioning, usually due to some form of dementia, also triggers the payment of benefits. The decline in mental functioning, however, is likely to be required by the policy to be severe enough that the insured requires daily assistance to care for personal needs and also requires supervision so that the insured does not wander away. The need for personal assistance and supervision must be fairly great. Most policies will not pay benefits during the early stages of dementia even though the individual may need some limited care and supervision. The policy may require the insured to prove their claim that they suffer from significant cognitive limitations by taking a standardized test that measures memory, orientation as to place and time, and executive functioning, that is, the ability to reason and solve problems.

Whether the cause of the need for care is physical or mental, either the policy will require the insured to be examined by a physician of its choice or require the insured to obtain a physician's certificate that authenticates the need for personal or medical long-term care. The insured should expect the insurance company to strictly enforce the terms in the policy that dictate when benefits are paid and to interpret the policy in a manner that favors the insurance company. The growth in the number of reported cases where an insured sues an LTCI insurance company in an attempt to be awarded benefits under a policy issued by the company suggests that the interpretation and enforcement of policy provisions can be contentious. Insureds should be aware that the conditions that they may think should trigger benefits may not be the conditions that the insurance company thinks trigger benefits.

Policies typically do not pay for care provided outside of the United States. Some policies will not pay for the cost of care that results from alcoholism, drug abuse, or mental illness that does not have an organic cause. Some older policies had a prior hospitalization requirement—typically three days—in order to trigger the payment of benefits the subsequent cost of long-term care. Newer policies rarely contain this requirement; some states do not permit LTCI policies to be sold if they contain such a requirement.

C. Premiums

The premium for an LTCI policy is a function of the age of the insured at the time the policy becomes effective. The younger the insured, the lower the premium. The savings in premiums can be considerable if LTCI is purchased at a younger age. Those who purchase a policy when younger pay less over their lifetime than those who purchase it when older, even though the younger purchaser will have paid premiums for more years if both collect benefits at the same age. The reason is that the company has more years to invest the premiums paid by the younger purchaser; it is the earnings on invested premiums that are critical to producing enough revenue for the insurance company to be able to afford to pay the benefits promised in the policy.

Many LTCI policies are sold to couples with shared benefits. For example, the policy may pay four years of benefits that can be used by one or both spouses. The alternative is to purchase a separate policy for each spouse. However, couples policies typically do not cost twice as much as a policy sold to an individual. The reasons for the "discount" arise from reasons such as couples having better health in old age and the tendency of a couple to care for each other long after a single person would have had to pay for care.

Once set, the premium for LTCI does not rise merely because the insured ages. The policy is almost surely guaranteed renewable; it cannot be canceled so long as the insured pays the annual premium unless the insurance company withdraws from selling insurance in the state where the insured resides. Although the individual does not pay higher premiums merely because of growing older, the insurance company may raise the premiums for policyholders in the same class, that is, a company could raise the premiums on all polices by a set percentage. Subject to state approval that may or may not be forthcoming, insurance companies raise premiums if they find that the premiums on outstanding policies are too low to sustain the product. The initial premium may prove too low if the insurance company made mistakes in its estimates of any of a number of future variables. The company may have overestimated the number of policy owners who let their policies lapse. From the standpoint of the company, policy lapses result in the collection of premiums without the possibility of ever paying benefits to those policyholders. A more likely reason for a request for an increase in the premiums is because the number of policyholders who qualify for benefits and the dollar amount of benefits paid has apparently been underestimated by many companies that sold LTCI. The result is that the premium levels have been too low to sustain the benefit payouts. Low rates of return on the insurance company investments may also have contributed to the need to request a premium increase. Whatever the cause, the lesson of the last decade is that a purchaser of LTCI should not be surprised if the premium is later increased by 10 to 20 percent or even more over the life of the policy.

Purchasers of LTCI must realize that they may be paying premiums for 20 to 30 years or even more. For example, the joint life expectancy for a couple both age 65 is 26 years. Of course, it is also possible that very soon after taking out the policy, one of the spouses will need long-term care, just as it is possible that neither will ever qualify for policy benefits. It is the nature of casualty insurance that it protects against the risk of a loss, not that it pays for a cost that is certain to occur. Therefore, the value of the insurance to the purchaser is not measured by the benefits paid, but by the reduction in risk of financial loss if the insured event, here the need to pay for long-term care, should occur.

Still, a potential purchaser of LTCI ought to consider the cost of the premiums as an offset against the benefits paid by the policy. A purchaser of LTCI at age 65 can reasonably expect that the need to pay for long-term care will rise sharply after age 80 due to the increase in the likelihood that the purchaser will experience dementia or other debilitating physical ailments. The purchaser can therefore assume that it is likely that premiums must be paid for 15 to 20 years before they will qualify for benefits. The result is the value of the benefits paid is reduced by the premiums paid.

For example, assume at age 65 the insured takes out a policy with annual premiums of $2,000 a year. At age 85, the insured begins to collect a daily benefit of $150 per day up to the policy limit of three years. The total benefits (after the elimination period) would be $164,250. But those benefits would have cost the insured $40,000 (20 years × $2,000/year) meaning that the actual benefit to the insured would be $124,250. Of course, if the insured qualified for benefits at an earlier age, the reduction would be less but if the insured did not qualify until later than age 85, the offset in the value of the benefits on account of the premiums paid would be more.

The policy will almost surely waive the payment of premiums during the period that benefits are paid. Many policies also do not initially lapse if the insured fails to pay the premium because of a mental disability such as dementia. The insured or a representative of the insured will be permitted to pay the premiums in arrears if done so in a time period set out in the policy. Some policies require the insurance company to notify an identified third party, such as an adult child, if the premium is unpaid. Absent such a provision, state law may permit the insurance company to cancel the policy for the nonpayment of the premium even if that occurred because the insured was mentally disabled such as having dementia.

Some policies feature a "paid-up" feature. After a period of payment, commonly ten years, no additional premiums are due, but the policy remains in effect for the life of the insured. Paid-up policies are in reality a form of prepaying premiums, which may appeal to those who are still employed and want to cease paying premiums at or soon after they retire and expect to experience a decline in income. This feature also appeals to those who want to minimize the possibility that the premiums will rise over the life of the policy as well as those who expect to live longer than their actuarial life expectancy and so desire to limit how many years they will be paying the premium. Whether prepayment is attractive also depends on whether the insured agrees that the discount rate that the insurance company applied to the future expected premium payments is accurate or whether the insured would be financially better off not prepaying future premiums and investing the funds not used to prepay the premium. Prepayment does not make sense if the insured anticipates becoming eligible for benefits prior to the end of the term of the premium prepayments.

D. Tax-Qualified Policies

Most LTCI policies sold since 1997 are "tax qualified." As such, these policies are eligible for certain tax benefits. To be tax qualified, the policy must meet the requirement of I.R.C. Section 7702B(b). That section requires policies to contain consumer protection provisions promulgated by the National Association of Insurance Commissioners in 1993 that include

- Guaranteed renewability,
- Prohibitions on certain limitations and exclusions,
- Protection against unintentional lapse by requiring the insurance company to give notice of the nonpayment to a designated third party;
- Availability of inflation protection of the benefits;
- Prohibition against a requirement of prior hospitalization as a condition for collecting benefits; and
- Prohibition against non-coverage of a preexisting condition. (The insurance company can refuse to sell a policy to someone with a preexisting condition, however.)

Tax-qualified policies may be offered by employers as a tax-free benefit to employees just like health care benefits.[5] The benefits paid by such policies are tax-free up to the greater of a daily limit of $360 in 2017 (adjusted annually for inflation) or the actual cost of care.[6] The premiums are deductible as I.R.C. Section 213 medical expenses to the extent such expenses exceed 10 percent of adjusted gross income if the insured claims itemized deductions. The amount of the premium deduction is capped, however, and the amount is higher for older insureds. In 2017 (adjusted annually for inflation) the limits were:

Age 40 or less	$410
More than 40 but not more than 50	$770
More than 50 but not more than 60	$1,530
More than 60 but not more than 70	$4,090
More than 70	$5,110

The deductions are permitted for each insured person, so a married couple can deduct the cost of two individual policies if they do not have a joint one.

The tax advantages of tax-qualified policies have resulted in the great majority of policies now being offered meeting the requirements. Nevertheless, the purchaser of LTCI should be careful to inquire as to whether the policy is tax qualified.

E. State Partnership Policies

The Deficit Reduction Act of 2005 permitted states to recognize "partnership" LTCI policies. The partnerships vary somewhat from state to state, but the programs permit those who are paid LTCI benefits to retain financial resources equal to those benefits when they apply for Medicaid as a source of payment for long-term care. For example, if the insured were paid $150,000 in benefits, the insured would be allowed to retain assets worth $150,000 and still qualify for Medicaid. For a discussion as to when and how to use the partnership program in concert with Medicaid, see Chapter 14, Medicaid.

To qualify for the partnership program, the policy must meet the requirements of "tax-qualified" policies. In addition, unlike qualified plans that only have to offer inflation protection of benefit payments, partnership policies must offer inflation protection if the policy is purchased by someone age 75 or younger. If the purchaser is age 60 or younger, the inflation protection must be compound inflation protection. Partnership policies must be portable among states that have elected to participate in the program. If the policy met the requirements in the state where it was sold, it must be recognized as satisfying the requirements in the state where the insured applies for Medicaid. Detailed information about the partnership program can be found at http://www.aaltci.org/long-term-care-insurance/learning-center/long-term-care-insurance-partnership-plans.php.

---

5. I.R.C. §§ 106(a), 7702B(a)(1).
6. *Id.* § 7702B(d)(2)(A)(4).

III. Reasons to Purchase Long-Term Care Insurance

The question as to who should purchase LTCI is difficult to answer. To claim, as some do, that the high cost of long-term care is reason enough to purchase LTCI is incorrect. Insurance should be purchased to protect against a financially unacceptable potential loss. Homeowners insure their houses against fire because they cannot risk the loss of the value of the house or the cost of repairing the house. Some seem to believe that cost of long-term care is analogous to the cost of replacing a house. It is not, however, because of the potential of Medicaid paying for long-term care.

A. Single Individuals

As explained in Chapter 14, Medicaid, if an individual is unable to pay the cost of needed long-term care, usually care provided in a nursing home, the cost of providing long-term care for that individual will be paid for by Medicaid. Significantly, the quality of care provided in a nursing home whether paid for by Medicaid or by the resident (referred to as "private pay" resident) is the same. In theory, a private pay resident could pay for superior care, such as single room (Medicaid pays only for a joint room), more personal care by nurses and staff, and more ancillary services. In reality, almost no nursing homes exist that offer better care to private pay residents because there is no viable market for a more costly, albeit higher quality, nursing home. Purchasing LTCI does not mean that if the individual resides in a nursing home that they will receive better care. The reality is that the private pay resident will share a room with a Medicaid qualified resident and the two will receive identical care. The private pay resident, however, will be charged a higher daily rate than the Medicaid qualified resident because Medicaid will only pay a predetermined amount that it believes appropriate, and that amount is always lower than the rate charged to private pay residents.

Medicaid is one reason why LTCI has not proven to be an attractive insurance product.[7] Most elderly individuals either expect to rely on Medicaid or else they have sufficient income and savings to self-insure against the risk of incurring costly long-term care. Although a few elderly may have enough income to pay for whatever long-term care they need, most do not; rather they rely on their savings, including the value of a house. For example, if the cost of care is $100,000 per year, even five years of care amounts to $500,000, which, if augmented by their income, is affordable for those with assets of at least $750,000, or more. A more realistic cost of care would be two years of assisted living at $50,000 per year and three years of nursing home care at $100,000 per year for a total of $400,000; a cost that those with annual income of $50,000 and savings of at least $500,000 can afford.

---

7. A 2004 study found that only 10 percent of the elderly own LTCI. Jeffrey Brown & Amy Finkelstein, *Supply or Demand: Why Is the Market for Long-Term Care Insurance So Small?* (NBER Working Paper 10782), http://www.nber.org/papers/w10782.

Even for single individuals with modest net worth, the purchase of LTCI is not compelling. For example, an individual with savings of $250,000 and a house worth $200,000 has a total net worth of $450,000. Even ignoring their income, they can afford nine years of assisted living at a cost of $50,000 a year or four and one-half years of nursing home care at a cost of $100,000 a year (approximately $275 per day).

However, individuals who can pay for long-term care out of income and savings often fear that paying for long-term care will greatly diminish the value of their estates. For example, if their estate is worth $400,000 and the individual must pay $260,000 for long-term care, the estate would have lost 65 percent of its value. Facing that possibility, some believe that purchasing LTCI is prudent. If a single individual has a compelling reason to maintain the value of their estate, perhaps to leave a legacy to a needy or disabled heir, LTCI may be a sensible precautionary purchase.

Some, who lack the income and savings to pay for potentially costly long-term care, purchase LTCI to avoid having to move into a nursing home in order to qualify for Medicaid. Although Medicaid is beginning to pay for care outside of a nursing home, such as home care and community-based care (see Chapter 14, Medicaid), in the past it paid almost exclusively for nursing home care. That is changing, however, as more states use Medicaid funds to support paid long-term care provided in the home. Yet at present, older individuals who need long-term care cannot be certain that Medicaid reimbursement will be available unless they reside in a nursing home. The prospect of having to move to a nursing home may be so off-putting that the individual buys LTCI in order to have a source of payment for care in the home or in an assisted living facility.

Thus envisioned, the purchase of LTCI serves as protection against an individual having no choice but to move into a nursing home in order to create Medicaid eligibility even though the individual's care needs could be met in a less institutional and restrictive setting. Of course, it is possible that the individual's need for care will only be met by moving into a nursing home. If so, the purchase of LTCI will not have served its purpose. Many individuals contemplating old age, however, may be willing to accept the lifetime cost of LTCI premiums to ensure that they have the funds to pay for long-term care and so hopefully delay or never have to move into a nursing home.

B. Married Couples

LTCI is attractive for married couples because it provides financial protection for the non-institutionalized spouse, or community spouse,[8] as referred to by Medicaid. Couples correctly fear that if one must pay for long-term care, the other may become destitute. For many middle and upper-middle class elderly, having

---

8. Medicaid refers to the spouse of the Medicaid applicant as the "community spouse" no matter where he or she resides. 42 U.S.C. § 1396r-5(h)(2).

one spouse eligible for Medicaid could only occur by imposing significant loss of income and financial well-being upon the community spouse. The cost of the care, particularly if provided in a nursing home, may exhaust their joint income thus forcing them to use their savings, but doing so may significantly deplete or exhaust their savings. As explained in Chapter 14, Medicaid, the institutionalized spouse can qualify for Medicaid without using any of the community spouse's income to help pay for the cost of care. But much of the savings of the couple must be spent on care for the institutionalized spouse, except for a community resource allowance for the community spouse, thus leaving the community spouse with many fewer assets for support. To avoid that outcome the couple should consider purchasing LTCI.

An LTCI policy will permit the couple to pay for long-term care for several years and so possibly avoid ever needing to resort to Medicaid. The couple can either purchase a policy that provides a set period of benefits for each of them or they take out a shared policy. With a shared care policy, the couple purchases benefits that can be split between them. For example, if they buy a policy with a five-year limit on benefits, if one spouse uses two years of the policy and dies, the surviving spouse would have three years of available benefits.

The value of the LTCI in the form of protection against the risk of the loss of investment income or savings that supports the community spouse must be measured against the annual cost of LTCI premiums for the couple for the rest of their lives. The question is whether it is worth it to them to accept a modest, but permanent, reduction in income by buying LTCI insurance to protect against a larger, but uncertain, reduction in income caused by paying for long-term care.

The value of the financial protection offered by LTCI for the community spouse depends on how long the community spouse lives after the death of the institutionalized spouse. The value of LTCI decreases if the institutionalized spouse only pays for long-term care for a short period of time before dying or if the community spouse does not live very long after the death of the institutionalized spouse. If the institutionalized spouse dies soon after incurring long-term care costs, the cost to the community spouse in terms of the need to spend their savings will not be very great; very likely a cost that the surviving spouse can absorb without much effect on their quality of life. If the community spouse dies soon after the death of the institutionalized spouse, the loss of savings used to pay for long-term care will be irrelevant since the community spouse will not have lived long enough to have need for those savings.

If LTCI is purchased to protect the community spouse, the result is to shift disposable income from the couple, due to the cost of the annual premium, to the surviving spouse by protecting her consumption of the future potential investment income that arises from the couple's savings. Without the LTCI, those savings would be at risk of being spent on long-term care for the other spouse.

In contrast, LTCI offers little value for couples with very modest savings because the exhaustion of their savings to pay for long-term care will have only a modest impact on the economic well-being of the community spouse. Even if the institutionalized spouse goes on Medicaid, the community spouse will retain a community spouse resource needs allowance (CSRNA) and their own income such as pension income or Social Security benefits. On balance, the cost of the LTCI in most cases outweighs it benefits to couples with a net worth of less than $300,000.[9]

C. To Facilitate Planning for Medicaid Eligibility

As discussed in Chapter 14, Medicaid, the transfer of assets for less than fair market value made within five years of applying for Medicaid may cause a period of ineligibility. One technique that can be employed, however, is to transfer assets to an irrevocable trust, collect the income from the trust, wait five years and then apply for Medicaid. Any transfers made five years before the date of the Medicaid application do not have to be reported. If the transferor or their spouse does not apply for Medicaid within five years, the transfer is irrelevant when determining their eligibility for Medicaid.

The transfer of the asset is to an irrevocable trust is a grantor trust because the grantor preserves the right to income from the trust assets. In order to protect the principal of the trust from being considered available to pay for the cost of long-term care, the trustee will not be able to distribute the principal to the grantor under any circumstances; presumably the grantor can afford to give up access to the principal. Even the amount of income that is distributed to the grantor is subject to a degree of manipulation based on how the assets are invested, which is determined by the trustee. The trust income can be maximized in the period before the grantor is on Medicaid. After the grantor becomes eligible for Medicaid, the trustee can invest the trust asset in a manner designed to minimize income that must be distributed to the grantor.

Five years after the transfer of assets to the trust, the transfer will not affect the eligibility of the grantor or the spouse for Medicaid. However, when funding the trust, the grantor cannot be sure whether within the next five years either the grantor or the spouse will need costly long-term care; so costly that they will not be able to afford it and so have to apply for Medicaid. Having transferred assets to the trust, however, they would have to disclose that transfer and likely find that they are not eligible for Medicaid for several months, if not years.

To deal with that possibility, a couple can purchase LTCI. If either should need costly long-term care, the LICI will pay enough to permit them to wait out the five-year transfer period before applying for Medicaid. To be sure that the policy will cover the need, they should purchase LTCI that pays a high daily benefit for at least four years. At the end of the five years, the grantor can let the policy lapse with the expectation that Medicaid will be available to pay for costly long-term care.

---

9. *See* http://www.consumerreports.org/cro/2012/08/long-term-care-insurance/index.htm.

Before transferring assets to a trust, the grantor should first apply for LTCI to ensure insurability. Next, the grantor should weigh the cost of paying the insurance premiums for four or five years (the grantor might be able to afford one year or even more of long-term care) against the value of the assets that the grantor expects to transfer to the trust, making sure that the value of the transferred property sufficiently exceeds the cost of the insurance to justify transferring assets into a trust.

D. Second or Later-Life Marriages

LTCI can be very valuable for couples in a second, later-life marriage who have children or other preferred heirs. Those who enter into a later-life marriage often sign prenuptial agreements to protect their assets in case of a divorce. A prenuptial agreement, however, is not permitted by Medicaid to protect the parties from having their assets spent down to pay for the cost of long-term care for the other spouse. This is particularly unfortunate for the spouse who owns more assets. It is very possible that if the spouse with less income and fewer assets needs costly long-term care, the income and assets of the well spouse will be called upon to bear the cost of that care. If both spouses have limited income and savings, the likelihood of either being required to pay for the care of the other rises dramatically. Even if both have high incomes or significant savings, it is possible that the medical costs and the long-term care costs of one could result in a significant depletion of the other, well spouse's savings.

The couple may fear that the well spouse's estate will be significantly reduced by the cost of care for the ill spouse, thereby reducing the inheritance of the heirs—typically children—of the well spouse. Many who enter into a later-life marriage are understandably concerned that the marriage not result in a reduced inheritance for their children or other designated heirs.

LTCI can be the solution. Each spouse can purchase (or they jointly purchase) LTCI that pays relatively generous benefits, and thereby greatly minimize the possibility that either will have to pay for the long-term care costs of the other. For example, an LTCI policy that pays benefits of $225 per day for up to five years has a potential total benefit of $410,850. This potential payout, of course, ultimately benefits the heirs of both the ill and well spouse.

Even if the couple has only modest income and savings, their children may decide that it is a good "investment" and so volunteer to help pay for the insurance as a means of protecting their inheritance as well as protecting their parent's financial well-being.

IV. "Hybrid" Long-Term Care Insurance Products

A purchaser of LTCI has two options: the traditional policy that only insures the cost of long-term care and a hybrid policy that combines LTCI with life insurance or an annuity. Hybrid policies are increasingly popular; sales of traditional policies have been declining while hybrids sales are rising, though their increase in sales has not equaled the decline in the number of sales of traditional policies. One reason is that most hybrid policies require a single, upfront premium that averages over $125,000. (Some insurance companies allow the insured to spread the payment over two to ten years.) The high premium means the policies are usually purchased by individuals with a high net worth. Because part of the premium is not paying for long-term care insurance, the premium on hybrid policies is not deductible (see Section II.D. Tax-Qualified Policies) and also does not qualify for the Partnership Program (see Section II.E. State Partnership Policies).

A hybrid life insurance and LTCI policy typically offers a maximum death benefit that initially exceeds the cost of the single upfront premium. How much so depends on the age of the insured and the insurance company's anticipated rate of investment return on the premium. The death benefit declines over a period of years, often ten years, down to the cost of the premium. Meanwhile, as long as the insured lives, they own LTCI, which, for example, might pay $175 per day for four years with the daily benefit compounding at 5 percent per year. The death benefit, after a period of decline is ultimately fixed; it is not affected by the payment or nonpayment of long-term care benefits. Essentially, the investment return earned by the insurance company on the premium pays for the cost of the LTCI coverage.

An alternative is a combined life insurance and long-term care insurance policy that offers a fixed death benefit that is reduced by any amounts paid for long-term care. The long-term care benefits, like a traditional long-term care policy, are subject to a daily limit and possibly a term of years. Usually such hybrid policies feature a single upfront premium and have lower daily benefit levels than traditional long-term care policies, and they often do not offer inflation protection.

A hybrid annuity policy is an alternative. One form is a hybrid-deferred annuity. The individual purchases a deferred annuity that never goes into pay status and is linked to long-term care coverage. The individual selects the amount of long-term care coverage, which is usually 200 percent or 300 percent of the face value of the annuity; if the annuity pays $3,000 per month, the long-term care benefit might be $6,000 or $9,000 per month, or $200 or $300 per day. The individual also can include inflation coverage of the benefit amount, and must select how long the benefit will be paid. The payment of benefits reduces the value of the deferred annuity. After a period of time, such as 20 years, if the policy has not paid long-term care benefits, the annuity can be redeemed for its accumulated value or it can be left to accumulate further interest and the long-term care policy will remain in effect. At the individual's death, the heirs will inherit the greater of the accumulated annuity value, if there have been no withdrawals or benefits paid, or the initial single premium less the amount of long-term care benefits paid.

The following is an example of how such a policy might work. A 60-year-old paid a premium of $50,000 for a long-term care, deferred (for 20 years) annuity with a 200 percent benefit or $100,000 at a daily rate of $150 per day with a

5 percent inflation coverage compounded annually. After 20 years, because of the annual compound 5 percent inflation, the policy pays a maximum $265,330 in long-term care benefits. Assume that in year 20, the annuity had a cash payout value of $180,000, which the insured can cash out or leave in the annuity and continue the LTCI. In the alternative, in years 15 and 16, the insured collected $100,000 worth of LTCI benefits and then died. The annuity will be cashed out by her heirs, but its value will be reduced by $100,000. The heirs will receive the greater of the cost of the initial premium of $50,000 or the value of the annuity less $100,000.

When considering the purchase of a hybrid LTCI policy, the potential purchaser must realize that the cost of the long-term care portion of the policy is difficult to calculate. The policies, which are likely to become even more complex in the coming years, offer multiple benefits. The cost of any one of those benefits is not usually broken out. For the purchaser, the question is whether it makes more sense to purchase pure LTCI and accept the possibility that no benefits will ever be paid. Doing so reflects the fundamental point of any insurance—to avoid the risk of a loss that the insured cannot afford. The purchase of pure LTCI should be the least expensive way of purchasing it because the cost reflects the actuarial estimate of the cost of the risk. No hybrid product can lower the estimated cost of the risk. Nevertheless, if the other product offered by the hybrid policy appeals to the potential purchaser, the policy may make sense. The purchaser, however, should ask what risk is being met by the other policy benefits. For example, does the insured need more life insurance? If not, why purchase a policy that has both long-term care benefits and death benefits. Merely because the purchaser likes the idea of being sure to be paid benefits may not be a sufficient reason to purchase unnecessary life insurance.

A third option is to use a life insurance policy to help pay for the cost of long-term care. The life insurance policy will have a long-term care rider that will meet the definition of a qualified long-term care insurance contract under I.R.C. Section 7702B, and so the benefits that are paid from the contract are not included in gross income subject to the dollar limits of that code section (see Section II.D. Tax-Qualified Policies). The policy benefits are "accelerated" because they are paid before the death of the insured. Depending on the policy, the long-term care benefit payment can either reduce the policy's cash surrender value or the death benefit.

Even a pure life insurance policy can be used to pay for long-term care costs. If the policy has a cash value, this amount can be accessed by a withdrawal or a policy loan to pay for long-term care expenses. To help pay for long-term care expenses, an owner of a life insurance policy may be able to access its value if the policy contains a life settlement option that permits the insured to a lump-sum payout that is less than the death benefit; the life settlement terminates the insurance. Another option is a viatical settlement; selling the policy to a third party who will receive the death benefit. Viatical settlements require the insured to be terminally ill with the sale price dependent on the insured's life expectancy and the amount of the death benefit. The proceeds from a sale of a life insurance policy are generally not subject to the income tax.

Later-Life Concerns

Part III reviews the legal issues associated with later life, usually meaning clients in their 80s or 90s. It begins with a description of the provision of long-term care in settings other than a nursing home. Next, Chapter 14 describes Medicaid, the federal-state program that pays for over half of the total cost of care for elderly. Part III continues with a chapter that examines guardianship and conservatorship as responses to elderly mental incapacity (Chapter 15). Another response to late life mental incapacity is trusts, which in Chapter 16 are discussed as possible alternatives to guardianship. The book ends with Chapter 17, which is devoted to the estate planning issues that arise when engaging in estate planning with a very old client.

Provision of Long-Term Care Outside of a Nursing Home and Hospice Care

13

I. Introduction

Long-term care is most often associated with a need to reside in a nursing home; it is true that many elderly who need long-term care reside in a nursing home.[1] However, nursing homes are very expensive; the annual cost can run from $70,000 to $120,000. They are often thought of as being impersonal and too often resemble a hospital. Many elderly greatly fear ever having to move to a nursing home, which they see as a bad place to live and a worst place to die. Happily, nursing homes are not the only setting in which long-term care is provided. There are several alternatives. More long-term care is provided in the home than elsewhere, with most of the care being provided by spouses and family, although many pay for long-term care in the home, and increasingly states are subsidizing home care for the elderly. Other alternatives to nursing homes are assisted living facilities and continuing care retirement communities. An older individual in need of long-term care must carefully consider the

---

1. For a detailed discussion of nursing homes including the legal rights of their residents, see Lawrence A. Frolik, Residence Options for Older and Disabled Clients, Ch. 11, Nursing Homes (ABA Publications 2008).

possible care alternatives and weigh their relative advantages in light of what the individual can afford and what they and their family consider to be acceptable. In the end, however, the source of payment for the care may determine where the individual receives long-term care. Therefore, any discussion of long-term care choices must begin with an overview of payment sources.

II. Payment Sources

Because of the cost of long-term care, most older individuals are unable to afford it. They may be able to pay for a few months or even years, but their ability to pay usually ends before their need for care is over. Fortunately, there are sources of payment; unfortunately, those sources often limit the available choices. The following is a brief overview of funding sources for long-term care. The topics are more fully covered in other chapters as indicated.

A. Private Insurance

Some individuals have long-term care insurance that will pay for some or all of the cost of their care without necessarily limiting by whom or where the care is provided (see Chapter 12, Long-Term Care Insurance). Long-term care insurance will pay a daily benefit rate after the individual has met the required deductible period, known as the elimination period. For example, the individual may not become eligible for benefits until they have resided in a facility, either a nursing home or an assisted living facility, or paid for their care for 90 days. Most long-term care policies essentially have a co-pay because the policy will only pay a stated daily benefit amount, such as $200 per day, which is often less than the daily cost of the care. In light of the nearly annual increase in the cost of long-term care, some policies have an inflation provision that raises the benefit annually by a predetermined percentage, such as 5 percent. Long-term care insurance policies sold in the last decade almost always pay for care wherever provided so that residence in an assisted living facility triggers the payment of benefits. Because assisted living costs much less than a nursing home, the daily benefit that was purchased to cover most of the cost of residence in a nursing home is usually higher than the daily cost at the assisted living facility. For example, the policy might pay $200 per day, while the assisted living costs only $135 per day. If that is the case, the individual will have the entire cost of the assisted living care paid for as long as the policy pays benefits.

Policies almost always have limits on how long they pay benefits, with three or four years being common. If the individual resides in assisted living at a cost less than the policy's daily benefit, the policy may credit the individual with additional days of benefits equal to the total in the difference of the cost of the assisted living and the policy's daily benefit amount. For example, if the cost of the assisted living was $135 per day and the policy paid a benefit of $200 per day, the $65 difference would be credited as providing additional days of coverage. If the individual lived in the assisted living facility for two years, 730 days, the individual would be credited with $47,450 ($65 × 730 days), which would translate into 237 additional days of coverage beyond the coverage limits stated in the policy.

Long-term care insurance usually pays benefits for home care. The daily benefit amount may be the same as for care in a facility, but some older policies pay only half as much for home care. Whatever the amount of the benefit, it may be less than the cost of the care unless the paid care is significantly augmented by free care, such as that provided by a spouse.

Wherever the care is provided, the policy will only pay benefits if the individual meets the policy requirements as to what condition will trigger the payment of benefits. Most policies require that the individual be certified by a physician as needing long-term care and either be unable to perform at least two activities of daily living—bathing, dressing, eating, toileting, and ambulation—or have a significant cognitive deficit, such as dementia.

Some newer life insurance policies also pay benefits for long-term care. Depending on the terms of the policy, the individual may be able to convert the policy's death benefits into payment for long-term care up to a limit stated in the policy. Alternatively, the policy may permit the insured to convert the death benefits into an annuity that the insured can use to help pay for the cost of long-term care.

B. Medicare

Medicare Part A pays for a limited amount of long-term care but only if it is provided in a skilled nursing facility (almost all nursing homes qualify as skilled nursing facilities). Care provided in an assisted living facility will not qualify for Medicare reimbursement. (See Chapter 5, Medicare.)

Medicare is designed to pay for acute care, not long-term care, but it does pay for a limited number of days in a nursing home if those days follow immediately after three days of in-patient (not observation status) hospitalization. The intent being that the nursing home is a less expensive source of skilled nursing care than continued residence in a hospital. Medicare pays only for skilled nursing care and rehabilitative services.[2] It does not pay for custodial care even if provided in a nursing home that also provides skilled nursing care.

After admission to a skilled nursing facility, Medicare will pay the cost for the first 20 days. For days 21 to 100, the individual has a co-pay of $164.50 per day (in 2017). After day 100, Medicare does not pay any additional benefits.

C. Medicaid

About one-half of all nursing home costs are paid for by Medicaid, which also pays an increasing amount for care in the home and community. Medicaid is a federal-state program that, among other things, reimburses nursing homes for

---

2. 42 C.F.R. § 409.31.

care provided to eligible individuals. Medicaid is known in some states as Medical Assistance and in California as Medi-Cal. Eligibility for Medicaid requires that the individual need skilled or custodial nursing home care and that the individual qualify financially. Medicaid is a welfare program; only individuals with few resources and income that is less than their cost of care are eligible (see Chapter 14, Medicaid).

Individuals can anticipate becoming eligible for Medicaid and can even take steps to accelerate eligibility, but in the end, Medicaid assistance requires the individual to have few countable resources, $2,000 in most states, and to devote almost all their income to the cost of care. To qualify for Medicaid usually requires an individual to reside in a nursing home. Many who reside in nursing homes would prefer not to, but do so because that is only way they can qualify for Medicaid.

However, Medicaid has been amended to permit it to issue waivers to states to use Medicaid funds (both federal and state) to pay for care in the community. The waiver programs were included in the Patient Protection and Affordable Care Act of 2010 (ACA) and provided authority for states to apply for five-year demonstration plans or projects that began in 2014.[3] There are several types of waivers that states may apply for, including a waiver to provide long-term care services in home and community settings rather than institutional settings. To qualify for the waiver, the state must establish home-based and community-based setting requirements that are "person centered" and create options based on an individual's needs and preferences. The actual form of the home care program depends on the manner that the state implements the waiver. As a result, it is difficult to generalize as to the available benefits and eligibility standards, but in general an individual can receive reimbursement for the cost of hiring home health care aides and other needed services if the individual meets the state's income and resource eligibility requirements, which may be less onerous than the requirements for eligibility as a resident of a nursing home.

III. Long-Term Home Care

Medicare will pay for home health care related to an acute medical condition but will not pay for the cost of long-term home care (see Chapter 5, Medicare). As discussed in Section II.C., Medicaid may reimburse long-term home care. If not, absent long-term care insurance, the individual must pay out-of-pocket for the cost of home care, arrange for its delivery, and monitor the quality of the care.

A. Hiring Private Home Caregivers

A private, home caregiver can be hired directly or through an agency that provides home care services. Hiring a caregiver directly can be done through an

---

3. 42 U.S.C. § 1396n.

employment agency, by looking for individuals on Craigslist or in the newspaper, or by names supplied by other elder service professionals such as geriatric social workers. Advertising for a home caregiver is usually unwise because it exposes the older individual to potential criminals who use the job interview to gain access to the older person and their property. The use of an employment agency is preferable to direct hiring because the agency should vet the caregiver and ensure that they are dependable and capable of performing as needed. If an agency is used, the older person should insist that the agency conduct a background investigation including credit and criminal checks. Ideally, the employment agency would accept liability or have insurance to pay the victim if the person who is hired abuses, neglects, or exploits the older person.

Those considering home care should first identify the specific services needed and, in particular, note whether the services needed are personal care or health care because the two require very different skills. If health care is the primary need, it is best to employ a home health care agency that supplies such services because of the need for professional training and supervision. If personal care is the motivating reason for hiring in-home assistance, it may be possible to hire such care directly, but it is usually better to hire a geriatric care manager or social worker to assess the older person's needs and either have them hire or recommend a qualified personal care attendant. Another alternative is to contract with an agency to provide the attendant.

How much care will be needed varies. The needs of some older persons can be met with one caregiver who works 8 to 10 hours a day for five days a week. Many older persons, however, will need either more hours of care or need hired care seven days a week. If the latter, the family should realize that because several caregivers may be needed it may be sensible to hire an agency or a professional, such as a geriatric social worker, to hire and coordinate the caregivers.

The caregivers must be supplied with adequate equipment and supplies, which will depend on the nature of the caregiver's duties. If meal preparation is expected, the caregiver will have to have the proper food to prepare. If household cleaning is needed the caregiver will need cleaning supplies. If walks or trips are expected, the caregiver will have to be instructed as to where, when, and for how long they should take the older person and perhaps be supplied with pocket money to purchase snacks or incidentals for the older person. The residence must also be adapted to the care needs, such as grab bars in the bathroom and possibly an elevated toilet seat. If the older person exhibits some degree of dementia, the residence doors must be secured to prevent the older person from wandering away.

Many families or spouses who decide that a loved one requires in-home care resort to an agency with which they contract to provide caregiving services. The agency should properly vet, train, and supervise the caregivers. The agency will also be responsible for supplying a substitute employee should a caregiver be unable to report to work because of sickness or other reason. The agency should be able to supply references, provide appropriate background checks on its employees, and be sure that the employee and the older person are compatible. The agency will also handle paying the employee, withhold and pay all wage taxes including Social Security and unemployment, and provide the employee with the annual W-2 federal income tax wage form as well as all city and state wage forms.

In lieu of engaging an agency to provide the caregiver, hiring a geriatric care manager or social worker is an alternative. Some geriatric care managers or social workers may insist that the older person contract with them to create a care plan before they will agree to assist in locating appropriate staff to meet the needs detailed in the care plan. Although it is more costly to hire a professional, such as a care manager, who in turn hires or locates a home caregiver, doing so significantly increases the likelihood of hiring a dependable, qualified caregiver. If the caregiver is hired by a professional, the professional will have the responsibility to ensure that the person hired has proper training. The professional should also be required to monitor the care provided and ensure that it meets the needs of the older individual.

All of this comes as a price, but in light of the weaken condition of the older person ongoing monitoring by a professional seems worth the cost. Spouses and family members of the older person can also supervise the home caregiver, but a professional should have more knowledge and experience about what can be expected from the caregiver and how to motivate them to properly perform their duties. The professional should also be better at noting when the level or amount of home care should be increased or modified based on the changing needs and condition of the older person.

Whether the caregiver is hired through an agency or directly by the older person or their family, there should be a formal written employment or engagement contract that details the work to be performed, the obligations of the employee, the responsibilities of the agency, the payment amount and timing, and the termination rights of both parties. The contract should also detail the hours and days of work, vacation, holiday, personal days, and paid sick days. The contract should also state the amount of notice that must be given—two weeks is common—and the right of the employer to terminate a caregiver for cause without notice.

If an agency is not used, the older person or their family will be responsible for withholding and paying income and wage taxes, including Social Security and unemployment taxes because a home caregiver is considered an employee rather than an independent contractor.[4] If cash wages exceed $2,000 (in 2017) to a household employee in a year there is a requirement to pay and withhold Social Security wage taxes or engage in withholding for income tax purposes. If a caregiver is paid $1,000 or more in a calendar quarter, the employer must pay the federal unemployment tax. If the employer is uncertain as to what forms must be filed and what taxes withheld, the employer should contact an accountant, either to

---

4. https://www.irs.gov/publications/p926/ar02.html.

perform those functions or for advice as to what they as an employer are required to do under federal, state, and local laws.

Under rules finalized in 2016, home health care workers must be paid the minimum wage and be paid overtime pay under the Fair Labor Standards Act (FLSA).[5] In 2017, the federal minimum wage was $7.25 per hour, but many states have adopted a higher minimum wage. Under FLSA those who provide "companionship services" are not required to be paid the minimum wage. Companionship services are defined as providing fellowship and protection rather than providing care for the individual. That exemption is not available, however, if the employee spends more that 20 percent of their workweek performing "care services," which are defined as assisting with the activities of daily living. Those, in turn, are defined as dressing, grooming, feeding, bathing, toileting, and transferring—moving the person from a bed to a chair—and also include other services such as preparing meals, driving, light housework, and assistance with taking medication. In short, because of what tasks most caregivers are hired to perform, it is almost certain that the FLSA minimum wage and overtime payment requirements will apply.

Hiring a home caregiver necessitates the older person purchase liability insurance to protect against the cost of paying for injuries sustained by the caregiver or caused by the caregiver. Even if the caregiver is employed by an agency, the caregiver may have an independent right to sue the homeowner for tort liability for injuries suffered on the job. If the caregiver is directly employed, an injury while on the job may give rise to a worker's compensation claim that in turn could require the employer, the older person, to make compensation payments for many weeks. The older person should also have sufficient insurance to pay for tort liability in the event the caregiver injures a third party. Finally, the older person also should take out insurance against theft or damage to the house or household effects by the caregiver.

B. Hiring a Relative to Provide Care

Most home care is provided for free by a spouse or an adult child. Often, however, the individual in need of care compensates the relative either because the caregiver needs the money or the older individual is attempting to lower the amount of their savings in order to become eligible for Medicaid assistance. For example, if the older individual wants to qualify for Medicaid Home and Community Based Services they must not have countable resources in excess of the amount permitted by the state. Giving away excess assets is not an option because doing so would invoke the Medicaid penalty period (see Chapter 14, Medicaid). Therefore, to spend down to the resource limit, the older individual may begin to pay a relative who had formerly had been providing their assistance for free.

Payment to a relative for personal care should be made pursuant to a written contract in order to rebut the presumption that the transfers to the relative were

---

5. https://www.dol.gov/whd/regs/compliance/whdfsFinalRule.htm.

gifts rather than payment for services. Such a contract should detail the services to be provided including the number of hours, the type of care to be provided, provisions for time off, such as for holidays or personal days, termination provisions and the amount of compensation. The contract should state that all payroll taxes will be paid and that the necessary withholding for income taxes will occur. Failure to do so may be grounds for Medicaid asserting that the agreement is a sham transaction and not payment for care services but rather an attempt to transfer resources to the relative in order to qualify the older individual for Medicaid.

Some older individuals attempt to prepay the relative by giving them a lump-sum payment for future care. By doing so, the older individual can more rapidly spend down their resources in an attempt to become eligible for Medicaid. Paying a lump sum can work, but Medicaid will closely examine the provisions of the agreement. Typically, such an agreement should detail the amount of care being purchased and do so by spelling out the hours and days of care as well as the form of care that the relative will provide. For example, the agreement might require the relative to provide the older individual with transportation to doctors' appointments or to a Senior Center where the individual can socialize. Most importantly, the agreement should state what happens if the older individual moves into an institution, such as a nursing home, before the expiration of the prepaid care time or if the individual dies before the relative has had time to deliver all the contracted for personal care services. Ideally, the contract would require the relative to return a portion of the lump-sum payment in proportion to the amount of services already provided. A return clause makes it apparent that the payment was for services and not a disguised gift.

1. Occupancy by Caregiver of the House of the Older Individual

Often relatives who provide home care move into the older individual's home and live rent-free, either to make themselves more available or as a form of compensation. If the free rent is the only compensation, the older individual does not need to pay wage taxes and there is no income subject to withholding.[6] Despite the possible informal or "friendly" nature of the arrangement, the parties should consider signing a formal Occupancy Agreement to be sure that both sides understand what is expected of the other. The agreement should state that the right to live rent-free in the older individual's house is dependent upon the provision of care giving services. The agreement should detail what part of the house that the caregiver has the right to exclusively occupy; parts of the house that may be off limits; the right to bring in furniture or use the older person's furniture; what, if anything, the caregiver must pay for, such as cable television; the caregiver's responsibilities as to household cleaning and maintenance; the caregiver's duties as to repair and maintenance of the exterior of the house, the lawn, and outbuildings; the right of the caregiver to park a car on the property or on the street; and how meals and groceries for the caregiver and the older individual will be

---

6. IRS Publication 926, https://www.irs.gov/publications/p926/ar02.html.

handled. The agreement should also list the caregiving duties in general terms and whether the caregiver has any responsibilities as to the older individual's medical needs and medications. The resident caregiver may also want the older individual to pay for health and disability insurance for the caregiver.

Either party should be able to terminate the agreement with adequate notice, such as two weeks. The agreement should also state how long the caregiver can continue to live in the house if the older person should move to a new house or apartment, an institution such as a nursing home, or upon the death of the older individual. The parties should also agree as to the protocol to be followed if the older individual starts to lose mental capacity. One solution is to have a third party empowered to terminate the agreement if the mental or physical condition of the older person deteriorates to the point that a more experienced or professional caregiver is needed.

2. Caregiver Compensation Provided by a Promise to Leave Them the House

Some older individuals not only provide free housing to a caregiver, they also promise to deed the house to the caregiver should the older individual move into an institution, or to leave the house to the caregiver in their will. An agreement to compensate a caregiver by a devise in a will is a validly enforceable contract, but it can lead to litigation if there is a question as to whether the caregiver carried out their part of the agreement by providing proper care. Although an oral agreement can be enforceable,[7] putting the agreement in writing is much preferable. The agreement should state in general terms the obligations of the caregiver, whether those duties must be carried out for a minimum number of years in order for the older person to be required to devise the home to the caregiver, what happens if the caregiver quits, becomes unable to perform the functions of a caregiver, or dies before the older individual. Provisions should also be made as to whether the caregiver can continue to live in the house if the older individual moves out for any reason and whether the caregiver has a right to the house even if they ceased to provide services because the older individual moved out of the house, such as into a nursing home but did not die for an extended period of time. The agreement should also detail which party is responsible for the maintenance, upkeep, insurance, and taxes of the house both while the older individual lives in it and after they have moved out. The agreement should also address whether the older individual is required to pay for health and disability insurance for the caregiver.

The timing of the transfer of the house to the caregiver must be carefully addressed. The parties likely contemplate the homeowner dying at home or only after a brief hospital stay. The more likely scenario is that the homeowner will be forced to move out because of an increasing need for nursing care that the caregiver is unable to provide. Dementia, for example, might force the homeowner to move into a secure facility that is able to provide the level of care needed and increase the extent of care as the dementia worsens.

---

7. *E.g.*, Estate of Jesmer v. Rohlev, 609 N.E.3d 816 (Ill. App. Ct. 1993).

If, for whatever reason, the homeowner moves out of the house, the caregiver will likely insist that they be permitted to continue to reside in it. Although that may be acceptable to the homeowner, the parties need to agree as to who is going to pay the taxes, repair, and maintenance on the house until such time as the older person should die. The parties will likely also agree that the deed for the house will remain in the homeowner's name until their death. If the homeowner moves from the home into a facility, the parties should address whether the caregiver can permit another party, such as a partner or spouse, to move into the house or even rent out the house. If the homeowner no longer resides in the house, the parties may want to agree that after a year or some other agreed upon passage of time, the house will be transferred to the caregiver as payment for the care that they provided.

3. Exchange of Home for Future Care

Some older individuals who lack enough savings or income to pay for their care enter an agreement to obtain in-home care by transferring the ownership of the house to the caregiver in exchange for a promise caregiver will provide lifetime care for the older person. The caregiver is often, but not always, a relative. Not surprisingly, such an arrangement raises a number of issues that should be addressed in a written contract between the parties. The issues to be addressed include

- What happens if the caregiver predeceases the older individual?
- What if the caregiver, due to mental or physical decline, is unable to perform the agreed upon care?
- What happens if the older individual requires care that is beyond the ability of the caregiver to perform?
- Can the caregiver insist that the older individual hire additional help, such as visiting nurses, to assist if the needs of the older individual exceed the ability of the caregiver? If so, who pays for such additional care?
- Who determines whether the older individual should move out of the house into an assisted living facility or nursing home?
- Does the caregiver have the right to permit a third party, such as a partner or new spouse, to live in the home while the older individual is still living in it?
- Can the caregiver sell the house and relocate on the condition that the caregiver permits the older individual to move into the new residence?

IV. Congregate Housing

The term "congregate housing" refers to housing for older individuals that provides services but usually not personal care or nursing care. Congregate housing is typically age restricted and only accepts older individuals as residents as allowed by the Federal Fair Housing Act. That act, which otherwise bars discrimination in housing, exempts housing for older persons.[8] The act permits housing intended for and solely occupied by persons age 62 or older. It also permits housing intended and occupied by persons age 55 or older if at least 80 percent of the units are occupied by at least one person age 55 or older. Congregate housing exists for both populations—all residents age 62 or older and housing having at least 80 percent of the occupied units having at least one person age 55 or older (see Chapter 8, Housing).

Most congregate housing is provided in facilities that contain apartments or condominiums designed for individuals who can live independently but desire some degree of shared living. The individual has a separate apartment or condominium but also enjoys access to common areas, such as a card room; a reading room with newspapers, magazines, and books; and even a craft or woodworking room. Some congregate housing features a dining room that doubles as a theater or common room. Typically the resident's monthly rent or condominium fee pays for upkeep of the common areas, landscaping, and also for some limited in-unit housekeeping and linen service. For an additional fee, the resident may procure additional services, such a laundry and dry cleaning. In-unit personal assistance is not typically provided, but the residents can purchase such assistance, such as a personal attendant, on their own. Some congregate housing facilities have a social worker on staff to help arrange needed services.

Some congregate housing has a common dining room, but such facilities rarely provide three meals a day. Some provide lunch and dinner, but most only provide an evening meal. Some facilities mandate payment for the evening meal, for others it is optional. The provision of meals has proved to be very costly and not always desired by the residents. As a result, it is becoming more common for the facility not to provide any meals to residents.

Congregate housing appeals to elderly who wish to remain independent but be freed of the chores that accompany home ownership. In essence, congregate housing is a bit like living in an upscale hotel with the added attraction of common areas and recreational facilities, such as tennis courts, that help provide a sense of community. An older person, however, who requires personal care should consider other forms of housing.

V. Assisted Living

Assisted living facilities provide supportive living for older individuals who need personal assistance but do not need health care assistance. Residents live in a single or shared small apartment or studio unit that will not have a full kitchen. The facility will have a dining area and provide all the resident's meals. Because

---

8. 42 U.S.C. § 3607(b).

what services are provided by the assisted living facility vary from state to state, the fees also vary, but usually an assisted living facility will cost about half as much or less than a nursing home operating in the same community.

Residents often have physical limitations; some have a loss of cognition, usually from dementia, or are too frail to live alone. Some have a physical condition that makes living alone unwise, such as the loss of vision from severe macular degeneration, and others simply want to avoid social isolation. Some desire that if they have a need for medical assistance, that they are living where someone will notice they need assistance and see such assistance is forthcoming.

Assisted living facilities are licensed by the state and are not permitted to offer skilled nursing care, which is a level of care that is available only in a licensed nursing home. Many who reside in assisted living do so because they need assistance with activities of daily living, including help with dressing, bathing, and toileting. Others can care for their personal needs but can no longer cook for themselves and so require the facility to provide them with three nutritious meals a day as well as necessary supplements or snacks.

Assisted living also frees the residents from what are called the instrumental activities of daily living, such as food shopping, food preparation, housekeeping, doing laundry, using the telephone to seek assistance, driving or using public transportation, and managing the financial aspect of a household. The goal of assisted living is to provide support as needed but also promote maximum independence, choice, privacy, and dignity. Assisted living facilities attempt to provide their residents with a safe, supportive environment where they can experience as much autonomy as is consistent with their mental and physical condition. Residents (other than those with dementia) are free to come and go, a few will own a car but most will rely on public transportation. The facility cannot provide medical care, but it will monitor the residents' prescription drugs and make sure the residents take them in the proper order and in a timely manner. The facility often has rooms in which residents can participate in physical and other therapies provided by outside providers that are often paid for by Medicare.

The quality of life in an assisted living facility depends on the individual facility. It also is dependent on the manner in which state licensure permits the facility to operate and what services it can provide. The number of assisted living facilities has grown rapidly over the last decade because many elderly correctly perceive assisted living as being less expensive, offering more privacy, and a less regimented life than a nursing home. It is also often a more practical alternative to paying for in-home care for an aging individual with declining mental or physical capabilities. Assisted living facilities typically try to create a home-like atmosphere with individual apartments, either studios or one-bedrooms. The units do not have a kitchen but may have a microwave oven and a small refrigerator. Most assisted living facilities feature common areas for recreation and socializing as well as comfortable dining rooms that feature chandeliers and individual table service. Staffing is usually dictated by state regulations, but many facilities provide more staff than is required in order to be able to provide services to residents in a timely and unrushed fashion.

Many residents of assisted living facilities have mild or moderate dementia. Although assisted living facilities are not licensed to provide medical care, they can provide supervisory care for individuals with dementia. In response to demand, many assisted living facilities have created floors or wings dedicated to the care of residents with mild or moderate dementia who need supervision and assistance with personal care and do not have other medical needs. One symptom of dementia is the propensity for individuals to roam or wander away from where they live and lack the awareness to know how to return. Known as "elopement," it is often the result of the individual trying to return home, to a work site, or to seek someone or something. The result is that a primary care need for those with mild or moderate dementia (as opposed to those with severe dementia) is supervision and keeping them on the premises. Their urge to wander is often a motivating reason for the family or spouse moving the individual into assisted living. The hope is that the facility will have means of preventing elopement, which can include an isolated floor that can only be exited by keying an elevator, a dedicated wing with the exit under supervision, or by the use of personal wrist or ankle bracelets that alert the staff if an individual attempts to leave the facility.

The facility can also provide an individual with dementia with personal care, such as grooming, dressing, making sure they eat, and providing them with appropriate stimulation. The facility cannot provide medical care, but mild or moderate dementia typically does not require medical assistance beyond ensuring that the individual takes their prescription drugs, which may have been prescribed to manage anxiety or other symptoms of the dementia. As the dementia progresses, however, the individual's care needs may grow beyond the level of care that the facility's license permits it to provide.

In particular, in most states, assisted living facilities cannot house non-ambulatory, bedfast individuals. If the individual with dementia is unable to leave their bed, the facility must transfer them to a nursing home. Still, many demented individuals can reside for many months in an assisted living facility just as individuals with manageable medical conditions, such as persons with congestive heart failure who are ambulatory and on maintenance prescription drugs, can live in assisted living rather than in a nursing home.

Although state licensure requirements dictate who an assisted living facility may house, at the margins the facility has discretion when to discharge a resident because of their declining medical condition. For example, if the resident has a stroke that leaves them physically impaired, the facility has to decide whether to wait and see whether and how much the resident may recover or in the alternative discharge the resident because of their medical needs. Some assisted living facilities are associated with a nursing home and as a consequence may be quicker to discharge the resident and recommend that they move to the associated nursing home. Facilities that have success in attracting new residents may be more aggressive in discharging medically needy residents than facilities that have open beds. State law may give residents the legal right to resist discharge beyond any contractual protections that were contained in the contract of admission signed by the resident.

The great majority of assisted living residents are private pay. There is little public reimbursement of assisted living, although in light of the lower cost of assisted living as compared to nursing homes, states are becoming more open to helping to pay for the cost of care. In some cases, partial reimbursement by the state as part of its home and community care program is available as states try to reduce or minimize the number of Medicaid reimbursed residents of nursing homes. If, however, a resident is not eligible for state assistance, private payment is the only option absent the individual having a long-term care insurance policy that will reimburse the cost of care (see Chapter 12, Long-Term Care Insurance). Residents who run out of funds to pay for their care may have no choice but to move into a nursing home where they can qualify for Medicaid reimbursement for their cost of care.

Before moving to an assisted living facility, the potential resident should consider the following:

- Is in-home care a financially viable alternative—at least for a period of time?
- Assuming I can afford it, is in-home care a practical alternative?
- If the need for care is dementia, is in-home care viable?
- Is in-home care sensible in light of the demands and stresses it puts on my spouse and family members?
- Can I afford the monthly fee?
- If the monthly fee exceeds my monthly income, do I have enough savings to afford to live in the facility for an extended period?
- If married, do my spouse and I have enough income and savings to bear the cost of assisted living and still comfortably support my spouse?
- If married, does it make sense for my spouse to continue to reside in our current house, condominium, or apartment, or should they relocate?
- Are there other viable alternatives such as congregate housing or a continuing care retirement community that might be better for both spouses?

Residents of assisted living facilities sign a contract of admission. Although there is no standard contract, the following terms or requirements are usually part of the contract:

- The date of occupancy starts the clock on the requirement to pay. A potential resident may try to negotiate a flexible date in case something should occur, such as a health problem that delays the resident's move into the facility.
- Identification of the unit to be occupied should be stated in the contract rather than leaving it up to the facility. At a minimum the contract should

describe the type of room—one-bedroom—and if possible the location—fifth floor or Tower A. The aspects of the room, such as whether it has a private bathroom and what cooking facilities it has, such as a microwave oven, refrigerator, or a sink, should be in the contract. The contract should state that the room will be fully cleaned before the resident moves in, which should include cleaning the carpets and possibly painting the walls in a color chosen by the resident within a range of choices supplied by the facility.

- The room furnishings, if any, should be described. Many residents fully or partially furnish the room, not so much as a way to save money, but to create a more familiar atmosphere. The resident should also know what items the facility will supply, such as window curtains or a shower curtain. What happens to the furnishings supplied by the resident upon the resident's discharge or death should also be stated in the contract. For example, if the resident installs a new light fixture, does the fixture remain with the facility?

- The resident's physical and mental condition will also be part of the contract. Before signing the contract, the facility will require that the potential resident be well enough to be permitted to reside in the facility. The resident will also have to meet the health requirements on the day of admission. A severe medical problem between the date of signing the contract of admission and the date of moving in might be grounds for the facility to refuse admission.

- The contract should also address whether the resident can make physical changes to the unit, such as repainting it, wallpapering it, putting in new carpets or other forms of flooring, modifying a closet, or removing or inserting a wall. Even if the resident is permitted to make such changes, the facility will likely require that it review and give prior approval to the resident's remodeling plans.

- The contract should state the services to be provided, including maintenance, cleaning of the unit, linen services, meals, any in-unit assistance, recreation, transportation to services such as medical appointments, whether the facility will have a nurse or other medical person on site for some portion of the day, and whether Medicare therapy providers are allowed to provide services in the facility.

- The contract should state whether the facility will sell additional services to the resident, such as in-unit personal care.

- Although the contract will likely state that the facility will provide meals that meet the medical dietary needs of the resident, it should also state whether the facility will provide meals that meet the resident's dietary preferences, religious or otherwise.

- The resident's rights should be spelled out. The right to have visitors, when they may visit, the right to apply for public assistance to help pay the monthly fee, and whether there is a resident's council that meets with management.

- The resident should assume that the contract will permit the facility to raise the monthly fee and to make reasonable changes in the form and kind of care provided to the residents.
- The potential liability of the facility to the resident should be spelled out. The resident should be careful to note possible limitations on liability, as some facilities impose a requirement that the resident assume certain risks of physical injury rather than holding the facility responsible. Allegedly such limits on liability help reduce the monthly fee.

Alternatives to assisted living are board-and-care homes and personal care or retirement homes that provide care much like an assisted living facility but often house older individuals with lower incomes and fewer assets. Depending on state law, these facilities, which predate the assisted living facility model, house individuals with varying care needs. At a minimum, they house and feed their residents. These facilities, which number in the thousands, vary greatly in size with some housing a handful of residents in a converted large, old family house to larger facilities that house hundreds in apartment-like compounds. Typically they cost less than newer assisted living facilities, in part because they often provide less assistance and fewer amenities. Some provide little more than housing and meals, but others provide a good deal of individual care and supervision. Many residents who lack a spouse and have limited incomes, choose to reside in the facilities because they are single and require a safe residence and meal preparation rather than needing personal care.

VI. Continuing Care Retirement Communities

Continuing care retirement communities (CCRCs) are communities reserved for older individuals that provide varying levels of care, typically independent living, assisted living, and nursing home care, although not all CCRCs provide all levels of care. Although traditionally a CCRC provided on-site nursing home care, a few provide nursing care off-site. The premise of a full-service CCRC is that once a resident enters the community, they will never have to leave even if their mental or physical health deteriorates.

CCRCs are found in cities and suburbs, small towns and metropolises; some are high rises, some feature garden apartments, others have a mixture of freestanding residences and connected units. Almost all have a central core structure that contains a dining room, recreational amenities, common rooms, assisted living units, and the nursing home facility. Many CCRCs are operated by nonprofits, some of which are affiliated with religious entities; others are owned and operated by for-profit entities.

Residents of CCRCs pay an admission fee and a monthly service fee. The individual initially moves into the CCRC independent living unit at a set monthly fee. (CCRCs usually will only admit residents whose health permits them to initially move into independent living.) The monthly fee typically rises over time as the cost of the operation of the entity rises. Annual increases of 3 to 6 percent are not uncommon. In the original CCRC model, the monthly fee did not rise, however, even if the individual's physical or mental condition necessitated a move from the independent living unit to assisted living or to the nursing home facility. In recent years, some CCRCs have retreated from the "fixed fee" model to charging a higher fee if the resident moves into assisted living, and even more CCRCs now charge a higher fee if the resident moves into the nursing home facility. By doing so, the CCRC can charge less for the independent living. In particular, because today fewer elderly require long-term nursing care—as opposed to assisted living—potential residents of CCRCs are more willing to accept the risk of having to pay more for nursing home care in exchange for paying less while they reside in independent living or in an assisted living unit.

CCRCs charge a high initial admission fee; $200,000 to $500,000 is common. Most residents finance it largely or entirely with the proceeds from the sale of their homes. Traditionally, the entry fee was essentially nonrefundable unless the resident died within a limited period of time, such as 30 days, or the entry fee might be fully refundable if the resident died in 30 days but the amount of the refund would decline over time so that it might be 60 percent refundable before the sixth month, 30 percent at the ninth month, and not refundable thereafter. If a couple moved in, the refundable feature would apply only if both spouses died within the time period. No refund would be available if the resident voluntarily moved out of the CCRC.

Today, most CCRCs offer a variety of admission agreements that provide a choice of whether to pay a nonrefundable entrance fee, a limited refundable fee, or pay a higher, but potentially fully refundable fee. Some admission fees are fully refundable but only when the individual's unit has been re-occupied and the new resident has paid another admission fee. A limited or declining admission fee, might, for example, initially be 100 percent refundable, but after three years decline to 85 percent, and then to 65 percent after five years, where it remains until the resident dies. Of course, even a 100 percent refund does not account for the loss of investment opportunity during the period that the fee is being held by the CCRC, but at least the estate of the resident recovers the entire admission fee. The general rule is the more refundable the admission fee, the higher it is.

In general, CCRCs offer three types of contracts:

- Type A contracts are extensive or life-care contracts that promise the unlimited use of health care services at little or no increase in the monthly fee.

- Type B, or modified, contracts permit unlimited use of the assisted living facility but limit the amount of health care services that may be accessed without any increase in the monthly fee, such as, for example, up to 30 days in the nursing home facility with no increase in the monthly fee. Beyond that, the monthly fee increases but it is still below the average monthly cost of nursing homes in the area.
- Type C, or fee-for-service, contracts require residents to pay market rates for any CCRC-provided health-related services and possibly for personal care provided in the assisted living facility of the CCRC. This contract is essentially the rental of an independent living unit with the option to purchase additional services. The contract may or may not permit the resident to a refund of the admission fee (assuming there is one) should the resident voluntarily leave the community in order to enter assisted living or a nursing home not affiliated with the CCRC. If there is no admission fee, the arrangement is essentially a rental agreement that is terminable by the resident but not the CCRC except under specified conditions.

Most residents of a CCRC live in independent living units with a smaller number living in the assisted living portion of the facility and an even fewer number occupying nursing home beds. The financial model of a CCRC depends on the appropriate mix of residents with most needing little care or supervision. As a result, CCRC residents are younger and healthier than those who move into a freestanding assisted living facility. Many enter in their 70s, although those who can prove that they can live independently (they may be required to pass a physical or submit proof of their health) can move in at any age. Many residents continue to drive and so bring a car with them. The independent living unit may be a studio, but one and two bedroom units are the norm, with some CCRCs offering a few three-bedroom units—one for him, one for her, and the third being used as an office or entertainment center. The unit will have a small, complete kitchen, but the CCRC will furnish at least one meal a day as part of the contract of admission. The meal serves to help the residents socialize and also permits the CCRC staff to observe the residents' health. If a resident unexpectedly fails to show up for dinner, the staff can contact the resident and inquire whether they need assistance. Some CCRCs also open the dining room for breakfast or lunch and charge an additional fee for those meals. The CCRC will also feature common rooms, such as a card-playing room; recreational facilities, such as an in-door swimming pool; and rooms for supportive services, such as a physical therapy room. Some larger CCRCs have a bank on site open for two or three days a week, a small gift shop that is sometimes operated by the residents, and possibly small garden plots. Clubs, such as a book club, are common. The facility often screens movies in a common room and brings in community groups, such as a high school choir, to entertain the residents.

If a resident's health declines too severely or if the resident shows signs of dementia, the contract of admission will permit the CCRC to move the resident to its assisted living facility. Typically the CCRC will engage the resident and the resident's family or spouse in a discussion as to whether the resident's physical health or mental cognition no longer permits them to live independently. But in the end, the CCRC has the authority to force the resident to relocate to the assisted living unit or the nursing home facility. For an additional fee, some CCRCs offer additional assistance in the independent living units. Such assistance may delay the need to move to assisted living that features small studio or one-bedroom units that lack a kitchen but may have a microwave oven, a small refrigerator and a kitchen sink. The CCRC will furnish three meals a day to its assisted living resident, often in a dining room separate from that used by the independent living unit residents. The resident will receive some in-unit care but for the most part the assisted living facility will operate very much like freestanding assisted living facilities and insist that the residents be able to walk to the common dining hall and care for most of their own personal care needs.

If the resident has ongoing, daily medical needs or severe dementia, the resident will be moved into the nursing home wing facility. A CCRC will not accept Medicaid; the resident must have enough income and assets to pay for a lifetime of care. Because the CCRC does not accept Medicaid, it may offer single bed nursing home rooms if the numbers permit. The nursing home wing will be licensed by the state to provide care that is similar to that provided in any nursing home, although many CCRCs contend that they offer superior care that is less institutionalized and more respectful of the resident. A CCRC will likely accept Medicare reimbursement for the first 20 days of care if the resident qualifies for Medicare reimbursement and for the partial Medicare reimbursement of days 21 to 100.

To be admitted to a CCRC, the potential resident must prove that they have enough income and assets to pay for their care no matter how long they live. Failure to pay the monthly fee is grounds for the CCRC to evict the resident, as is behavior by the resident that is deleterious to the CCRC. Otherwise, the CCRC cannot evict the resident even if their health deteriorates badly and much sooner than expected. The resident, in turn, because of the guarantee of lifetime care, does not need to pay for long-term care insurance. In fact, a CCRC can be understood as a form of long-term care insurance if the monthly fee does not rise even if the resident's care needs become more costly to provide. A few nonprofit, religiously affiliated CCRCs offer subsidies for individuals who become unable to afford the monthly fee, but there is no guarantee that the CCRC will do so or, if it provides a subsidy, that it will do so until the death of the resident.

Residents who have a dispute with the CCRC over its attempt to evict them must rely on the contract of admission that will define the respective rights of the parties. They can also claim that their eviction would violate the federal Fair Housing Act[9] but usually the contract of admission will determine the legality of the eviction, and that typically favors the CCRC over the resident.

---

9. *Id.* § 3604.

Because a portion of the admission fee represents prepayment of the provision of possible future health care, it, and some or all of the monthly fee may be tax deductible as a medical expense under I.R.C. Section 213, subject to the limits of that section. The CCRC will inform the resident whether any portion of the admission fee is deductible and whether the monthly fee is deductible. If the admission fee is refundable, it will not be deductible until it or some portion is no longer refundable. I.R.C. Section 7872, which imputes interest on below-market loans, does not apply to CCRC refundable admission fees so long as the resident or the spouse is at least age 62.[10]

The large amount of the entry fee makes the financial stability of the CCRC a paramount concern for its residents. To financially function, the CCRC must manage several variables.

- The average age of the residents at time of entry and their expected life expectancy.
- How soon, if ever, the new resident will require personal assistance and health care that will necessitate their move into the assisted living unit or the nursing home facility.
- The expected increase in the cost of operating the facility such as for labor, food, and utilities.
- The expected return on the invested entry fees until they are either returned or spent down to provide care for the residents.

Miscalculation of any of these variables can result in the need to raise the entry fee, raise the monthly fee, or cause the CCRC to be more aggressive in attracting or admitting younger, healthier residents who will not need assisted living or nursing home care for several years. Potentially, CCRC that badly miscalculates its future revenue and expenses may go bankrupt.

To protect CCRC residents from the CCRC having financial difficulties, states regulate their financial operation. (States also regulate the assisted living and nursing home facilities that are part of the CCRC.) There is no federal regulation or licensing of CCRCs, although if the CCRC nursing home facility accepts Medicare it will have to qualify as a Medicare certified facility, and the state may require that it license the assisted living facility and the nursing home. Before signing an admission agreement, the potential resident should ask the CCRC which state agency regulates it, and then make inquiries with that state agency about the CCRC's financial stability. The CCRC should be asked for its excess margin ratio that compares current income to current expenses. If the ratio is negative, the CCRC should be avoided. The potential resident should also inquire as to the amount of long-term debt compared to cash reserves that represent retained admission entry fees (cash reserves should equal at least 50 percent of the debt). If the CCRC is owned by an entity that operates more than one facility,

---

10. I.R.C. § 7872(h).

the resident should inquire whether each CCRC is financially independent or whether the financial success of the entity can be affected by the financial conditions of the other affiliated CCRCs.

The potential resident should also inquire as to how long the CCRC has successfully operated, the occupancy rate (over 90 percent is the norm), the annual turnover rate, the average age of the residents, the relative number of women and men, and the percentage of residences occupied by couples as well as the number and percentage of residents living in the assisted living and in the nursing home facility.

VII. Hospices and Hospice Care

Hospice care is often recommended for the terminally ill. Hospice care is palliative care for terminally ill patients that focuses on pain relief and acceptance of death; it does not try to cure the patients or extend their lives. The goal is to keep patients comfortable, as pain-free as possible, and enable them to live out their lives in a peaceful and dignified manner. It provides compassionate care along with emotional and spiritual support as desired by the patient.

Hospice care, or hospice, as it sometimes called, is provided in a variety of settings. There are freestanding hospices and hospices located in hospitals, in assisted living facilities, and in nursing home facilities, but most commonly hospice care is provided in the patient's home. About 40 percent of hospice care is provided in the home of the patient and another 25 percent in nursing homes or assisted living facilities. About a quarter is provided in freestanding hospice facilities and less than 10 percent in a hospital. Over 40 percent of hospice patients are age 85 and older.[11] Home hospice care features a family member as the primary caregiver who is supported by hospice staff who assess the patient's needs, regularly visit the patient, and provide some direct care and services. Home hospice care provided by the family is typically augmented with limited periods of care by licensed nurses. If the patient's pain becomes unmanageable or if the family is not available to provide in-home care, the patient may be moved into an in-patient hospice facility.

An estimated 1.5 million patients receive hospice annually. The numbers have increased steadily over the past decade and the number of hospice providers has grown to over 4,000. Medicare pays for almost 90 percent of all hospice patients. Still, only a minority—likely about 40 percent—of deceased Medicare beneficiaries used hospice for three or more days, with cancer patients being the most likely to use hospice. About a third of hospice patients die within seven days of admission.

---

11. *See generally* National Hospice and Palliative Care Organization, *NHPCO's Facts and Figures, Hospice Care in America—2014 Edition,* http://www.nhpco.org/sites/default/files/public/Statistics _Research/2014_Facts_Figures.pdf.

Almost half die within 14 days of admission; only about 10 percent remain in hospice for six months or more.

Together with the patient, the hospice staff develops a care plan that features pain management and control of symptoms. The staff is an interdisciplinary team consisting of the patient's attending physician; the hospice physician or medical director; nurses; social workers; clergy or spiritual counselors; and speech, physical, and occupational therapists. At the center of the "team" are the patient and the patient's family who work together to guide and monitor the hospice care. As a condition of participating in Medicare hospice, the provider must have at least 5 percent of the care provided by volunteers, who undertake tasks such as providing clerical assistance, fundraising, or direct patient support.

The hospice interdisciplinary team will

- Manage the patient's pain and symptoms;
- Provide assistance with the emotional and other nonphysical aspects of dying;
- Supply prescription drugs, medical supplies, and equipment;
- Instruct the family and volunteers on how to care for the patient;
- Provide therapies as needed, for example, speech therapy;
- Provide respite care for family caregivers; and
- Provide spousal and family bereavement counseling.

The team members have defined roles. The hospice physician or medical director has overall responsibility for the patient's medical care plan with the key component being pain and symptom management. Nurses manage the care plan and monitor the prescription drugs, social workers and clergy focus on the patient's and the family's attitude and help them come to accept the impending death, and therapists provide care designed to minimize the patient's pain and reduce symptoms.

The hospice will likely employ home health aides, nonprofessional caregivers, who will usually have the most contact with the patient. These aides provide personal care, such as assistance with bathing and backrubs. The aides typically have only a high school education but their positive attitude can bring comfort to the patient, and their presence gives the family caregivers some respite. While the aide is present, the family can tend to their own needs or leave the premises to shop, take care of their affairs, or seek out recreation. The hospice may provide music therapy to assist the patient to relax and hopefully find some degree of peace. Art therapy is also employed. Patients are supplied with materials that enable them to express feelings about their condition that are difficult or impossible to articulate. Note that Medicare does not pay for music or art therapy. Hospices are required to make reasonable efforts to involve clergy or other spiritual advisors if requested to do so by the patient. Even without a formal invitation, clergy often visit the patient, in part because if they do so, the hospice is credited with having used a volunteer whose time counts toward the requirement that 5 percent of the care be provided by a volunteer.

Medicare pays for over 90 percent of hospice care. As a result, the Medicare guidelines dictate how hospices operate.[12] For example, Medicare requires that patients be kept comfortable and safe, be permitted 24-hour visiting rights, and be able to select their food and mealtimes.

Medicare Part A will pay for hospice only if the patient's physician and the hospice physician certify that the patient is terminally ill with a life expectancy of six months or less.[13] The patient must agree in writing that they will accept palliative care rather than curative care. The patient, in other words, must agree to end attempts at curing the illness or condition and accept only comfort care in lieu of the services reimbursed by Medicare Part A and Part B. The patient, however, can terminate hospice care at any time. Prior to accepting hospice care, the patient has a right to a one-time only consultation with the hospice physician or medical director to go over the care options and how the hospice plans to manage the patient's pain and symptoms. The patient then has the choice of accepting or refusing hospice. If the choice is hospice, Medicare will cover everything that is needed for palliative care including the cost of physicians (including the patient's regular physician if desired by the patient); nurses; social workers; medical equipment, such as a wheelchair; medical supplies, such as bandages; prescription drugs; home health and homemaker aides; therapies; dietary counseling; grief counseling for the patient and the patient's family; short-term in-patient care if needed for pain management; and any other Medicare-approved services deemed necessary by the hospice team. If the patient's family needs respite care, Medicare will pay to house the patient for up to five days in a Medicare-approved facility, such as a hospital, each time respite care is required.

Medicare will not pay for room and board for the patient but it will pay for respite care for which the patient may be required to pay a small co-payment. If the patient resides in a nursing home, Medicare will not pay the charges for room and board. However, the patient can be on Medicaid, which will pay for the nursing home room and board while Medicare pays for the patient's hospice care. Medicare hospice care also does not pay for care in an emergency room, inpatient care in a facility, or an ambulance unless it was arranged by the hospice or is unrelated to the patient's terminal illness. Medicare reimbursement or payment for hospice care is the same whether the patient was enrolled in original Medicare Parts A and B or in a Medicare Advantage Plan. Non-hospice medical care will continue to be paid for by traditional Medicare or by the patient's Medicare Advantage plan, which will also continue to offer its additional services, such as dental care. Patients who have a Medigap policy can expect it to pay for the hospice cost of drugs and respite care that might otherwise be billed to the patient.

---

12. 42 C.F.R. §§ 418.1–418.205.

13. For a detailed description of how Medicare hospice operates, see the Centers for Medicare and Medicaid booklet, *Medicare Hospice Benefits, available at* https://www.medicare.gov/Pubs/pdf/02154-Medicare-Hospice-Benefits.PDF

There is no deductible for Medicare hospice care; the only co-pays are up to $5 per prescription for drugs prescribed for pain and symptom management and a 5 percent co-pay for respite care. Although Medicare hospice is intended for patients who have a life expectancy of six months or less, if after six months of hospice, the patient is still alive, hospice care will continue if the hospice medical director or other hospice doctor recertifies that the patient is terminally ill and has a life expectancy of six months or less. Hospice care is initially provided for two 90-day benefit periods that are followed by an unlimited number of 60-day benefit periods. At the start of each period, the hospice medical director or other hospice doctor must recertify that the patient is terminally ill and has a life expectancy of six months or less.

The patient has the right to change providers once during each benefit period and also has the right to terminate hospice care and return to the type of Medicare coverage the patient had before choosing hospice. If the patient is later eligible, they can return to hospice at any time that they choose.

Medicaid 14

I. Introduction

Medicaid is the federal program designed to pay for the medical expenses of low-income individuals who are aged, blind, or disabled.[1] Created in 1965, it provides money to the states to help reimburse the cost of medical care of those eligible. Medicaid participation is voluntary by states, which pay a significant portion of its cost, with the state cost of Medicaid varying from approximately 25 percent to 50 percent. Responsibility for administering Medicaid rests with the Centers for Medicare and Medicaid Services (CMS), which are part of the Department of Health and Human Services. CMS provides funds to state agencies that, in turn, reimburse providers of medical care.

Federal law establishes minimum requirements as to eligibility and for what forms of medical assistance the state must pay. So long as states meet the federal requirements, they may establish more liberal eligibility requirements and provide more generous assistance.

Because it is a jointly funded program, individual state Medicaid or medical assistance programs are subject to both federal and state laws and regulations. Consequently, state Medicaid programs differ. Moreover, federal law permits states some choices in how to structure their Medicaid, which further adds to differences among the state Medicaid programs. Finally, states

---

1. 42 U.S.C. §§ 1396–1396r.

use different names to identify their programs. Some call it Medicaid, others Medical Assistance, and California uses the term Medi-Cal. Whatever they call it, every state participates in Medicaid. To participate each state must submit to CMS a state medical assistance plan that meets the requirements of the federal law. Changes in the state Medicaid program are subject to federal review to ensure that the program still complies with the federal law.

Medicaid provides benefits to a variety of individuals, but this chapter only discusses Medicaid benefits for the elderly, those age 65 and older. The chapter is also limited to Medicaid benefits for long-term care such as provided in a nursing home; it does not address other Medicaid benefits that are available to impoverished elderly persons.

II. Eligibility

Only U.S. citizens and certain qualified aliens[2] are eligible for Medicaid. Individuals must document their citizenship inter alia by a passport, a birth certificate, by religious records of the birth or by a written affidavit signed by two citizens.[3] The eligibility requirements for aliens are complex. Some, but not all, aliens in the following categories are eligible for Medicaid:

- Permanent residents,
- Lawful aliens,
- Asylees, and
- Refugees.[4]

All citizen residents of a state are eligible. Individuals are considered to be a resident of

- The state where they live with the intent of staying permanently or indefinitely, or
- The state from which the individual receives a state supplement to Supplemental Security Income.

Individuals who live in an institution, such as a nursing home, are considered to be a resident of

- The state where they live with the intent of staying permanently or indefinitely,
- If they are unable to express a preference, the state in which they are physically present,[5] or

---

2. 8 U.S.C. § 1641.

3. https://www.cms.gov/Regulations-and-Guidance/Legislation/DeficitReductionAct/Citizenship.html.

4. 8 U.S.C. § 1612.

5. Matter of Kashmira Shah, 733 N.E.2d 1093 (N.Y. Ct. App. 2000).

- If the state places the individual in an institution in another state, the state that made the placement.[6]

States cannot impose additional residency requirements or deny benefits due to a temporary absence from the state. An individual is eligible for Medicaid where they reside even if they move from another state directly into a nursing home in the state in which they apply for Medicaid.[7]

A. *Categorically Needy*

Federal law requires that state Medicaid programs must provide eligibility for financially needy individuals who are classified as being "categorically needy" including those who are aged, blind, or disabled who receive Supplemental Security Income (SSI) and also those would be eligible for SSI but for the cost-of-living increases in Social Security since 1977.[8]

Eligibility for Medicaid based upon the receipt of SSI benefits is very important for younger disabled individuals because of the importance of the subsidized medical care provided by Medicaid.

In 1974 when the SSI program was enacted, some states did not want to expand Medicaid eligibility to include those receiving SSI. In response, the federal Medicaid law granted states the right not to define those eligible for SSI as being eligible for Medicaid. Those states are known as section 209(b) states. They are

- Connecticut
- Hawaii
- Illinois
- Minnesota
- Missouri
- New Hampshire
- North Dakota
- Ohio
- Oklahoma
- Virginia

Among these 209(b) states, the income and resource criteria for Medicaid eligibility differs. With the exception of Hawaii, however, the Medicaid income eligibility standards for the 209(b) states are very similar to the federal Supplemental Security Income eligibility income limit.

B. *Optional Categorically Needy*

States have discretion to extend Medicaid eligibility inter alia to institutionalized (living in a nursing home) individuals whose incomes are low enough to qualify for SSI but because they are institutionalized they are not eligible for SSI.

---

6. 42 C.F.R. § 435.403.
7. *Id.* § 1396a(r).
8. *Id.* § 435.135.

States may use the income cap test to extend Medicaid eligibility to individuals who live in a nursing home who meet resource requirements (discussed in Section II.E.). The income cap is equal to 300 percent of the maximum SSI benefit for a single individual. In 2017, the maximum SSI benefit for a single individual was $735, meaning that the income cap was $2,205 per month. In 2017, in an income cap state, individuals who met the resource test and whose income was less than $2,205 per month were eligible for Medicaid. The income cap dollar amount is absolute; even one dollar of extra income results in ineligibility, although if the individual can divert income into a qualifying trust (discussed in Section III), they can become eligible.

For example, if an individual residing in a nursing home in an income cap state who has no resources has income of $2,000 a month (below the income cap), the individual must spend that $2,000 less a personal needs allowance (federal law requires states to permit a personal needs allowance of at least $30 a month) on their care with Medicaid paying the remaining cost. If the individual has $2,000 a month income and the state permits them to retain $50 a month as a personal needs allowance, and if the individual has a monthly nursing home cost of $7,000, the individual will pay $1,950 a month for the cost of their care with the state Medicaid program paying the remaining cost.

Medicaid eligibility is determined monthly. An individual may be ineligible in one month because of excess income, but be eligible the next month if their income should decline below the amount of the income cap.

The income cap states are Alabama, Alaska, Arizona, Colorado, Florida, Iowa, Idaho, Louisiana, Mississippi, Nebraska, New Mexico, Oklahoma, Oregon, South Carolina, South Dakota, Texas (only applies to Medicaid assistance for the elderly), and Wyoming. Connecticut applies the income cap test only to those applying for Medicaid home health care benefits.

C. Optional Medically Needy Coverage

States have the option of extending eligibility to the medically needy,[9] defined as those whose countable resources are within the SSI limits, but who are not eligible for SSI because they have too much income. To become eligible for Medicaid, the individual must "spend down" their income on medical care, such as the cost of nursing home care.[10] (States that use the income cap method to determine eligibility do not use the "spend down" method.) If, having spent all their income on their care, the nursing home resident still does not have enough income to pay the remaining cost of care, they are eligible for Medicaid. The individual must spend all their income on their care less a personal needs allowance of $30 a month (higher in many states).[11] At that point, Medicaid will begin to pay for the cost of their care.

---

9. 42 U.S.C. § 1396a(a)(10)(C).
10. 42 C.F.R. § 435.814.
11. *Id.* § 435.832.

For example, if an individual lives in a nursing home that charges $7,300 a month and has monthly income of $3,350 a month and the state permits them to retain $50 a month as a personal needs allowance, the individual will pay $3,300 a month toward the cost of the nursing home and the state Medicaid program will pay the remainder.

As with income cap states, in states that use the income spend-down test Medicaid eligibility is determined monthly. If the individual's income varies, the amount of income they must apply to their care will similarly vary. Failure to spend down income on their medical care results in the individual being ineligible for that month. In some instances, the individual applying for Medicaid is mentally incapacitated and their finances are being handled by an agent under a power of attorney. If the agent does not spend the individual's income on their care, the individual will not be eligible for Medicaid. For example, when an agent paid for a personal companion for the individual who applied for Medicaid, that expenditure was held not to be for medical care and so did not qualify as a spend down that could lead to Medicaid eligibility.[12] However, Medicare premiums are valid spend-down expenditures.

The spend-down states are California, Connecticut, Georgia, Hawaii, Illinois, Kentucky, Maine, Maryland, Massachusetts, New Hampshire, New Jersey, New York, North Carolina, North Dakota, Pennsylvania, Rhode Island, South Carolina, Tennessee, Vermont, Virginia, Washington, West Virginia, and Wisconsin as well as the District of Columbia.

Note. Whether an income cap or a spend-down state, the state will not necessarily pay the rate charged by the nursing home to the individual—a rate known as the private pay rate. The state will determine a "fair" reimbursement rate to nursing homes, a rate that varies across the state and reflects the state estimate of the cost of operating a nursing home. For example, if the private pay rate is $200 a day, the state may pay only $187 a day. Not surprisingly, nursing homes prefer to serve private pay residents rather than those on Medicaid. To be financially sustainable, most nursing homes need an adequate percentage of private pay residents.

D. Determination of Income

Medicaid determines the applicant's income the same as it would be determined for an application for SSI, which defines income as cash and any in-kind provision of food and shelter.[13] Income is broadly defined and includes earned or unearned income, gifts, wages, dividends, interest, rents, royalties, alimony, pensions, disability benefits, veterans' benefits, and capital gains. The individual cannot turn their back on income; if it is available to them it is countable income even if the individual does not take possession. Note that federal income tax refunds and federal tax credits are not income.[14]

---

12. Sunrise Healthcare Corp. v. Azarigian, 821 A.2d 835 (Conn. App. Ct. 2003).
13. 20 C.F.R. §§ 416, 1102.
14. PMS 16771-450; PMS 16771-350 (July 2013).

Annuities paid to the institutionalized individual are considered income and not counted as a resource. The purchase of an annuity by the Medicaid applicant is not considered a transfer that causes ineligibility if the annuity meets the federal requirements. The annuity must be irrevocable and non-assignable, be actuarially sound, and provide for payments in equal amount during the term of the annuity with no deferral of payments and no balloon payments.[15] The state must be named as the first remainder taker if the annuitant dies before the end of the term of the annuity. (The state must be named the second remainder taker if the first remainder taker is a minor or disabled child.) The state as remainder taker has the right to be reimbursed up to the total amount of medical assistance paid on behalf of the institutionalized spouse. Retirement annuities purchased with proceeds from a retirement plan or an IRA are not treated as a transfer that might cause a period of ineligibility.

E. Resource Eligibility Requirements

To be eligible for Medicaid the individual must not have more than $2,000 in countable resources. A married couple cannot have more than $3,000. States have the option of using a higher dollar amount. Countable resources include all property that can be reduced to cash. Certain resources, however, are excluded and do not affect eligibility. They are

- the home (the individual's residence) and the land appurtenant up to an equity value of $560,000 or $840,000 at the option of the state (in 2017, adjusted annually for inflation),
- household goods and personal effects,
- one automobile if needed for the individual's transportation or for that of a member of the individual's household,
- burial plots,
- the cash surrender value of insurance if the face value of the policy does not exceed $1,500, and
- a prepaid funeral up to the dollar amount allowed by the state.

A house is excluded so long as it is occupied by the community spouse (or a dependent relative such as a disabled child), or if the institutionalized individual has no spouse, for as long as the individual intends to return to the house.[16] Once the individual has no intent to return to the house and so it is no longer their principal residence, the house becomes a countable resource. States differ on how they determine whether an individual has an intent to return to the house. Although some states require a doctor's statement that the individual may recover enough to return to the house, other states use an arbitrary time period, such as

---

15. 42 U.S.C. § 1396p(c)(1)(G)(ii).
16. 20 C.F.R. § 1212(c).

six months residence in a nursing home, and thereafter presume that the individual does not intend to return.

If the house is an excluded resource and sold, the proceeds from the sale continue to be treated as an excludable resource if they are intended to be used to purchase another house within three months of the date of receipt of the sale proceeds. If no replacement house is purchased within the three-month time period, the value of the receipts, including a promissory note or mortgage, are countable on the first day of the month following the three-month exclusion period.[17]

Whether an Individual Retirement Account (IRA) owned by the individual is considered an available resource depends upon the applicable state law. Some states count an IRA as a resource; other states do not. The alternative to counting an IRA as a resource is to count the distributions as income as they are made to the individual, including the required minimum distributions that must be made beginning in the year after the individual turns 70½. The state might even count the IRA of the community spouse as a countable resource.[18]

F. Effect of Marriage upon the Determination of Income and Resources

Married couples face special rules as to income and resource eligibility requirements if one spouse enters a nursing home and applies for Medicaid.

1. Income

A married individual who is in an institution such as a nursing home and applies for Medicaid must meet the income requirements; but only the income of the institutionalized spouse is counted. The income of the non-institutionalized spouse, known as the community spouse, is not counted and is not considered available to pay for the cost of care of the institutionalized spouse. Income is determined by "the name on the check"; income is considered to belong to the spouse in whose name the income is paid.[19] If income is paid in both names, each spouse is considered to be the owner of one-half of the income.

The effect of the name on the check rule is that the community spouse retains all their income. In theory, that could be a considerable sum, but in reality the community spouse's sources of income are typically Social Security retirement benefits, a pension, and income from a trust from a third party such as deceased parents. If the couple receives investment income, most if not all of those resources (assets) that produce the investment income will have to be spent down before the institutionalized spouse will be eligible for Medicaid.

If the community spouse owns an IRA, state law determines whether the IRA is treated as an available resource that counts against the eligibility for the

---

17. *Id.* § 1212(e).
18. Ark. Dep't of Human Services v. Pierce, 435 S.W.3d 469 (Ark. 2014).
19. 42 U.S.C. § 1396r-5(b).

institutionalized spouse. Some states do not count an IRA and instead permit the community spouse to retain the income that is distributed by the IRA.

One exception to the income rule arose in Illinois where a court upheld the right of the state to seek restitution for Medicaid paid on behalf of an institutionalized spouse from the income of the community spouse to the extent their income exceeds Minimum Monthly Maintenance Needs Allowance (MMMNA) (discussed in the next subsection).[20] The court held that the state spousal support laws were not preempted by the federal Medicaid statute that only required that the state permit the couple's income, including that of the institutionalized spouse, to be used to supply the community spouse with the MMMNA. The state did not have to permit the community spouse to retain income in excess of the MMMNA.

2. Community Spouse and the MMMNA

Although the general rule is that all of the income of the married, institutionalized spouse must be spent on their care, an exception exists if the community spouse has too little income. In order to mitigate community spousal impoverishment, the community spouse has a right to some of the income of the institutionalized spouse. The community spouse has a right to have income that is at least equal to the MMMNA,[21] which is equal to 150 percent of the federal poverty level for a two-person household. That amount is revised for inflation every July 1. As of July 1, 2017, the number was $2,030.00 per month (higher in Alaska and Hawaii). If the community spouse's income is less than the MMMNA, the institutionalized spouse must provide enough income to raise the community spouse's income up to the amount. There is also a Maximum Monthly Maintenance Needs Allowance that sets the limit on what states can set as the income allowed to the community spouse, which was $3,022.50 as of July 1, 2017.

The MMMNA can be increased additionally if the community spouse is eligible for an excess shelter allowance up to $609.00 as of July 1, 2017, if their housing costs exceed a state-determined amount (higher in Alaska and Hawaii). Shelter costs are calculated by adding together the community spouse's housing expenses, such as rent, mortgage, taxes, insurance, and condominium fees, and utility costs or a standard utility allowance.

Other circumstances that can raise the MMMNA include a family member who is defined as a dependent child or sibling of either the institutionalized or community spouse living with the community spouse.[22] A community spouse may also have a right to an increased MMMNA if they have unreimbursed medical expenses. A court order that dictates payments from the institutionalized spouse, such as alimony, must be enforced even if that results in the community spouse having income in excess of the MMMNA.[23]

---

20. Poindexter v. State of Ill. Dep't of Human Services, 890 N.E.2d 410 (Ill. 2008).
21. 42 U.S.C. § 1396r-5(d)(3).
22. *Id.* § 1396r-5(d)(1)(c).
23. *Id.* § 1396r-5(d)(5).

A community spouse can be granted an allowance that exceeds the Maximum Minimum Monthly Maintenance Needs Allowance by a showing of exceptional circumstances or if in financial distress. If the community spouse is denied additional income because the state does not find their circumstances rise to the level of financial distress, the community spouse has a right to appeal the rejection to an administrative hearing.[24] However, the community spouse will not be granted an increase allowance merely because they prefer to live a costly lifestyle, for example if they chose to live in an apartment that has a very high rent.

Finally, if the institutionalized spouse's income is insufficient to raise the community spouse's income to the MMMNA, in addition to transferring income, the institutionalized spouse will also have to provide resources to the community spouse that are valuable enough to produce sufficient income to raise the community spouse's income to the MMMNA. How many resources must be transferred depends upon how the state calculates the income that the resources can produce.

3. Resources

Just like single Medicaid applicants, a married Medicaid applicant must spend down resources until they have met the state maximum resource allowance that must be at least $2,000. In the determination of the resources available to the institutionalized spouse, a snapshot or determination of the couple's resources is made on the date of the entry into the nursing home, or as worded in the statute, on the first date of a continuous period of institutionalization that is expected to last 30 days.[25] In some states, if the individual entered the nursing home directly from a hospital, the first day of hospitalization may be the date as of which the resources are valued. The resources that are counted are as described in Section II.E.

All of the countable resources of the couple are counted without regard to how the resources are titled. The community spouse's, the institutionalized spouse's, and jointly held resources are all counted. Although the institutionalized spouse cannot have resources that exceed the state limit, Medicaid does recognize the need of the community spouse to be allowed to retain some resources. The amount permitted to be retained is known as the Community Spouse Resource Allowance (CSRA). The amount of the CSRA is based on the total value of the countable resources and state law. The CSRA granted to the community spouse is not liable for the cost of the care of the institutionalized spouse.

The amount of the CSRA depends upon state law and the total value of the countable resources. Federal law, however, stipulates a minimum and a maximum amount that are adjusted annually for inflation. In 2017, the minimum CSRA was $24,180 and the maximum $120,900. If the couple's resources are less than the minimum, the community spouse retains all the resources. If the resources exceed the minimum, state law determines the amount of the CSRA. A few states permit the

---

24. *Id.* § 1396r-5(e).
25. *Id.* § 1396r-5(f)(2).

community spouse to retain all the resources up to the maximum amount allowed by federal law. Most states permit the community spouse to retain the greater of the minimum CSRA amount or 50 percent of the resources not to exceed the maximum CSRA.

The following examples illustrate the 50 percent CSRA rule.

Value of resources	Amount of the CSRA in 2017
$15,000	$15,000
$25,000	$24,180
$40,000	$24,180
$60,000	$30,000
$200,000	$100,000
$300,000	$120,900

After the CSRA is determined, the institutionalized spouse must spend down their share of the remaining resources until they retain only the amount permitted by the state. The institutionalized spouse is not obligated to spend down their excess resources for the cost of their care. The institutionalized spouse cannot give away the resources, however, for doing so might create a period of ineligibility (see discussion of gifts in Section II.H.), but otherwise they are free to spend the resources as they see fit. In reality, an institutionalized individual will be limited in how they spend their excess resources because they will need to pay for the cost of the nursing home until they become eligible for Medicaid.

The community spouse has no obligation to use their CSRA to support the institutionalized spouse; they may spend or save the resources as they see fit.

G. Dealing with Excess Resources

If a couple foresees one of them likely entering a nursing home in the near future, steps can be taken that will improve the financial situation of the community spouse.

1. Using Annuities to Create Additional Income for the Community Spouse

The couple can convert countable resources into income for the community spouse that does not have to be used to support the cost of care of the institutionalized spouse. (This may not be permissible in some states despite the apparent legality of doing so under federal law.) The couple can buy an annuity payable to the community spouse. It does not matter whose resources are used to purchase the annuity because the determination of countable resources does not depend on which spouse owns which resources. Therefore, transfers between spouses are not subject to a transfer penalty.

For the annuity not to be treated as a transfer that might cause of period of ineligibility, the annuity must name the state as the first remainder beneficiary for at least the total amount of the medical assistance paid on behalf of the institutionalized spouse, or the state can be named as the second remainder beneficiary if the first taker of the remainder is a minor or disabled child who disposes of their remainder interest for less than fair market price. The annuity must also be irrevocable and non-assignable, actuarially sound, and provide for equal payments and no deferral of payments and no balloon payments.[26]

The most common form of a spousal annuity used in Medicaid planning is one that is paid for a set period of time, such as ten years or any period that is actuarially sound, meaning that the payment period is equal to or less than the life expectancy of the community spouse. For example, suppose a couple has $350,000 in countable assets and that the CSRA is $120,900. If they do nothing, when one spouse enters a nursing home, the community spouse will be allowed to keep $120,900 but the remaining $229,100 will have to be spent down by the institutionalized spouse, probably almost all of it for the nursing home costs. Instead, prior to entry of the institutionalized spouse into the nursing home, the couple purchases a 5-year annuity (shorter than the life expectancy of the community spouse) at a cost of $200,000 that pays $3,400 a month or $40,800 a year to the community spouse for 60 months. The annuity names the state the first taker of the remainder. A week later, the institutionalized spouse enters the nursing home. The couple's resources total $150,000 of which the community spouse can retain a CSRA of $75,000. The remaining $75,000 must be spent down but that is far less than the $229,100 that would have had to have been spent down if the couple had not purchased the annuity.

States have pushed back against community spouse annuities, claiming that the value of the annuity should be treated as a resource. Courts, however, have generally held that a spousal annuity must be treated as income and not valued as a resource.[27] In 2015, the Third Circuit held that short-term annuities were income, not resources, even though the terms of the two annuities, 14 months and five years, were shorter than the annuitants' life expectancies.[28] A federal district court found that North Dakota could not limit an annuity to an amount not in excess of the Maximum Monthly Maintenance Needs Allowance: to do so would violate the federal law that permits a spouse to have unlimited amounts of income.[29] The North Dakota Supreme Court, however, held that because the community spouse annuitant could sell the future income paid by a non-assignable annuity, the annuity was a resource and not income.[30] A year later, however, in another case, the same court held that because there was no potential buyer for a stream of income paid by an annuity, the annuity had to be treated as income and not as a resource.[31]

---

26. *Id.* § 1396p(c)(1)(G)(ii).

27. E.g., Weatherbee v. Richman, Commonwealth of Pa. Dep't of Pub. Welfare, 351 Fed. Appx. 786 (3d Cir. 2009).

28. Zahner v. Sec. Pa. Dep't of Human Services, 802 F.3d 497 (3d Cir. 2015). *In accord*, J.P. v. Mo. State Family Support Div., 318 S.W.3d 140 (Mo. 2010); Vieth v. Ohio Dep't of Family Services, 2009 WL 2331870 (Ohio Ct. App. July 30, 2009).

29. Geston v. Olson, 857 F. Supp. 2d 863 (D.N.D. 2012).

30. Estate of Gross v. N.D. Dep't of Human Services, 687 N.W.2d 460 (N.D. 2004).

31. Estate of Pladso v. Traill Cnty. Soc. Services, 707 N.W.2d 473 (N.D. 2005).

The court noted that in the earlier case, the annuitant had the authority to change the payee; but in the case before it the annuitant could not change the payee and there was no evidence that a third party would be willing to purchase the income stream.

2. Converting Excess Resources into Excluded Resources

Because only countable resources determine Medicaid eligibility, it is possible to preserve more resources for the community spouse by converting countable resources into excluded resources.

The value of the house (up the dollar equity limits discussed previously) is excluded so that improvements or repairs to the house present the opportunity to convert countable resources into an excluded resource. If the CSRA is at the maximum—$120,900 in 2017—every dollar converted into an excluded resource is a dollar saved.

For example, if the couple has $262,900 in countable resources and the CSRA is $120,900, and the institutionalized spouse is permitted to retain $2,000 of resources, the institutionalized spouse must spend down $140,000 ($260,900 − $120,900) to become eligible. But if, for example, $20,000 can be converted into excluded resources, the institutionalized spouse will only have to spend down $120,000.

There are several ways to convert countable resources into excluded resources. A new car can be purchased. Any mortgage debt can be paid off, the roof and driveway can be repaired, new landscaping may be in order, new carpets are an option, as is repainting the inside or outside of the house. The couple can prepay for their funerals and purchase burial plots.

For example, a couple has $200,000 in countable assets plus a house worth $175,000. The house is an excluded resource. After the ill spouse enters the nursing home, the CSRA is set at $100,000 (50 percent of the countable resources.) The couple trades in their old car for a new one at a cost of $20,000 and also pays $20,000 for house repairs including a new furnace. The result is that the institutionalized spouse now has to spend down on $60,000 in countable resources. Next the couple purchases a five-year annuity (the wife's life expectancy is 12 years) for $50,000 that will pay the community spouse $10,000 a year. The result is that the institutionalized spouse has spent down to $10,000 and will soon be eligible for Medicaid.

Business property essential to self-support is also excluded, but the state can limit the exclusion to $6,000 of equity value.[32] Some states do not impose a dollar limit. In those states, it is common to use resources to purchase rental property, such as a condominium that is titled in the name of the community spouse. The income from the rental property is paid to the community spouse and so is not liable for the care of the institutionalized spouse. And because the condominium is business property, the value of the condominium is an excluded asset. At the death of the institutionalized spouse, the rental condominium can be sold by the

---

32. 20 C.F.R. § 416-1222.

surviving community spouse with no obligation to repay the state for the Medicaid reimbursement for the cost of nursing home care for the institutionalized spouse.

H. Transfers of Resources and Periods of Ineligibility

The prior transfer of resources by either the institutionalized or community spouse may result in a period of ineligibility for Medicaid. Since 2006, Medicaid applicants have been required to disclose any uncompensated transfer of resources—a gift—during the 60 months prior to the date of the application.[33] Commonly referred to as the five-year look back rule, it is triggered by transfers that include any uncompensated transfer of resources, even when a joint owner removes funds from an account that was funded by the Medicaid applicant. The failure to demand the payment of funds owed to the applicant is also a transfer. If a married Medicaid recipient has a right to a statutory share of their deceased spouse's estate, a failure to file a claim for that share is considered a transfer that will trigger a period of ineligibility.

If the applicant made a gift within the 60-month look back period, the amount of the gift determines the length of time of ineligibility. The total value of all gifts is divided by the state average monthly or daily cost of a nursing home (the amount is determined annually by the state and is often on the low side). The result is the number of months or days of ineligibility. For example, suppose 20 months before the date of the Medicaid application, the applicant gave $70,000 to a child. The average monthly cost of a nursing home in the state is $7,000. The applicant is ineligible for Medicaid for ten months.

If both spouses made transfers that cause a period of ineligibility, the penalty is based upon the total transfer amount and is applied against the first spouse to enter a nursing home. If later, before the penalty period has expired, the second spouse also enters a nursing home, the state has the option of applying the remaining penalty period to either spouse or to divide it and apply it to both.[34]

The period of ineligibility begins on the date of the gift if the donor is already receiving Medicaid or the date the donor applicant would otherwise be eligible for Medicaid and is residing in a nursing home, receiving care in any institution equivalent to that of a nursing home, or is receiving, or in some states is eligible for, home- or community-based services paid for by a Medicaid waiver. The most common scenario is the applicant who made a disqualifying gift will enter the nursing home, spend down resources to become eligible, which will trigger the period of ineligibility. Because the applicant will not be able to afford the cost of the nursing home, a third party, often the recipient of the gift that caused the ineligibility will pay for the cost of the nursing home until the period of ineligibility has passed.

---

33. 42 U.S.C. § 1396p(c)(1)(B)(i).
34. Transmittal 64 § 3258.6 (Jan. 30, 2004).

Some states permit the Medicaid applicant to make a gift and later purchase an annuity payable to themselves that will pay most, but not all, of the cost of a nursing home, but because the applicant cannot afford the cost of the nursing home, the applicant is otherwise eligible for Medicaid and so the penalty period begins to run. For example, the applicant, who is single, has Social Security income of $2,500 a month and $62,000 in countable resources. A week before entering the nursing home, the applicant gives $40,000 to a daughter and uses $20,000 to buy a short-term immediate pay annuity. (The applicant is permitted to retain $2,000 of resources and still be eligible for Medicaid.) The state divisor to determine the period of ineligibility is $8,000 with the result that the gift of $40,000 results in a 5-month penalty period. The individual who made the gift enters the nursing home, which charges $8,500 a month for a private pay resident. The individual, except for the transfer penalty, would be eligible for Medicaid because he lives in a spend-down state. If he spends his entire $2,500 Social Security benefit on the cost of the nursing home (disregarding any personal needs allowance), he will be short $6,000 a month. But he will incur a five-month penalty. During those five months, he applies the $4,000 of the annuity to pay for the nursing home and augments it with another $4,500 out of the gift of $40,000. After five months the penalty period is over, and the individual is eligible for Medicaid. The annuity payout period is over; the daughter has paid $22,500 of her father's nursing home expense out of the gift but retains $17,500 ($40,000 - $22,500 = $17,500). Note some states do not permit the use of an annuity and a gift as a planning device.

Federal law states that promissory notes owed to the applicant are not resources; the interest paid on the loans is income as received and when the note comes due and is repaid, the repayment, if not spent down, is a resource.[35] An individual contemplating entering a nursing home can loan money to a third party thereby diminishing the countable resources. The income paid on the note must be spent on the cost of the nursing home, but if the individual dies before the note is paid off, the principal of the loan can be passed on to an heir. Under federal law, to be treated as a valid loan, the promissory note must have an actuarially sound repayment term that has payments of an equal amount, no deferral of payments and no balloon payments, and the note is not cancelled upon the death of the lender. The note must also be non-assignable, otherwise it will be held to be capable of being reduced to cash and so be considered an available resource. Finding a borrower for a promissory note can be difficult. Some loan money to their children. Case law is split on whether a promissory note based on a loan to a child is a valid loan or is akin to a trust-like device and so an available resource.[36] States vary as to whether they will challenge the validity of a promissory note as being a trust-like device that is a countable resource.

---

35. 42 U.S.C. § 1396p(c)(1)(I).
36. Not a valid loan, Able v. Velez, 437 Fed. Appx. 73 (3d Cir. 2011); valid loan, Lemmons v. Lake, 2013 WL 1187840 (W.D. Okla. Mar. 21, 2013).

Federal law requires states to provide hardship waivers if the imposition of a penalty period would endanger the applicant's life due to the lack of medical care or would deprive the applicant of food, clothing, shelter, or other necessities of life.[37] A hardship application can be filed by either the Medicaid applicant or by the nursing home in which they reside.[38]

I. Personal Service Contracts

Excess countable resources can be used to purchase a personal service contract. The payments will not be considered a gift if the contract provides for the provision of services equal in value to the payments made to the service provider.[39] Typically, the potential Medicaid applicant enters into a contract with a provider of services, often a child or other family member, and pays a lump sum in return for a promise by the other party to provide personal services for a designated period of time. The key to the transfer not being classed as a gift is to ensure the personal services contract details the services to be provided, and that the lump sum payment accurately reflects the value of the services anticipated to be provided.

Although the care will initially be provided at the home, if the older individual enters a nursing home or assisted living facility, the care provider can still provide valuable assistance by augmenting the care provided by the institution and also by monitoring the quality of the care in the nursing home and by advocating for better and more appropriate care.

The contract must provide a payment rate, usually an hourly rate that is comparable to market rates for such care. If the older individual dies before the contract has been completed or if the provider is unable to continue to provide services, the contract should call for a return of a portion of the original lump sum that is proportional to the amount of care not provided.

Many courts have examined the validity of these contracts in the face of state claims that the lump sum transfer is not a payment for services but a partial gift. Courts have upheld the validity of the agreements where the parties can prove that the services to be provided are equal in value to the amount of the lump sum payment, and that services were actually provided according to the terms of the agreement.

III. The Use of a Medicaid Asset Protection Trust

Transferring assets to a revocable trust has no impact on Medicaid eligibility. Assets held in a revocable trust, whether created by the Medicaid applicant or the spouse, are considered to be available resources in the determination of Medicaid eligibility.[40] Distributions from the trust to the Medicaid applicant or the spouse

---

37. 42 U.S.C. § 1396p(c)(2)(B).
38. *Id.* § 1396p(c)(2)(D).
39. *Id.* § 1396p(c)(1)(J).
40. *Id.* § 1396p(d)(3)(A).

are treated as income. Distributions from the trust to third parties are treated as transfers subject to the five-year look back rule.

Irrevocable trusts can be used for Medicaid eligibility planning but only if done properly. The applicant will be treated as having established any trust that was created by the applicant's spouse, a guardian or agent under a power of attorney acting on behalf of the applicant or their spouse, or a person or court acting at the direction of the applicant or their spouse.[41] The assets will be considered to be available resources in the value of any income or principal that can be paid to the applicant regardless of whether such income or principal is actually distributed and regardless of the discretion of the trustee or any restrictions on such distributions.[42] An irrevocable trust that can benefit third parties is considered a transfer and is subject to the five-year look back.

As discussed, uncompensated transfers can lead to a period of ineligibility for Medicaid. However, after five years have passed since the date of a transfer to an irrevocable trust, a Medicaid applicant does not have to reveal the transfer. In light of this, some elderly individuals who believe that someday they may need to apply for Medicaid to pay for nursing home expenses make transfers to an irrevocable trust with the plan not to apply for Medicaid until five years have passed. A transfer to an irrevocable trust is sometimes referred to as creating and funding a Medicaid Asset Protection Trust, or MAPT.

The essence of an MAPT is to protect assets from being considered an available resource and protecting the asset from Medicaid recovery if the state does not include self-settled trusts as being subject to estate recovery. The settlor of the trust (the potential Medicaid applicant) can retain the right to receive the income of the trust and is taxed on the income. And, of course, the income is considered available to pay for their nursing home care. Because the trust is a settlor trust, the value of the trust assets are included in the settlor's estate and so receive a step-up in basis. As a result, settlors typically transfer appreciated assets to the trust.

Because the trust is a grantor trust for income tax purposes, a residence transferred to the trust remains eligible for the I.R.C. Section 121 exclusion of $250,000 for a single taxpayer and $500,000 for a joint return of capital gains resulting from the sale of the residence. A settlor often transfers their house to the trust. The settlor will retain a life estate in the house and so has the right to occupy it. If married, the community spouse of the institutionalized spouse has the right to continue to occupy the house after the institutionalization or death of the other spouse. If they sell the house, the capital gains exclusion is still available. If the house is not sold before they die, the house receives a step-up in basis. If the settlor eventually goes on Medicaid, because the house is owned by the trust, it is not subject to estate recovery and can be passed on to the children or other heirs. Because of the need to meet the five-year look back rule, the trustees must not be able to distribute principal to the settlor

---

41. *Id.* § 1396p(d)(2)(A).
42. *Id.* § 1396p(d)(3)(B)(i).

beneficiary; the mere right to distribute principal under any condition makes the trust assets available resources.[43] But the trustee should be required to distribute all the income of the trust to the settlor, thus ensuring that the trust is a grantor trust for income tax and estate tax purposes. The trust should also provide that if for any reason it is terminated the settlor cannot receive any of the trust principal. At the death of the settlor, or both spouses if both are settlors, the assets transferred to the trust will be distributed to the remainder takers of the trust.

Any assets transferred to an irrevocable trust are subject to the five-year look back rule. If the trustee can make distributions from the trust to the individual or their spouse, the amount of the trust principal that can be distributed is considered to be an available resource even if it is not distributed. For example, if the trust requires all the income to be distributed to the trust and also as much of the principal that the trustee believes necessary for the settlor's support and maintenance, the entire value of the trust is counted as an available resource because the trustee might distribute it.[44] Therefore, the trustees should not be permitted to distribute principal to the settlor under any conditions.

Ideally, the settlor will not need to move into a nursing home until at least five years have passed after the creation and funding of the trust. If the settlor never enters a nursing home, the only "cost" of the trust will have been the loss of access to the principal. Presumably, the settlor had sufficient other assets not to need access to the principal of the trust after funding it. In any case, the settlor will have access to the income produced by the trust principal.

If the settlor does enter a nursing home and becomes eligible for Medicaid, the income distributed to the settlor will be counted in the determination of whether the settlor is eligible for Medicaid. The amount of income produced by the trust, however, can be manipulated by the trustee by the form of investment of the trust principal. By careful selection of the trust investments, the trustee can minimize the trust income and thereby minimize the income of the settlor that must be applied to pay for their long-term care.

Settlors who transfer assets to an irrevocable trust sometimes purchase long-term care insurance to help pay for the cost of long-term care if they should have to enter a nursing home before the passage of the five-year look back period. The settlor must determine how many months of long-term care that they can afford to pay without any benefits from a long-term care insurance policy. In making that calculation the settlor should include the projected income from the trust, other sources of income such as Social Security benefits, and other savings not included in the trust. Based on those projections, the settlor can decide whether they will need additional benefits paid by a long-term care insurance policy and, if so, for how many months. The insurance benefits should be sufficient in terms of the duration and amount of the monthly benefit to enable them to pay for the cost

---

43. Doherty v. Dir. of the Office of Medicaid, 906 N.E.2d 390 (Mass. App. Ct. 2009).
44. 42 U.S.C. § 1396p(c)(1)(B).

of the nursing home (or other form of care), and to forego applying for Medicaid, until five years have passed after the creation and funding of the trust. After or even before the passage of the five-year look back period, if the insurance benefits are not triggered, the settlor can let the policy lapse.

Trusts funded by third parties for the benefit of the Medicaid applicant or their spouse over which the applicant or their spouse have no control may be considered available resources depending on the limits on distributions from the trust. If the trustee must make distributions for the benefit of either the institutionalized or community spouse, such as under a support standard, the trust is considered an available asset even if the trustee does not make the mandated distributions. If the third party funded trust is a pure discretionary trust, such as might be the case if the trust beneficiary is disabled to the extent that they are otherwise eligible for public benefits including Medicaid, because the trust beneficiary has no power to compel distributions, the trust assets will not be considered to be an available resource. An example is:

> The Trustee may distribute to or expend for the benefit of (name of beneficiary) so much of the principal and the current or accumulated income therefrom, at such time or times and in such amounts and manner as the Trustees, in their sole discretion, shall determine.[45]

To be a pure, discretionary trust the language should not say that the trustee "shall distribute" because that term can be interpreted as mandating distributions. The trust also should not state that distributions may be made for any identifiable reason or standard, including such terms as "support," "maintenance," "health," or "education" for fear that a state court might hold that the trustee can be required to make distributions and therefore the beneficiary has the power to compel distributions. If such is the case, the trust assets can be considered to be an available resource for purposes of determining Medicaid eligibility.[46]

The trust should also state that it is the intent of the settlor that "the trust should supplement rather than supplant otherwise available public benefits." Otherwise, a court might decide that the settlor intended the trust to provide at least a minimum level of support to the beneficiary.[47]

IV. Home- and Community-Based Services

States are increasingly expanding Medicaid coverage to pay for care provided at home, known as Home and Community Based Services (HCBS).[48] This approach to

---

45. Pack v. Osborn, 2008 WL 4907545 (Ohio App. Nov. 14, 2008).

46. Strojek *ex rel.* Mills v. Hardin Cnty. Bd. of Supervisors, 602 N.W.2d 566 (Iowa Ct. App. 1999); *but see* Pohlmann v. Neb. Dep't of Health & Human Services, 710 N.W.2d 639 (Neb. 2006).

47. Shaak v. Pa. Dep't of Pub. Welfare, 747 A.2d 883 (Pa. 2000).

48. 42 U.S.C. §§ 1396n, 1915; https://www.medicaid.gov/medicaid/hcbs/authorities/1915-c/index .html.

caring for the elderly is promoted as being a less costly way for the state to support an individual who needs long-term care. HCBS operates on the premise that many who need long-term care assistance do not need the degree of care offered in a nursing home. If they live at home they may receive help from a spouse or adult children and so only require supplemental paid professional care. For example, they may have sufficient support overnight but because their volunteer helpers have jobs, the older individual may need personal attendants to assist them during the day. Or volunteer helpers may not be able to carry out all the needed care, such as bathing the elderly individual. Whatever the individual's particular needs, their care through HCBS will cost the state less each month than if paying to maintain the older individual in a nursing home.

Federal regulations require that states operate their HCBS programs by way of a person-centered planning process that addresses the individual's health and long-term service needs in a manner that reflects the individual's preferences and goals. To be eligible for HCBS, the individual must have a need for care that would meet the state's eligibility requirements for institutional care, that is, have a need for nursing home care as certified by a physician. The income and resource requirements vary from state to state.

States set a limit on the number of individuals that they will serve under the HCBS program. Services offered can include a combination of standard medical services and non-medical services. Standard services include, but are not limited to, case management (i.e., support and service coordination), homemaker, home health aide, personal care, adult day health services, habilitation (both day and residential), and respite care.

V. Long-Term Care Insurance Partnership Program

Federal law permits states to create long-term care insurance partnership programs to encourage their residents to purchase long-term care insurance.[49] Such programs allow Medicaid applicants to disregard resources in an amount equal to the benefit payments that they received from long-term care insurance if the policy meets the federal requirements, which are

- The insured was a resident of the state at the time the policy coverage began.
- The policy is a qualified long-term care insurance policy as defined by Internal Revenue Code Section 7702B(b).
- The policy has been certified by the state insurance commissioner as meeting the requirements of Long Term Care Insurance Model Act.
- If sold to an insured under the age of 62, the policy must contain a compound annual inflation rider that increases the benefits. Some level of inflation protection must also be provided for purchasers age 61 to 75.

---

49. 42 U.S.C. § 1396p(b)(1)(C)(iii).

- The state Medicaid agency must provide information and advice to potential purchasers of such insurance.
- The issuing insurance company must regularly inform the state Medicaid agency of the date and amount of benefits paid under such policies and other information that the state may require.
- The state cannot impose requirements on partnership policies that are not also imposed upon other long-term care policies sold within the state.

A Medicaid applicant who has received benefits under a partnership policy gets a dollar for dollar exclusion of otherwise countable assets. For example, suppose the applicant received $50,000 in insurance benefits and then applied for Medicaid. If the applicant has $70,000 of countable resources, only $20,000 is counted and must be spent down before the applicant is Medicaid eligible. The other $50,000 of assets is not required to be spent down in light of the individual having received $50,000 in long-term care insurance benefits.

In practice, the partnership program has had only limited success. Those who purchase long-term care insurance and receive substantial benefits, such as $200 a day for two years, or $146,000 total benefits, are very likely to still not qualify for Medicaid because the disregard of the $146,000 typically will still not bring their resources low enough to qualify for Medicaid. Those whose total countable resources are low enough to be offset by the benefits paid by long-term care insurance typically cannot afford the insurance premiums or they do not see enough value in passing on to their heirs resources equal to the value of the insurance benefits to justify paying the premiums for many years. They realize that they may never incur substantial long-term care costs and so never benefit from purchasing the insurance.

The partnership is most attractive if the insured must pay for long-term care for an extended period of time beyond the period for which the insurance paid benefits. For example, if the insurance pays for two years, and the insured continues to pay for long-term care for care for another three years, it is likely that the insured will have spent so much on their care that they will qualify for Medicaid. If so, the partnership will protect the assets worth value of two years' worth of insurance benefits, although whether that amount is worth the cost of the insurance depends on how important it is for the insured to protect assets that will benefit a community spouse or heirs. For most elderly, the answer is that the cost of the insurance is not worth the possible benefit.

VI. Medicaid Estate Recovery

The federal Medicaid statute requires states to attempt to recover from the estates of Medicaid beneficiaries the amount paid as Medicaid benefits.[50] An

---

50. *Id.* § 1396p(b)(1)(B)(1).

estate is defined as "all real and personal property and other assets included within the individual's estate, as defined for purposes of the state probate law."[51] All assets that are part of the probate estate are subject to estate recovery. Even, for example, the proceeds of life insurance payable to the estate even if the insurance contract permits the insurance company to pay the proceeds directly to family members who are the heirs of the estate rather than paying the proceeds to the estate. States have the option to extend the recovery to assets not included in the probate estate including property owned in joint tenancy or in a living trust.[52]

Because estate recovery is limited in most states to the probate estate, many assets are not subject to recovery, including joint property with right of survivorship, property held as tenants by the entireties, life insurance payable to a named beneficiary other than the estate, brokerage accounts with Transfer on Death designations, assets in irrevocable trusts including "Totten Trusts" or "In Trust For" accounts payable at death to a named beneficiary, and such amounts of assets that the state permits the estate to retain under the undue hardship exemption permitted by federal law.[53] If, for example, the state permits the Medicaid beneficiary to retain $2,500 and still be eligible for Medicaid, the state might also permit the retention of $2,500 by the estate.

Estate recovery is required only for payments made for individuals who were age 55 or older when they received Medicaid assistance for nursing home or community-based long-term care or, at the option of the state, the value of other benefits provided by the state.[54] The latter include hospital and prescription drug services provided to an individual over age 55 that were provided while the individual was

- A resident in a nursing home or was receiving home- and community-based services;
- On temporary leave from a nursing facility; or
- In a hospital after being transferred from a nursing home.

Assets that are exempted under a state long-term care insurance partnership are not subject to state recovery.[55] Medicaid cannot recover for payments made to Medicare for Part A or Part B premiums, deductibles, co-insurance or co-payments.[56]

Upon the death of a Medicaid beneficiary, the personal representative of the estate must notify the state Medicaid agency of the death and inquire as to whether the state intends to file a claim. The personal representative must be cognizant of the law of the state because states differ on the particulars of estate recovery.

---

51. *Id.* § 1396p(b)(4)(A).
52. *Id.* § 1396p(b)(4)(B).
53. *Id.* § 1396p(b)(1)(C)(v).
54. *Id.* § 1396p(b)(1)(B)(1).
55. *Id.* § 1396p(b)(1)(C)(ii).
56. *Id.* § 1396p(b)(1)(B)(ii).

For example, how to make the notification, such as by certified mail or by e-mail, and to whom, depends on state law. The state will have some number of days to respond to the notification by the personal representative assuming the notification met the state requirements as to what kind of information must be provided. If the beneficiary owned a house that is occupied by their spouse, the state will likely file a lien on the house to protect its estate recovery claim.

After it has received proper notification, the state will file a claim for reimbursement for the Medicaid benefits that it provided to the deceased. The claim should not be taken at face value. The personal representative should carefully examine it to ensure that the claimed amount is correct. States have been known to miscalculate the benefit payments or even include non-Medicaid benefits in the estate recovery claim.

If the Medicaid beneficiary is married at the time of their death, estate recovery cannot be made until the death of the surviving spouse and only if there is no surviving child under the age of 21, blind, or permanently and totally disabled.[57] Because of the resource spend down rule, a Medicaid beneficiary rarely has an estate of a value beyond what the state permits, which can be as little as $2,000 in assets. However, the state can attempt to recover against excluded resources with the house being the most likely resource. At the death of the Medicaid beneficiary, if the house is owned by the surviving spouse, the state will place a lien on the house, which it will collect either when the surviving spouse sells the house or dies. Similarly, if the house is jointly owned and occupied by a disabled child, the state cannot collect on its lien until the sale of the house or the death of the disabled child. In the same manner, the state cannot enforce a lien upon a house if a sibling of the Medicaid beneficiary has an equity interest in the house and resided in it for at least one year before the date of the Medicaid beneficiary's admission to the nursing home.[58]

If the state only enforces Medicaid recovery against the probate estate, recovery against the house can be avoided by the use of a "Lady Bird Deed," whereby the Medicaid applicant transfers their interest in the house to whomever they want to eventually own the property after their death.[59] The applicant retains a life estate that includes the right to sell or convey the property during the applicant's lifetime. The retention of the right to sell or convey the property means that the applicant has not made a transfer that would result in a penalty period that would delay benefits. At the same time, however, the Lady Bird Deed prevents Medicaid recovery because, upon the applicant's death, the house passes immediately to a named transferee by virtue of the deed rather than passing through the applicant's probate estate.

57. *Id.* § 1396p(b)(2).
58. *Id.* § 1396p(a)(2).
59. HCFA Transmittal 64, § 3258.9.

VII. Medicaid Right to Collect against Third Parties

A Medicaid application effectively assigns the beneficiary's rights against third parties to the state Medicaid agency.[60] States are required to "ascertain the legal liability of third parties"[61] and to seek "reimbursement for such assistance to the extent of the legal liability."[62] Typical claims against third parties include those arising from personal injury, workers compensation, health insurers, and other possible payers of the long-term care costs of the Medicaid beneficiary.

Although there is no dispute as to the requirement that the Medicaid beneficiary must repay Medicaid if the long-term care expenses are also paid for by a third party, litigation has arisen over the amount of such repayment. Medicaid beneficiaries have asserted that full reimbursement is not due unless the beneficiary received full payment for all of their claims. For example, if the Medicaid beneficiary settled a tort claim for less than all of the alleged damages, the beneficiary will claim that they do not have to fully repay the state Medicaid agency, but need only repay in proportion to the amount that the settlement represents to the claim for damages. If the Medicaid beneficiary settled for 40 percent of the claim, the beneficiary would only repay 40 percent of the Medicaid reimbursement claim. This view was upheld by the Supreme Court, which ruled under federal law that a state is entitled only to that portion of the settlement that represents payments for medical care.[63] The Supreme Court later held that states could not create by law an irrebuttable statutory presumption that imposes a fixed percentage of a settlement that is owed to the state as repayment for Medicaid payments.[64] If the Medicaid beneficiary and the state Medicaid agency disagree as to the proper allocation of the settlement, they must submit the dispute to a court; the state cannot rely on an arbitrary allocation.[65]

VIII. Appeals from Denial for Medicaid

Federal law requires that states provide that individuals have the opportunity to apply for benefits and that such benefits will be "furnished with reasonable promptness."[66] The state must determine whether the applicant is eligible within 45 days of the application.[67] If the application is denied or if benefits are reduced or terminated the state must afford the applicant the opportunity for a fair hearing

---

60. 42 U.S.C. § 1396a.
61. *Id.* § 1396a(25)(A).
62. *Id.* § 1396a(25)(B).
63. Ark. Dep't of Health & Human Services v. Ahlborn, 547 U.S. 268 (2006) (citing 42 U.S.C. § 1396p(a)(1)).
64. Wos. v. E.M.A., 133 S. Ct. 1391 (2013).
65. *Id.*
66. 42 U.S.C. § 13961(a)(8).
67. 42 C.F.R. § 435.912(c)(3).

at which they can challenge the state's determination. The time limit to file an appeal for a fair hearing must be reasonable, but under federal law it cannot exceed 90 days.[68] State time limits are often shorter. If a Medicaid beneficiary has their benefits terminated, they must file an appeal within ten days of the mailing of the notice of the termination.[69] The Medicaid beneficiary can request that the benefits continue pending the outcome of the appeal, but if the appeal is denied, the state can require repayment of the benefits paid after the initial termination.

The filing of an appeal for a fair hearing will result in the state Medicaid agency sending a notice of appeal to all parties and later a notice of hearing that contains the date, time, and location of the hearing in front of an Administrative Law Judge (ALJ). Prior to hearing there may be a prehearing or settlement conference for which discovery is permitted, and the ALJ must have access to the relevant information in the hands of the state agency.[70] State law determines how soon after the hearing and closing of the record that the ALJ must file a decision. After the ALJ's decision, the director of the state Medicaid agency has 90 days to affirm, reverse, or modify the decision or remand the matter for further hearings.[71] The right of the applicant to appeal a final denial depends on state law as to which court the appeal can be made.

In lieu of requesting a fair hearing, the applicant can sue directly in state or federal court.[72] If doing so, the client is best served by engaging counsel who has experience in suing for Medicaid benefits in state and federal courts.

68. *Id.* § 431.221.
69. *Id.* § 431.231.
70. *Id.* § 431.240.
71. *Id.* § 431.244.
72. 42 U.S.C. § 1983.

Guardianship and Conservatorship

15

I. Introduction

For many, advanced age results in a decline of mental capacity. The reasons vary, but in most cases dementia is the cause. It is estimated that over five million individuals age 65 or older suffer from dementia. Over one-third of those age 85 and older have some degree of Alzheimer's dementia.[1] Other elderly suffer mental decline because of Parkinson's disease, strokes, and even the effects of prescription drugs.

The loss of mental capacity by an individual creates problems for the law, which assumes that every adult individual has mental capacity and so has the right to autonomy and independent self-determination. Individuals therefore have the right to make decisions as to their person and property. The law does not assume that an individual will make rational decisions or even make decisions that are in their best interest; they can even make decisions that are harmful. The law creates the opportunity for the individual to make a reasonable decision but not require that the individual act reasonably. All the law requires is that individuals have the opportunity to make their own decisions.

The law, however, does not permit individuals who lack sufficient mental capacity to make decisions about their person and

---

1. https://www.alz.org/documents_custom/2016-facts-and-figures.pdf

property. An individual who lacks mental capacity to make a reasonable decision has no legal right to make decisions as to their person or property. In particular, the law fears that someone who lacks capacity may make decisions or take actions that are harmful to their person or property. It is critical, therefore, for the law to define who lacks mental capacity and to establish a method to determine whether someone lacks mental capacity. If an individual has been identified as lacking mental capacity, the law must ensure that there is something in place that will permit someone to make legally binding decisions on behalf of the incapacitated person. Some elderly will have executed durable powers of attorney (see Chapter 10, Management of Property of a Person Who Is Mentally Incapacitated), perhaps revocable trusts to manage their property (see Chapter 16, Trusts), and appointed a surrogate health care decision maker (see Chapter 11, Health Care Decision Making) and so not need a guardian or conservator.

If, however, the individual has not planned for possible mental incapacity, they will lack an individual or entity to make binding legal decisions for them. If so, the court may appoint a guardian or conservator to make decisions for them. That, in turn, raises the issue of who or what should be named as the decision maker and what powers that decision maker should have. Finally, the law must have some standard for how the decision maker should perform and who should monitor their performance.

Every state has adopted statutes that provide for substitute decision making for individuals who lack mental capacity. State laws differ as to terminology, the definition of mental incapacity, the procedure or process used to determine incapacity, when it is appropriate to name a substitute decision maker, the powers delegated to a substituted decision maker, and how the substitute decision maker is monitored. Typically, states delegate the probate courts the authority to determine who is mentally incapacitated, the right to appoint a substitute decision maker, and the duty to supervise that person or entity.

States use two terms for a legally appointed substitute decision maker: a guardian who operates under a guardianship, and conservator who operates under a conservatorship. Some states use both terms; guardian for the substitute decision maker who makes decisions concerning the person, and conservator for the substitute decision maker who makes decisions concerning the individual's property, that is, the estate. California reserves the term "guardian" for adults having supervision over children and uses the term "conservator" for those handling an adult incapacitated person's property or person.

In this chapter the terms "guardian" and "guardianship" will be used to include conservators and conservatorship. The individual under the guardianship will be referred to as the incapacitated person. In some states, that person is called a ward and a few states use the term "incompetent." In addition to guardianships, states also provide for statutorily appointed surrogate or proxy decision makers for health care. (See Chapter 11, Health Care Decision Making.) The relation between a guardian and a surrogate health care decision maker depends on state law, but usually the guardian's authority supersedes that of the surrogate health care decision maker.

II. Defining Who Is an Incapacitated Person

States define who is incapacitated and in need of a guardian somewhat differently but the common theme is an incapacitated person is an adult who is not capable of making or communicating reasonable decisions. Many states draw upon the definition in the Uniform Probate Code that defines an incapacitated person as someone who is "lacking sufficient understanding or capacity to make or communicate responsible decisions."[2] Arizona, for example, tracks that language while also requiring a finding that the person is "impaired by reason of" and lists several causes including mental illness or mental disorder.[3] Pennsylvania, in addition to requiring impaired decision-making ability, also requires that the person be "impaired to such a significant extent that he is partially or totally unable to manage his financial resources or to meet essential requirements for his physical health and safety."[4] Florida defines mental incapacity not by an inability to make reasonable decisions but rather as "the lack of capacity to manage at least some of the property or to meet at least some of the essential health and safety requirements of the person."[5]

No matter how the state statute defines mental incapacity, most courts will declare an individual incapacitated only after proof that the individual lacks the ability to make reasonable decisions because of a physical or mental condition or illness. Because of their diminished capacity, the individual cannot manage their financial affairs and cannot make essential decisions about their person or health care. In the past, individuals were placed under a guardianship because of their status or condition such as being demented. Today, courts are less concerned with the individual's diagnosis and instead focus on the individual's need for assistance because the individual is incapable of caring for themselves or their property.

The current emphasis on how well individuals appear to be able to take of their person and property is sometimes referred to as a functional approach. Rather than trying to analyze why the individual is making bad decisions, the court is more interested in the results of the decisions made by the individual. Functional assessment reflects the view that guardianship is a way in which society assists and protects those who lack the capacity to care for themselves. A court that is responsive to functional assessment should be more willing to accept lay

---

2. U.P.C. § 5-103(7).
3. ARIZ. PROBATE CODE tit. 14, § 14-501(1).
4. 20 PA. CONS. STAT. ANN. § 5501.
5. FLA. STAT. ANN. tit. 21A, § 744.102(12).

testimony about the quality and the effect of decisions made by the alleged incapacitated person and be less concerned about the medical explanation for the individual's behavior.

Nevertheless, anyone filing a guardianship petition should present adequate medical testimony that provides an explanation for the behavior of the alleged incapacitated person. Most courts will insist upon a medical confirmation that the irrational behavior arises from a loss of capacity. Lacking such testimony, the court may be reluctant to impose a guardianship for fear that the individual, though making "bad" decisions, has capacity. Guardianship is not a solution for irrational or even destructive behavior or for misusing or wasting assets. It is only appropriate if the individual is incapable of making rational decisions because of an illness, disability, or condition that causes the irrational, destructive, or wasteful behavior.

A state that recognizes both guardianships and conservatorships may have a different, less rigorous definition of being incapacitated for purposes of having a conservator appointed to manage the individual's property. That is the case in the Uniform Probate Code, which focuses on the waste or dissipation of assets rather than the mental state of the individual.[6] Voluntary conservatorship is permitted in some states. Essentially an individual can petition the court to place the individual and the individual's property under the control of a conservator without a finding that the individual lacks mental capacity. Voluntary conservatorship allows a physically infirm individual to ask a court to appoint a conservator with limited authority to deal with the particular property and asset management needs of the individual.

III. Types of Guardianships

As discussed in Section IV, Guardianship Procedures, a guardianship is initiated by the filing of a petition requesting that the court find the respondent is mentally incapacitated and in need of a guardian. The petition must state the type of guardianship being requested. Typically a state will recognize plenary guardians, guardians of the person, guardians of the estate (property), and limited guardians. States also have provisions for the appointment of temporary or emergency guardians.

A. Plenary Guardians

A plenary guardianship grants the guardian authority over both the person and property of the incapacitated person. It is the most common form of guardianship. Often the guardian is a spouse or adult child who is empowered to take charge of all aspects of the incapacitated person's life. The plenary guardian has control

---

6. U.P.C. § 5-401.

of the estate of the incapacitated person and collects the income of the incapacitated person, pays their bills, invests their assets, and manages their property. The specific authority of the guardian depends upon state law and local court procedures; the court will instruct the guardian as to their authority and responsibilities at the time of their appointment.

A plenary guardian also makes decisions concerning the person of the incapacitated person. The most important decisions about the person are those involving health care, including end-of-life decision making. State law determines the extent of a guardian's health care decision making authority and when the guardian must have prior court approval to undertake certain actions. The guardian also decides where the incapacitated person lives. The physical or mental condition of the incapacitated person may necessitate moving them from their house into an apartment or an assisted living facility.

B. Guardian of the Person

A court can appoint a guardian of the person who does not have authority over the estate of the incapacitated person, but only over their person, such as determining where they reside and their medical care. A guardian of the person has no authority over the incapacitated person's property. Courts often appoint a guardian of the person in the event that no one is willing or available to serve as plenary guardian. In such cases the court often appoints two guardians, one as guardian of the person and the other as guardian of the estate. The court also may appoint only a guardian of the person if it does not perceive a need for a guardian of the estate because the incapacitated person has taken adequate steps for the management of their property, such as appointing an agent under a power of attorney or having placed their property into a trust where it is adequately managed by the trustees. A court may find someone who is willing to act as the guardian of the person but is not willing to take on managing their assets because the guardian does not believe that they have the time or skill needed to manage the property of the incapacitated person. Sometimes a relative or friend of the incapacitated person is willing to act as guardian of the person, but because that relative or friend does not live near the incapacitated person or because of their lack of knowledge or experience, the court does not believe that they can effectively manage the property of the incapacitated person, pay the bills and oversee the quotidian responsibilities associated with property management.

A guardian of the person may find their ability to make decisions as to the person hampered, if not blocked, by the person, such as a guardian of the estate, who has control over the incapacitated person's finances. The guardian of the person who wants to relocate the incapacitated person must first ensure that whoever controls the finances, whether it is a guardian of the estate, an agent, or a trustee with discretionary authority, will be willing to pay for the new living arrangement. As a result, whereas the guardian of the person may have unfettered authority to make health care decisions, the guardian of the person may find that for many other decisions the ultimate power rests with the guardian of the estate. The latter can block what the guardian of the person wants to do by refusing to pay the costs associated with the proposed course of action. If the guardian of the person believes the guardian of the estate is thwarting their attempts to improve the life of the incapacitated person, or making decisions as to the property that are not in the best interest of the incapacitated person, the guardian of the person can go to the court and ask it to require the guardian of the estate to finance the decision of the guardian of the person.

The extent of the authority of the guardian of the person depends on state law. Some powers require prior approval by the court. For example, agreeing to or instigating divorce may require court approval or it may not be permitted at all.

As the decisions about the person's life become more critical, the more likely it is the guardian will be required to ask the court for prior approval. For example, a guardian of the person may have the authority to move the incapacitated person from a house into an apartment, but many states require court approval to move the incapacitated person into a nursing home. Court approval may be required if the guardian wants to terminate life-sustaining treatment, although more states now permit guardians to make the decision without resorting to the court.

C. Guardian of the Estate

An incapacitated person can have a guardian of the estate. In some states, a guardian of the estate is called a conservator. Whatever the name, a guardian of the estate controls the finances and assets of the incapacitated person subject to any limits or instructions by the appointing court or of the state statute authorizing the appointment of a guardian of the estate.

Although the authority of the guardian of an estate is very broad, many states or appointing courts limit or prohibit the guardian to spend principal without prior court approval. This is designed to protect the incapacitated person from a guardian spending down principal to the point of impoverishing or severely impacting the income and the well-being of the incapacitated person. Selling real estate or entering into long-term leases on property owned by the incapacitated person may also need court approval, as may providing support to the spouse or family of the incapacitated person. Making substantial gifts to help qualify the incapacitated person for Medicaid eligibility may be permitted but the guardian may be required to, or may feel the need to, request prior court approval. Other substantial gifts may be permitted as long as the gifts do not transgress the estate plan of the incapacitated person. Transfers of the assets to a trust usually also require court approval and must be consistent with the estate plan of the incapacitated person. The guardian may be permitted to amend a trust created by the incapacitated person if doing so does not thwart the incapacitated person's estate plan.

A guardian of the estate cannot execute a will for the incapacitated person but, depending on state law, may be able to exercise a power of appointment, disclaim a devise under a will, or claim the statutory share of the incapacitated person.

State law determines whether the guardian of the estate needs court approval to initiate or settle a tort claim of the incapacitated person.

D. Limited Guardianship

Most states permit a court to appoint a limited guardian if the court finds that the alleged incapacitated person, although suffering a loss of mental capacity, retains sufficient capacity to be permitted to control part of their life. In the past, when petitioned to declare an individual incapacitated, a court had only two alternatives; either the person was or was not incapacitated. Today, many states permit the court to find that an incapacitated person is partially incapacitated and in need of a guardian with limited powers designed to meet the particular needs of the incapacitated person. For example, the court may find an individual incapable of handling their investments, but capable of handling day-to-day finances. The court could appoint a limited guardian with the authority to take over the investment decisions but not the more mundane daily finances of the incapacitated person.

Limited guardianship was conceived as part of the doctrine of least restrictive alternative, which promoted the concept that guardianship should not interfere with an individual's autonomy and independence any more than necessary. It was hoped that limited guardianship would be the norm and that many fewer plenary guardians or guardians of the person or estate with unlimited authority would be appointed. That has not proven to be the case; limited guardians are not commonly appointed. In practice, particularly with older alleged incapacitated persons, a guardianship petition is only filed after the person has lost a significant degree of mental capacity and so is in need of a plenary guardian. Those appointed with authority over the estate of the incapacitated person also contend that shared control over the finances is impractical, too costly, and exposes the guardian to liability in the event that the guardian oversteps their limited authority. Most courts apparently agree and so rarely employ limited guardianship of an estate.

Proponents of limited guardianship for the person have had some success in obtaining limited guardianships, but, as with guardians of the estate, for the most part petitioners have not requested limited guardianships and courts have not appointed them. If, however, the state permits limited guardianship, a petitioner should consider requesting it. The needs of the incapacitated person should be carefully considered to see what kind of assistance the individual needs, and the court should be asked to grant authority to the guardian only to the extent needed to meet those needs. However, for older persons with loss of mental capacity, limited guardianship is usually not a realistic option, particularly because the older person is likely to continue to lose capacity over time. The fear that the older person might be a victim of financial exploitation or neglect by caregivers also undermines the court's comfort with limited guardianship. When coupled with the court's familiarity with plenary guardianship, the need for greater involvement of the court in designing a limited guardianship, and the desire of financial institutions and many professional guardians to have plenary authority, the use of limited guardianship can be expected to remain the exception rather than the norm.

E. Temporary or Emergency Guardians

Every state has accelerated procedures that facilitate the appointment of a temporary or emergency guardian in the event of the need for immediate protection of the incapacitated person's property or person. As the name suggests, temporary or emergency guardians—the name used varies from state to state—are limited in time. Typically, the temporary or emergency guardian is followed by a petition for a guardianship, and that petition is subject to the normal procedural requirements.

The procedures used to respond to a petition for a temporary or emergency guardian vary, but they usually include the requirement that the incapacitated person is in danger of or is suffering from immediate and irreparable injury that necessitates a time-shortened resolution. The temporary or emergency guardian procedures often permit a court hearing before notice of the petition has been given to the incapacitated person (after-the-fact notice is required), professional assessment of the incapacitated person may be waived (lay testimony about the condition of the incapacitated person may be sufficient), and counsel for the incapacitated person may be waived. Assuming the court finds a need for a guardian, the court can appoint a temporary or emergency guardian whose authority may be limited to dealing with the immediate need of the incapacitated person, such as removing them from a physically abusive living situation. The temporary or emergency guardian will often petition the court to appoint them as a permanent guardian, although in a few cases, the temporary or emergency guardian may decide that because they have successfully dealt with the immediate needs or problem, the individual no longer needs a guardian.

IV. Guardianship Procedures

A. Jurisdiction and Venue

Guardianship is initiated by the filing of a petition with the appropriate court, asking that the court find the named respondent—the alleged incapacitated person—to be mentally incapacitated and asking the court to appoint a guardian for them. Almost all states permit a guardianship petition to be filed by any "interested person," although in practice most petitions are filed by spouses, adult children, other family members, hospitals, or public agencies concerned with the alleged incapacitated person's well-being. A few states limit who may file a petition; for example, California bars most creditors of the alleged incapacitated person from filing a petition.[7]

---

7. CAL. PROB. CODE § 1820(5)(c).

The petition must be filed with the appropriate court that has jurisdiction, usually the state's probate court. Courts have jurisdiction over individuals physically in their state, including those who are just "passing through," such as a tourist. Courts also have jurisdiction over an individual expressly brought into the state for the purpose of seeking a guardianship for them.[8] Courts have rem jurisdiction over property in their state even if owned by someone not present in the state at the time of the filing of the guardianship petition. A summer home, for example, could be put under the protection of a guardian of the estate for a nonresident if the court determines that the owner is incapacitated. In some cases, the nonresident may be under a guardianship in their state of residence, but the court that appointed the guardian did not have jurisdiction over the property not in the state. The state in which the property is located may be permitted to rely on the determination of incapacity in the state in which the alleged incapacitated person is located as the basis for determining the alleged incapacitated person to be incapacitated and in need of a guardian for their property.[9]

The petitioner must select the venue, or the location, of the court in which to file the petition. Usually the proper venue is the county in which the alleged incapacitated person lives or is present. For example, the alleged incapacitated person may reside in County A, but currently be living in a nursing home in County B. State law determines in which county the petition must be filed—County A or B. State law also determines whether the alleged incapacitated person can waive proper venue. If the guardianship is sought for property of a nonresident, proper venue is the county in which the property is located.

B. *Contents of the Petition*

State law and local court rules determine what the guardianship petition must contain. Usually the petition must contain the name, age, residence, and mailing address of the alleged incapacitated person; the nature of their incapacity; and a list and the value of their assets. It may also have to contain the name of the alleged incapacitated person's spouse, children, other relatives, and intestate heirs. The petition may also be required to state if the alleged incapacitated person lives in an institution or has a caregiver. The petition should state the nature of the guardianship requested and the name of the proposed guardian.

State statutes increasingly require a petition that contains detailed information about the alleged incapacitated person, such as the petitioner's relationship to the alleged incapacitated person, a description of the disability causing the mental incapacity, specific allegations as to why the alleged incapacitated person's person or property are at risk, why less restrictive measures are not effective, and whether the alleged incapacitated person has an agent under a power of attorney or a health care surrogate decision maker. In essence, the petition must present

---

8. *See, e.g., In re* Vena HH, 756 N.Y.S.2d 300 (2003).
9. *E.g.,* 20 PA. CONS. STAT. ANN. § 5511(b).

a case as to the cause and extent of the alleged incapacitated person's mental incapacity and explain why the imposition of guardianship is the most appropriate response.

C. Notice

State law will require adequate notice to the alleged incapacitated person and may also require notice to a list of individuals, including the alleged incapacitated person's spouse and children. The timing of the notice required varies from state to state; it often is as little as three days prior to the date of the hearing on the petition. In some states it must merely be "reasonable." Failure to give proper notice may or may not be grounds for dismissal of the petition; it may merely delay the date of the hearing. States often require the notice to the petitioner to be in a language that they understand and the font used in the petition to be at least a minimum size.

D. The Hearing

1. Right to a Jury

The filing of a guardianship petition will lead to a court hearing to determine whether the alleged incapacitated person is mentally incapacitated as defined in the state statute, whether to appoint a guardian, and, if so, what powers to grant to the guardian. State law likely requires a jury trial unless waived by the alleged incapacitated person, which is frequently the case. Most counsel for the alleged incapacitated person prefer to waive the jury and rely on a judge who is more experienced and knowledgeable about what behavior and medical conditions prove mental incapacity as defined by the state statute. If, however, the alleged incapacitated person wishes to contest the need for a guardian, they may prefer a jury that they believe may be sympathetic to their desire to avoid a guardian and continue to control their life. The jury, of course, only determines whether the individual is incapacitated. If it so finds, the judge determines whether guardianship is appropriate and identifies who will be appointed as guardian.

2. Presence of the Alleged Incapacitated Person

States vary as to whether the alleged incapacitated person must be present at the hearing. A few states mandate their attendance but most states leave it up the court whether to hold the hearing in the absence of the alleged incapacitated person. Usually state law provides that courts will not require the alleged incapacitated person to be present if doing so would be potentially injurious to their health. Their presence may also be waived if it would be unhelpful, such as if the person is in a coma. Often, where the health of the alleged incapacitated person would prevent them from attending the hearing, the court will hold the hearing where the alleged incapacitated person resides, for example in an assisted living facility, if the alleged incapacitated person is healthy enough to be present at a hearing but not healthy enough to be transported to the court house.

3. Right to Counsel

The alleged incapacitated person has a right to counsel. Some states mandate that the alleged incapacitated person have counsel; if the alleged incapacitated person cannot afford counsel, the state will provide one. Other states permit the alleged incapacitated person to waive the right and to hold the hearing with no counsel representing the alleged incapacitated person. The counsel for the alleged incapacitated person should act as a zealous advocate. Some courts prefer that counsel temper advocacy with an attempt to act in the best interest of the alleged incapacitated person, which may mean conceding the need for a guardian and, instead, focusing on who should be appointed as guardian and what powers the court should grant them. However, the Rules of Professional Conduct state that counsel for an individual with impaired mental capacity should attempt to maintain a normal client-lawyer relationship.[10] That means meeting with the individual, reviewing the evidence, advising the individual as to the best course of action, inquiring how the client wishes to proceed, and advocating for the outcome that the individual desires.

If the individual is found to be incapacitated, counsel should attempt to ensure that the person or entity nominated to be the guardian is appropriate and will act in the best interest of the incapacitated person. The powers granted to the guardian should also be monitored; the powers should not exceed the needs of the incapacitated person. If, for example, the incapacitated person's property is at risk, but their person is not because they reside in a nursing home and have appointed a health care decision maker, counsel might accept a guardian of the estate but resist the appointment of a plenary guardian.

State law usually places the cost of guardianship upon the estate of the incapacitated person if the court grants the petition for guardianship. Courts rarely award fees to the counsel for the petitioner if the petition is denied, but will award fees to the successful counsel for the alleged incapacitated person. If the court appoints a guardian, counsel for both the petitioner and the incapacitated person can request the court to approve their fees from the estate of the incapacitated person. (Not all states permit the petitioner's counsel to be awarded fees from the incapacitated person's estate.) The amount of the fee depends upon the complexity of the work involved, the skill of the lawyer, the time expended, and the value of the incapacitated person's estate.

4. Evidentiary Standards and the Burden of Proof

The burden of proof is on the petitioner who must convince the court that the alleged incapacitated person has a mental condition that prevents them from adequately caring for their person or property. Most states require a determination of mental incapacity by a showing of clear and convincing evidence. That standard arises either by virtue of a statute or by common law holdings. In other states, a

---

10. MODEL RULES OF PROFESSIONAL CONDUCT R. 1.14.

preponderance of the evidence is the standard. Typically, the petition will have to introduce sufficient evidence that the alleged incapacitated person lacks the ability to recognize or understand the facts relevant to the care of their person or property, as well as the ability to make reasonable decisions due to a medical disease or condition. Courts typically require specific examples of acts by the alleged incapacitated person that demonstrate the lack of capacity as well as acts and decisions made by the alleged incapacitated person that prove their person or property are at risk of harm due to their inability to make reasonable decisions. If the petitioner has requested only a guardian of the estate, or conservator, as it is called in some states, the burden of proof is not to show global incapacity but only that because the alleged incapacitated person is incapable of effectively managing their property, it is likely that the property will be wasted or dissipated or that the alleged incapacitated person could be the victim of financial exploitation.

To impose a guardian requires the petitioner to prove that the alleged incapacitated person is incapacitated as that term is defined in the statute. Once the alleged incapacitated person has been declared incapacitated, in most, but not all, states if the incapacitated person wishes to reverse the decision on the basis that they have regained capacity, the burden of proof is on the incapacitated person to convince the court that their capacity has been restored.

5. Use of Court Visitors

Many states grant the court independent authority to gather information about the alleged incapacitated person. State law may permit the court to send a court visitor—also known as an investigator—to visit the alleged incapacitated person at their residence and to report back to the court as to the condition and apparent needs of the alleged incapacitated person.[11] The right of the court to seek out information is based on the long-standing belief that if an individual is incapacitated, the appointment of a guardian is in their best interest because the guardian will protect the incapacitated person and their property. The use of visitors also reflects the reality that the alleged incapacitated person may not be represented by counsel. The visitor thus serves as a safeguard to help ensure that the court has an objective understanding of the condition and life circumstances of the alleged incapacitated person. Who may serve as visitor depends upon state law, but often they are volunteers who are paid only a modest honorarium. Hopefully, the visitor will have been adequately trained and be capable of accurately assessing the condition and needs of the alleged incapacitated person, but that is not always the case. Some courts have full-time investigators on their staff whom the court can use to gather information about the alleged incapacitated person, including an interview with the alleged incapacitated person.

A few states permit the court to appoint a guardian ad litem for the alleged incapacitated person. The guardian ad litem, who is frequently an attorney, acts as the court's eyes and ears. In addition to gathering information, the guardian

---

11. *E.g.,* U.P.C. § 5-303(b).

ad litem usually will present a recommendation to the court as to how the court should proceed—whether to find the alleged incapacitated person to be legally incapacitated, what powers to grant to the guardian, and who to appoint as guardian. Some courts routinely appoint a guardian ad litem if the alleged incapacitated person does not have counsel and instruct the guardian ad litem to determine whether the court should appoint counsel to represent the alleged incapacitated person.

State law and local court rules determine the function of a guardian ad litem. Some require the guardian ad litem to determine what the alleged incapacitated person wants while other states require the guardian ad litem to determine what would be in the individual's best interest. In no case, however, is the guardian ad litem, even if an attorney, the counsel for the alleged incapacitated person. If counsel is needed, the alleged incapacitated person should hire an attorney or the court should appoint one.

When representing either the petitioner or the alleged incapacitated person, counsel must respect and acknowledge the findings and recommendations of a visitor, investigator, or guardian ad litem, but counsel should emphasize that the ultimate decision as to whether to appoint a guardian is up to the court. In particular, counsel for the petitioner should be prepared to argue that the needs of the alleged incapacitated person can be met by arrangements that are less restrictive than that of guardianship. Even if the court finds the individual to be incapacitated, petitioner's counsel must offer sufficient proof that the appointment of a guardian is necessary to protect the incapacitated person from future harm to their person or property and so justify the appointment of a guardian.

6. Selection of the Guardian

If the court or jury determines that the alleged incapacitated person is legally incapacitated, the court determines whether the appointment of a guardian would best serve the needs of the incapacitated person, and the court determines what kind of guardian to appoint, for example, a plenary guardian, and what powers to grant to the guardian. The court must also decide who or what entity to appoint as guardian. Usually the court will appoint the guardian nominated in the petition although the guardianship laws do not require that they do so. Typically, state statutes call for the appointment of suitable or competent individuals or entities. Some states bar individuals or entities that have a particular relationship to the incapacitated person from serving as guardian, such as an employee of a nursing home in which the incapacitated person resides.

If the court chooses not to appoint who the petition nominated, state law may establish a preference of suitable guardians, including the spouse, adult children, and other relatives, such as siblings. Such lists are precatory; the court can ignore the list if it finds that the preferred person would not be appropriate or if another person or entity would be better suited by virtue of their training, temperament, or geographical location. If the incapacitated person nominated a guardian when they still had capacity, perhaps in a power of attorney, state law may require the court to appoint the nominee unless the nominee is not willing or not capable of performing as a guardian. Some states require the court consider the incapacitated person's preference for guardian even if the individual never formally nominated anyone, but the court has the discretion to ignore those wishes if it believes that doing so would be in the best interest of the incapacitated person.

Although most guardians of older individuals are spouses or family members, many incapacitated older individuals lack a spouse or family member willing or able to perform as guardian. In the past, banks often served as guardian, but today banks are much less likely to agree to serve as a guardian. To fill the void, alternative entities or individuals serve as guardians, which include professional guardians, public guardians, and nonprofit corporations that serve as guardian.

Professional guardians are individuals, often social workers or individuals having gerontology training or experience, who are available for hire as a guardian. The estate of the incapacitated person pays for the services of the professional guardian to the extent that the estate has the resources to do so. They charge by the hour and sometimes contract with others, such as caregivers, who provide goods and services needed by the incapacitated person. Professional guardians typically are aware of the state requirements as to obligations to the incapacitated person and to the court. They should also be conversant with what authority they have, when they should contact the court for its advice or consent, any limits on spending the income or principal of the incapacitated person, and reporting requirements. Many professional guardians are certified by the National Guardianship Association,[12] and there are also state level professional guardianship associations.

Some states have created public guardians who are available to act as guardians when there is no other available guardian. Public guardians can be state employees, a state agency, or a state official. Some operate at the county level, others statewide. Some states limit the authority of the public guardian, particularly in regard to health care decisions. A few states permit public guardians to initiate guardianship petitions, but most states do not. The degree of involvement of a public guardian depends largely on the size of their caseload, with most having more guardianships than desirable, which limits the time that the public guardian can devote to any one incapacitated person. A public guardian may have the right to seek payment for their services from the estate of the incapacitated person. If the state has no public guardian, many courts routinely appoint local attorneys as guardians when there is no alternative. These are not considered public guardians, but in reality they fill a similar role. They are compensated by a charge on the estate of the incapacitated person.

Some states deal with the problem of a lack of qualified guardians by making grants to a nonprofit corporation to serve as guardian as needed or by hiring the nonprofit on an individual basis to act as guardian. Some of the nonprofits are

---

12. http://www.guardianship.org.

social service agencies that provide other services to the elderly. As such, they often combine the role of guardian with caregiving or overseeing the provision of needed services for the incapacitated person. Usually the incapacitated person's estate is not large enough to pay for the cost of the nonprofit guardianship, but if it is, the court may require the incapacitated person's estate to bear the cost of the guardianship.

Guardians are subject to the oversight of the appointing court and can be removed if the court determines that they are unable or unwilling to adequately perform their duties or are not acting in the best interest of the incapacitated person. A court can remove a guardian in response to a petition or on its own recognizance. Sometimes the guardian is replaced because of changed circumstances, including a move to a new residence by the incapacitated person or the guardian, because of changing needs of the incapacitated person such as health issues, changes in the health of the guardian, or a change in the incapacitated person's finances, such as inheritance. Some guardians lose the physical or mental ability to perform and so must be replaced.

Courts determine whether and how much compensation is provided to a guardian subject to state law and local court procedures. Spouses and family members typically serve without compensation; professional guardians, attorneys, banks, and nonprofits are usually compensated. The rate of compensation depends upon local court practices but it is usually an hourly rate. From the standpoint of the guardian, the hourly rate that a court will approve is often low. Moreover, courts will often only pay the guardian rate for acts that require a guardian, such as arranging for health care and managing investments; a lower rate is paid for non-guardian acts, such as providing transportation or grocery shopping for the incapacitated person. The lower rate is to prevent guardians from running up their fees and to encourage them to use less costly means of meeting the needs of the incapacitated person. Family members who serve as guardian typically will not be compensated for performing family obligations such as visiting the incapacitated person, but can be paid for their acts as a guardian, including meeting with a physician to discuss the health care needs of the incapacitated person.

V. Authority of the Guardian

Guardians have only the authority granted to them by the court. State statutes and the common law of the state determine the extent of power that can be delegated to the guardian. Although most states grant similar authority, critical variations exist among states that the guardian's counsel must be aware of.

A. Guardian of the Estate

A guardian of the estate is authorized to take possession of the incapacitated person's property, manage it, protect it, and use it for the benefit of the incapacitated person. Because of the potential for theft or misuse of the property, courts often require the guardian to post a bond. Although the guardian will have to account for their actions to the court, day-to-day the guardian of an estate acts on their own with no court supervision. The need to eventually account, however, makes it imperative that the guardian keeps accurate records of their activity, including income received, payments, and investment decisions. How frequently the guardian will have to report to the court varies. At a minimum, the guardian of the estate will have to give an accounting at the death of the incapacitated person (which terminates the guardianship) or if the guardian is removed, resigns, or dies. Typically the guardian of the estate is required to give a preliminary report to the court, such as after the first six months of the guardianship. At that time the guardian may be required to provide an inventory of the assets and provide an indication of how they intend to handle the estate. Many states now require annual reports to the court by the guardian. Such reports are often made on court designed forms that are intended to reveal whether the guardian is misusing, abusing, or failing to properly manage and expend the assets of the incapacitated person. Courts can also order a guardian to report on their demand, which might arise from a third party informing the court that the guardian may be misusing the incapacitated person's assets.

The guardian of the estate must maintain an inventory of the assets of the estate, keep detailed records of income and expenditures, and record and be able to justify investment decisions. Although the guardian is required to pay the legitimate bills incurred by or for the incapacitated person, the guardian may have to request court approval to spend principal; such approval could be on a case-by-case request or could be part of a plan of support approved by the court. Whether the guardian can make gifts depends on the authority granted by the court. Usually smaller gifts, such as birthday presents, do not require prior court approval, but larger gifts, such as paying college tuition for a grandchild are best undertaken only with prior court approval, as are substantial gifts of property taken to facilitate eligibility for Medicaid or to avoid federal or state estate taxes.

The guardian of the estate is not personally liable for the debts or expenses of the incapacitated person, and is not personally obligated to pay for the expenses incurred by the guardianship, such as paying for professional or legal advice. However, if the guardian incurs unnecessary expenses or disburses funds in a manner that violates the guardian's fiduciary obligations to the incapacitated person, the guardian may be liable to reimburse the estate for those expenses.

A guardian of the estate must productively invest the assets of the estate subject to state law and court restrictions. The standard is that of a prudent investor, which includes the possible loss of value from investments such as stocks that were a prudent investment even though they might decline in value. Merely following the investment philosophy of the incapacitated person may not be prudent, either because they were an imprudent investor or because changes in circumstances, including the financial needs of the incapacitated person, may dictate a different investment approach. Whenever the guardian has any doubt about how to proceed, they should request the advice of the court.

Some rights held by the incapacitated person many not be granted to the guardian of the estate, including the power to revoke a trust, change beneficiaries on insurance policies or retirement benefit plans, withdraw funds from a joint bank account, elect against a will, or exercise a power of appointment. If the guardian believes that any of these or similar acts is warranted, they should explain to the court why they desire to act and why such act would be in the best interest of the incapacitated person, and ask for court approval of the proposed course of action.

The guardian of the estate must act in the best interest of the incapacitated person. How to identify what is the best interest is not always easy. Some courts believe it includes using the assets to assist others who the incapacitated person had been assisting, such as a spouse or a disabled child; other courts define the term more narrowly. A court might, for example, refuse to permit the guardian to pay the rent of an adult child even though the incapacitated person had done so in the past for fear that to continue to do so might eventually reduce the quality of life of or impoverish the incapacitated person. In particular, courts will carefully examine any expenditure that does not directly benefit the incapacitated person to ensure that it does not financially disadvantage them or potentially reduce their quality of life. If a guardian of the estate has any doubt as to whether an expenditure is within their power, they should seek court approval. Otherwise, the guardian is potentially personally liable for the misuse of the assets of the incapacitated person.

B. Guardian of the Person

A guardian of the person or a guardian with plenary power has been delegated by the court with the authority to make decisions that affect the person. Chief among these are determining where the incapacitated person lives and making decisions about their health care. State law determines the extent of the guardian's powers and how those powers are to be implemented. Several states, while generally permitting the guardian to determine the residence of the incapacitated person, have placed limits on the ability of the guardian to admit the incapacitated person into a nursing home or similar facility. And as a practical matter, if the guardian of the person is not also the guardian of the estate, the guardian of the person must gain the consent of the guardian of the estate to relocate the incapacitated person because only the guardian of the estate has the authority to pay for the relocation, such as rent or monthly support fees.

Usually the most important decisions made by the guardian of the person center on the personal care and health care needs of the incapacitated person. The guardian is obligated to ensure that the incapacitated person is properly cared for and safe. In conjunction with the guardian of the estate, the guardian of the person must arrange for proper care such as personal attendants or placing the incapacitated person into a supportive facility such as assisted living. The guardian of the person also makes health care decisions for the incapacitated person ranging from routine care, such as a flu shot, to end-of-life decision making. In the past, courts often wanted the guardian to seek prior court approval of very serious medical decisions, such as the termination of life-sustaining treatment, but today courts often freely delegate serious medical treatment decisions to the guardian and permit them to act as they see fit. Depending on state law, the guardian may be expected to employ substituted judgment, meaning to make decisions consistent with the values and choices that the incapacitated person would have made. Alternatively, the guardian may be expected to act in the best interest of the incapacitated person regardless of the prior express wishes of the incapacitated person. States vary as to whether termination of life-sustaining treatment, such as feeding tubes or respirators, can ever be in the best interest of the incapacitated person.

State law determines whether a guardian can make health care decisions if the incapacitated person has previously appointed someone else as their health care surrogate decision maker. Depending on the applicable state law, the appointment of a guardian may override any rights of a previously appointed substitute decision maker, the guardian may have the authority to choose to remove the surrogate, the guardian may be required to ask the court for authority to remove the surrogate, or the surrogate may continue to have sole authority to make health care decisions for the incapacitated person consistent with the authority granted by the document in which the surrogate was appointed.

Some actions may require prior court approval, such as moving the incapacitated person out of state or voluntarily admitting them to a mental hospital. A guardian cannot initiate divorce without prior court approval, but in some states the guardian can acquiesce to a divorce. Even so, the more prudent course is for the guardian to seek court approval before agreeing to a divorce initiated by the other spouse.

VI. Obligation to Make Reports to the Court

States and local courts increasingly demand regular reports from the guardian. After an initial inventory of the assets of the incapacitated person and a report about their physical condition, personal care needs, and health, the guardian will often be required to file an annual report. The initial report might require the guardian to lay out a plan of care for the incapacitated person. The later annual reports will be expected to detail whether that plan has been carried out and whether changing circumstances dictate a change in the care plan. The guardian is expected to report changes in the mental and physical condition of the incapacitated person, whether they have any unmet needs and whether the guardian's authority should be modified in order that they can better serve the incapacitated person's needs. If the incapacitated person has serious health problems, the guardian should detail what steps have been undertaken to deal with those problems. The guardian of the estate must report the receipt of income and what expenditures were made since the last report, and detail the investment activities.

Annual reports are supposed to permit effective court supervision of the guardian. Unfortunately, too many courts lack sufficient staff to effectively review the reports and monitor the actions of guardians. Nevertheless, a guardian should take care to file the reports in a timely manner and ensure that the reports are accurate and complete. Failure to file reports as required can result in the removal of the guardian.

VII. Termination of Guardianship

Guardianship terminates upon the death of the incapacitated person or upon a court terminating the guardianship, which can occur because the incapacitated person has recovered mental capacity or because the incapacitated person has moved out of the court's jurisdiction and another court has taken over supervision of the guardianship. At the death of the incapacitated person, the guardian's authority ends. If the guardian has control over the assets of the incapacitated person, those assets will have to be turned over to the personal representative of the incapacitated person's estate. Upon learning of the death of the incapacitated person, the guardian should maintain control of the assets, protect them from third parties, and inventory them while awaiting court instructions as to how to proceed. Termination of a guardianship usually results in the guardian being required to give an accounting to the court as to how the guardian had dealt with the person and property of the incapacitated person during the period of the guardianship or since the last report filed by the guardian.

Trusts | 16

I. Introduction

As clients age, due to declining mental or physical vigor, many find it more difficult to manage their investments. Some aging clients may feel comfortable managing their financial affairs but fear that an illness, such as a stroke, or mental decline brought on by dementia may someday cause them to be unable to effectively manage their finances. Even though they have executed a power of attorney that appoints an agent to handle their day-to-day financial affairs, such as paying their bills, they do not necessarily want the agent to handle their investments, which they believe requires a higher level of knowledge and skill than what the agent possesses. To meet the current or potential need for assistance in managing their investments they create a trust.

Many older clients want a revocable trust that they can amend or revoke at will. A few, who intend to give away assets, will create and fund an irrevocable trust. The possible reason for doing so is discussed in Section III. Irrevocable Trusts. The revocable trust, however, is the overwhelming choice for older clients who are not interested in giving away assets, but only in creating a vehicle that will ensure effective management of their assets in the event that they are no longer capable of doing so.

Another reason to create a revocable trust is to permit the use of a pour-over will that leaves all or the bulk of the testator's assets to the trust, which upon the death of the testator, becomes irrevocable. Many leave their estates to a trust in order to avoid public disclosure of how they have chosen to distribute their estate. Unlike a probated will, a trust is not a public document. Although many states recognize the validity of an unfunded revocable trust, some do not. To avoid any chance that the trust might be disallowed for lack of funding, it is best to nominally fund it, such as by clipping a $10 bill to the trust document as the trust corpus. To avoid a possible challenge to the trust on the grounds that the trust corpus was not productively invested, the trust could be funded with a small denomination U.S. savings bond.

By creating a revocable trust that is not part of the will, the settlor can amend or revoke the trust without changing the will. The trust can also receive gifts or legacies from third parties who want the transferred assets to eventually be distributed according to the terms of the trust. For example, some settlors create a trust that after their death will benefit their children so that other relatives may make inter vivos or testamentary gifts to the trust with the assurance that the assets transferred to the trust will not be available to the children until their parents are deceased. Of course, third parties who leave assets to the trust take the chance that the settlor may amend the trust and not leave the assets to the children as expected by the third party.

II. Revocable Trusts

A. Creation of a Revocable Trust

Under the common law, unless otherwise stated, a trust is irrevocable.[1] To create a revocable trust, the settlor must state that the trust is revocable and by whom and under what conditions. Typically the trust will be declared to be unconditionally revoked by the settlor by giving written notice to the trustees. If the settlor has named an agent under a power of attorney, the settlor must decide whether the agent should be granted the power to revoke or amend the trust. Often that power will not be granted because an agent granted such powers has the ability to overturn the settlor's testamentary plans.

The trust should also state that the settlor can amend the trust at any time by providing the trustees with written notice and a copy of the amendment. Again, the settlor should consider whether the settlor's agent should be granted the power to amend the trust. Usually the answer should be no, unless there is a compelling and specific reason for doing so. Although the Uniform Trust Code permits an agent acting under a power of attorney to amend or revoke a trust only if the trust or power of attorney so provides, to ensure that there is no confusion or doubt as to

---

1. The common law rule is reversed by some state laws so that a trust is revocable unless it declares that it is irrevocable. E.g., the Mo. Unif. Trust Code (MUTC), § 456.6-602(1).

the agent's authority, the trust document also should state whether the agent can amend or revoke it.

Although many who are married create separate revocable trusts, some married couples create a single, joint trust, particularly if they own real estate jointly. Joint trusts are more common in community property states because spouses own undivided interests in the community property; ownership by a joint trust is not a significant change. Some married couples in common law states employ a joint trust, particularly in states that recognize tenancies by the entirety. The joint trust permits the couple to maintain their joint ownership, rather than severing it in order to accommodate two separate trusts.

A joint trust usually provides that both are beneficiaries of the trust and that both can revoke and amend it. In community property states that might not be possible. The Uniform Trust Code permits a trust holding community property to be revoked by either spouse but the trust can only be amended by joint action of both spouses. To the extent the trust holds non-community property, each settlor can revoke or amend the trust only as to the portion of the trust property attributable to that settlor's contribution.[2]

At the death of the first spouse, the assets of a joint trust are divided into those of the deceased spouse and those of the surviving spouse with the trust continuing and owning the assets of the surviving spouse. The assets of the deceased spouse are either distributed according to the terms of the trust or, if the trust language provides, the assets remain in the trust.

B. Advantages of a Revocable Trust

Older clients create and fund revocable trusts to ensure continuity of the management of their assets in the event they lose the ability to effectively manage their financial affairs because of the loss of physical or mental capacity. Although an agent acting under a durable power of attorney can be delegated the power to manage their assets, a trust may be preferable because third parties such as banks, brokers, and other financial institutions are often hesitant to accept an agent's authority, particularly if the power of attorney authorizes the agent to act only if the principal, the settlor, has become incapacitated.

The funded revocable trust can also lower the chances that the settlor will have a guardian or conservator appointed to manage their assets. State guardianship and conservatorship statutes usually require that the person for whom the guardianship or conservatorship is sought not only to be mentally incapacitated as defined in the state statute, but also be in need of the protection offered by a guardianship or conservatorship.

An incapacitated person who has appointed an agent to handle their day-to-day financial affairs, such as paying their bills, a surrogate health care decision maker to make decisions concerning their medical care, and also has a revocable

---

2. UTC § 602(b).

trust to handle their investments, should not qualify as needing a guardian or conservator even if they are found to be mentally incapacitated.

The revocable trust also means that if the settlor loses mental capacity, the management of the trust assets will continue without interruption. Similarly, the death of the settlor will not mean a change of management other than a change in trustee, and assets owned by the trust will not have to be retitled or reregistered at the death of the settlor. The trust assets are also immediately available at the settlor's death without the need to wait for a probate decree or issuance of letters testamentary and so can be distributed as dictated by the terms of the trust.

The trust, which typically owns the bulk of the settlor's assets, functions as a will substitute, which means that the trust assets will not be subject to probate. Though the advantage of the avoidance of probate depends on state law and local circumstances, if the settlor transfers real estate located in two or more states, the ownership of the real estate by the trust eliminates the need to open up probate in more than one state. However, because the trust will not own all the assets of the settlor, it is likely that probate will have to be opened in at least one state.

C. Federal Taxation of Trusts

Under the Internal Revenue Code, the settlor of a trust is called the grantor.[3] A revocable trust is a grantor trust and as such the trust is disregarded for income tax purposes; all items of income and all deductible expenses are reported on the grantor's Form 1040. Because of the grantor's retained right to revoke the trust, the grantor is treated as if the trust did not exist. The grantor must give the trustee Form W-9, which supplies the trustee with the grantor's social security number. The trustee, in turn, supplies the grantor's social security number to the mutual funds, brokers, and the like who hold trust assets so that they can report the income to the IRS and issue a Form 1099 to the grantor. The attribution of the trust income to the grantor occurs without regard to whether the grantor serves as trustee and even if no trust distributions are made to the grantor. The grantor reports the amounts on the Form 1099 on their individual income tax form. If the trust provides the proper information to the grantor, the trust does not need to file a separate tax return.

Reflecting that a revocable trust is essentially ignored for income tax purposes, if the grantor's residence is placed in the trust, the I.R.C. Section 121 exemption of $250,000 for a single tax payer or $500,000 for a married couple filing a joint return is not lost.[4]

D. Selection of Trustees

To be viable, a trust must have one or more trustees who manage the trust and own the legal title to the assets of the trust, which they hold for the benefit of the

---

3. For details as to the federal income tax treatment of revocable trusts, see I.R.C. § 671 and the regulations thereunder.
4. IRS Private Letter Ruling 1999-12026, issued on March 26, 1999.

beneficiary who owns the beneficial interest. The initial trustees are named by the settlor. (The term "settlor," rather than "grantor," is used here in recognition of the historical use of that term to designate the creator of a trust.) Almost all settlors who create a revocable trust, which they expect to fund while alive, name themselves as trustee. They do so because they want to continue to manage the trust assets and control distributions from the trust. By naming themselves as a trustee, they deal with the trust assets as if they continued to own them outright. Married settlors often name their spouse as co-trustee because the couple may have always mutually managed their financial affairs. By naming their spouse, their joint management continues. Sometimes each spouse creates a trust and both name the other as co-trustee. If a spouse is not named as trustee, someone else or some entity, such as a bank, should be named as a co-trustee to ensure that if the settlor suddenly ceases to be trustee, the trust will have a trustee, because under trust law, a trust must have at least one trustee. If not, someone will have to go to the appropriate court and file a petition asking the court to appoint a trustee.

The settlor will cease to be a trustee because of death, because of the loss of mental incapacity or because they resign as trustee. A settlor might resign if they thought that because of a decline in physical or mental ability, they were not up to the task of managing the trust. If they do not choose to resign, the other trustee can go to court to have them removed. However, the involuntary removal of the settlor as trustee because of a loss of mental capacity can be difficult. State law likely creates a presumption that a settlor of a revocable trust has capacity and that presumption probably applies to a settlor in the capacity of a trustee. A judicial adjudication of incapacity in a guardianship or conservatorship hearing should be definitive proof that the settlor/trustee is incapacitated and so should be removed as a trustee. State law may provide a method short of a determination of guardianship or conservatorship to declare a trustee as incapacitated, such as a physician's certificate.

It is preferable, however, for the trust to provide a mechanism for one trustee to confirm the incapacity of another trustee. First, the trust should define what is meant by "incapacitated" such as "unable to understand or communicate rational decisions about the management of the trust." Next the trust should identify who will make the determination of incapacity. Of course, that could be a court, but the better solution is to name a party, such as "Dr. Jane Doe" or if she is not available, "a geriatric physician or geriatric psychiatrist." Alternatively, the trust could appoint an entity, such as the trust department of a bank to make the determination. The bank could make the decision on its own, which might be appropriate if the trustee had become severely demented, or the bank could request an opinion from a physician or other appropriate professional. A trustee who does not agree with a determination that they are not mentally capable of carrying out the duties of a trustee, can petition the court to overturn the determination and keep the individual on as a trustee.

The privacy protections of the Health Insurance Portability and Accountability Act of 1996 (HIPAA) may interfere with a physician releasing information about the settlor's or a trustee's health. Fortunately, the regulations permit the release of otherwise protected health information to an individual's personal representative,[5] who is defined as a person with authority to act on the behalf of the individual. The trust could state that anyone who agrees to act as trustee must designate another trustee of the trust as a personal representative to the extent necessary to obtain health or medical information relevant to a determination of the trustee's capacity to serve as trustee.

If the trust does not terminate upon the death of the settlor and continues, it becomes an irrevocable trust. As such, it is discussed in Section III, Irrevocable Trusts.

E. Beneficial Interests

Because a revocable trust is funded as a means of ensuring continuity of asset management, the settlor will be the named beneficiary of the trust with the trustees having the discretion to distribute income and principal to the settlor as they see fit. Because the trust is ignored for income tax purposes and all the income is attributable to the settlor, there is no tax advantage in distributing or not distributing income. Typically, however, the settlor only distributes income and principal as needed, leaving excess income to accumulate in the trust.

The settlor must decide whether the trust can make distributions to other parties. If married, or in a long-term relationship, the settlor is likely to permit distributions to the spouse or partner. If the settlor loses capacity, distributions to the spouse or partner would permit that person to financially maintain the household. Some settlors will restrict such distributions to income in order to protect their plan of distribution of the corpus of the trust. If the spouse or partner is a trustee or a successor trustee upon the settlor's incapacity, the settlor may want to limit trust distributions after they cease to be a trustee, such as by limiting distributions to only the trust income in order to prevent the spouse or partner from having access to the principal of the trust.

Some settlors provide that the trustee can make distributions to a named class of beneficiaries, such as their children and grandchildren. This permits the settlor to make gifts to them directly from the trust, as opposed to distributing the assets to the settlor who in turn makes a gift to the class members. It also permits a successor trustee to make distributions to the class if the settlor has lost capacity and is no longer serving as a trustee. The settlor, however, should consider placing limits on the amount and the frequency of the distributions in order to ensure the trust is not drained of assets to the extent that it would impair adequate support of the settlor and also to protect the plan of distribution of the trust assets that will occur at the death of the settlor. Additionally, limits on distributions to third

---

5. 45 C.F.R. § 164.502.

parties should be included if a successor trustee, such as an adult child, is a potential beneficiary.

Settlors should also consider whether to permit the trust, after the settlor has lost capacity and is no longer serving as trustee, to make charitable gifts or to fulfill the settlor's charitable pledges. If the settlor, for example, annually made a donation to a charitable institution or entity, the trust might be permitted to continue to make a donation in the name of the settlor. As with any power to make a distribution, the settlor should limit charitable donations by a trust by identifying the appropriate recipients and limiting the amount of such donations.

The settlor must decide whether the trust terminates upon their death. If it does, the trust assets can be distributed to the estate of the settlor or be distributed to such persons or entities as provided in the trust. Married settlors must choose whether to distribute the trust to their spouse and, if so, whether outright or into a trust for the benefit of the spouse. The state's forced or statutory share statute requirements must be considered; the fact that the assets are held by a revocable trust most likely makes them subject to the state forced share requirements.

After the death of the settlor, the trust can continue as an irrevocable trust or it can pour its assets over to another trust, perhaps a revocable trust established by the settlor's spouse. If the trust is to continue after the death of the settlor, the trust must provide for successor trustees for the settlor and the other named trustees. Adult children are the obvious choice if the trust distributions are mandated, such as "all income equally to my children." If, however, the trustee has some discretion over distributions, such as a discretionary power to distribute principal or the power to distribute income "as necessary for the support of" a beneficiary, the settlor may not wish to name the children as trustees if they are potential beneficiaries. Even if the only power of the trustees is the power to choose trust investments, if the trust must distribute all its income, the children as trustees can increase the trust distributions by investing in income-producing assets, such as bonds, rather than investing in assets that may grow the principal, such as stocks, and thereby increase the income distributions to themselves at the expense of the future income beneficiaries or the takers of the remainder. The factors that should be considered in the selection of trustees and successor trustees are discussed in Section III, Irrevocable Trusts.

III. Irrevocable Trusts

A. In General

An irrevocable trust cannot be revoked or amended by the settlor. It is an independent legal entity that is managed by the trustees for the benefit of the beneficiaries. Any assets transferred to an irrevocable trust are beyond the control of the settlor unless the settlor is a trustee. In the past, irrevocable trusts were frequently used as a means of avoiding federal estate taxes because the trust assets, if they could not benefit the settlor and if not transferred within three years of death, were not part of the settlor's taxable estate. With the present very high federal estate tax exemption, very few estates are subject to the tax and so there is little reason for most elderly to attempt to avoid the tax by transferring assets to an irrevocable trust. There is also rarely any income tax advantage because undistributed income in a trust in excess of modest amounts is taxed at the highest marginal rate, assuming that the settlor did not retain any powers over the trust that would make it a grantor trust with the income attributed to the settlor.[6] As a result, there is little incentive to create and fund an inner vivos irrevocable trust unless the settlor wishes to make an irrevocable decision as to the disposition of assets. That might occur if the settlor fears that in the future third parties might attempt to reach the assets—such as in a later-life marriage—or to change the plan of disposition—again in the context of a marriage or because heirs attempt to gain access to the funds while the settlor is alive.

B. Choice of Trustees

If the settlor creates an inner vivos irrevocable trust, the settlor can name themselves as trustee. As with any trust, the settlor must decide whether to name co-trustees, which is usually advisable in case they lose capacity. If that should occur, the co-trustee can take steps to ensure that the incapacitated settlor no longer serves as trustee and is replaced by a successor trustee named in the trust instrument.

The settlor should name successor trustees. The longer the trust is expected to last, the greater the need for successor trustees because with the passage of time the likelihood increases that the successor trustee will be called upon to act as a trustee. The alternative to naming several sequential successor individual trustees is to name a corporate trustee, such as the trust department of a bank, as successor trustee with the expectation that the corporate trustee will not need to be replaced. If that need should occur, however, the corporate trustee could petition the court to name a successor corporate trustee. Alternatively, the trust could provide that a corporate trustee has the right to resign and appoint a successor corporate trustee.

Beneficiaries of irrevocable trusts are often granted the power to remove a corporate trustee and replace it with another corporate trustee. They are permitted to do so "without cause." They are granted this power to protect themselves and the trust from an incompetent, inadequate, or inattentive corporate trustee. Sometimes the beneficiary has no particular complaint but has moved far away from where the corporate trustee is located and would prefer a trustee located to where they, the beneficiary, lives. Often if a beneficiary has the right to remove the trustee, the mere threat of removal will cure the problem. When faced with

---

6. *See* I.R.C. §§ 671–677.

possible removal, a corporate trustee will likely meet with the beneficiary and attempt to resolve whatever is causing the beneficiary to threaten to remove the trustee.

The beneficiary is granted the right of removal "without cause" to prevent the corporate trustee from attempting to block its removal by going to court and claiming that the power granted to the beneficiary to remove the trustee was subject to conditions that were not met, such as the trustee not being sufficiently attentive to the financial needs of the beneficiary. Typically, trusts require the beneficiary who has the right to remove a corporate trustee to name a successor corporate trustee. This prevents the beneficiary from naming an individual as trustee who might be willing to carry out the wishes of the beneficiary without regard to whether that would be consistent with the settlor's intent or in the best interest of the beneficiary.

C. Trust Protector

In response to the desire for more flexibility and adaptability of trusts, many settlors appoint a trust protector. Some of the increase in the use of protectors is due to the Uniform Trust Code (UTC), which, although it does not use the term "protector," authorizes the settlor to "confer upon a person . . . to direct certain actions of the trustee"[7] that permits the appointment of a protector. The "law" of protectors is not well defined, as only a few states specifically authorize their appointment. The absence of state protector statues and the lack of cases[8] that discuss the duties and responsibilities of a protector means that in most states settlors are free to grant such powers to a protector as they see fit.

Protectors are a means for a settlor to attempt to ensure that in the future the trustees will carry out the intent of the settlor. Trust protectors are also a response to the greater powers and discretion that modern trust law confers upon trustees. The UTC, for example, lists 26 possible trustee powers as well providing liberal standards for judicial modification of the trust.[9] A settlor may be worried whether those expanded powers or judicially sanctioned trust modifications will be used in ways inconsistent with the settlor's intent. Moreover, in the past, an irrevocable trust was not only irrevocable but also unamendable. Today the opposite is true. A truly irrevocable, unamendable trust hardly exists, as state statutes and courts often permit the modification of an "unamendable trust" as well as permit decanting the trust assets into a new trust.

Settlors who create a perpetual or dynasty trust are likely to appoint a protector. The expected extended term of the trust makes it advantageous to have

---

7. UNIF. TRUST CODE § 808(b), cmt. ("Subsections (b)–(d) ratify the use of trust protectors and advisers.").

8. *E.g., In re* Eleanor Pierce (Marshall) Stevens Living Trust, 2015 WL 672549 (Feb. 18, 2015); Midwest Trust Co. v. Brinton, 331 P.3d 834 (Kan. App. Ct. 2014); Minassian v. Rachins, 152 So. 3d 719, 722 (Fla. Ct. App. 2014).

9. UNIF. TRUST CODE, art. 8 and art. 4 (2010).

someone empowered to modify the trust in light of changing law, changing beneficiaries, or questionable actions by the trustee. As a general rule, the longer a trust is expected to last, the greater the need for a protector who can adapt the trust to changing law and to changes in the needs and abilities of the beneficiaries, some of whom may not have yet been born at the inception of the trust.

The extent of the authority granted to the protector is up to the settlor. Some states, however, have enacted protector statutes that provide a list of powers that are granted to the protector absent language to the contrary in the trust. The settlor, however, should not rely on a statutory, default grant of authority, but should carefully select what powers to grant to the protector in light of the settlor's concerns about how the trust will operate in the future and how best to ensure that the trustee carries out the settlor's intent.

1. Powers of the Protector

The settlor should enumerate the powers granted to a protector in the trust document. If a state lacks a "protector" statute, settlors are free to empower a protector as they see fit.[10] Even if the state has a statute that defines and authorizes a trust protector, the statute likely does not limit what powers may be granted to the trust protector.[11]

The most significant power granted to a protector is the right to remove and appoint a trustee and to fill a trustee vacancy. All other powers of the protector that relate to the trustee are merely more specific grants of authority that could be accomplished if the protector threatens to use the power to remove the trustee. Granting the protector the power to name successor trustees is a response to the ever lengthening of the duration of trusts. The longer the trust lasts, the more likely it is that none of the trustees will have been appointed by the settlor. Even the original named successor trustees will have died, become incapacitated or resigned. Although the settlor could leave the appointment of future trustees up to a court,[12] many settlors prefer to appoint a protector with the authority to name successor trustees should the need arise.

The settlor should also grant the protector the power to remove and replace the trustee, but in most cases limit the selection of the new trustee to a corporate trustee. The protector should have the power to remove a trustee even though the appropriate court also may have that authority. The right of a court to remove a trustee depends upon the applicable state law. The Uniform Trust Code, however, is instructive. Under the Uniform Trust Code, Section 706, a court may remove a trustee for listed reasons that include when "the trustee has committed a serious breach of trust" or "because of unfitness, unwillingness, or persistent failure of the trustee to administer the trust effectively, the court determines that removal of

---

10. Minassian v. Rachins, 152 So. 3d 719, 722 (Fla. Ct. App. 2014).
11. *E.g.*, Ariz. Rev. Stat. Ann., art. 8, 14-10818.
12. Unif. Trust Code § 704 (amended 2010).

the trustee best serves the interests of the beneficiaries."[13] Although the grounds for judicial removal are broad, they nevertheless require proof that the trustee is not performing properly. A settlor might want to avoid having that improper performance revealed to a court to avoid the cost of bringing a court action and the public nature of that request and the resulting publicity. Moreover, the settlor may empower the protector to be able to remove a trustee for reasons other than the reasons that permit removal by a court. For example, if a beneficiary and a trustee do not get along, but the trustee is not performing in a way that would permit judicial removal of a trustee, the protector may believe it best to remove the trustee and replace it by an entity that the beneficiary can get along with.

Other powers that can be granted to a protector include the right to change the situs of the trust, decant the trust, terminate the trust under defined conditions, and to amend the trust in response to changes in other state or federal law or changes in the Internal Revenue Code or state income tax law. Any amendment, however, would have to be consistent with the settlor's intent.

Most of the powers that can be granted to a protector that concern trust administration, including the power to modify the trust instrument, can be done by a court. Granting a similar power to a protector is essentially duplicative. Yet a settlor may prefer a protector because doing so creates a means to solve a problem with the trust that is less expensive and quicker than resorting to requesting court action. Moreover, the settlor may have more confidence in the judgment of the protector, rather than in an unknown judge.

A settlor can give the protector the power to effect the beneficial enjoyment of the trust, such as a power to veto otherwise mandatory distributions, discretionary distributions, or delay beneficiary withdrawal rights. The protector could also be granted a limited power of appointment among designated beneficiaries or a power to add or remove beneficiaries.

Although a settlor could grant the protector a power to modify beneficial interests, it is difficult to imagine why a settlor would do so. If the settlor is fearful of changing circumstances that might necessitate such a change, the settlor can provide that specific, listed events trigger a change in trust distributions or create a power in the protector to change the beneficial interests.

2. Selection of the Protector

The settlor appoints the initial protector who should be qualified and willing to undertake the responsibilities of the position. Who is qualified depends to a great extent on the powers delegated to the protectors. Who is willing to serve depends upon the effort expected of the protector and whether the protector is considered a fiduciary.

(a) WHO IS QUALIFIED TO ACT AS PROTECTOR? The kinds of powers granted to the protector suggest inter alia, that the protector must understand what a

---

13. Unif. Trust Code § 706(b) (amended 2010).

trust is, how it functions, the law of trusts and trustees, federal and state taxation of trusts, and the relative advantage of one state trust law over another. The list suggests that a protector be an attorney knowledgeable about trust law or an entity that regularly handles trust affairs. The alternative is to appoint a lay person as protector with the expectation that they will seek out professional guidance. But if the lay protector is unqualified to carry out the responsibilities absent professional assistance, in reality the functions of the protector have been delegated to the professional advisors. Therefore, the appointment of a professional with special knowledge and expertise would usually be the preferred choice.

The appointment of a professional as protector, however, risks creating a conflict of interest if the protector has business or professional dealings with the trustee or any of the beneficiaries. Possible conflicts of interest should give a settlor pause and should be avoided if possible.

A settlor who wants the protector to monitor the trust for changes in the law should appoint an attorney, a corporate entity such as a trust company, or an individual who is a professional, like an accountant. Conversely, if the settlor grants the protector the power to modify beneficial interests, such as by delaying a distribution, naming new beneficiaries, or decanting the trust, the settlor might reasonably prefer a lay person, including a relative, who the settlor has confidence in, to change beneficiary interests in a manner consistent with the intent and values of the settlor. But even a power to alter beneficial interests might better be left to a professional protector, such as an attorney, who has no personal interest in how the trust operates or who benefits from it.

(b) WILLINGNESS TO SERVE AS PROTECTOR. Whether an individual or corporate entity is willing to serve as a protector depends on a number of factors, but three stand out: the potential trustee's relation to the settlor, the duties to be performed, and the level of exposure to liability. Ideally, the settlor should consider appointing someone who has a close, personal relationship to the settlor and feels obligated to accept the appointment. Yet such a person might decline to serve as protector if the duties seem too onerous or if they fear personal liability.

Corporate entities will agree to act as protector only if the cost of acting as protector, in terms of effort and possible liability, is adequately offset by the compensation paid for their acting as protector. The most important concern for a corporate entity is likely the possible liability that may arise from being a protector. That, in turn, may be a function of the duties that arise from being a protector, particularly any fiduciary responsibilities. See subsection 3, The Protector as a Fiduciary. In some instances, the trust settlor may have to negotiate with a corporate entity and adjust the duties of the protector in such a way as to make the position one that the entity is willing to undertake.

(c) POSSIBLE PROTECTORS. Who is capable of successfully performing as protector depends to a great degree on what the settlor envisions and what powers have been delegated to the protector to fulfill that vision. If the settlor is most concerned that the trustee acts in a manner that meets the needs of the beneficiary, an individual protector who knows both the settlor and the beneficiary may be the best choice. The appointment of an individual also suggests that the settlor wanted the protector literally to be a "protector" of the beneficiary. If the trust continues for a considerable time after the initial beneficiaries die, however, the settlor may prefer an entity, rather than an individual, serve as the successor protector.

Some individuals who are professionals, such as attorneys, are named as protectors because of the knowledge and skills that they bring to the position. The settlor, though wanting a skilled protector, may be more comfortable with an individual who is a professional rather than a corporate entity, such as a bank, at least during the initial years of the trust. Yet, sometime during the trust's existence, an individual protector may die or resign and so necessitate a successor trustee. The preferred choice for a successor is an entity because an entity will likely be in existence throughout the life of the trust.

Further support for naming an entity as protector is found in the fact that very often the duties assigned to the protector require a sophisticated understanding of trust law and when it would be appropriate to act, which is consistent with the appointment of an entity as the initial protector and even more so as the successor protector.

(d) IDENTIFYING THE SUCCESSOR PROTECTOR. In addition to having the necessary knowledge and expertise, and not having a potential or actual conflict of interest, the protector has to have longevity. Trusts can last for many years and several generations. If the settlor initially appoints an individual, that individual is unlikely to live long enough (or be capable of serving effectively) to serve as protector for the duration of the trust. The settlor can name another presumably younger individual as successor protector, but in time the successor will also die. Even a corporate protector might resign as protector and so necessitate the appointment of a successor protector. Regardless of the how it comes about, at some point, a successor protector will likely be needed.

The settlor has several options for providing for a successor protector. The settlor can name the successor, the settlor can delegate to the protector the right to appoint a successor, or the trustee or beneficiary can be empowered to name a successor protector. The longer the trust is expected to last, the better it is to permit the protector to name their successor. All else failing, the settlor can provide that a court name a successor protector.

3. The Protector as a Fiduciary

A few states mandate that a protector is a fiduciary.[14] In the absence of state law, the trust can declare its protector to be a fiduciary. Holding the protector to a

---

14. *See, e.g.,* N.C. GEN. STAT. § 36C-8A-1-11; 14A V.S.A. §§ 808, 1101–1105; VA. CODE ANN. § 64.2-770; WYO. STAT. §§ 4-10-808, 4-10-710-711.

fiduciary standard can be justified on the grounds that most of the powers held by the protector would be subject to a fiduciary standard if held by a trustee. For example, a trustee granted the power to amend the trust is subject to a fiduciary standard of care.[15] Some state statutes that provide for a protector to be a fiduciary do not provide that the settlor can waive that requirement.[16] But in other states, the settlor can insert a clause in the trust that negates the statutory imposition of fiduciary status on a protector and limit under what conditions, if any, the protector is a fiduciary.[17]

The minimum requirements that a settlor must require of a trustee or a protector depends on state law. The UTC states that the terms of a trust prevail over the provisions of the state statute except that inter alia the trustee must act "in accordance with the terms and purposes of the trust and the interests of the beneficiaries."[18] If the settlor can exculpate the trustee from fiduciary status, it would seem that the settlor can also declare that a protector is not a fiduciary.

Even if the protector is not a fiduciary, the protector must act in good faith.[19] The UTC permits the trust provisions to prevail over the Code except for a list of powers that include the "duty of the trustee to act in good faith."[20] A protector, who like a trustee, has powers that can affect the beneficial enjoyment of the trust, presumably must also act in good faith. In interpreting an exoneration clause in trust and demonstrating the fundamental nature of the requirement of good faith, the Pennsylvania Supreme Court held that the trust exoneration clause would govern but it "becomes inapplicable if it would allow a fiduciary who acted in bad faith or with reckless indifference to the beneficiary's interests to escape liability."[21] Apparently, even if the settlor provides in the trust that the protector is not a fiduciary, the settlor cannot exonerate the protector from acts or omissions arising from bad faith.[22]

The settlor may also want to ensure that mere negligence by the protector will not create liability. The settlor can define "good faith" to provide that an act of ordinary negligence does not violate the good faith standard. However, the settlor

---

15. *See, e.g.*, Rubinson v. Rubinson, 620 N.E.2d 1271 (Ill. App. 1993).

16. *See, e.g.*, Miss. Code Ann. §§ 91-8-808 ,91-8-1201; Mo. Rev. Stat. § 456-8-808; N.C. Gen. Stat. § 36C-8A-1-11; S.C. Code Ann. §§ 62-7-808, 818; Tenn. Code Ann. §§ 35-15-808, 35-15-1201–1206; Vt. Stat. Ann. tit. 14A, §§ 808, 1101–1105; Va. Code Ann. § 64.2-770; Wyo. Stat. Ann. §§ 701.0808, 0818.

17. *See, e.g.*, Alaska Stat. §§ 13.36.370–375; Ariz. Rev. Stat. Ann. §§ 14-10808, 10818; Del. Code Ann. tit. 12, § 3313; Idaho Code Ann. § 15-7-501; N.H. Rev. Stat. Ann. §§ 564-B, 8-808, 12-1201; 760 Ill. Comp. Stat. Ann. § 5/16.3; Ind. Code Ann. § 30-4-3-9; Mich. Comp. Laws § 700.7809; Ohio Rev. Code Ann. § 5808.8; Or. Rev. Stat. §§ 130.685, .735; and Wash. Rev. Code § 11.100.130.

18. Unif. Trust Code § 105(b)(2) (amended 2010).

19. Robert Whitman, *Exoneration Clauses in Wills and Trust Instruments*, 4 Hofstra Prop. L.J. 123, 125 (1992).

20. Unif. Trust Code §§ 105(b)(2), 1008.

21. *In re* Estate of Niessen, 413 A.2d 1050, 1053 (Pa. 1980).

22. William W. Brown, Trusts § 30.25 (2014).

cannot exculpate a trustee, and presumably a protector, from liability for acts taken in bad faith or with reckless indifference (gross negligence).[23]

4. Protector Affirmative Duties

The protector must act consistent with the language and purposes of the trust, the intent of the settlor, and the interests of the beneficiaries.[24] The settlor, however, should also state that the protector has a duty to inquire and seek information relevant to the powers held by the protector. For example, if the protector can amend the trust in response to changes in the law, the protector should have the obligation to monitor changes in state and federal laws that impact the trust.

To facilitate the protector carrying out their duties, the trust should specifically provide that the trustee is required to provide information to the protector when requested by the protector or preferably the trust should require the trustee to provide regular reports to the protector. The information to be conveyed should be listed in detail in the trust.

The protector should have the duty to take appropriate and sufficient action to protect the interest of the beneficiaries and see that the trust carries out the settlor's intent. A failure of the trust to state what is expected of the protector can lead to litigation and require judicial interpretation.[25] Merely stating that the protector has absolute or unlimited authority, such as to remove a trustee, is not adequate. The UTC states that even "absolute" or "uncontrolled" discretionary powers must be exercised "in good faith and in accordance with the terms and purposes of the trust and the interests of the beneficiaries."[26] A Minnesota court noted that a trustee will not be permitted to act in a manner that is an abuse of discretion, and the motives of the trustee in exercising or not exercising a discretionary power is one factor used to determine whether an abuse has occurred.[27] Though the case refers to trustees, it is highly likely that a protector would be subject to similar oversight. The trust should therefore state that the protector has absolute discretion but must nevertheless act in good faith.

The trust should also require the protector to be proactive and seek out appropriate information, particularly in regard to the behavior of the trustee. The trust should require that the protector act in the manner of a prudent person. What is prudent depends on the facts and circumstances, but at least the standard puts the protector on notice that they have a duty to monitor the acts of the trustee and to take action when appropriate.

---

23. RESTATEMENT (THIRD) OF TRUSTS § 96(1) (2003).
24. The Uniform Trust Code does not define "good faith," but surely it would be bad faith to act in a manner inconsistent with the purposes of the trust, the intent of the settlor, or contrary to the interests of the beneficiaries.
25. *See, e.g.,* McLean Irrevocable Trust v. Ponder, 418 S.W.3d 482, 484 (Mo. Ct. App. 2014).
26. UNIF. TRUST CODE § 814(a) (amended 2010).
27. *In re* Trusts A & B of Divine, 672 N.W.2d 912 (Minn. App. 2001).

5. Protectors of trusts with beneficiaries with mental disabilities

A compelling reason to appoint a trust protector arises when a trust beneficiary has diminished mental capacity. Under the law of trusts, the beneficiary has the right to sue the trustee to preserve and protect the beneficiary's interests by asking the court to require the trustee to act according to the provisions of the trust and in a manner consistent with the best interest of the beneficiaries.[28] That right, however, may be meaningless if the beneficiary, due to diminished mental capacity, is incapable of protecting those rights, which might be the case if the beneficiary is mentally ill, suffers from dementia, has an intellectual or developmental disability, or has traumatic brain injury. Such a beneficiary might be unaware that the trustees are not acting in good faith or is not in compliance with their duties and obligations.

A solution for a mentally disabled beneficiary is the appointment of a protector who is empowered to monitor the actions of the trustee, the trust investments, and changes in trust law. Perhaps the most important duty of a protector is to monitor the amount and frequency of trust distributions to the beneficiary, particularly if the trustee has some degree of discretion as to the distributions, whether the discretion is unlimited or limited by a standard, such as the support needs of the beneficiary. No matter if the distribution power of the trustee is unlimited or limited, the settlor can reasonably be concerned that the trustee might be too parsimonious or, less likely, too generous, in making the discretionary distributions. Because the beneficiary with reduced capacity may not be capable of raising a protest as to the trustee's actions, the settlor should appoint a protector to monitor trust distributions and consult with the trustee as to the appropriateness of the distributions.

A settlor should consider appointing a protector even if a trust does not have a beneficiary with diminished mental capacity at the time of its creation of the trust. Settlors must plan for possible future, unborn beneficiaries of the trust who may have reduced mental capacity from birth or experience it at some point in their lives. A very real possibility is that aging trust beneficiaries may become demented and lose mental capacity and so be incapable of protecting their beneficial interests. As trusts last longer and serve beneficiaries over their lifetimes, the likelihood increases that beneficiaries will live long enough to become demented. Other very old beneficiaries may not suffer from dementia, but due to chronic illness, reduced hearing and vision, or extreme frailty may not be physically capable of protecting their interests by monitoring the trustee's acts.

6. Oversight of and Compensation for a Protector

The trust should provide oversight of the protector. If the trust lasts for a number of years, the original protector will very likely have resigned or died. Even if the settlor had named a successor protector, that person or entity may, too, have

---

28. RESTATEMENT (THIRD) OF TRUSTS § 78 (2011).

resigned or died before the termination of the trust. If the original protector or named successor protector is a corporate entity, although it may continue to perform to the letter of the duties of a protector, it may lack any sense of personal obligation to the settlor to carry out the intent of the settlor. Moreover, a corporate entity can rightfully expect to be compensated.

A settlor has several choices as to how to provide effective oversight of the protector. The trust could state that the protector is held to a fiduciary standard. Doing so, however, will make it more difficult to find any individual or entity willing to serve as protector. An alternative is to have the trust periodically compensate the protector in order to create a contractual obligation with the protector. The protector should sign a contract that spells out the protector's obligations (and limits of obligations) and the compensation to be paid by the trust. Ideally the contract should detail the remedy for a breach by the protector, such as removal, specific performance, repayment of the compensation, and payment to the beneficiary for any damages caused by the protector's malfeasance.

The settlor should also provide a means to remove and replace the protector and identify the conditions and standards that signal when the protector should be removed. The settlor should state that the beneficiary, or the beneficiary's representative, can petition the appropriate court to remove the protector based on the protector not fulfilling their obligations.

Estate Planning with the Very Old Client

17

I. Introduction

Every client's estate plan is different. Each client presents a unique combination of problems, concerns, and needs. One of the factors is the age of the client, or if a couple, the clients. Experienced estate planners know that the client's age is an important component. Creating an estate plan for a 45-year-old is different than creating a plan for a 65-year-old. And certain life events motivate many to seek out estate planning. Turning age 65 or retiring is a spur for some clients to revisit their estate plan. The death of a spouse is another event that causes many to amend their estate plan. For others, merely becoming very old motivates them to make a "final" estate plan. As a result, estate planning attorneys are increasingly seeing clients age 80 or older. Many of these very old clients have similar problems and concerns.

II. Time Is Short

Attorneys and their clients often seem to be living in different worlds when it comes to time. What an attorney thinks is a reasonable time to research the law and draft documents, to clients may seem like a long time. Because attorneys have many clients and many demands on their time, they must manage client expectations and be clear that the client understands that "soon" does not mean tomorrow. Though the need to make the client understand why things go slowly is understandable, it may not be the best response when dealing with clients age 80 and older.

In terms of time, the very old client differs in two ways from younger clients. First, the very old client is almost always retired and has also fewer obligations to community or other groups. As a result, the very old client has more available time and fewer distractions. Very old clients also often become very fixed on the problems they raise with their attorney and become impatient for a resolution. The passage of a week to the attorney may seem like very little time has passed, but to many very old clients, a week to reflect on the meeting with the attorney, to think about what was discussed, and to wait for the attorney's answer can seem long enough to expect a response from the attorney. This sense of compressed time in many very old clients means the attorney should inform the client when they can expect to hear from the attorney and to provide a date by which the client can expect to receive documents. These dates should be provided in a letter or other communication that is separate from the attorney engagement letter.

The letter that provides the client with a probable timeline as to when various stages of the work will be completed should be in hard copy as well as e-mail. It should be short and succinct, with the expected completion dates presented as bullet points. The goal is to make the information obvious and easily reviewed by the client. The hope is the letter will forestall the client from calling or e-mailing asking when they can expect to see some progress on their legal problems. The projected completion dates should be relatively soon; the longer the time frame the more likely the client will eventually contact the attorney to complain about the lack of progress even if the completion deadlines in the letter are being met. Finally, the attorney should make every effort to meet the completion dates in the letter. When circumstances make it impossible to conform to the timeline, the attorney should proactively inform the client of the delay, give a brief explanation of why it occurred, and provide an updated timeline and completion dates.

Second, an attorney must be cognizant that if the attorney delays too long a very old client may lose mental capacity, become too ill to continue the planning process, or even die. Of course, merely being age 80 or older does not mean that a client is about to lose their mental capabilities or die. However, clients of an advanced age are statistically more at risk of suffering a loss of mental capacity, perhaps due to dementia or as a result of a physical condition or illness, such as a stroke. They also have a higher likelihood of suffering a debilitating incident or illness, such as a broken hip condition or just general decline. And, of course, morbidity rates rise with age. For example, an 85-year-old woman has a life expectancy that is about half as long as that of a 75-year-old woman, approximately 7 years versus 13 years, and the 85-year-old woman is three times more likely to die within a year than is a 75-year-old woman.[1] A 90-year-old woman is five times more likely to die within a year.

Moreover, the very old who seek out an attorney are more likely to either be suffering from mental or physical decline because it is often the existence of that decline that motivates many to put their affairs in order or to make what they expect to be their final estate plan. Thus, the very old clients seen by an attorney are often more sick or frail than the average very old person. That form of adverse selection should impel the attorney to shorten the time that it takes from the initial client interview to the signing of documents.

An attorney dealing with very old clients, therefore, should attempt to resolve the legal issues in a timely fashion. Gathering the necessary information from the client, discussing the options with the client, and getting the client's signature on documents should be accomplished as soon as possible. In some cases, the client's age and declining health may dictate that the legal work be simplified so that it can be completed sooner, with the idea that the best can be the enemy of the good. A good plan, even if not the best plan, is better than letting the client die with no plan. For clients of advanced age who have suffered a decline in mental capacity, the attorney may simplify the plan so that the client can understand it. Although it is not necessary that clients completely understand their estate plan, particularly in light of some of the complex planning solutions that are employed, the client must at least understand the broad contours of the plan and comprehend what the plan hopes to accomplish. At times, even to meet these modest levels of comprehension may mean that the attorney must draft a more basic plan that accomplishes most of the possible desired outcomes even if it falls short of achieving all that might have been done had the client been more mentally capable.

III. Communication Problems

Communicating adequately with a very old client can be difficult for several possible reasons: cliental lack of hearing, vision, physical frailty, a painful condition, or loss of mental acuity. Attorneys who engage with very old clients must be alert to possible problems in communicating and devise strategies for overcoming them.

The loss of hearing is very common is the very old; more than half of those age 80 and older suffer from hearing loss. Hearing loss associated with aging is called prebyacusis or age-related loss of hearing. Its cause is unknown, but it is thought to be genetic in origin and is part of the general decline in physical function. There is no cure. The use of a hearing aid can help, but only a third of those with hearing problems employ a hearing aid.

The loss of hearing in a client can be pernicious because clients often attempt to hide the loss or do not even realize the extent of the loss and so are unaware

---

1. http://life-span.healthgrove.com.

that they are not hearing all that the attorney is saying. If the client does not have a spouse or partner present, their lack of hearing can create a barrier to a proper attorney-client relationship because communication between the attorney and the client is essential. If a couple is meeting with the attorney, and only one has a hearing problem, the spouse who can hear will take the lead in the conversation and often repeat important points to the poor hearing spouse. The couple may not even be cognizant of doing this, as it has become the way in which they typically function. Though this behavior may be comfortable to the couple, it is not acceptable for the attorney because each spouse is a client of the attorney, and each spouse must hear, understand, and concur with the plans being formulated.

When meeting with very old clients, the attorney should not assume that the client can hear what the attorney or others are saying. Early on in the conversation the attorney can determine if the client has a hearing problem by asking the individual a question that cannot be answered by yes or no or by a rote, conventional answer. Often a person with diminished hearing can hear just enough of a question to intuit what it was. Even if they hear almost nothing, if they heard a noun or two, they can respond in a way that gives the impression that they heard the question. For example, if the attorney asks, "It is great to finally see the sun," if the client only hears the word "sun" they will assume they have been asked about the weather, and so answer, "It certainly is a beautiful day." If they have no idea what the attorney said, they might respond, "I always feel better on a sunny day." Even if not responsive to what the attorney said, the statement might seem appropriate as a standard way to respond to the attorney's initial greeting. Moreover, the well hearing spouse may respond if the attorney asked a question and thus cover for the spouse with a hearing problem.

To avoid being misled, the attorney should ask the client, or both spouses individually, a question that reveals whether they heard the question. For example, "Betty, how was the traffic on the freeway this morning?" or "Bob, I see you live in Smallville. How long have you lived there?" Both questions require a specific answer from an identified person. If in the example, however, Bob interrupts and answers for Betty, a follow up question to Betty might be, "Betty, where did you grow up?"

If the attorney believes a client has a hearing problem, it is best to state that to the client and ask how the client wants the attorney to deal with it. When dealing with a couple, the attorney must explain that both spouses are clients and so both spouses must understand what is being said.

When talking with a client with impaired hearing, the attorney should sit next to the person rather than talking across a desk. A round table for client meetings is desirable because it permits everyone to see the face of whoever is speaking. The attorney should look directly at whoever is being addressed, speak a bit slower than usual, pause after major points and avoid going off on tangents or adding unnecessary details. With some clients, it may be necessary to give the client a memo with bullet points to read during the discussion. Often if an individual knows the general topic being discussed, they can hear and comprehend more of the discussion.

Clients with vision problems are usually more open about the problem. The most common causes are cataracts and macular degeneration. If the client has a problem reading, they are likely to admit it when asked to review a document or memorandum. An attorney who is alerted to the problem should ask the client how they want to deal with it. Some will be able to read if the document has a larger font. Some have a machine at home that throws the document on a screen in a greatly enlarged font. A few will ask for a recorded version of the information in the document. Others will rely on a spouse or child reading the material to them. The attorney should adapt to whatever the client is comfortable with, but keep in mind that a very old client may also have a poorer memory that is exacerbated by their inability to read.

IV. Testamentary Capacity

A testator must have testamentary capacity to execute a valid will. With most clients, this is not a problem. However, because the loss of mental capacity rises with age, when dealing with very old clients the attorney must take care to assure themselves that the client has the requisite level of capacity. If not, the will can be declared invalid.

The common law test of testamentary capacity has four elements:

1. Did the testator understand the nature of the act, that they were writing a will?
2. Did the testator know the nature and extent of their property?
3. Did the testator know the identity of those who were the natural objects of their bounty?
4. Did the testator understand the plan of disposition of their assets in the will?

The attorney has the obligation not to permit a client who lacks testamentary capacity to execute a will. Conversely, the attorney should attempt to ensure that a client with low, but sufficient, testamentary capacity, is provided with sufficient assistance so that they are able to execute a valid will.

The attorney should have a standard procedure used to determine whether a client has testamentary capacity and should employ it whenever the attorney suspects the client's capacity might become an issue. Asking the client a series of questions about their family and heirs, what they own, and how they want to distribute their estate should reveal the state of the client's capacity. If the attorney has any doubt about whether the client has testamentary capacity, an expert in geriatric assessment should be called in to evaluate the client. Of course, because doing so may annoy the client and their family, the attorney must carefully explain why the assessment is necessary and how doing it is in the best interest of the client.

If the attorney concludes that the client has capacity, the attorney must be sure to maintain a file of evidence that will support that conclusion. The best way to discourage a claim of the lack of capacity is to have proof that the attorney took appropriate steps to establish that the client had capacity. In particular, because the client's testamentary capacity is determined at the moment of signing the will, the attorney should have a will signing procedure that will yield evidence that the client had capacity. The witnesses to the will should be told of the importance of the event and the need for them to be satisfied that the testator has capacity. They may need later to testify, and so the will signing should be done in a formal enough manner and be free of distractions so that it is memorable to the witnesses. The independence of the witnesses is also important. If possible, the witness should not be the attorney's employee or partner, but the attorney should know them well enough so that in the future they can be located if that becomes necessary. They should also be mature and perceptive enough to be able to judge whether the testator seemed to be aware of what they were doing. Because of the doctrine of a moment of clarity, the testator need only have the requisite capacity at the time of the signing of the will. The fact that they might have lacked testamentary capacity before and after the time of the execution of the will, it is not determinative. For that reason, the impressions and conclusions of the witnesses as to the mental capacity of the testator can be crucial.

V. Presence of Third Party

Often a very old client or a very old couple will want a child or other party to be present during the interviews with the attorney, either to explain later to them what occurred or to observe what had occurred and be available to discuss what the attorney advised. Although having a third party present is acceptable, the attorney should insist on meeting with the client or the couple alone for a period of time to ascertain whether they actually want the third party present, why they want them present, and whether they do not want the third party present during discussions about certain topics. Whatever the reason for the presence of the third party, the attorney must deal with the issue of confidentiality. The client who wants a child or other person present must sign a statement that they waive their right to confidentiality and are willing to share all information revealed during their meetings with the attorney when the third party was present.

The attorney should also be alert for possible undue influence by the third party. Not just influence that rises to the level of being sufficiently undue to call into question whether the will is a valid document, but also influence that results in the client making decisions that they might not have been made if the third party were not present. The client may not wish to annoy or anger the third party and thus concurs in decisions with which they may not agree. The client may also be less forthcoming about certain topics in the presence of the third party. Sometimes the attorney will be requesting information or discussing matters that the client never thought would be inquired about and would prefer not to reveal to the third party but does not want to reveal their reluctance to do so to the third party. The attorney, therefore, must listen carefully and determine when it would be best to ask the third party to leave the room and request that they do so even if the client or the third party objects. Better to offend the third party and to meet alone with the client than to permit the third party to unduly influence the client. The attorney must insist on meeting privately with the client both at the beginning of the planning process and at the end before the client takes any action or signs any documents. In the end, the attorney is responsible for ensuring that the client's actions represent the true desires of the client and not those of the third party.

VI. Undue Influence

A will can be invalidated if it was the result of undue influence. Although testators have the right to devise or give away their property as they see fit, those acts must reflect the will and autonomous choice of the testator and not that of a third party, the influencer. The elements of undue influence vary somewhat from state to state, but in general it is necessary to prove four components in order to substantiate a claim of undue influence.

1. The testator was susceptible to the influence of others.
2. The testator and influencer had a confidential relationship.
3. The influencer used the confidential relationship to effect a change in the distribution of assets in the will.
4. The change in the will did not express the true or autonomous desire of the testator.[2]

Although the age of the testator is not a formal component of undue influence, in reality the testator's age is relevant because very old testators are believed to be much more susceptible to undue influence.

Claims of undue influence are also often joined with the claim that the testator lacked testamentary capacity. The claims are in the alternative because if the testator lacked testamentary capacity, the will is invalid. A claim of undue influence can only arise if the testator had capacity to execute a valid will, but a successful undue influence claim almost always requires a showing that the testator had diminished mental capacity.

---

2. Lawrence A. Frolik, *The Biological Roots of the Undue Influence Doctrine: What's Love Got to Do With It?*, 57 U. PITT. L. REV. 841, 850 (1996).

Although no attorney wants to write a will that is the result of undue influence, it can be difficult to ascertain whether a client is being a victim of undue influence or is just writing a will that reflects the client's gratitude or admiration of the person to whom they are making a testamentary disposition. To help in making that distinction, the attorney should have a checklist of possible indicators of undue influence.

The first is the age of the client; the older they are the more likely they may be a victim. Next is their mental condition. The lower their mental capacity or the more physically dependent they are on others, the more susceptible they may be to undue influence. Third is the existence of a confidential relationship. The attorney should be alert to a testamentary gift to someone in a confidential relationship, which is defined as a relationship in which there is special trust and confidence between the parties. Sometimes it is a fiduciary relationship such as that of a guardian, agent, or trustee. Other relationships that have found to be confidential include those with an attorney, physician, nurse, caregiver, housekeeper, or a member of the clergy. Family members such as spouses, children, adult lovers, and siblings have been found to have a confidential relationship. Even charitable organizations and universities have been held to be in a confidential relationship with decedents.

The two additional critical elements of undue influence are active procurement and a change in the will that favors the influencer. Active procurement has been found when the influencer was present at the signing of the will, having recommended the attorney, instructed the attorney how to draft the will, paid the attorney, secured the witnesses to the will, or kept possession of the signed will. In short, whenever a third party has been involved in the planning process, the attorney should be alert for possible undue influence or for a possible challenge to the will based on a claim of undue influence.

Finally, the attorney should pay special attention to a will that has a significantly different distribution scheme than that of the prior will. If so, the attorney should question the client for the reasons for the change, both to ensure against drafting a will that is the product of undue influence or to be able to protect the testator's wishes against a claim of undue influence. With a very old client, the attorney should be alert to testamentary gifts to nurses, caregivers, and housekeepers. Depending on the amount of the gift relative to the size of the estate, it is possible that the gift is merely an acknowledgement of the assistance and comfort provided to the testator, but it might be a result of undue influence. Gifts to new friends and companions should also be scrutinized carefully, particularly if the client exhibits any sign of dementia.

If the client leaves unequal shares to their children, the attorney should document in the file the reasons why the client did so. If any heirs are cut out of the will, the attorney should be sure that the client knew of their existence and deliberately left them nothing. If a client is leaving property to descendants beyond their children, such as grandchildren, the attorney should question the client's knowledge of these heirs, particularly if one heir is favored over the others. It is possible that the very old client may not have much knowledge about their grandchildren's lives, capabilities, prospects, and personal issues. The client should be encouraged to learn as much as possible about possible heirs to ensure that the amount and form of the gift reflect the realities of the heirs' lives. If one grandchild is favored more than others, the attorney should keep in mind that grandchildren have been found to have been the source of undue influence. In the end, of course, as long as the client understands what they are doing and the will reflects their autonomous decision, the client can leave their estate as they see fit.

VII. Use of Trusts

Trusts are often appropriate for very old clients; some of whom are best served by placing most of their assets into an inter vivos trust as a means of managing those assets if they should lose the capacity to do so. Others will be capably served by the appointment of an agent acting under a power of attorney (see Chapter 10, Management of Property of a Person Who Is Mentally Incapacitated). Older clients may also decide that they should leave their estate in trust rather than by outright gift.

For couples, if both are very old, the survivor should not be given an outright gift. The assets should be left in trust to protect the survivor in case they are not capable of managing the inheritance. The limits on access to the trust depends on what each spouse considers wise. Some may fear the assets going to the spouse of a second marriage or may fear that the survivor will spend the inheritance at the expense of the children. Others may want the survivor to have full access to the inheritance. Some will provide the surviving spouse with all the income but limit their access to principal. Still others will want to sharply limit access to assets by the survivor, and prefer to give an independent trustee, who is not the surviving spouse, the discretion to make distributions as they see fit in light of the surviving spouse's financial needs.

Making testamentary gifts to trusts for the children and other heirs is often wise for a very old client. Use of a trust can enable generation skipping planning, though with the few number of estates subject to the federal estate tax that motivation has become less compelling. Ignoring possible estate or inheritance tax advantages, a trust may still be a wise choice because it can be used to ensure that the gift will not be totally spent by the first recipient, usually a child, but will still be available for grandchildren and other descendants. A very old client is likely to have old children. For example, an 85-year-old could have a child age 60 or older. If the client intends to leave their estate to their children, consideration should be given to reality that the child might be age 70 or older at the time of the client's death and the grandchildren might be age 45 or even older. If so, in many instances it might be wiser to leave the inheritance to the child in a trust with limitations on the child's ability to access the trust or at least limit their access to the principal of the trust and so ensure that the grandchildren will eventually benefit from the trust.

The possibility that a child might someday need to pay for costly long-term care is one reason for leaving a gift to a child in a trust to which the child has limited access. A very old client may have children who themselves are over age 60. If the child should suffer early on-set dementia or another debilitating illness, the child might need costly long-term care. As discussed in Chapter 14, Medicaid, the child will not be eligible for Medicaid payment of their long-term care until they have spent down their assets. In light of the child's other financial resources and the needs of their spouse and other family members, it might be more sensible to have them go on Medicaid and hold back funds left in a trust for their benefit so that those assets can be used for the benefit of the grandchildren or other heirs.

The child may never encounter the need to pay for costly long-term care, but they may lose the ability to handle their financial affairs. Leaving an inheritance in trust for them ensures that the assets will always be under capable management. Likewise, leaving the inheritance in trust can protect an aging child from being victimized by others who prey upon the elderly who are financially well off, but due to aging are unable to protect themselves from financial exploitation.

If a trust is used to protect the assets so that the grandchildren will benefit after the death of their parents, the child beneficiary will not have access to the trust assets. This raises the question whether the trustees should have the authority only to make fixed distributions to the child, such as all the income, or have the authority to make discretionary distributions to the child including those limited by a standard such as health, education, and maintenance. When creating a trust for a young beneficiary, many believe it wise to grant the trustee discretion to make distributions of principal as needed in light of how the life of the beneficiary unfolds and what needs arise over time. With an older beneficiary, however, the needs of the beneficiary are more apparent and so it may be advisable to have a fixed standard of distributions and not rely on the discretion and judgment of the trustee. Doing so has several advantages. The beneficiary knows what will be distributed by the trust and can plan accordingly and if the beneficiary needs to apply for Medicaid to pay for long-term care, the trust assets will not be an available asset that will disqualify the beneficiary.

Not granting discretion to the trustee also makes it easier to find an acceptable person or entity to act as trustee. If the trust is for the benefit of a child, a grandchild could be named trustee who has no discretion as to distributions to their parent and so avoid possible family disharmony that could arise if the child refused a parental request to make a distribution. In addition, corporate entities should be willing to charge a lower fee as trustee if they are not authorized to make discretionary decisions about distributions.

A non-discretionary trust could be required to distribute all the income of the trust to the beneficiary but that creates issues as to how the trust assets are invested because investments can be selected by the trustee that either increase or decrease the annual trust income. An alternative that avoids the trustee control over the amount of income is a unitrust that directs the trustee to distribute a fixed percentage of the average year-end value of the trust for the past five years. (The number of base years can be fewer.) The settlor selects the percentage distribution based on the anticipated value of the trust, the income needs of the beneficiary, and the willingness of the settlor to create the possibility that the trust will be exhausted due to the mandated distribution rate. For example, if the trust is expected to have a value of approximately $500,000, a percentage distribution rate of four percent would mean the beneficiary would receive about $20,000 per year. The amount could increase or decrease over time depending upon the rate of return on the trust investments. If the settlor desired that the child have more income, the distribution could be set at seven percent or approximately $35,000 a year. That amount, however, could begin to delete the principal of the trust, which in turn would later reduce the amount of the annual distribution. If the settlor is not bothered by the possible exhaustion of the trust, the settlor could have an annual distribution equal to the greater of 7 percent or $30,000 per year. Note that even by distributing $30,000 a year, and ignoring any investment returns, a trust funded with $500,000 would last for over 16 years. If, however, the settlor wants to ensure that the trust will continue through the child's life, the annual distribution percentage likely should not exceed four percent. At the death of the child, the settlor could either provide that the trust continue for the life of a grandchild or the lives of grandchildren, or provide for the trust to terminate and the assets be distributed to the grandchildren, to other individuals, or to a charity.

Whatever powers are granted to the trustee, the older client needs to take care as to whom they select as trustee and successor trustee. Once the client has suggested possible candidates to act as trustee, the attorney should ask the client several questions. How long has the client known the individual? What is the client's relationship to the individual? What is their occupation and where do they live? Does the individual have the necessary knowledge and temperament to fulfill the duties of a trustee? Of course, the most important question is whether the client trusts the individual.

VIII. Charitable Gifts

Many very old clients want to make a testamentary gift to charity. The simplest way is merely to make a gift outright to the charity in the will. Never accept the client's assurances that they have the proper name of the charity, however. The attorney should contact the charity to be sure that it is correctly identified and that the gift is directed toward the proper entity, such as to a local unit or to the national entity.

If the amount of the proposed testamentary gift is not insubstantial, the client should consider instead making a lifetime charitable split interest gift, by which from the income produced by the principal of the gift is paid to the donor, but the remainder, the principal of the gift, eventually is distributed to the charity. A split interest charitable gift produces an immediate income tax deduction for the value of the gift of the remainder interest, permits the sale of assets without recognition of capital gain, and reduces the value of the donor's estate.

For many, a charitable remainder annuity trust (CRAT) is appealing.[3] The clients, a couple, create an irrevocable trust that pays the client an annual percentage return of the principal. At the death of the second to die of the couple, the trust terminates and the principal is distributed to the named charity. The clients receive an immediate charitable deduction for the present value of the remainder gift to the charity. The payout must be at least 5 percent of the initial fair market value of the property placed in the trust. A CRAT assures the client that they will receive a specified amount each year during the term of the trust because the amount of the required annual distribution is determined at the date the assets are transferred to the trust, regardless of the amount of the trust's income. Of course, a fixed annual payout provides no protection from inflation.

An alternative to a CRAT is the charitable remainder unitrust or CRUT, which pays the income beneficiary a fixed percentage of not less than 5 percent of the fair market value of its assets determined annually. The CRUT distributions fluctuate annually with the value of the assets, and so provide protection from inflation and allow the beneficiary to share in the benefits of the trust assets growing in value. The distribution can be limited to the trust's income in years when the trust income is not sufficient to meet the required percentage payout. If so, the donor can also provide that any resulting deficiency in the annual payout will be made up in years when the trust income exceeds the required payment.

The CRAT and CRUT provide an immediate income tax deduction so long as the value of the remainder going to the charity equals at least 10 percent of the value of the property donated to the trust. The value of the remainder interest, and so the amount of the charitable income tax deduction, depends upon the percentage payout to the income beneficiary and the age of the beneficiary. The lower the percentage payout to the beneficiary and the older the beneficiary, the greater the value of the deductible charitable contribution. If the clients are very old, the creation and funding of a CRAT or a CRUT can result in a significant charitable income tax deduction. The income tax savings that result from the deduction represent additional wealth for the client that can be passed on to their heirs. If, instead, the same amount of funds were donated to the charity as a gift under the will, unless the client's estate were great enough to be subject to the federal estate tax, the gift would not generate a charitable deduction.

---

3. Charitable remainder trusts are governed by I.R.C. § 664(d)(2) and the regulations thereunder.

A CRAT or CRUT also enables the client to realize the value of capital appreciation without incurring the federal capital gains tax. If the client transfers appreciated assets to the CRAT or CRUT, they can use that value to determine the resulting charitable income tax deduction even though the transfer does not trigger realization of the appreciated capital gain. Of course, if the client held the appreciated asset until death, because of the step up in basis at death, the capital appreciation would not be taxed. However, by making a gift to the CRAT or CRUT, the client is able to convert the asset into a stream of income without having to sell the asset and pay the capital gains tax on the appreciation.

If an older client wants to leave a testamentary gift to a grandchild who is below college age, the attorney should ask the client to consider creating a 529 plan account, which is an education savings vehicle established under the Internal Revenue Code Section 529. States create the right of an individual to establish a 529 plan, and most states permit individuals to open a plan in that state whether they are a resident or not.

A 529 plan permits an individual to create an investment account to which they make contributions to be used to pay for the higher education expenses of a designated beneficiary. The investment manager of the account is selected by the 529 plan; the individual who opened the account, the account owner, does not direct the investments. The account owner, not the beneficiary, determines when distributions are made from the plan. The account owner can also change the designated beneficiary of the account.

The account is exempt from the federal income taxation. Distributions from the account that are made to pay for qualified higher education expenses are also not taxed and can be paid directly to the educational institution. Most states also do not tax distributions for educational expenses. Any distribution not made for higher educational expenses is subject to the federal income tax plus an additional 10 percent penalty tax. Many states permit the contributor to a 529 plan to deduct the contribution from their state income tax return.

Contributions to a 529 account are treated as completed gifts to the designated beneficiary and as such qualify for the annual gift tax exclusion of $14,000 (in 2017). Additionally, a contribution of up to five times the available annual exclusion amount may be made to a 529 account without incurring gift taxes, although the gift is then prorated over the next five years as if the donor had given a gift each year.[4] For example, if the annual exclusion is $14,000, an account owner can give $70,000 to an account for a designated beneficiary, and treat the $70,000 for gift tax purposes as if it were given at a rate of $14,000 per year over five years.

The value of a 529 account is not included in the account owner's estate at death unless the account owner either elected to have contributions prorated over five years and died during that period or died after funding the account but prior to naming a designated beneficiary.

---

4. I.R.C. § 529(c)(2).

IX. Powers of Attorney and Surrogate Health Care Decision Maker

The very old client should review their prior estate planning documents and revise them as needed. In particular, most should execute new power of attorney, if only to have a more recently executed document that may calm the fears of third parties as to whether the power is still valid. The client should also review who they named as agent and successor agents in light of changing circumstances, both in the lives of the agents and in the nature of the client's assets. If the client has transferred much of their assets to a revocable trust, the duties of the agent will be much less onerous. A child who might not have had the time to be agent before, might be able to handle the reduced obligations when only a modest amount of assets would be under the control of the agent. Of course, the client should also reconsider who are the trustees or successor trustees of their inner vivos trust in light of the nature of the current trust assets and the life circumstances of the trustee.

The very old client should also sign a new surrogate health care decision maker form (see Chapter 11, Health Care Decision Making). If the client has executed a more recent form, third parties are more likely to respect and abide by the directions contained in the document. Next the clients should review who they named as the surrogate and successor. A change in circumstances of either the client or the designated surrogate may necessitate a change in who is named surrogate. Finally, the client should consider tailoring the document to any known illness or condition that they suffer from. At a minimum, the document should state that the client is aware of the illness or condition and nevertheless grants the surrogate authority to make health care decisions including the right to terminate life-sustaining treatment. The goal is to make clear to third parties that the client was aware of the implication of granting full authority to the surrogate and the possibility, that in light of the client's illness or condition, the surrogate was likely to invoke the powers granted to them in the document.

The document that appoints the surrogate may give them full discretion as to health care treatment decisions, but the client should provide a nonbinding advisory letter to the surrogate that details the kind of treatment decisions that the client would like the surrogate to make. Even though the client may not have previously provided such a letter, and depended instead upon oral discussions with the surrogate as the way to instruct the surrogate as to the client's wishes and values, with advanced age the client should put down those desires in writing. First, because the likelihood that the surrogate may have to act increases markedly as the client ages. Next, because some surrogates may not credit the aging client with really meaning what they say in a conversation; writing is always more compelling as evidence of the client's desires than oral statements. Furthermore, if the client writes down their wishes, the client will have to give more time and consideration in determining how they want the surrogate to act. If necessary, the attorney can assist in the creation of the advisory letter to be sure that the letter accurately reflects what the client wants and covers the possible medical care decisions that the surrogate may be faced with.

If the client suffers from early stage dementia, but still retains sufficient capacity to sign a valid surrogate medical decision maker document, the client should be asked to consider what kind of medical treatment they desire in the event the dementia progresses to a severe condition. If possible, the client should state in the document that if they are severely demented whether they authorize the surrogate to refuse or terminate medical treatment of a condition, such as pneumonia, that if not treated might cause death. Some clients would prefer to die from an otherwise treatable illness rather than suffer increased dementia; other clients would prefer to be provided medical treatment regardless of the dementia. The client should also consider whether they want to be fed by hand if the dementia progresses to the point that they no longer have the mental capacity to feed themselves. Some do not want to be hand fed or even hydrated, as they would prefer to die from lack of nutrition and hydration. Others will prefer to be fed by hand.

The attorney should emphasize to the client that the goal is for the client to be treated and cared for in a manner consistent with the client's values. Although the documents drawn up by the attorney can help to achieve that, in the end it is the client who must talk to their spouse, children, and physician and explain the kind of end-of-life medical care that they want. Only by so doing can the client be sure that the surrogate is aware of what the client wants and understands the obligation to try to carry out what the client wanted. Making end-of-life decisions as a surrogate can be extremely stressful. The client can help reduce that stress by assuring the surrogate, preferably in writing, that when appropriate the client wants the surrogate to permit the client to die.

Index

marriage effect on eligibility for,
219–22
Medicare Part C and, 73
Minimum/Maximum Monthly
Maintenance Needs Allowance
considered with, 220–21
optional categorically needy
threshold for, 215–16
optional medically needy threshold
for, 216–17
overview of, 213–14
periods of ineligibility for, 225–27,
228–30
personal service contracts and, 227
residency requirements for,
214–15
resource eligibility requirements
for, 218–19, 221–22
resource transfers and ineligibility
for, 225–27, 228–30
spend-down tests for, 216–17
Supplemental Security Income and,
214, 215–16
third party collection rights under,
235
trusts protecting assets with,
183–84, 227–30, 233, 284
209(b) state requirements for, 215
veterans benefits and, 82, 84, 85
medical issues
aging bodies and, 25–32
aging brains and, 32
cancer as, 26, 27–28, 98, 169, 209
dementia as (*see* dementia)
depression as, 35
elder protection statutes on, 98–99
estate planning with very old clients
consideration of, 276–77
health insurance coverage of, 38, 58,
63, 72, 73 (*see also* Medicaid;
Medicare)
hearing and vision issues as, 30–31,
105, 200, 213, 215, 277–79

heart conditions as, 26, 30, 32, 35,
99, 161–62, 169, 201
HIPAA privacy issues with, 262
housing choices influenced by,
105–6, 111
joint, muscle, and bone diseases and
conditions as, 28–30, 99, 105
overview of, 25
Parkinson's disease as, 34, 35, 98,
106, 169, 237
skin diseases and conditions as,
26–28
strokes as, 32, 34, 35, 106, 133, 152,
169, 201, 237, 257, 276
veterans medical care coverage of,
84–88
See also health care decision making
Medicare
appeals of claim denials with, 78–79
co-pays with, 74, 75, 76, 77, 78, 212
coverage under, 74–78
deductibles with, 74, 76, 77, 78, 212
eligibility for, 48, 71–74
finance sources for, 69–71 (*see also*
taxes and *premiums subentries*)
hospice care coverage under, 74, 75,
77, 209, 211–12
lifetime reserve days with, 74
long-term care alternatives coverage
under, 74, 75, 77, 191, 207, 208,
209, 211–12
Medigap policies, 79–80, 211
overview of, 69
Part A (hospital/skilled care), 69,
71–72, 74–76, 211
Part B (physicians/outpatient
services), 69, 70–71, 72, 75,
76–77, 211
Part C (Medicare Advantage/
managed care), 69, 71, 72–73, 77,
79, 211
Part D (prescription drugs), 69, 71,
73–74, 77–78